LHOTSE
27890

Geneva
Spur

NUPTSE
25850

Camp IV
24900

m

Camp III
22900

BARUNTSE
23688

CHO POLU
22093

Imja
Glacier

Namche Bazar, 18 miles

BERANN

Drawing by Berann, © 1963, National Geographic Society

AMERICANS ON EVEREST

AMERICANS ON EVEREST

The official account of the ascent
led by Norman G. Dyhrenfurth

BY JAMES RAMSEY ULLMAN
AND OTHER MEMBERS OF THE EXPEDITION

J. B. Lippincott Company

Philadelphia and New York

To the memory of

JOHN E. BREITENBACH

who lies on Everest

CONTENTS

viii CONTENTS

Part II
THE COMPONENTS

ILLUSTRATIONS

COLOR

BLACK AND WHITE

FOREWORD

by Norman G. Dyhrenfurth

THE TRAIL LEVELED OFF GENTLY. Dense forest gave way to grassy slopes. Gabriel Chevalley and I walked together at the rear of the column. That morning we had left the ancient lamasery of Taksindu as the sun rose over a sea of clouds, with the mountains of Solu Khumbu outlined in bold relief. The date: December 7, 1952. It was a clear, glorious Himalayan morning, a perfect occasion for daydreaming. Our feet moved along the narrow path in rhythmic monotony, like those of well-trained animals. They had covered much ground that year.

An ancient Buddhist *mani* wall came into view. Gabriel pulled up short. I almost bumped into him before I looked up, for my thoughts had been far away. Together we gazed off into the distance. Beneath us the gently rolling hills stretched to the horizon, growing higher and wilder until they met the great peaks, crowned with shimmering glaciers and lofty ridges: the Jugal and Langtang Himal, Gaurisankar, Cho Oyu, and many others. And then there was *our* mountain—dark, grim and remote—reaching for the very sky in one final, supreme gesture: Chomolungma, Goddess Mother of the World!

Silently we took off our packs and stretched out among the alpine flowers. Soft tufts of brownish moss were a welcome change from the windswept slopes of Mount Everest. It felt good to be alive. We stared at the distant horizon, reliving the past weeks and months. It had been quite a struggle.

Twice that year the Swiss had assaulted the mountain. On May 28, Raymond Lambert and Tensing Bhotia (now known as Tenzing Norgay) had reached the highest point ever attained by man on this earth: 28,200 feet of thin air, just below the south summit of Everest. Here they had entered the so-called "zone of death"; and exhaustion, plus oxygen failure, put an end to their desperate struggle. More dead than alive, they succeeded in descending to camp on the South Col; then the monsoon storms were upon them. The mountain was evacuated hurriedly but in good order. No lives were lost. By July everyone had reached home.

But the Swiss were not discouraged. Nor were they ready to concede the mountain to others. By early October they were back at the old Base Camp. Of the original team only Raymond Lambert and Dr. Gabriel Chevalley were able to return. Chevalley was the leader, with Lambert as climbing leader. The rest of the group was new. Tensing Bhotia again was in charge of the Sherpa team, the high-altitude porters. I was the only American and the official photographer as well as film maker.

At first everything went well. The dreaded Khumbu Icefall was negotiated in short order, and two camps were established in the Western Cwm, the "Valley of Silence." By the end of October we were ready for the move to the South Col. Nothing, we felt, could stop us this time; our hopes for the summit were high. Then, on October 31, disaster struck: an ice avalanche swept through the Lhotse Couloir. Three Sherpas suffered minor injuries, but Mingma Dorje, one of the best, died two hours later. Crushed ribs had punctured his lungs. He was buried on a small moraine at 22,000 feet, beneath the huge obelisk of the mountain that had claimed his life.

Grimly we continued the struggle. A new route was found through the glaciated Lhotse Face. High camps were established. The days were getting short; winter was just around the corner. Temperatures dropped to 40 below zero, and up high the storms were raging. At last, the South Col was reached on November 19, but at a heavy price: Lambert, Reiss, Tensing and seven young Sherpas—the only ones more or less fit, from an original team of twenty-seven—spent one frightful night on the Col. The thermometer dropped to 45 below, and icy gales swept across "the most desolate spot on earth" with near-hurricane strength. The next morning dawned clear, but it was bitterly cold and the winds continued with unabated fury. The Sherpas had reached the limit of their endurance. They refused to remain in this inferno and started the long descent. But Lambert, Reiss and Tensing decided to make one last desperate effort. A few hundred feet above the Col, at the entrance to the steep couloir, they too met their master. The enraged elements had fought them to a standstill. There was no use denying the obvious: winter had come to Everest. To continue the struggle could have meant death for the entire assault team. With heavy hearts we admitted defeat. To use Gabriel Chevalley's words: "We were 'purged' from the mountain."

And now all this lay behind us. We were headed out toward Kathmandu and home. I don't remember how long we remained there on that hill beneath the *mani* wall, drinking in the warm sunshine and looking back on another phase of our lives. There was Everest: dark, remote, and incredibly high. Even at this distance there were unmistakable signs of violent storms. The famous "plume" of snow extended for miles toward the east. And yet we looked at the mountain with great longing. It had been a terrible antagonist, but now that we had to leave it we felt close to tears. Neither of us spoke, each alone with his thoughts. The following year, 1953, the British would have their turn. Their chances for success were good. And even if their attempt should fail, the government of Nepal had given 1954 to the French.

"*Les avant-premières à l'Everest—c'est tout. On n'aura plus de chance.*" Gabriel's softly spoken, nostalgic words expressed my own feelings. We were among the forerunners to Everest, and now it would be someone else's turn to run the final lap. It was very much like a relay race, as the baton passed from one team to another. And that is as it should be.

"*Eh bien, mon cher, on-y-va?*"

It was getting late, and two tired men prepared to move on. The end of a great adventure drew near. Ten more days on the trail before Kathmandu, then the long flight home to that "other" life. Right now the thought seemed almost unbearable. One last look— and Everest was gone. We were on our way.

I knew then that I would return.

I was seated at my desk. Outside, students passed back and forth on their way to classes. The sign on the door carried my name. Head of the Motion Picture Division, Department of Theater Arts, University of California at Los Angeles. A medium-sized frog in a somewhat confining pond.

This was my third day back at the old job, after a six-month leave of absence without pay to join the Swiss on Everest. The desk was piled high with unfinished business: letters to be answered, committee meetings, agendas, budgets to be prepared, schedules to be drawn up, lists of students to be counseled, films to be completed. The windows were opened wide, the California sun shone brightly. Yet the air felt stuffy. Everything seemed to close in on me. The thought of returning to this kind of life filled me with dread. Telephones kept ringing, typewriters made infernal noises, and students stuck their heads through the window to ask unanswerable questions. There I sat, staring dully at a desk littered with reminders of a former life. Slowly a picture came into focus: deep, green valleys, clear mountain streams, primitive stone huts, Buddhist chortens, ceaselessly turning prayer wheels, and above all the High Himalaya. Faces appeared on my memory screen—brown, happy and proud faces. There was the Sherpa Ang Dawa, my good friend, waving a final farewell as our plane taxied down the runway at Kathmandu. His last words: "Sah'b, please come back!" There had been tears in his eyes.

The loud ring of the telephone interrupted my dreams: "Professor Dyhrenfurth, I am to remind you that there will be a faculty meeting at twelve noon. Please try to attend." The departmental secretary sounded both cheerless and efficient.

I glanced at my watch. Almost an hour's time before the meeting. The watch brought back other memories. It had been presented to me with an inscription: *"Souvenir Expédition Suisse a l'Everest,*

Automne 1952." How out of place this seemed in Southern California, and particularly in the Department of Theater Arts!

But so was I.

To help create a new department within a large university, devoted to the development of a new and better generation of film makers, had once offered a great challenge. But now, suddenly, it seemed terribly stale and uninspiring. The initial impetus was gone; someone else could take over, someone content to spend the rest of his days in the academic world.

Kenneth Macgowan's office was next to mine. As usual, he sat behind his desk, in one corner of the room, his attention divided equally between his pipe and his dictating machine. Not only was he Chairman of the Department, but also my very good and understanding friend. Turning off the machine, he took a few puffs on his pipe and asked, "What's on your mind, Norm? Any problems?"

"I'm afraid I can't take it any more, Kenneth. Everything seems different. The job bores me to death; nothing makes much sense. I'm afraid I'll have to resign."

"After only three days? Are you sure?"

"Positive. It isn't just the job. Everest has changed my whole outlook on life. I don't know what it is, but something drastic happened to me up there. What seemed terribly important before just —well—isn't any more."

Kenneth did not appear to be surprised. "What are you planning to do?" he asked. "You can't keep going on expeditions forever. Besides, how will you support your family?"

"I don't know yet. I'll think of something."

Kenneth knew me well enough to realize that nothing could change my mind. After expressing his personal regrets at my decision, he agreed that this was something I had to do if I was to live with myself. By the time I left his office, I felt like a new man. Even the air was fit to breathe again. I decided to call it a day. The committee meeting would have to get along without me.

Wives and families are a wonderful invention. That is, if you are lucky. Sally, our son John, and our German Shepherd Rocky greeted me at the door.

"Darling, how wonderful—you're early," said Sally. "How about a drink?"

"I'd love one."

"You look happy and relaxed. What happened?"

"I told Kenneth I was resigning. He understands."

"I couldn't be happier. Now you can really relax and regain those 40 pounds you lost on the mountain."

"Well, some of it."

John was pleased, too. "Duff (that's my family nickname) congratulations! I think it's terrific!" he said. And while Rocky made no comment, he also seemed not displeased.

I had been given an overwhelming vote of confidence.

Life in the Los Angeles suburb of Reseda was very pleasant. Weight was soon back to normal, and then some. Our tiny swimming pool was surrounded by a high wall, offering complete privacy plus the chance to get a fine tan. There was no telephone. Anyone wanting to reach me had to send a wire or drive out in person. What more could a man ask for?

Alas, money, for one thing. Money to implement the dream of return to Everest—of launching the first American Expedition to Everest. For six years I worked on the project in every way I could think of: planning books, writing magazine articles, lecturing, making radio and television appearances, and trying to interest Hollywood motion picture producers in documentary films with a Himalayan background. Here and there I managed to raise a few hundred dollars toward the realization of my one great hope, but they were the merest drops in the bucket.

One of my projects called for a photographic flight over Mount Everest. While I was trying to interest one of the West Coast's leading airplane manufacturers, word reached the world of the British triumph. Days later the Indian Air Force made several flights over the summit. The resulting pictures, which were magnificent, appeared everywhere, and my own plans died a-borning.

I then tried to get the backing of newspapers and magazines. I pointed out to them that The London *Times* had for many years lent a helping hand in financing Himalayan expeditions, and that now was the time for Americans to follow suit.

But with Everest just climbed, the inevitable reaction was, "It's been done. Why do it again?" And the chances for an American expedition seemed remoter than ever.

These were years of hopes, frustrations, economic doldrums—and, on the brighter side for me, three other expeditions:

The 1955 International Himalayan Expedition to Solu Khumbu and Lhotse, Everest's closest neighbor.

The 1958 Slick-Johnson Snowman Expedition to the Arun Valley and Solu Khumbu, in search of the elusive yeti.

The 1960 Swiss Dhaulagiri Expedition, which placed a total of eight men on the summit of the world's sixth-highest mountain, the highest peak ever scaled without oxygen.

Between expeditions, there were seemingly endless lecture tours, a Fulbright Research Grant for a year's study of the Italian motion picture industry, dozens of films for the United States Air Force on the development of the Atlas missile, and a picture on the first isotope-powered unmanned weather station in the Arctic. Throughout it all, I tried not to lose sight of the ultimate goal. There was always the memory of that day in December of 1952, when Chevalley and I had looked back on *our* mountain with great sadness and longing.

At last, upon my return to Kathmandu in June of 1960, after the Dhaulagiri Expedition, I decided to make one final, supreme effort and applied to His Majesty's Government of Nepal for permission to lead an American expedition to Everest in 1961. Months went by and soon it was too late for 1961. The next year had been reserved for a government-sponsored Indian team. So I reapplied for 1963. By now I was back home, and several months went by without word from Kathmandu. But finally a letter reached our embassy, dated May 10, 1961, and signed by the Chief of Protocol of the Ministry of Foreign Affairs:

"I write to acknowledge with thanks the receipt of your letter dated May 2, 1961, and attached cheque for $320 in payment of one half of the royalty charged for Mr. Dyhrenfurth's proposed expedition to Mount Everest in 1963. I suggest that you kindly inform Mr. Dyhrenfurth confirming His Majesty's Government's final approval of his proposed expedition to Mount Everest in 1963. . . ."

Now all that remained was the financing, organization, selection of team, and a few other details such as how to support my family in the interim. When Nick Clinch, who had organized and led two successful American Himalayan expeditions, had his first unbelieving look at my original budget estimate of $186,000, his first comment was: "Norm, you're crazy! You'll never get that kind of money in this country. Remember, this isn't Europe, but the U.S.A. Nobody gives that much of a damn about mountains or mountaineering." As an afterthought he added: "If you do get it, you don't even have to climb the mountain; you'll deserve a medal just for raising the dough."

Well, "raise the dough" we did. Climb the mountain we did. That is the story that follows. But again and again, as the adventure unfolded, I found myself thinking back to those other times when all effort had ended in disappointment and frustration: in 1952, with the Swiss; in 1955, on the International Himalayan Expedition. On October 29, 1955, I had written in my diary:

". . . our last evening at Base Camp, at the foot of the Icefall. The sun has set some time ago; I am sitting on a rock above camp, lonely in the gathering darkness. The last light fades from the surrounding peaks. I am torn between two emotions: happy to be returning home, and at the same time sad and nostalgic. Hard weeks and months lie behind us, yet the parting from these great mountains weighs heavily. . . ."

That had always been the way before.

But now no longer.

This time, as we left Base Camp on May 25, 1963, it was all different. The job was done; the challenge had been met at last. I knew I would never return.

Everest has been friend and foe for the past eleven years, but now the time has come to turn my back on it. In passing through the Buddhist monastery of Thangboche on the way out from the mountain, we stopped to pay our respects to the reincarnate High Lama. As we took our leave, he looked very frail, lonely and forlorn. We had become good friends over the years. But I don't expect to see him ever again. When I left Thangboche, the "Sacred Meadow," in the past, there was always, for me, the strong feeling of having lived there before, in a previous incarnation. Each time I was deeply moved and close to tears, as James Hilton's Hugh Conway must have felt when turning his back on Shangri-La. I knew that I was leaving part of myself behind, and that some day, somehow, I must return.

This was no longer the past. It was the present. There still was a moment of regret as we passed through the lamasery's gateway, but the mountains were enveloped in heavy clouds, and Everest was hidden from view. This made the parting somewhat easier.

All that remains now is the return to that "other" life. . . .

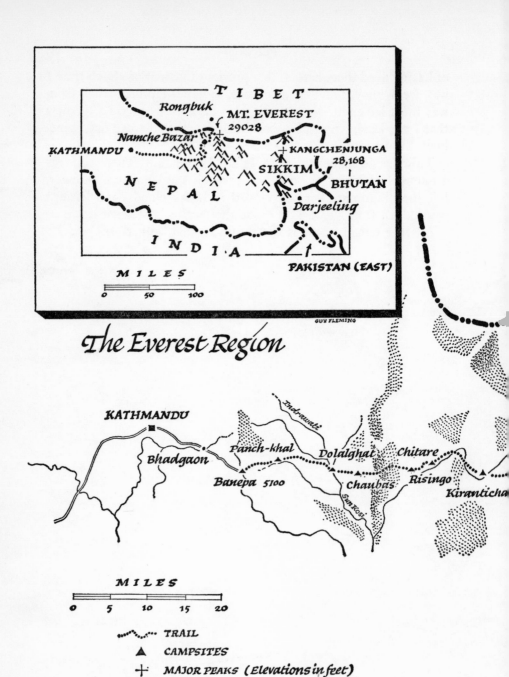

The Everest Region

MILES
0   50   100

TIBET

Rongbuk   MT. EVEREST
           29028
Namche Bazar
KATHMANDU   KANGCHENJUNGA
                           28,168
           SIKKIM
NEPAL   BHUTAN

           Darjeeling

INDIA

PAKISTAN (EAST)

GUY FLEMING

KATHMANDU

Indrawati

Bhadgaon   Panch-khal   Dolalghat   Chitare

Banepa 5100   Chaubas   Risingo
                        Sun Kosi   Kiranticha

MILES
0   5   10   15   20

•••••᠁•᠁ TRAIL

▲ CAMPSITES

✛ MAJOR PEAKS (Elevations in feet)

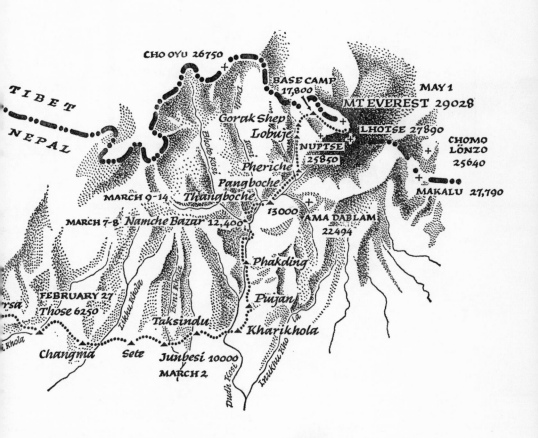

The Approach March

Drawn by Guy Fleming, adapted from
a National Geographic Society map

PART I

THE ADVENTURE

1. VISION

BEGIN AT THE BEGINNING—yes. But for this story there are many beginnings. One of them is in the streets of Calcutta on the morning of February 13, 1963.

It is not yet six when we troop heavy-eyed from the Oberoi Grand Hotel and board the bus for Dum Dum Airport. A gray haze hangs over the city; there are few people about, and the only sound is the thump and chug of our antique engine. For a while we are in a commercial and governmental district. But only a little while. Then, for the rest of the way to the airport, we are in the slums, and slums, and slums for which Calcutta is unhappily famous.

Swiftly the dawnlight brightens. The rising sun burns molten through the haze, and the vast warren comes to life. We are in a world of shacks and alleys; and from the shacks come human figures, tattered, barefoot; and in the alleys they cook, eat, wash, urinate, defecate. In the favored places cows lie contemplating the sunrise. From the less favored places bundles of rags rise and become men. We pass a legless woman dragging herself through the dust. A small boy raises his head to the rumble of our passing, and

3

his eyes are blind with film and pus. The city flows by us in a scabrous tide: in its hundreds, thousands, millions.

Then it is gone. We are at Dum Dum. We are in a DC-3, old but valiant, of the Royal Nepal Airlines Corporation—roaring, rising, banking—and Calcutta is lost behind us. Below are the dry brown plains of West Bengal, as we bear north by west toward Kathmandu, Nepal.

There are fifteen in our party, plus some half-dozen other passengers including a Buddhist monk with shorn head and saffron robe; and the fastest plane boarders are in the right-hand window seats, for we know that what we have waited so long to see will best be seen from that position. During the first hour and more, however, right and left make no difference; there are only the brown plains. Then there is a break in the plains, a glint, a long snaking across the face of the land, and we pass over the Ganges. But even this, one of the world's great rivers, draws only casual notice, for rivers are not on our minds.

It is not until almost a second hour has passed that the true change takes place. Within the plane, an almost visible tautening of bodies and senses. Beneath it, a change in the earth; for now at last the Indian plains are gone and we are flying over the forest country of southern Nepal, called the Terai. The land slopes upward gently. Then more steeply. And then it is no longer merely a slope but a range, broken into hills and valleys, crests and gorges. Here are Nepal's southern ramparts, the outliers of the Himalaya,* and as we cross them they thrust sharply, menacingly upward, until they seem about to nudge the wings of the plane.

But this is not all that is happening. What lies below us is nothing compared to what lies ahead. For now before us, to the north and east, are the true Himalaya: a huge white sweep of mountains poised like a wave against the bare blue sky. The mist and dust of the lowlands are far behind. Blue and white are pure, flawless, in all-but-blinding brilliance. And as we fly on, the wave becomes a tide, the tide an ocean, and that is all there is between heaven and earth: the high white ocean of earth's greatest mountains.

---

* In English, the name of the range is often rendered in the plural: i.e., Himalayas. In its basic Sanskrit meaning, however, it is a singular concept—*Himalaya*: Abode of Snow—and it is therefore used in this form throughout this book.

Everyone in the plane, Buddhist monk included, is crowded over into the right-hand seats, craning and staring. And out of the white ocean we pick the crests that are the topmost peaks. Straight out from the windows, a bit to the north of east, rises the mass of Kangchenjunga, third highest of earth's summits. Diagonally ahead, beyond an intervening sweep of lesser giants, is Makalu, fifth highest. Beyond that Lhotse, fourth highest. And beyond that— "There it is," we say together, as if all with one voice. And there It is, indeed. Everest. The king—dwarfing all the others; the white crest of ocean frozen into a radiant pinnacle, its snow plume streaming eastward in the wild west wind.

Some of us are seeing it for the first time. Some have seen it before. But in the magic of these moments it makes no difference. For all of us, everything else is gone. A scant two hours past we were in the very heart of earth's ugliness and squalor, but now the slums of Calcutta are remote, unimaginable. Our own homes, too, are dim and distant; the whole world of planes and seas, cities and nations, men and the works of men gone and lost behind us. All that is real is that white vision in the sky.

We seem to have passed not only beyond the earth, but beyond time itself, to a realm above the earth, fixed and changeless. But it is not so. For presently, once again, there is change. The vision has tilted. The white ocean has tilted. They are sliding away; and now we see it is the plane that has tilted; it is banking, descending, the earth rising to meet us; we are coming back to earth, back to the world, and before us is the Valley of Nepal and Kathmandu.

Now it is the vision that is gone.

But we shall see it again.

2. *STILL THERE*

THERE WERE OTHER BEGINNINGS TOO, and one of them was not vision but computation. This was 111 years earlier, in 1852, when a clerk in the office of the Survey of India looked up from a maze of figures and announced to his superior: "Sir, I have discovered the highest mountain in the world!"

The mountain, to be sure, had not sprung suddenly into being. Though geologically young as mountains go, it had stood there upon the Tibetan-Nepalese border—at latitude 27°59'16" North and longitude 86°55'40" East—for some few million years before Tibet and Nepal, or even man himself, existed; and for several years before 1852, known to the Indian Survey as Peak XV, it had been recognized as *one* of earth's highest summits. It was not, however, until after many computations that it emerged unchallenged as *the* highest, and soon thereafter it was named in honor of Sir George Everest, an early British Surveyor General of India.*

* It was not then known that the peak already had a Tibetan name: *Chomolungma*—Goddess Mother of the World. For the long run and for the world at large this is certainly the better name for earth's highest pinnacle; but it would seem likely that, for Westerners, *Everest* is here to stay. At least we can be grateful that Sir George's surname was not Jones, Brown or Smythe-Tewksbury.

6

At the time, its altitude was calculated at 29,002 feet. In 1905 the figure was raised to 29,141, and in the most recent survey, in 1952–53, it was again readjusted, this time to 29,028 feet. This is the figure that is currently accepted, giving the peak a margin of 778 feet over its nearest rival, 28,250-foot K2, in the Himalayan sub-range of the Karakoram.

For the Western world, Everest was discovered, measured and named at a distance, and it was not until many years later that any-one, other than Himalayan hill people, even got near its base. In the early days of this century, however, the approach at last began —carried on mostly by Englishmen based in what was then British India—and slowly the net closed in about the remote, secret place where rose the highest mountain on earth. At that time both Nepal and Tibet were tightly shut to Westerners; the few who crossed their borders went disguised as Hindu or Buddhist traders. But in 1904 one of the old-style British military missions, on a march to Lhasa, partially pried open the door to Tibet; and in 1920, after long negotiation, permission was granted for an exploratory moun-tain expedition to enter the Forbidden Land.

In the following year came the first confrontation of moun-taineer and Everest. And what had begun as an exercise in higher mathematics was presently to become one of the great adventures of modern man.

The 1921 British venture was a reconnaissance, not an all-out climbing attempt, for every foot of the mountain was then terra incognita. Setting out from Darjeeling, in northeastern India, the pioneers followed a long, roundabout route: first north through Sikkim, then west through southern Tibet, finally approaching Everest from the north by way of Rongbuk and its ancient Bud-dhist monastery. South of Rongbuk, there It was, a vast lopsided pyramid of rock, ice and snow, towering three vertical miles above the high Tibetan plateau; and following the Rongbuk and East Rongbuk Glaciers, the mountaineer-explorers moved up into the unknown world and spent three months probing for ways to the heights.

In the course of these investigations, George Leigh-Mallory, who was soon to become one of the most noted of all Everesters, had an experience that, in the light of later events, was significant and ironic. For, climbing to the top of a high pass called the Lho La, at the base of Everest's West Ridge, he looked across at a narrow snow- and ice-choked valley that was later to become famous in climbing history as the Western Cwm. Indeed it was Mallory who then gave it this name—using the nomenclature of the mountains of Wales, which he had often visited; but little did he realize that this would ultimately be the road to the summit. "I do not fancy it would be possible," he wrote later. And, furthermore, that area of the mountain lay in Nepalese territory and was therefore politically closed to the reconnoiterers of 1921.

Mallory and his companions therefore turned their attention elsewhere, and presently, in a long, high saddle abutting from Everest's Northeast Ridge, they found what they believed to be the key to the ascent. This saddle, which they named the North Col, was reachable only by steep and hazardous slopes of snow and ice; but the climbers managed the ascent, gaining the crest of the Col at about 23,000 feet. Above it, the rock of the Northeast Ridge, slanting skyward, seemed to present no insuperable difficulties. They were equipped to go no farther, however, and it remained for subsequent expeditions to push on along the trail they had blazed.

The wait was not a long one; for the very next year the British were back again, this time prepared for an actual attempt on the summit. Spearheaded by Mallory and other topflight climbers, they gained the North Col, continued on up the Northeast Ridge and out onto the North Face, reaching the then incredible height of 27,300 feet.* But here wind, cold and exhaustion called a halt, and the high climbers had to retreat to camp beneath the snow slopes of the Col. From there, another attempt was mounted; but it ended quickly in disaster—the worst in Everest's history. For on the steep snow, some 600 feet beneath the Col, an avalanche descended on a column of Sherpa porters, carrying seven of them in a white torrent to their deaths. And that was the tragic end for the expedition of 1922.

In 1924, however, the siege was resumed, and the expedition of that year was destined to become one of the most famous in moun-

* This was the first expedition on which oxygen was used—though only experimentally by a few of the climbers. In those days the apparatus was so cumbersome and undependable that it seemed as much a liability as an asset. And besides, its use was considered by many to be not quite "sporting."

taineering history. Mallory and several of the other 1922 climbers were back again, augmented by a group of able newcomers, and following the now-familiar route, they once more worked their way up to the heights. In a magnificent effort—without benefit of oxygen—Col. E. F. Norton and Dr. T. Howard Somervell angled up across the vast North Face to a height of 28,000 feet; and from there Norton alone struggled on for another hundred feet or so, setting an altitude record that was to endure for twenty-eight years. Then, a few days later, came a second assault that was soon to become legend. This time Mallory was first on the rope, and his companion was Andrew Irvine, an Oxford undergraduate and the youngest man on the expedition. They did not take the Norton-Somervell route. Instead of traversing the North Face, they climbed straight up to the crest of the Northeast Ridge, hoping to follow its jagged skyline all the way to the summit. During the course of their ascent one of their companions below had a brief glimpse of them on the ridge: two tiny specks against the sky, moving upward, less than 1500 feet from the goal. Then mist closed in. Dusk came; then night. Another day passed, and more days, and the two climbers never returned. Where and how death overtook them no one knows. And whether victory came before the end no one knows either. On a subsequent expedition one of their ice axes was found lying on the slabs of the North Face below the ridgeline, but it shed no light on mountaineering's greatest mystery.

After 1924, Tibet again shut its doors to Westerners; but after a lapse of some years they were opened again, and during the 1930's there were four more British ventures on Everest. Of these, the first, in 1933, was the most successful, achieving almost the identical height reached in 1924. But the next three, in 1935, 1936 and 1938, were plagued by bad weather and fell short of this mark. It seemed almost as if a magical line had been drawn beneath the ultimate heights, saying to man and his aspirations, *"Thus far but no farther."*

Then came World War II and another, even longer hiatus in the battle for earth's highest mountain. During this period the startling possibility was presented that Everest might not even be the highest mountain, for various wartime airmen flying the Hump between India and China reported that from a height of 30,000 feet they had looked *up* at a distant mountaintop, known as **Amni Machen**, far to the northeast of the Himalaya. They were wrong, however. Subsequent explorations by the Chinese, in whose territory Amni Machen stands, proved that it was a mere 23,000 feet or so, and Everest's supremacy remained inviolate.

By late 1945 the world was again technically at peace; but with Asia in turmoil—notably in India and China, where vast political upheavals were in process—it was not until the 1950's that large-scale Himalayan mountaineering was again possible. When at last it was resumed, however, it was on a scale, and with results, that had been theretofore undreamed of. A century before, there had been what has come to be known as the Golden Age of mountaineering in Europe: a period of some twelve years, during which a whole host of the Alps' greatest peaks were climbed for the first time. Now in the 1950's the Himalaya was in turn to have a Golden Age; for at the beginning of the decade not one of its fourteen Eight-thousanders* (peaks that rise more than 8000 meters, or roughly 26,250 feet, above sea level) had been successfully scaled, and at the end all but one—and that the lowest—had felt the tread of boots on their summit snows.

First came Annapurna, won by the French in 1950. Then in succeeding years came Everest and Nanga Parbat (1953), K2 (1954), Kangchenjunga and Makalu (1955), Lhotse (1956) and Dhaulagiri (1960), together with five other giants, in a record of success that was sensational and dazzling. Had the war years given birth to a new breed of supermen? The answer, of course, is no. Part of the reason for the successes, at least after Annapurna, is unquestionably psychological. Once a barrier has been broken, its subsequent breaking is an easier affair, whether it be in space or the four-minute mile or the climbing of mountains. But aside from this, in mountaineering as in astronautics, foot racing, or any other human activity, it has been a matter of increased experience and knowledge, of improved techniques and equipment.

The old Everesters confronted their mountain in Norfolk jackets and felt hats. They used the same boots, gloves and climbing gear that they had used in the Alps. Their oxygen equipment was rudi-

---

* There are no Eight-thousanders outside the Himalaya. The highest non-Himalayan peaks are less than 25,000 feet.

mentary, their food stores bulky, and their understanding of the problems of high-altitude living was gained bit by bit, through hard and bitter experience. Not, to be sure, that postwar climbers have solved all the problems or know all the answers, but they have gained hugely from the trials and errors of their predecessors. They know that the Himalaya are not merely outsized Alps, but mountains of totally different scale and scope, requiring different tactics and logistics. And they have had the benefit of all the scientific and technological advances of recent years, with such end products as concentrated foods, lightweight but warm clothing, light but strong metals, efficient packaging, reliable instruments, effective medicines. Mountaineers like to think of their realm as being beyond and above the twentieth century world of laboratory and factory, industrialism and mass production. And so it is, once they are there, to both eye and spirit. But they must also acknowledge the fact that the road to earth's rooftop is paved not only with good intentions—not only with human strength and courage and aspiration (of which earlier climbers had no less a share)—but also with the "advances" of a civilization which in many ways they deplore.

In terms of Everest, the gap between 1930's and 1950's brought about not only such changes as these, but also a drastic shift of scene. For if the physical world remained the same as before, the political world had altered greatly. Tibet, which before had provided the only permissible route to the mountain, was again being sealed off from the outside world, this time by Communist China. But in rough counterbalance, Nepal, which for centuries had been tightly shut to foreigners, had begun to open up. The one possible road to earth's summit no longer led in from the north but from the south. And it is from this side—almost as if it were another mountain—that Everest, in the postwar years, has been challenged and climbed.

The first party to approach it, in 1950, was not a mountaineering expedition but a small group of five Americans and one Englishman, who had received permission to explore in northeastern Nepal, and who, like climbers the world over, were filled with curiosity as to what the mountain might present from this direction. Traversing regions never before seen by Westerners, they came to the Sherpa country, called Solu Khumbu, due south of the peak; and from there two of them—Dr. Charles S. Houston, a top American climber, and H. W. Tilman, a veteran British Everester and Himalayan explorer—went on to the very foot of the mountain. Here, at the head of the Khumbu Glacier, was the base of Everest's vast West Ridge. To its left was the snow saddle called the Lho La, which George Mallory had climbed from the other side twenty-nine years before. And to its right, visible from a vantage point across the glacier, was the high hidden valley which Mallory had called the Western Cwm.

The Cwm, however, was separated from the lower glacier by a monstrous icefall, a frozen cataract of ice plunging steeply downward through a narrow gap between Everest and a neighboring peak called Nuptse; and Tilman and Houston liked its looks no more than had Mallory before them. In any case, they were equipped to go no farther, and presently they rejoined their companions in the Sherpa country below. No actual climbing had been done. The way to the heights looked dangerous and difficult in the extreme. But at least they had pioneered a route to the mountain that was far shorter than the old Tibetan approach. And they had seen sights of majesty and beauty on which no man had ever laid eyes before.

Confront *homo curioso* with a closed door and he will turn the knob. Open the door a finger's width and he will insert a foot. Houston and Tilman had reached Everest's southwestern gate in the fall of 1950, and exactly a year later a full-scale British expedition followed after them, prepared, if not to climb Everest, at least to give this unknown side a thorough reconnaissance. It was led by another old Everester of the thirties, Eric Shipton, but the other members were of the younger postwar generation, and among them was a tall raw-boned New Zealander named Edmund Hillary. As their predecessors had predicted, the Icefall proved sticky going. Day after day, then week after week, the climbers labored up through its white wilderness of towers and chasms, hacking steps, stringing ropes, striving constantly but futilely to find a route that would not be menaced by toppling cliffs and crumbling footways. At last they reached the top of the Icefall. Or, rather, almost the top. For just beneath its final pitch, where it levels off into the Western Cwm, they were confronted by a huge crevasse that split it across from side to side; and here Shipton called a halt. They

had proved that the Icefall would "go." Even the crevasse at its
top could be managed with the proper bridging materials. But,
with winter approaching, they were running out of time and good
weather, and it would remain for others to push on into the Cwm
and beyond.

"Others," as it developed, were very much others. For the political pressures that swung back the gates of Nepal had opened them
to all nations of the West, and now for the first time a wholly non-
British assault was made on Everest. In 1952 the Swiss had their
turn, and they all but snatched the prize for which the British had
been struggling for three decades. Working their way up the Icefall, they entered the Western Cwm, and at the head of the Cwm
climbed the steep slopes on the flanks of Lhotse, the world's fourth
highest peak, which with Everest and Nuptse forms an awesome
juxtaposed trinity of mountain masses. This brought them to what
the British had named the South Col, a 26,200-foot saddle between
Lhotse and Everest. And from there the French-Swiss climber,
Raymond Lambert, and the remarkable Sherpa, Tenzing Norgay,
launched a tremendous effort, getting to within 800 feet of Everest's summit before wind, cold and exhaustion turned them back.
This was in the spring of 1952. In the early fall the Swiss were back
again—marking the first occasion on which the mountain had been
tried twice in one year. But this time, in worse weather, they were
stopped a short distance above the South Col.

In that same fall there may or may not have been another expedition on the Tibetan side of Everest: to wit, a Russian attempt
on the top of the world. No official announcement about it was
ever made, but rumors of such a venture soon began filtering along
the Himalayan and then the international grapevine. There was
talk of an ascent to about 26,000 feet and of a subsequent disaster
which took six lives. How much, if any, of this is true is still unknown in the Western world, for the facts have remained hidden
in clouds of Communist secrecy. But at least the Russians made no
claim of having reached the summit.

Then came 1953—the ninth British expedition—and victory.

The details of this great exploit are too well known to need
cataloging here, and besides, they are frequently mentioned in the
pages that follow. In its overall aspect the essence of the thing was
that it was a supreme all-out effort, stronger in both manpower and

materiel than any that had been mounted before. Over the years of struggle and aspiration Everest had become, very specially, a "British" mountain. But now the British no longer had the exclusive franchise. A French expedition had already staked its claim for an attempt in 1954, the Swiss for another try in 1955; and it was obvious that if the British didn't climb "their" mountain in short order, someone else surely would. Under the leadership of Sir John—then Colonel—Hunt they therefore launched an attack which drew on every source, human and logistical, at their command; and the outcome, as all the world knows, was a shining triumph. Following the route pioneered by their own reconnaissance party of 1951 and the Swiss in 1952, they made their way up the Icefall, the Cwm, the Lhotse Face, to the South Col, pitching their highest camp above the Col at about 27,900 feet on Everest's Southeast Ridge. And on May 29 Edmund Hillary and the Sherpa Tenzing—the latter now on his seventh Everest expedition—went all the way to the top.

Earth's pinnacle had been reached at last. As with the North and South Poles before it, an ultimate had been won. "Very well, it has been done," said the world at large. "Let us turn our attention to other things." But mountaineers felt otherwise. Granted, Everest climbed would never again have quite the magic allure of Everest unclimbed. But it was still the summit of our planet. Unwon or once won, it was still an ultimate. And there would be many attempts to win it again.

The first, in 1956, was by the Swiss. And this time they pushed past their previous near miss to a brilliant success, putting two 2-man teams on the summit on successive days and, for good measure, making a first ascent of Lhotse as well. Then, in 1960 and 1962, came two Indian expeditions, both of which were a blend of achievement and disappointment. For neither reached the top. On the first try the climbers got to within 700 feet of the summit, on the second, even higher, only to be forced down in heartbreaking defeat. But for a nation with no mountaineering tradition, and which a few years before had numbered scarcely a single expert climber in all its vast population, India, even in its almost-but-not-quite efforts, had done itself proud.

It has remained for another Asian nation, the Chinese, to place a third claim to going all the way. In 1960, they say—at the same time that the Indians were on the Nepalese side of Everest—an expedition of their own was scaling the Tibetan side, during the course of which three men reached the summit and left a plaster bust of Mao Tse Tung, no less, as a memento of their visit. Unlike the mysterious Russian venture of 1952, the Chinese climb is known to have taken place and to have carried fairly high on the mountain. But the account of it, as released to the world, is so saturated in Communist propaganda, so vague in mountaineering detail, that most non-Chinese mountaineers (including Russians) have strong doubts that their summit claim is true.

These, through 1962, were the major expeditions to Everest: a total of fifteen, including reconnaissances in force but not the Houston-Tilman approach or the quasi-mythical Russian venture. In addition, over the years, there have been four bootleg raids, so to speak, on the mountain, three by lone-wolf adventurers (an Englishman, a Dane and a Canadian) and one by a quartet of three Americans and one Swiss. All were from the Tibetan side, with minimal equipment and no political authorization; and the results, for the solo climbers, ranged from death by exposure for the Englishman to respectable, though low-level, performances by Dane and Canadian. Most recent, occurring in 1962, was the American go (the one Swiss was more or less an afterthought), led by Woodrow Wilson Sayre, a grandson of our late President and a philosophy professor at Tufts University. Sayre & Company approached the mountain through Nepal, telling Nepalese and American officials that they were bound for one of Everest's neighbors, a peak called Gyachung Kang, which was itself of forbidding dimensions for a four-man party. But once in the wilderness, they crossed a pass into Tibet (i.e., Communist China), reached the northern base of Everest without being intercepted, and climbed to more than 25,000 feet, above the North Col, before reaching the end of their tether. They had little mountaineering experience, a scanty stock of food and gear, and no porters. And there is no denying that it was a remarkable junket. But it is no less remarkable that they did not either kill themselves or trigger a ripsnorting international "incident." As it was, they caused a vast amount of work and worry for our ambassador to Nepal and his staff—plus the embarrassment of apologies to the Nepalese Government. And Sayre himself, breaking down on the return trip, almost surely *would* have died

had it not been for the presence in Kathmandu of our own leader-
to-be, Norman Dyhrenfurth, who, at the risk of his life, flew out by
helicopter into the wilds to bring Sayre back to civilization. In
retrospect, as told by Sayre, the exploit was all fun and games. It
made for lively reading in *Life* and a good story on the lecture circuit. But it is exactly this sort of harebrained adventuring that
makes the lowlander think all climbers are mentally deficient. And
it hasn't the remotest resemblance to what true mountaineers
mean by mountaineering.

From 1920 to 1962, from Mallory to Sayre—thus stood the
Everest record as our Royal Nepal Airlines DC-3 took off from
Calcutta and droned its way northwestward above the Indian plain.
And now here we were, we Johnny-come-latelies, about to add to
that record as best we could.

Why?

That is the eternal blank-faced question forever put to the
climber by the nonclimber. Why turn your back on comfort, ease,
security? Why walk when you can ride, climb when you can fly,
struggle when you can rest? What is the lure of Old Baldy, Mount
Washington, Rainier, the Matterhorn, McKinley, Aconcagua, Annapurna, Kangchenjunga, Everest? To "why climb Everest?"
George Mallory long ago gave the answer that is now so famous it
is a bromide. "Because it is there," he said. And if cryptically un-
satisfactory to the unbeliever, it at least had the virtue of brevity.

For us, some forty years later, the question had an added barb.
Now it went, "Why—doubly why—climb Everest when it has already been climbed?" And for an answer we needed to add one
word to Mallory's statement: "Because it is *still* there."

The mountain—and the challenge.

Particularly was it still there for American mountaineers—our
true mountaineers—who had never yet had a try at it. Twice or
thrice climbed, besieged by fifteen or twenty or a hundred predecessors, it was still there, every inch of it, with its storms and its
battlements, its peril and its glory.

From our plane, presently, we were looking up from the drab
brownness of earth, across rising foothills, to a white vision in the
sky.

3. GLINT IN THE EYE

You DON'T JUST DECIDE to go to Everest, and go. Before our expedition moved an inch toward its objective, we had been through a struggle on the precipices of organization and finance, compared with which, we sometimes felt, the climb itself would be what Baedeker used to call "an easy day for a lady."

For me, the long long trail had begun some two and half years earlier, in the late summer of 1960. I was at home in my apartment in New York City; the phone rang, and at the other end was Dick Johnston, the assistant managing editor of *Sports Illustrated*.

"How would you like to go to Mount Everest?" asked Dick.

There was a slight pause.

"Please repeat that slowly," I said.

"Are you available to go on an expedition to Everest?"

Another pause. Something had happened to my heartbeat.

"I am," I said.

"Good. We'd like to have you represent us," said Dick. "An American expedition is being organized for next spring by a chap named—"

"Dyhrenfurth," I said.
"How did you know?"

I knew all right. I knew, because I knew Norman Dyhrenfurth. At the time I had not seen him for three or four years. I lived on the East Coast, he on the West. We had not recently crossed paths in our travels, nor had we corresponded. But we were friends of more than twenty years' standing, and I was as sure as I had ever been of anything in my life that if someone in the United States of America was planning an expedition to Everest, it was he and no other.*

Norman was a true man of the mountains. Before that he had been a boy and a child of the mountains. Indeed, mountains had been in his blood and bone from birth, for his father, Professor Günter O. Dyhrenfurth, a Swiss geologist and expedition leader, was—and is—perhaps the world's foremost expert on the Himalaya; and his mother, Hettie, had, on one of her husband's ventures, established a climbing altitude record for women that had endured for years. Born in 1918 and raised in Switzerland, Norman had come to the United States when in his early twenties, had become an American citizen and married an American girl. Trained as a motion picture photographer, he had worked in that capacity for documentary film companies in New York and elsewhere; then, moving to the West Coast, became first the head of the Department of Cinematography at the University of California in Los Angeles and subsequently a producer-director of his own films.

From his boyhood days in the Alps, however, mountains had remained (with due respect to wife Sally) his first and truest love. He climbed whenever and wherever he could. And the climbs grew in number and scope until he had behind him four major Himalayan expeditions: to Everest with the second Swiss venture of 1952; to Lhotse, Everest's great neighbor, in 1955, with an American-Swiss-Austrian group; again to the Everest region in 1958 on an American-sponsored search for the Abominable Snowman (no Snowman obliged); and in 1960 with an international party that climbed Dhaulagiri, the highest peak in central Nepal. On the

---

* With no apologies to Mr. Sayre, our venture is here and hereafter referred to as the first American Everest expedition.

Lhotse climb he had been leader; on the Snowman venture, deputy leader; on all four, a combined mountaineer-cameraman, leaving him with a backlog of expedition experience unmatched by anyone in this country. That Everest should be on his mind was as natural as that fire should leap upward or water flow down.

I had known Norman since soon after his arrival in the States. We had climbed together on the rock faces of the Hudson River valley, in the Tetons of western Wyoming, and I had learned from him much of what I knew about mountaineering: not merely the physical aspects of getting where you wanted to without falling off, but the meaning of mountaineering—the love of mountains —that underlies all the rest. It was not only natural, it was heart-warming, that he should now be involving himself in the greatest of all mountain adventures. For I knew that he would bring to it not only the knowledge, skill and determination that are essential for such an enterprise, but something else as well. Something without which a confrontation with the greatest mountain on earth would be purposeless and meaningless; something for which, I think, there is only one word; and the word is *reverence*.

Presently it was no longer Dick Johnston to whom I was speaking on the phone, but Norman himself, in Santa Monica, California.

"Well, at last!" I said. And then there was much talk, about this, that and the other—but all of it about Everest—and I think the excitement in our voices must have shaken the wires across the span of the continent, as we discussed the dreams and desires of two lifetimes.

Then, finally and inevitably, realism raised its ugly head.

"We're not there yet, Jim," said Norman. "It will still take some doing."

And it did indeed.

As of that September of 1960 the plan was that the expedition would take place in the spring of the next year. The first step in any nonbootleg Himalayan operation is to secure permission for the climb from the nation through which the mountain will be approached, and in the case of Everest this of course meant Nepal. Such permission, for 1961, had been granted some time ago by the Nepalese Government to Major O. William Hackett of the United

States Army (as a mountaineering private citizen), and Hackett had then sought out Norman, suggesting that he join in the venture. Norman, who had already been dreaming about Everest for years, had at once gone to work on its organization and financing (which was where *Sports Illustrated*, as a possible partial backer, came in). But even at the time of our first phone talk it seemed doubtful to him that the project could be mounted in a mere six months or so.

Soon doubt became fact: it could not. Everest in 1961 was simply an organizational impossibility. The following year was out too, for it had already been "reserved" by the second of the two Indian expeditions. So, with Major Hackett withdrawing from the enterprise, Norman made application to the Nepalese Government for permission for 1963. And 1963 it became.* "That gives us more than two years," he wrote to me late in the fall of 1960. "That should be enough."

And it was—though not by much.

For it is the ironic fact that in the great and wealthy United States it is harder to raise money for mountaineering purposes than in any other major, or even minor, country on earth. In Western Europe, with the Alps as its fulcrum, the climbing of mountains has long been a highly popular and organized activity, with funds for expeditions available from governments, foundations, Alpine Clubs, and various other sources. Since the beginning of large-scale Himalayan climbing early in this century, nations like Britain, France, Germany and Switzerland have sent out expedition upon expedition to the Roof of the World. Even in classically poor countries like Italy and Austria, mountaineers have found little trouble raising the funds to get them to their objectives and back. In nations of the non-Western world, such as Russia, India, and even China, interest in mountaineering, though new, has recently become intense, and here the expenses of expeditions have been borne entirely by governments.

Not that we in America would wish for this last. An expedition financed by a government—whether democratic, communist or in-

* We handed over a down payment of $320, against a total of $640. In recent years Nepal has charged a fee to foreign expeditions for the climbing of its peaks, ranging from this top amount for Everest down to $100 or so for lesser fry.

determinate—is certain, to a degree, to be *run* by that government, with all the inevitable concomitants of bureaucracy, red tape, regimentation and "official" status. And we who love mountains —at least in our part of the world—want as little of this as possible. On the other hand, however, those of us who were to become involved in the American Mount Everest Expedition of 1963 found ourselves wishing fervently, during the thirty-odd months that it took to launch it, that the process were less like wandering the streets with a tin cup. This state of affairs stems from the fact that, though there are not a few mountain lovers in these States of ours, their name is not legion and they control no potent purse strings. Indeed, in New York, California and points intermediate, the raising of money for an Everest expedition proved only slightly less difficult than, say, soliciting funds for a statue of Karl Marx on the White House lawn.

To be sure, there had been many American climbing expeditions before this one. To Alaska. To the Andes. To the far Himalaya. In this last category there had been Norman's own venture on Lhotse and an attempt on nearby Makalu by a team from the Sierra Club of California. There had been three notable assaults on K2, earth's second highest mountain; climbs on Masherbrum and Hidden Peak, two other giants of the Karakoram region; expeditions to other, only slightly lesser summits along the whole great uplift from Afghanistan to Assam.* All of these had somehow got themselves off the ground and to their distant objectives. But most had operated financially very close to the shoestring level. And none had been remotely comparable in size and scope to what Norman had in mind for the first American try at Everest.

Here we run—and ran—into a question that is forever hotly argued among mountaineers: to wit, what *is* the optimum size and scope of an expedition? Much of the appeal, and meaning, of mountaineering is a withdrawal from the "bigness" of the world we live in; from the complexities of a highly organized society into the simpler and purer world of nature as God made it. No climber worth the name wants to climb in a crowd. His beau ideal of a

* Several members of the 1963 Everest Expedition had taken part in these earlier climbs. Reference to some is made in the text that follows; reference to all is made in the "Who's Who" beginning on page 295.

mountain party is a small group of friends, away from the crowd, bound together by shared tastes and skills and aspirations in an adventure all their own. This is the way in which most mountaineering is done—and should be done; and there are those who extend this *should* to the greatest mountains, believing that even a Kangchenjunga, a K2 or an Everest can best be experienced, and even won, by a small and homogeneous party. High apostles of this creed have been the old and noted British Everesters, Eric Shipton and H. W. Tilman; and there are many in the States who agree with them—among them Dr. Charles Houston and Robert Bates, who have twice led expeditions to K2 and rank among the top mountaineers our country has produced. Indeed, during the organization of *Everest-1963*, a lively running debate developed between Norman and Charlie Houston, with the latter charging that the size of Norman's contemplated venture was in violation of the true mountaineering spirit.*

Norman, for his part, begged to differ. Though yielding precedence to no one in the "purity" of his mountaineering spirit, he believed that a major objective called for a major campaign. True, he conceded, there had been some notable climbs by small expeditions, among them Houston and Bates's own forays on K2. But the fact remained that they had not reached K2's summit. It was a large Italian party that finally did it. And on Everest itself, the British, after their many gallant but unsuccessful tries by comparatively small teams, had at last triumphed only when they put a powerful task force in the field.

It was such a force that Norman now planned. Not six or eight men, but eighteen or twenty, with all the porterage and equipment that such a number would require. Great care would be taken in their selection to insure a happy and congenial team, but it must also be a strong team, in personnel and all other resources. Man proposes, Everest disposes; and there is no foolproof passport to its heights. But Norman at least wanted its first American challengers to have every advantage that manpower, materiel and money could provide.

* There was, however, no animosity in the argument; and at expedition's end both Houston and Bates were warm in their praise and happy to concede that a case could indeed be made for a large-scale venture.

—American challengers. And such we would be. Yet presently another controversy was to arise over the use, or alleged overuse, of the very word "American"; for in the lexicon of mountaineers nationalism is a touchy and tricky subject. For better or worse (far *worse*, I would say) we of the second half of the twentieth century live in a world in which national allegiance is the primary index which splits man into separate categories; and in most fields of human activity, from armament to education, from space exploration to Olympic Games, it is taken for granted that organization and development are national in structure. But in the mystique of mountaineering—and this is one of its glories—things are otherwise. For the true mountaineer believes that, just as the physical mountains rise above the plains of the earth, so should his feeling for the mountains be above the pettiness of jingoism and flag waving. "Everest is too great to belong to anyone," said the Sherpa Tenzing when he and Hillary had come down from the first climb to its summit. "It is for all men." And to that the only answer is a quiet "Amen."

Nevertheless—and here we are back to the world we live in—most expeditions are "national," at least by label. There are times, one must concede, when it has been more than label; when jingoism has been carried to ugly extremes, as by the pre-World War II Germans, in both Alps and Himalaya, with their creed of *Führer und Vaterland*, victory or death. But in most cases expeditions are assembled along national lines simply because that is the most logical and practical way of doing things. During its organization period, *Everest-1963* was accused by the mountaineering purists not only of being too big but of being too "American"; of laying too much stress, in our efforts at promotion and financing, on our being the *first American* expedition to Everest. To which our answer was simply that (1) this statement was the simple fact, and (2) it was only by emphasizing it that, in a country not greatly dedicated to mountaineering, we were able to arouse interest in our venture. Neither in Norman Dyhrenfurth nor in any of us who were to become associated with him was there the slightest vestige of strident nationalism; of the notion that we were bigger, better or stronger than anyone else. We said rather, both to ourselves and others: "Yes, we are Americans—in which we find nothing to be particularly ashamed of. We are Americans who know and love mountains, and now for the first time we have a chance to go to the greatest of all mountains. We shall go eagerly, joyfully, reverently—and, we hope, with a strong enough team to give us a reasonable chance for success."

Thus we asked for support. And in the end we got it.

This, however, is getting well ahead of the story. For in that fall of 1960, and for more than a year thereafter, we had nothing at all; indeed, an even more absolute nothing than a few months earlier, for *Sports Illustrated*, which had been the one semicommitment for 1961, presently declared itself uninterested in a project as remote as 1963. That left Norman with his permission from Nepal and the glint in his own eye. But it was a glint that went deep, that never faded; and it was to carry him across mountains of labor, disappointment and frustration that often seemed to loom higher than Everest itself. There were times when I myself was convinced that the project would never materialize. But then, early in 1961, Norman came East, and we met at last after that lapse of several years. He had aged some in those years—as who hadn't?—and was far removed from the youngster I had climbed with back in prewar days in the Tetons and on Hudson cliffs. He was now a man in his forties, long since a husband and family man, carrying about 190 pounds on his sturdy six-foot frame. But the wavy shock of his brown hair was the same as ever, with no touch of gray. The thrust of his jaw was the same, the warmth of his handshake—and that glint in his gray eyes. "We're going to make it, Jim," he said. "Hang on, we're going to make it." And I heard the voice, and I saw the glint, and I stopped doubting.

Back home in Santa Monica, he had long since given up his workaday jobs of teaching and film making to devote himself entirely to the expedition. He lived on savings, credit and hope. While bankrupting himself, he made the telephone company rich and presently was doing the same for the airlines, in successive trips about the country in quest of team members and financing. The big foundations from which so many bounties flow—Ford, Rockefeller and the like—were not interested in mountaineering. (Nor, for that matter, were the little foundations.) In the Federal government there was no one authoritative source of funds to go to, but rather a variety of subsources, in many different departments, which might or might not prove interested in some aspect of the project; and soon Norman was in touch with more of these than he had previously known existed. For the food, clothing and equipment the expedition would need, there were letters, phone calls and calls in person to firms all over the country, in quest of donations of their products. There were negotiations with newspapers, magazines, book publishers, television networks—indeed with anyone and everyone who, for reasons sane or insane, might conceivably put a dollar or a penny into an expedition to Everest.

Or, rather, Everest-plus; for Norman had now broadened the scope of his plans to include not only Everest itself but its two great neighbor peaks, Lhotse and Nuptse. Both had also been previously climbed: 27,890-foot Lhotse by the same Swiss party that ascended Everest in 1956; 25,850-foot Nuptse by a British team in 1961. But no one had yet even attempted to include all three in one venture; and it was Norman's feeling that the triple climb, if successful, would be a notable mountaineering feat ("a real grand slam," as he called it) and that even in prospect it would serve as answer to possible backers who were forever saying, "But Everest has been climbed. Why climb it again?" Of this second theory I myself was dubious; for "why climb it again?" was asked only by strictly nonmountaineering types who would probably think Lhotse and Nuptse were a pair of TV comedians. But regarding the first proposition there was no room for argument. The ascent of the three great peaks, all by one expedition, would indeed be a notable "first" in the history of men and mountains, and it was a measure of Norman's ambition and imagination that he dared even think of it.

We prepared a brochure that presented our plans, our projected timetable, a roster of expedition members (which we shall get to presently), and—deep breath—a budget. Norman's original total for this was $186,000; but allowing for the hoped-for donations of food and materiel, by no means all of it would have to be in cash. As enterprises go in today's United States it was an almost picayune amount. But for mountaineering it was an unheard-of sum, and for a time it seemed that we could have stricken out the the three zeros and still not have made the quota.

At last, however, there came the first "breakthrough." And ironically it was with *Life*, a sister-magazine of *Sports Illustrated* in the Time, Inc. Empire, which had first encouraged us and then defected. The initial advance from *Life* was, to be sure, for no vast amount—a modest $2500—but at least it helped cover the endless drain of postage, phone calls and travel; and also it was a potent morale booster that *someone* was willing to gamble on us. Other than the *Life* advance, all there was to go on in those early days were advances from the more solvent prospective members of the expedition, all of whom had been solicited for $500 loans, returnable when and if (fantastic thought at the time) the enterprise ever emerged into the black. Meanwhile on other fronts there were prospects, prospects, prospects—all of whom had to be found, approached, seen, and briefed on various aspects of the project (including the spelling of Lhotse and Nuptse). And gradually we began to find friends and believers. In the governmental sector we won a few supporters—notably Secretary of the Interior Stuart E. Udall, Senator Warren G. Magnuson of Washington, and Senator Clair Engle of California—who helped clear the way to Federal agencies that might help us. Manufacturers of food and clothing, fabrics and equipment, began to turn a sympathetic ear. The American Alpine Club, the most prestigious mountaineering organization in the country, endorsed our venture and made us a small loan. Other climbing and outdoor clubs, with larger memberships, allowed us to use their publications for solicitation purposes. *Summit*, a West Coast magazine, small but influential in the mountain world, devoted most of an issue to our plans and needs. And through all these we began receiving support from individual contributors.

It was soon obvious, however, that we would never finance ourselves by a drib here, a drab there. What was essential was a nucleus of major backers; and here our main hope—along with government agencies—was the National Geographic Society. Unlike *Life*, the *Geographic* is not simply a magazine. It is also a foundation, with large resources available for the endowment of science and exploration, and over the years it had had a hand in

many expeditions, including Peary's and Byrd's—although never to
date in a strictly mountaineering venture. This, thought Norman,
was an omission that should now be rectified; and from the beginning of his planning he had made pilgrimages to the *Geographic's*
headquarters in Washington, D.C. On the helpful side was the
fact that we had a strong ally on the "inside" there: Barry C.
Bishop, of the magazine staff. Barry was a young man of many hats
and talents: a geographer, writer, photographer and mountaineer.
Representing the *Geographic*, he had been a member of Sir Edmund Hillary's Himalayan Scientific and Mountaineering Expedition of 1960–61; he was bursting with enthusiasm for a try at
Everest; and he did everything possible to plead our case in court.
But working against him—and us—was an opposed and potent factor that was to stretch negotiations out for almost a year.

This factor was simply that the *Geographic* shared with most of
the rest of the United States a notable lack of interest in mountaineering per se. Its involvement in the Hillary expedition had
been principally because of its scientific aspects (cartography, geology, meteorology, physiology), and almost its first question to us
was: what scientific work were *we* going to do? Norman was not
unprepared for this. Like every true mountain man he preferred
his mountaineering "straight" and believed that the climbing of a
great peak, for its own sake, justified itself a thousand times over:
in adventure, in depth—or height—of human experience, in the
interplay of challenge and response to challenge that is the very
essence of man's function in life. But he had not been born yesterday. He knew that it was hard, all but impossible, to "sell" mountaineering as an end in itself; that even in countries with a stronger
mountain tradition than ours it is often necessary to take on scientific commitments, to make an expedition "useful," "practical"—
and financible. And he was prepared to do this.

The problem was *how* to do it. How to launch and conduct an
expedition dedicated to both mountain climbing and scientific research without permitting its two disparate aspects to come into
conflict. And the solution, Norman felt, was twofold. One part of
it would be that mountaineering and science must be integrated;
that all scientific work must have a direct relationship to the climbing of a mountain, with no aims or purposes pulling in other direc-

tions. And the second part was that the scientists who came along would, insofar as it was possible to effect, *also* be mountaineers.

Negotiations with the *Geographic*, with government agencies, manufacturers, suppliers, and contributors went on and on. Meanwhile Norman was simultaneously working on the one aspect of the expedition without which all the rest would add up to exactly nothing: the composition of the team that would go with him to Everest.

In financing, he faced a realm of scarcity; in manpower, a world of abundance. For while there are not as many mountaineers in the country as there are bowlers or golfers or even skin divers, there are an ample number—and good ones—and most would give all they have, plus a bit more, for a chance at Everest. Unlike the world of mountains, the world of climbers is rather small and closely knit; its members are apt to be known to one another, if not personally, at least by reputation; and it was largely to men he knew, or knew of, that Norman went for his team.* He wanted a good spread in ages, from the middle twenties to the middle forties†—for mountaineering, unlike more competitive sports, is not the exclusive province of the very young. He wanted a spread in experience; from rock climbing to snow and ice climbing, covering the many skills and techniques that mountaineering embraces. He wanted no prima donnas or virtuosos good only for a short spectacular performance, but a group with endurance as well as ability, patience as well as daring, who could withstand, both physically and mentally, the ordeal that two to three months on Everest were sure to impose. Above all, he wanted a team that would get on together; that in spite of differences in individual background and personality would be bound together in firm companionship by their shared knowledge and love of mountains.

Also he wanted, and needed, specialists of various sorts: in medi-

* All told, there were about 100 applicants—three of them women. As regards the latter, there was no anti-female plank in the expedition's platform, for there are many first-rate women climbers. But it was felt that Everest itself would present sufficient hazards without our courting the possible added one of petticoat fever.

† A range which, to be sure, did not include myself, who am in the middle fifties. But my function on the expedition would be that of a scribe, not a climber; my goal, the base of Everest, not the summit.

cine, communications, photography, oxygen equipment. Not to forget those mountaineer-scientists who would—hopefully—beard the *Geographic* and other scientific organizations in their dens and emerge trailing clouds of lucre.

As early as mid-1961 an almost full tentative team had been lined up. There were subsequent dropouts, of course—owing to career, money and family problems—with new men coming in as replacements; but more than two-thirds of those originally selected were still on deck when 1963 arrived, a remarkable figure when one considers the time lapse and all that could happen in the interim. Most of the men were from the West; not unnaturally, for that is where our big mountains are. All but four of the final twenty were married, with a total, on departure, of twenty-six children (to which one was added during the expedition). The educational level was positively frightening, with no less than three M.D.s, five Ph.D.s and five M.A.s or M.S.s (three of whom were working for Ph.D.s), leaving the expedition scribe, with a lowly B.A., among the illiterate riffraff. Nine could technically be called professional climbers, in that at one time or another they had served as paid mountain guides; but in all cases this was as avocation, not full-time career. In their low-level incarnations, three of the twenty were in business, all the rest in some form of profession, of which the dominant one, by far, was teaching.

Second in command to Norman, as Deputy Leader, would be William E. Siri, biological physicist at the University of California, and himself the leader of several earlier expeditions (including the 1954 attempt on Makalu), making him the ideally sought-for combination of scientist-*cum*-mountaineer. Siri would not only conduct his own research projects in the field but would further serve as coordinator of all the expedition's scientific work. Also, like Norman, he hoped himself to go high on the mountain, although both, in their middle forties, were at a borderline age in terms of their chances of reaching the top. Physically they were antitheses: Norman big and powerful; Will small, slim and wiry, and with high forehead and glasses, pipe and tobacco pouch, looking every inch the research scientist. But both were equally men of the mountains, in experience, in love and in desire.

Also high on the roster* was William F. Unsoeld, aged thirty-six, one of the top climbers in the country, and in his nonmountaineering life a professor of philosophy and religion and a father of four. Willi—as distinguished from Will—was a three-time Himalayan veteran and was to rank as one of the expedition's elder statesmen: meaning that he would be consulted on all major decisions, and that if Norman and Will, for reasons of age or otherwise, could not go as far as they hoped, he would be the chief tactician for the summit attempts. That he was a man of action went without saying. But he was also a philosopher of the mountains, no less than of the classroom, and we knew his contribution to the team would be not only of leg and lung but of spirit as well.

Unsoeld was from the Pacific Northwest. And so too were James W. Whittaker, thirty-four, the manager of a Seattle sporting goods store, and Luther G. Jerstad, twenty-six, a speech instructor at the University of Oregon—both longtime summer climbing guides on Mount Rainier, scalers of Mount McKinley, and past masters of snow and ice craft. From the Rocky Mountain region came four other team members: Allen Auten, thirty-six, and Richard Pownall, thirty-five, of the Denver area, and John E. Breitenbach, twenty-seven, and James Barry Corbet, twenty-six, of Jackson, Wyoming. The latter three had all—as had Willi Unsoeld—been guides in Grand Teton National Park, one of the most challenging ranges for rock climbing in the United States. And Auten was both a practiced mountaineer and an electronic technician, in which second guise he would serve as our radio-communications expert. In the workaday world he was an editor of a Denver publication, *Design News*; Pownall was a public high school teacher; Breitenbach and Corbet were partners in a Jackson skiing and climbing equipment store, with Corbet further functioning as proprietor of a mountain lodge.

Our three physicians were Gilbert Roberts, twenty-eight, fresh from the United States Air Force; Thomas F. Hornbein, thirty-two, even fresher from the Navy (indeed, with the aid of official Washington, we had pried him loose before his term of service expired); and David L. Dingman, twenty-six, resident in surgery at Univer-

* More detailed biographies of the team members appear in "Who's Who," in Part II.

sity Hospital in Baltimore. All, too, were experienced mountain men—Dingman having climbed in Alaska and Peru, and Roberts and Hornbein as members of earlier Himalayan expeditions. In our party, Roberts would serve as senior M.D. Hornbein, an anesthesiologist, would, in addition to climbing and special doctoring duties, be the expedition oxygen expert and had already designed new apparatus which would be used on the mountain. As added distinction, he topped Willi Unsoeld as team paterfamilias, with a total of five children.

From the realm of the sciences, along with these and Will Siri, came four others: Richard M. Emerson, thirty-eight, a sociologist from the University of Cincinnati; James T. Lester, thirty-five, a Californian psychologist; Maynard M. Miller, forty-one, associate professor of geology at Michigan State University; and Barry W. Prather, twenty-three, who several times in the past had served as Miller's assistant, and now would do so again. Of these, Emerson had had wide mountaineering experience in the Rockies, Alps and Himalaya; Miller, ranking as perhaps the foremost glaciologist in the country, had been almost literally everywhere where there were mountains with snow and ice on them; and Prather, in spite of being expedition "baby," was already an old climbing hand, as well as geologist, physicist, radio operator and all-around handyman. Only Jim Lester, of the whole team membership, had had virtually no previous mountain experience; but no sooner had he been signed on than he began making up for lost time.

As still another specialist-plus-climber there was Daniel E. Doody, twenty-nine, a freewheeling cameraman and film maker who had long been a friend and associate of Norman's in Southern California. To be sure, Norman himself was of the same profession. But with the myriad duties he would have as expedition leader, he felt he himself could not do justice to a first-class motion picture job; and thus Doody came onto the team, with Norman moving up and sideways as prospective part-time cameraman and producer-director.

Then there was Barry Bishop, thirty-one, of the *National Geographic*—already introduced—who would certainly be one of us, when and if the Society gave its fiscal blessing. There was, of course, Norman himself. There was myself, as historian—bringing the roster to nineteen. And as the twentieth there would be the one non-American expedition member, Lt. Col. James O. M. Roberts, forty-six, of the British Army (retired), former officer in the Gurkha Rifles, more recently military attaché of the British Embassy in Nepal, and still, in retirement, a Nepalese resident. Jimmy, as he was to become known to us, was, and is, perhaps as experienced and knowledgeable a hand in the Himalaya as any man living. A veteran of some dozen major expeditions, and countless minor ones, from Everest to the Karakoram, he knew not only the mountains themselves, but the language and ways of the mountain people; and Norman (who had met him on his own previous Himalayan ventures) had from the beginning been hopeful of getting him as our transport officer. The hope was realized. And though the rest of us were not to meet him until our arrival in Nepal, we were all eventually to be grateful that he was one of us.

Such was our roster; and it was one that Norman—and everyone else—was well pleased with. In age balance there were seven men in their twenties, eight in their thirties, four in their forties, and one—shall we say courtesy member—in his fifties. In experience, eight had been on previous Himalayan ventures; six had climbed Alaska's Mount McKinley, the highest peak in North America; and all, save only Jim Lester, had been involved in high mountain exploits, ranging from Rockies to Andes, and Alps to Antarctica. We had our climbing scientists. We had the needed specialists. And of the lot, all but three (Miller because of specialized duties; Lester, because of inexperience; and I, for multiple reasons) rated as at least potential candidates for the summit teams.

Yes, we were pleased. And hopeful.

All that was missing was—money.

4. SOLVENT

IT CAME HARD. But come it did, at last.

The corner was turned when the *National Geographic* said yes. And it was a very big *yes* indeed. As the deal finally materialized, it involved funds for both the mountaineering and scientific aspects of the expedition, for Barry Bishop's participation as climber-geographer-writer-photographer,* and for the production of the expedition motion picture film. The total sum involved was about $114,000, well over half of our original budget. And, no less than the Chinese with their alleged bust of Mao Tse Tung, we would have been happy to take along a statue of Melville Bell Grosvenor, the *Geographic*'s president, to plant on Everest's summit.

Meanwhile, Norman's long campaign was beginning to bear fruit elsewhere. Most importantly, this was on the governmental front, where additional financing, in the form of grants or contracts, was secured from The National Science Foundation, the Office of Naval Research, the Air Force Office of Scientific Research, and the Army Quartermaster Research and Engineering

* Bishop and others would write the expedition story for the *National Geographic Magazine*; I, the story for *Life*, plus the expedition book.

Center. As its share of the bargain the expedition agreed to conduct research programs in glaciology, solar radiation, physiology, psychology and sociology—the last three to be concerned with the changes, physical, mental and communal, undergone by men under severe and prolonged stress.

An ironic concomitant of our increasing affluence (perhaps a subdivision of Parkinson's Law) was that the more money we got, the more we needed. For these scientific grants were, *ipso facto*, mainly for scientific ends, with only a fraction of the funds, in most cases about a third, available for general expedition purposes; and the result—with a scientific budget now added to a mountaineering budget—was a gradual and vast increase in the original figure. From $186,000 it climbed up an Everest of its own to more than $400,-000, while those of us who had long been struggling for a dollar here and a dollar there, began to feel less and less like mountaineers and more and more like executives of General Motors.

Still, as originally projected, far from all of the ledger figures represented actual cash; for now, too, the hoped-for contributions of food, clothing, climbing equipment, and all manner of materiel were coming in from many sources.* Indeed, there was occasionally an embarrassment of riches—as with the matter of liquor, which a certain company would have been particularly happy to supply us with and which we (for the traditional medicinal purposes, of course) were by no means loath to accept. In the end, however, we did not accept. For it was the essence of any deal involving free donations that the contributing company would be permitted to advertise that the expedition was using its product; and we foresaw possible future awkwardness in an announcement that our performance on Everest was thanks to the consumption of so and so's finest 90-proof gin or whiskey.

So, sadly—but we think wisely—we paid for our liquor.

Climbing a great mountain is a complex procedure. But all these preliminaries, we found, were even more so, and, to handle them, we had to organize along business as well as mountaineering lines. A corporation was formed: *American Mount Everest Expedition, 1963*—soon to be known as AMEE. A Board of Directors was

* For a listing of such contributors to the expedition, see Appendix I.

formed and an international Advisory Committee.* Corporate tax exemption was sought and finally won (an item of major importance in the quest for individual contributors). And the handling of finances was put on a professional basis. In this last sphere we were fortunate in now having the services of Charles B. Huestis, financial vice-president of the Hughes Aircraft Company, of Culver City, California, who had heard Norman lecture on one of his previous expeditions (with mentions of Everest), became fascinated with our project, and subsequently took over AMEE's fiscal affairs with a vast amount of savvy and dedication. Indeed, it seems altogether possible that, without his help, the expedition would have been squashed flat, before take-off, between the pages of its ledgers.

In the getting done of all that had to be done a prime problem was that the team members were scattered all over the country. In a small-sized nation such as Britain or Switzerland a group meeting can easily be called for a week end in, say, London or Zürich; but even in the jet age the United States is a large place, and most communication had to be by mail or telephone. By the spring of 1962, however, everyone was at work on some aspect of the expedition. The scientists were preparing their research projects. The doctors were assembling their medical and surgical stores—with Tom Hornbein, on the side, at work on the oxygen apparatus. Al Auten was readying the radio equipment; Dan Doody, the motion picture gear; and I, in the East, was involved in miscellaneous negotiations ranging from airlines to book publishers. Two of the most formidable jobs were handled by Dick Pownall in Denver and Jim Whittaker in Seattle, with the former in charge of all manner of food and the latter of all clothing, tentage and general equipment. From Santa Monica, Norman somehow kept track of everything, issued periodic newsletters and instructions, and every few weeks took off on a trip to one sector or another.

Then, in the early summer, he went all the way around the world. Partly it was to consult with mountaineering experts in various countries—including his own father in Switzerland; partly to secure certain specialized items of mountaineering gear that were more easily obtainable in Europe than in the States. But most

* See "Who's Who."

particularly it was to visit Nepal, to confer with Colonel Jimmy Roberts, and, with him to set in motion the machinery that, some eight months later, would produce the huge number of porters that an expedition of our size would need.* (It was during this visit, significantly, that he effected the rescue of Woodrow Wilson Sayre, the all-but-dead champion of the small, casual and porterless assault on Everest.)

So far so good. But there was better ahead. For a few months later, in September, 1962, came Operation Rainier. This was a long-planned affair in which, for the first time, the expedition came together as a unit, for the purpose of getting acquainted, testing food and equipment, and conducting shake-down trials in the many aspects of mountain climbing and mountain living. Assembling in Seattle (where Jim Whittaker and wife Blanche hosted us in their suburban home), we moved on to Mount Rainier National Park, took off from Paradise Lodge, at road's end near timberline, and hiked up to 10,000-foot Camp Muir, which was to be our base for the next week.

Though it is the third-highest mountain in the United States, outside of Alaska, Rainier is not quite half as tall as Everest. Jim Whittaker had already climbed it no less than fifty-five times, Lute Jerstad thirty-five times, and Barry Prather, as a member of one of Maynard Miller's geological expeditions, had once spent two months camped on its 14,410-foot summit. Still, it is no negligible peak. Its glaciers, twenty-six in number, are more numerous and larger than those on any other mountain in the country (again excluding Alaska). Its winds are wild, its snowfalls enormous. And close to Camp Muir, perched on a rocky outcrop between the Cowlitz and Nisqually Glaciers, was much the same steep frozen terrain of snow and ice slope, wall and crevasse, that we would later find, though at far greater altitude, in the high Himalaya.

Muir was scarcely a de luxe installation: a huddle of two aged stone huts plus a privy that is ordinarily the overnight shelter for climbing parties on their way to Rainier's summit. Now, however,

* At this time, Norman also sought permission from the Nepalese Government for a pre-expedition photographic flight over the Everest region. This, however, was refused—presumably for political reasons.

after Labor Day, the official "season" was over; Paradise Lodge and the guide service had closed for the year, and we had the place largely to ourselves. Mornings and afternoons we moved out onto the glaciers. We practiced climbing techniques. We tested the variety of clothing and equipment that we had brought up with us (some by pack train, some on our own backs): down-filled parkas and hoods and boots and mittens and ropes and ice axes and crampons and ice screws. We had our first workouts with two-way portable radios, with oxygen masks (sans oxygen), and with specially designed motor-driven winches that, though weighing only 16 pounds, could pull thirty times that weight up a snow or ice slope at the end of a wire cable.

Meals were experimental too—with stoves, cooking utensils and tableware (minus tables) undergoing close scrutiny, as well as a vast assortment of canned, packaged, dehydrated and freeze-dried foods. By no means all of these were of the simple camp-out variety, for it is well known that on a long expedition at great altitude appetites are apt to languish, demanding the stimulus of "special" foods; and among the stews and soups and powdered eggs we had also such exotic items as artichoke hearts, watermelon rind, smoked oysters and chutney. Most spectacular of all was a polyethylene-packaged, glacier-chilled dry martini presented to me with a flourish by Dick Pownall as I trudged into camp the first night at the fag end of the procession. But this, alas, was a one-shot gesture; there were to be no further martinis on either Rainier or Everest.

After lunch and in the evenings there were sessions on all manner of subjects. Samples of clothing and equipment were produced and tried out, and their pros and cons debated. The various specialists—doctors, scientists and technicians—spoke about their specialties. And of course there was nonstop talk of the end to which all the rest was directed—of Everest itself—until even those of us who had not yet been within thousands of miles of it felt we knew it step by step, inch by inch. Finally, even with night and bedtime, came more testing: of sleeping bags and air mattresses, and of a half-dozen tents varying in size and design which had been pitched on a small level snowpatch close by the huts.

Simultaneously with all this, a not dissimilar process of familiarization was taking place on another plane—the human plane. Some of the men, of course, were old intimate friends and climbing companions. Others were known to each other only casually or by reputation. But here on Rainier, for the first time, AMEE became a manifest living breathing entity; a hodgepodge of individuals and small groups were now a team. True, it was not quite *all* there; we were eighteen, not twenty. For Jimmy Roberts was in distant Nepal, and Willi Unsoeld was at the time in training for an administrative post with the Peace Corps, which would, happily, also be in Nepal, and from which he would be given leave, when the time came, for the duration of the expedition. These two shaped up in the advance book as two of our most indispensable members. But even without them we were a going concern. Out of two years of letters and phone calls, budgets and ledgers, hopes and despairs, there had at last emerged a flesh-and-blood group of *men* who were going out to Everest. There on Rainier's high glaciers the glint in Norman's eye brightened to a gleam. And I was very happy for him.

Eighteen we were—with a great bond, a single purpose. In short, a team. But still, as with every team, the basic component was the individual; and for me, who was now meeting most of the men for the first time, these individuals began emerging as more than names on a roster. To begin with (logically, because he was always the first to catch the eye) there was Jim Whittaker, 6 feet 5 inches of long bone and lean muscle, with shoulders that looked capable of nudging aside a small house and legs that ate up terrain like Paul Bunyan's. In counterpoint there was Lute Jerstad, Whittaker's longtime guiding partner on Rainier, who was 5 foot 8 including vertical crewcut hair, and was a maestro on the ukulele, in recitations of "The Shooting of Dan McGrew" and an expert at carrying loads so huge that only his legs appeared beneath them. There was Dr. Tom Hornbein, he of the oxygen gear and five children, who was even smaller, and who looked, in climbing rig plus mask (which he was forever testing) as if he had just emerged from a flying saucer. There were Jake Breitenbach and Barry Corbet, lean keen young mountain men from Wyoming—via Dartmouth; Dan Doody, of the five legs (three of them his camera tripod's), red beard and wondrous shaggy-dog stories; Dr. Gil Roberts, one-third physician, one-third mountaineer and one-third existentialist, with paperbacks of Sartre and Kierkegaard oozing from his sleeping bag;

and Dick Pownall, quiet, gentle, powerful, who, as our "food man," now found himself missing only the tailcoat in his role as Maître D' of Camp Muir.

These are first impressions I still remember. And there were others too. Of Barry Bishop, Al Auten and Maynard Miller, half buried under, respectively, piles of photographic, radio and geological gear. Of Dick Emerson and his tape recorder, which he would unobtrusively turn on during the evening powwows whenever the conversation grew "sociologically" interesting. ("Beware, Big Brother is listening.") Of Dr. Dave Dingman, who was somehow always unmistakably young Kildare-Casey, even when swathed in parka, hood and mittens. Of Barry Prather, who combined the roles of expedition baby and strongman (rivaled in the latter only by Jim Whittaker) and was as gently goodhumored as he was huge. Of Jim Lester, the lone nonmountaineer among us, who was deftly and tactfully feeling his way from "outside" to "inside." And of course of Norman and Will Siri, who, with quiet effectiveness, were running the show—to the degree that running was necessary —for it would be hard to imagine a group of men who, brought together for a common purpose, could have fused more readily into a working team.

Among the ramifications of the getting-acquainted process was a certain essential reshuffling of first names; for, as the reader may by now have noted, we were awash in Barrys and Jims. James Barry Corbet, an offender on both counts, paid the stiffest price, losing both first and second names and becoming, for identification purposes, "B.C." For reasons not unmeaningful to the naked eye, Barry Bishop became "Barry the Barrel" and Barry Prather "Barry the Bear." Jim Whittaker was easy; he was "Big Jim." Psychologist Jim Lester became, first, "Freud," then "Sigmund," then "Sig." And I, in tribute to my grandfatherhood—and with a glance ahead toward Asian linguistics—was soon favored with the title of "Gramps Sahib." All of which still left Colonel James Roberts, in Nepal, to be dealt with; but he was not a "Jim" but a "Jimmy," and in the end he was the only one to keep his name intact.

For the first few days on Rainier the weather was magnificent. Viewed from Muir's rocky ledge, the world was composed of but three elements: the white of mountain, the blue of sky, and below, sweeping away to eye's limit, the dim miles of the lowlands. Rainier stands alone; there are no other mountains close by. But off to the south rose other snowy peaks of the Cascades—Washington's Adams and St. Helens and Oregon's Hood and Jefferson—gleaming all day in the brilliant sunlight. On the fourth day clouds moved in. They were white gentle clouds, however, not around or above us, but far below, forming a vast white floor that shut out the lower world and left us and the mountaintops in high isolation.

Into that isolation, up the long trail through the cloud deck, came a trickle of visitors. One was Lou Whittaker, Big Jim's identical twin, who had been on the original expedition roster but had had to withdraw for business reasons; and seeing him in the flesh made one even more regretful than before that he had had to drop out, for the double portion of Whittaker was a sight to make even Everest quiver. Two others were Charles—now Chuck—Huestis, our financial wizard, and his teen-aged son Steve. And there were also Ira Spring, one of the country's foremost mountain photographers, some of the more rugged representatives of the Seattle press, and a variety of fellow mountaineers, most of them known to most of us, who made their home in the Pacific Northwest. These last, particularly, watched our activities with keen and practiced eyes; and if there was a cloud of envy in them too, that was after all, for mountaineers, only natural.

From a Rainier notebook: "Climb on icewalls and in crevasses. Big Jim W. the prize crevasse leaper. . . . Try out winch on Cowlitz Glacier. Wear crampons and oxygen masks. . . . Later, session on clothing. Decide to have parkas lengthened 4 inches to protect behinds when sitting in snow. Vote against climbing boot C: stitching invites leaks and blisters. . . . Back to glacier. Test ropes, pitons and ice screws. Practice rescue techniques. Work with wire ladders, Prusik slings, Jumar ascenders."*

And so on, each day.

There were two near-accidents, both involved in "testing." In the first, an ice screw supporting a rope gave way as Dick Pownall made a semifree leap from a 40-foot ice cliff; but a second screw held, stopping his fall—as it was intended to—just before he hit bottom.

* There is a glossary of mountaineering terms at the end of the book.

In the second, Maynard Miller was testing (i.e., sleeping in) one of the tents at night, when a gale wind arose, wrenched the tent from its mooring, and started carrying it off down the mountain. Maynard's shouts quickly brought help from others who had been sleeping nearby, but not before he and his nylon shroud had been blown almost to the lip of a wide-jawed crevasse.

This was the first blast to hit us, but not the last. For the weather, which for five days had been perfect, soured on the sixth, and for the next thirty-six hours we, our camp, and the whole of upper Rainier were battered by storm. It began slowly, with clouds massing, gray but quiet, and someone—Dan Doody probably—said, "Don't take it cirrus." "But "cirrus" it became, and more and more so, until the wind was howling demoniacally and snow beat in on horizontal tides. Theoretically, bad weather was what we wanted (for that eternal "testing"). But also, for our last two days on Rainier, we had planned a climb to the summit; and the two did not dovetail very well. Toward morning of the first storm day a small but valiant group set off up the mountain—not to try for the top, which would have been insane in such conditions, but to try out heavy-duty clothing and walkie-talkie radios. And with the latter, particularly, there was notable success, for the climbers' voices came down to us clearly from some 2000 feet above, even through the roar and crash of the storm.

Notes from the final day: "Now it's practice for 'indoor survival.' Huts a shambles, as windy in as out, and we huddle in sleeping bags in full clothing. . . . Drink half cupful of kerosene for breakfast. (Not on purpose.) Then out to privy—ah!—which features vertical upwinds and toilet paper streaming in banners toward the mountaintop. . . . Back to the sack. Freezing. Question: 'What in hell are we doing here?' "

Answer: We were preparing for Everest, and in comparison this was life at the Ritz.

"How was the view from the top?" came the inevitable query when we were down from Rainier. In reply, we adroitly changed the subject. And fortunately there were ample subjects to change to; for now the long siege of preparation was in its final phase, and there were a thousand and one things still to be done on every front.

Most important was the assembling, packaging and shipping of the vast amount of materiel that had been tested, approved, ordered, and had now to be dispatched across half the world: food and clothing, tents and cookers, oxygen and medicines, and flashlights and windburn creams—to a staggering total of 54,000 pounds. Making the operation more complex was the fact that all this was not to be packed any whichway, but according to careful plan in some 900 cartons weighing about 60 pounds apiece: each one containing certain cataloged items for use at a specific time and place, each ready to be hoisted, properly marked but unopened, onto a porter's back when at last we set out for Everest from Kathmandu.

This Labor of Hercules was performed in Seattle by a professional packing company, with Jim Whittaker and Dan Doody supervising. And by early December the job was done, and off went the 27 tons on a Calcutta-bound freighter. Meanwhile Norman was still ferrying back and forth across the country, involved in contracts, commitments, high and low finance; and the rest of us were busied both with our expedition specialties and such miscellany as passports, visas, immunization shots, and the little matter of how our families were going to eat during our absence.

One major problem that still had not been solved was that of plane transportation, a far from negligible item of eighteen round-the-world tourist-class passages (roughly the same in cost as Nepal-and-return tickets, so we opted for the former) at $1263.10 apiece. As one of my preliminary assignments, I had for more than a year been in touch with various international airlines trying to get us free or at least cut-rate rides—but with no success; and by mid-autumn of 1962 things looked a bit gloomy. Once again, however, Norman waved his magic wand, and we had the last of our big windfalls: a grant of $82,000 in blocked Indian rupees from the State Department's Bureau of Educational and Cultural Affairs. This would not only cover our transportation expenses but also leave a handsome balance for the payment of porters, our own travel costs, and other yet-to-be-met expenditures that could be paid for in Indian or Nepalese currency.

Also during this period there arose spectres of a different kind, about which we could do nothing but pray. First there was the Cuban crisis and its ominous international tensions. Then, far closer to home—our expedition home—there was the Chinese invasion of northern India, and we dreaded that momentarily we would have word from Nepal (which was bracketed by the invasion) that our entry and climbing permissions had been revoked. Finally, on a far different scale—a scale so small as to be ludicrous, but still one with threatening possibilities—*l'affaire Sayre*, with which Norman had been involved the previous summer, was now coming to public attention, with Sayre giving lectures and preparing a magazine piece on his Everest attempt; and we were concerned that Red China (which so far had been strangely silent on the subject) might now put strong pressure on Nepal to bar any further potential border jumpers. None of these fears, however, materialized. Somewhat to our surprise, and much to our joy, the political road to Everest remained clear. All we had to do was to climb it.

Financially, too, we were now in the clear. AMEE was, miraculously, solvent. And in December, at the annual meeting of the American Alpine Club, Norman had the proud moment of repaying with thanks the loan it had made the expedition the previous year when the going had still been sticky.

Then, directly after New Year, 1963, came the second occasion on which the expedition team assembled.* Now, however, the locale was no mountain. It was the University of California, in Berkeley, and for three days, at the Donner Laboratory and the Institute for Personality Assessment Research (IPAR), the team was subjected to intensive physiological and psychological testing as the first step in Will Siri's and Jim Lester's expedition projects. As far as can be gathered (though scientists are secretive about such things), no one flunked. The three days over, there was another scattering homeward. But not for long.

For now, at last, dream was about to become reality.

It had been decided that the expedition would fly to Asia in two contingents. The first and smaller would consist of Norman, Barry

---

* This time there were seventeen on hand. Willi Unsoeld was by now in Nepal with the Peace Corps; Jimmy Roberts had been in Nepal all along; and I was showing my age by being ill in Boston.

Bishop and Dan Doody—plus Norman's wife Sally, who was to serve for the duration as our liaison officer in Kathmandu, and Barry's wife Lila, who was planning a Nepalese trek of her own. Leaving three weeks ahead of the rest, they would fight the battle of customs in India and Nepal, and shepherd some 29 preshipped tons of ours from Calcutta dockside to Kathmandu.* On January 14, on schedule, they flew off from Los Angeles into the Pacific. And on February 3 the remaining fifteen of us assembled at San Francisco's International Airport.

There were no wives in this contingent. Wives had either been said good-bye to at home or—a few of them, whose homes were nearby—were standing around the airport concourse trying hard to smile; and we needed no one to tell us who, of all those involved in our venture, were sacrificing the most to make it come true. Outside in the foggy morning planes were roaring. Soon we were in our own plane and it was roaring. Beyond the windows, in the distance, there were figures waving: the three or four wives, Chuck Huestis and family, and others who had come to see us off. Then they were gone. The airport was gone. San Francisco and fog were gone, and there was blue sky, blue ocean.

On my flight across the continent the day before I had had as fellow passengers the members of a basketball team. No one had told me what they were; I could just *see* they were a basketball team. And now I found myself wondering if our fellow passengers could tell what we were. I rather think not. For outwardly we were not at all of a piece: in age or size or manner or any identifiable characteristic. It was inwardly that we were of a piece. And though for the first hours of flight we tended to be quiet and meditative, I knew that within that quietness there was enough concentration of energy, excitement and anticipation to have powered our plane if all its jets had failed.

Norman's father, Professor Günter Dyhrenfurth, had, in one of his many books about the Himalaya, given the range a new and provocative name. "The Third Pole," he had called it. And now we were off for that pole; the pole of poles above the other poles; and, God willing, we would climb it to the top.

---

* Roughly 2 tons had been shipped from Europe.

5. *"THE FACTS OF KATHMANDU"*

". . . the wildest dreams of Kew are the facts of Kathmandu. . . ."
Thus Kipling, when East was East and West was West. And
though the twain have done some meeting since, it is still true.

But that, again, is getting ahead of the story.

First there was the endless day of a jet flying westward, almost
keeping up with the sun. There were the Pacific miles, and Hawaii,
and more miles, and a sudden midday leap at the heart of nowhere
from occidental Sunday to oriental Monday. There were the stew-
ardesses serving chain lunches at three- or four-hour intervals, and
at last, after fifteen hours (or days? or weeks?) there was Japan.

Our timetable was not leisurely, but at least it was humanitarian,
and in Tokyo we had a three-day layover. Highlights were the Imperial Hotel (small resemblance to Camp Muir), Turkish-Japanese
bathing (steam plus masseuses), nightclubbing (last view for a
while of the frames of dames), and simply feeling the swarm and
pulsebeat of the ten-million-hearted city. Lowlights were the danger of being wiped out en masse by the schizophrenic traffic and a
fair amount of rumblings from homesick stomachs. On the diges-

tive front AMEE's doctors promptly moved in, specifying firmly what, thereafter, should and should not be eaten; and the situation soon improved. But to my mind, as a somewhat case-hardened traveler, there was both a plus and minus aspect to the matter. On the one hand, there was the unarguable proposition that a team such as ours should be delivered to its scene of performance in as good physical shape as possible. On the other, there was the rather depressing aspect of a group of young Americans, already well imbued with the idea that all food not cooked by mom in the U.S.A. was probably poisonous, being further indoctrinated with this nationalistic myth. Personally I did a fair amount of surreptitious cheating; but, then, the well- or non-well-being of my own innards would have small bearing on our mountaineering fortunes.

In terms of our purpose and function, the feature of the Tokyo visit was the opportunity, afforded us by the Japanese Alpine Club, of seeing the film of the alleged Chinese ascent of Everest in 1960. That they had had an expedition *on* the mountain was unquestionable; and it was fascinating to see, in panoramic color, the now-forbidden north side of Everest, with which, from the accounts of the early British expeditions, we were all familiar. But the film offered no more proof than had the written reports that the climbers had actually reached the top, and the agit-prop tone of the commentary was such as to make truth seem false even if truth were being told. "It grew dark. It was cold. All were close to exhaustion. But the brave pioneers of the People's Republic thought of Comrade Mao, took strength, and moved onward and upward"—with that plaster bust. Came a burst of music, a shot of three garlanded climbers being greeted by cheering crowds, then the fade-out. And we were no wiser than before.

After Tokyo there was Hong Kong (three days) and Bangkok (two days), with Will Siri as *Obergruppenführer*, doing the dirty work at hotel desks and airline counters, and the rest of us disporting ourselves in shops, fleshpots and sight-seeing buses, while struggling to assimilate the thousand sights, sounds and smells that pressed in upon us. In Hong Kong one could not but be conscious of the shadow of mainland China, invisible but vast, hemming in this tight bright little world of stores and banks and ships and skyscraper hotels. In Bangkok, our one dip into the true tropics, shorts and swimming pools, gilded Buddhas and soft brown laughter made Everest, with its savage heights and bitter storms, seem as remote as if it were a mountain of the moon.

But it was *not* remote. No longer. With each thrust of a plane's jets we were getting closer. From Bangkok we came to Calcutta (where the advance guard had already taken care of our shipped equipment, leaving us with no chores to perform). And on the morning of February 13—with jets behind us and the old DC-3 in their place—off we flew, north by west across the Indian plains. For the past ten days we had lived a life of fleeting and dizzying impressions, in an airborne limbo between the world of home and the world ahead. But now at last the change came. Now at last the great white wave, the Third Pole, rose up on the horizon ahead; and limbo was gone, the crowding images of the myriad world were gone; and there was only one image, one fact, one goal plain before us.

There it was. By God, *there it was.*

Then, instead, there was Kathmandu's airstrip. Waiting on its apron were the advance guard, plus Willi Unsoeld, plus Jimmy Roberts, plus many others who had come to greet us. And we were trooping out of the plane, and Dan Doody was behind his tripod, and Norman was shouting. "Don't look at the camera!"

It is a stern assignment for a writer confronted with Kathmandu to write about anything but—Kathmandu. For if there is a more writeaboutable city in the world, I have yet to see it. To us of the West its name is almost a synonym for remoteness—no less from New York and Washington and San Francisco than from Kipling's Kew. But remoteness is relative. In its own world of historic Asia it is a hub, a fulcrum; indeed the very quintessence of Asia, in its blend of races, of Hinduism and Buddhism, of the ancient tides of men and cultures that have flowed through it for millennia.

As if we had been dropped suddenly into the Land of Oz, we looked around and about us at "the facts of Kathmandu." At the brown people and the yellow and at the brown and yellow, with round and almond and Mongolian eyes, with Indian and Tibetan and in-between features—walking, squatting, smiling, staring, carrying loads (most of all carrying loads, for here man is his own beast

of burden), barefoot and boot-shod, some almost naked, some
swathed in rags, in scarves, in veils, in bangles. At teeming bazaars.
At pagoda-lined squares. At the dusty-red brick houses, two to four
stories high, festooned with ancient and intricate woodwork, that
are the indigenous structures of the city; and the huge whitish
gone-to-seed *bhavans*, or palaces, which the long-ruling Ranas built,
over the years, in imitation of European mansions. At the cows,
who own the streets, and the dogs (who have the first mortgage)
and, now and then, the elephants—for though elephants are not
native to Kathmandu's 4000-foot-high valley, they are brought up
from the warmer Terai country to take part in holiday ceremonials;
and there are holidays at what seems an average of three per week.
At the carved erotica that adorn many buildings: huge phalluses
and scrotums and friezes of copulating gods and goddesses. Above
all, at the temples. And there are temples everywhere: on the city
streets, on the surrounding hills, on the banks of the Bagmati River.
Some are Hindu, filled with images of Siva in his many incarnations, of Hanuman the monkey god, and Ganesh the elephant god;
and one, called Pashupatinath, is among the holiest places in the
Hindu world. Some are Buddhist, with rounded domes, spinning
prayer wheels, fluttering prayer flags; and from the two greatest of
these, called Bodhnath and Swayambhunath, tall towers rise. On
each of the four sides of the towers are two vast painted eyes—
unblinking, all-seeing—and these are the Eyes of God. "Who are
you?" they ask, as we look up at them. "What are you doing here?
Where are you going?"

Yes, where indeed?

These aspects of Kathmandu were as they had been through the
centuries. So too were the surrounding hills, and beyond the hills,
to the north, the white rampart of the Himalaya. Everest was not
visible; it was too far to the east, hidden behind an intervening
screen of lesser peaks. But the nearer mountains rose high above
the valley in a mural of gleaming snow, clear and dominant in the
bright winter sunlight.

Along with the rest of the world, however, the city has in recent
years seen its changes, as Nepal—to quote one of its leading citizens—"struggles to leap from the tenth to the twentieth century."
For a long time, until after World War II, the country was domi-

nated by a huge interlocking family called the Ranas, who, through a succession of hereditary prime ministers ruled it like a medieval fief, hermetically sealed off from the outside world. Though there had been kings during this period, they had been mere puppets, virtually prisoners. But in the late 1940's the reigning monarch, Tribhuvan, made his escape, and a few years later, with the help of newly independent India, staged an almost bloodless coup which returned him not only to his throne but to power as well. In this case, not at all according to Hoyle, monarchy spelled "progress," as against reaction. Nepal at last began to open up to the modern world; and on Tribhuvan's death, in 1955, his son, the present King Mahendra, continued the same policy. The Ranas are still very much in evidence, only a few of the most obstreperous having been exiled. But they seem content, for the time being at least, to play a nondominant, but very affluent, second fiddle.

In size and power Nepal is negligible as a sovereign state. Its population is about ten million, its area about 500 by 100 miles—most of it wildly mountainous—and for years its only exportable resource has been its Gurkhas, the famous fighting hillmen who have contributed manpower, color and unexampled courage to the British and Indian Armies. Along with the newly opened door has come the beginnings of tourism, plus the hope that in time Nepal will become a sort of Switzerland of Asia. A few other industries are in their infancy or prenatal stage. But in a country that is ninety per cent illiterate and (except for Ranas and art treasures) abjectly poor, progress thus far has been rather less than jet-propelled. Such, too, has been the case politically. With the overthrow of Rana rule, the theory was that the monarchy would be of limited power, subject to checks and balances; but—not alone among small emergent nations—Nepal soon found that democracy, Western style, worked better on paper than in practice. King Mahendra, with the army behind him, is now absolute boss, and the official phrase "His Majesty's Government" means exactly that.

Small and backward though it is, however, the country has been receiving plenty of outside attention. And not only from mountaineers. Indeed, lying in a geopolitical vise between India and Red China, it has become a cockpit of pressures and intrigues in the Asian sector of the Cold War. When I had previously been in

Kathmandu, in 1954, the whole Western community had numbered less than fifty and the only embassies had been those of
Britain and India. To these had now been added American, Russian
and Chinese embassies, with an Israeli legation thrown in for good
measure, and there were also delegations from the United Nations
(specialists helping the Nepalese in various aspects of government)
and from the International Red Cross (involved largely with the
problems of Tibetan refugees). Overall, the foreign population ran
to well over a thousand.

By far the largest group was the American, comprising not only
the embassy proper but a U.S. Agency for International Development (AID) Mission and a platoon of the Peace Corps. With
veteran mountaineer Bob Bates as its director and our own Willi
Unsoeld as its deputy director, the Peace Corps seemed almost to be
an adjunct of our expedition, but it was far from alone in extending
a welcoming and helping hand. From Ambassador Henry E. Stebbins on down the line, all America-in-Kathmandu gave us the
warmest of welcomes: not only wining and dining us to repletion,
but also supplying all manner of assistance in our struggles with
red tape (customs, currency exchange and the like) vis-à-vis the
Nepalese Government.

Headquarters for AMEE was the Hotel Royal—but the word
"hotel" must be quickly qualified by adding that any resemblance
to a Hilton or Sheraton was purely coincidental. A former Rana
bhavan, or palace, it was a rambling cave of the winds, featuring
marble staircases, galleries of Rana portraits, and huge ornate rooms
furnished with broken-down cots, early Cro-Magnon plumbing,
and patterns of drilled holes in the ceiling to afford easy egress for
evil spirits. (Also, there was an antique trailer on the front lawn,
for use on occasions—such as now—when cots were outnumbered
by guests.) Staffing this wonderland was a brigade of servants, at
a ratio of about three per guest: all male, all happy and dirty, all
invisible when wanted and ubiquitous when not. And as proprietor-
host there was Nepal's foremost non-Nepalese fixture, Boris Lissanevitch.

Boris is a White Russian. As a teen-aged boy, soon after the
Russian Revolution, he got out of his homeland as a member of a
touring ballet troupe and for years thereafter pursued a career in

the Orient as restaurateur, club proprietor, and internationally known friend of almost everybody. Among the friends, after World War II, was the then expatriated Tribhuvan, King of Nepal, and when he regained his throne he invited Boris to his country to become its first non-Asian hotelier and all-around entrepreneur. Boris accepted. In due time the Hotel Royal came into being. And in due time, too, he found himself in jail; for the government, which had initially promised him tax exemptions for the setting up of his enterprises, subsequently changed its mind and presented him with a whopping bill, which Boris could not and would not pay. As is proper in a fairy-tale kingdom, however—whether it be Oz, Graustark or Nepal—it all culminated in a happy ending. King Tribhuvan died, his son Mahendra succeeded him, and in the whole of Nepal no one other than Boris was remotely capable of catering the dinners and receptions with which the coronation was to be celebrated. So he was forthwith released from jail and restored to freedom, eminence, and the Hotel Royal.

There have been times since when he has thought a life term would have been the better alternative, for running a hotel geared to Western tastes in Nepal is not unlike running a beach resort in Antarctica. Boris, however, is a good White Russian; hence a philosopher. He has a beautiful young Danish wife, a lively cosmopolitan family and roster of guests, and has discovered that if he doesn't look too closely into his kitchen or ledgers—or expect results when he gives an order—he can live a fair approximation of the good life in fabled Kathmandu. What he lacks in the requisites for modern hotelkeeping, he more than makes up for in warmth and hospitality. And the Royal's Yak and Yeti Bar ("yeti" being the indigenous name for the Himalaya's Abominable Snowman) is as congenial a place for a drink as any east of Suez or west of New York's Third Avenue.

Boris is even capable of coping with Everest expeditions (which I think might not be the case with a Hilton or Sheraton), and it was without plaint from him—indeed with his full cooperation—that we turned the north compound of the Royal into a replica of the freight yards of Chicago. Thanks to the labors of our advance guard, everything—well almost everything—was on hand. They had fought the good fight, first in Indian and then in Nepalese customs.

In between, they had ferried the bulk of the shipment by truck convoy from Calcutta to Patna, India, and by several charter-plane flights from Patna to Kathmandu—with Barry Bishop going all the way by truck as shepherd of inflammables (oxygen, butane, gasoline, kerosene) which could not legally be flown. And here at last were those 29-odd tons of ours, half a world away from their starting point, stacked in cardboard mountain ranges in the Royal's compound.

This, during our Kathmandu phase, was the nerve center of the expedition. In overall charge was Colonel Jimmy Roberts, who, armed with his huge experience in such matters, deftly brought order out of chaos; and working with him, often from early morning to dusk, was the rest of the team—sorting and resorting, opening and distributing the Seattle-packed items that would be used on the approach march, marking and cataloging the rest for use at the right place and the right time. Dick Pownall and helpers applied themselves to food. Jim Whittaker and others handled clothing, tentage, climbing gear. Tom Hornbein checked the oxygen equipment, Al Auten the radio apparatus, Maynard Miller his geological paraphernalia (which the nongeologists claimed added up to 10 tons in itself). And the rest worked either on other specialties or on general logistics of what was where and why—or why not.

The army of low-level porters who would carry all this in toward Everest was not yet on the scene. But very much there, and very importantly, were thirty-two of the high-climbing Sherpas who would be with us for the duration. Slight of build, broad of smile, incredibly tough in lung and limb, these now almost legendary hillmen have over the years become as essential a part of Himalayan mountaineering as the outlanders who hire them. And here in the Royal's compound they piled into the work at hand with as much zest as they would later show on the mountain itself. On their first appearance a few were dressed in their native homespun clothing and wore their hair in the traditional long braids wound about their heads. But the great majority had long since adopted Western ways. Their hair was short; they wore the shirts and trousers and boots that had been given them by previous expeditions; and now to these were added, much to their delight, the brand new clothing and equipment which AMEE supplied.

Of the thirty-two, twenty-eight were from the Solu Khumbu region of northeastern Nepal, the longtime homeland of the Sherpa people which lies just to the south of Everest. These had come down the long trail to Kathmandu, led by the veteran Passang Phutar, a man in his indeterminate forties (Sherpas are vague about their ages) who was to be sirdar, or headman, of the expedition porters. The other four were from Darjeeling, in India, to which many Sherpa families had migrated in the old days, when it was the starting place for the trek to Everest by the route through Tibet. Two of these were already famous in the Himalayan world. One was Ang Dawa IV (there being a plethora of Ang Dawas in Darjeeling), thirty-eight years old, barely 5 feet tall, looking for all the world like a tiny brown doll, who had been Norman Dyhrenfurth's personal aide and good companion on his previous four expeditions. And the other was Nawang Gombu, a nephew of the illustrious Tenzing Norgay, who, like his uncle, was on the staff of Darjeeling's Himalayan Institute of Mountaineering. Gombu, aged about thirty, had an outstanding climbing record, dating back to the 1953 British triumph on Everest and culminating in the Indian Everest expedition of 1960, on which he had been one of the two members who got to within 700 feet of the top. Further, he was far better educated than most Sherpas, knowing how to read and write and boasting a range of tongues from his native Sherpa, through Hindi and Nepali, to fluent English. Most significant of all, he brought to mountaineering—again like Tenzing—not only great physical qualifications, but also spirit and drive. No man among us, Eastern or Western, burned with greater desire to reach the top of Everest; and we were all convinced from the beginning that he would stage a magnificent performance.

Another addition to the party—Nepalese but not Sherpa—was a young man glorying in the name of Captain Prabakher Shumshere Jung Bahadur Rana, which for expedition purposes was mercifully shortened to "Noddy." Assigned by the Nepalese Army and Foreign Ministry as our liaison officer, Noddy proved a valuable acquisition, for he was friendly, knowledgeable and enthusiastic, and (unlike not a few liaison officers, who tend to go along for the ride) would show that he could pull his full weight on the expedition, particularly as aide to Jimmy Roberts in the eternal problems of logistics. On the other side of the coin, however, we were at this time worrying about the possible loss of one of our most essential team members, Willi Unsoeld. Back in Washington months before, we had been assured by the Peace Corps (indeed, by Sargent Shriver in person) that Willi would be made available to us for the whole period of the climb. But, as is the way of governments, the papers had not yet come through, and with take-off now only a few days away, he was still at his desk in Kathmandu Peace Corps headquarters.

Also largely missing from the compound was Norman himself, who was currently confronting crisis upon crisis—these of the Nepalese variety—in the labyrinthine governmental secretariat building called the Singha Durbar. There was a long hassle about our permit to use our radio-communications equipment. (Permission finally granted.) There was a demand for advance payment of a fee for climbing Lhotse and Nuptse, as well as Everest. (Credit finally established.) But these were only minor roadblocks. To quote Norman: "I spent most of my waking hours battling the Foreign Ministry about their insistence on the use of United States dollars for all expenditures within Nepal, whereas our State Department grant provided us with Indian rupees for that purpose. For several days there was a complete impasse, and it looked as if we might never get off if we didn't produce the dollars. But fortunately for AMEE we had the complete and determined support of Ambassador Stebbins, and at last, two days before our scheduled departure, I was told that we would be permitted to proceed as planned."

The timetable for all Everest expeditions, except those few which have taken place in the fall,* has to be reckoned backward from the probable coming of the summer monsoon. For this warm wet wind from the Indian Ocean blows up into the eastern Himalaya each year toward the end of May or the beginning of June and turns the high peaks into a death trap of melting ice and crumbling snow. Most previous parties had set out for the mountain in mid- or late

---

* One of these was the second Swiss expedition of 1952, in which Norman had been a participant. The weather encountered had been mostly fair but bitterly cold; the increasing shortness of the autumn days had been a major problem; and Norman was convinced that the spring season offered better chances for success.

March. But it was part of Norman's basic strategy to allow as much time for the ascent as was humanly possible, and he had long ago set a February departure date—specifically February 20. This gave us exactly a week in Kathmandu, and for a while, in both the Singha Durbar and Compound Campaigns, it seemed certain we would never make it. In the end, though—manfully, and a little pridefully—we did.

Meanwhile—

Had everything arrived that should have? Answer: no. Three last-minute air shipments from San Francisco were still somewhere en route and would have to be shipped after us.

Were there any items to be bought in Kathmandu? Answer: yes. One of them was umbrellas—surely a strange-sounding requisite for an Everest expedition; but previous parties had found them a boon on the approach march, and particularly on the return trip during the monsoon rains.

Was everyone (other than Unsoeld) present and accounted for? Answer: not always. At a checkup in the compound one of the younger Sherpas, a son of sirdar Passang Phutar, turned up missing. But Passang explained that he had gone off for only a few hours to get married, adding that his bride would be useful on the march as an added load carrier. Which she was.

Despite a dozen flaps a day, however, there was no major breakdown. Even Willi Unsoeld's official release at last came through from Washington—though so late that he had to spend the morning of the twentieth in the Peace Corps office and come dashing after us to our first night's campsite. And the rest of Operation Take-off proceeded with wondrous smoothness. On the nineteenth our mountains of impedimenta, accompanied by Jimmy Roberts and all the Sherpas, went off in fourteen truckloads to the village of Banepa, 15 miles eastward, which marks the end of navigable road near the rim of the Valley of Kathmandu. And the next morning, dead on schedule, the rest of us followed in a convoy of Jeeps and Land Rovers.

The scene that followed, in an open field beyond Banepa, was something to set the late Cecil B. De Mille to turning in his grave. For now, suddenly, our cast of characters multiplied itself some twenty times. There were ourselves.* There were our Sherpas and baggage. There was a great crowd of seer-offers, most of them from Kathmandu's American community, all of them laden with cameras and good wishes. Most essentially for the job at hand, there was our horde of low-level porters now joining us for the first time— hillmen and valley men, male and female, children, oldsters and in-betweeners—and through the whole of the morning they filed past in jostling, jabbering procession while their loads and identification tags were assigned to them. The total was 909 loads. At about 65 pounds each (including the porters' meager personal possessions) they made our 29-plus tons. And now, slowly but surely, all those tons began to move. In single file, bent under their burdens and headstraps, our armless army moved out of the field at Banepa onto the trail beyond, in a file so long that it took two hours to pass a given point. Among the porters, spaced at wide intervals, were ourselves and our Sherpas: the Sherpas moving briskly, happily, on toward home and highlands; ourselves turning, waving, taking a last lingering look at the twentieth century—then facing to the east and trudging on.

There had been many beginnings, of many kinds, to our adventure. But here at last was the real thing.

* Plus one invited "camp follower": Ewald W. Schnitzer—known as "Spark"— a friend of Norman's from UCLA who was to hike in with the team as far as Solu Khumbu.

A NOTE ON "WE" AND "THEY"

THUS FAR this has been a "we" book, in the first person plural, with the author participating in the story. From now on it will be largely a "they" book, in the third person, for my own physical participation in the expedition ended a day out of Banepa.

During the preceding year I had begun to suffer from faulty blood circulation in the right leg, and in the fall, after the Mount Rainier workout, I had undergone two operations, hoping to improve matters enough so that I could accompany the team at least to Base Camp. But it was not to be. Thanks to Norman, I remained, officially, an "expedition member." Thanks to the team doctors, I was permitted to travel as far as Kathmandu. But, for me, that was the virtual end of the trail. There was—as even I had to admit—no way, physical or rational, for me to get in even to the foot of Everest, and I was destined to perform my functions as expedition scribe from a strictly rear-echelon base.

One concession I wrung from our M.D.s. They allowed me to go along, half on foot, half on ponyback, on the first brief day from Banepa to a place called Panchkal, so that I could get a bit of the "feel" of the approach march. At day's end camp was pitched beside a network of converging streams. For acres around, as night came, the cookfires of the porters gleamed in the darkness, and beyond them the black hills sloped up toward the stars. Already the world of Jeeps and trucks, hotels and secretariats, seemed remote beyond imagining.

By four the next morning the porters were stirring. By sunrise they were on their way. And soon, too, the expedition members—nineteen of them now, not twenty—were shouldering their packs and starting off on the trail. Standing beside it, I shook hands with them as they passed. "Good-bye. God bless." What else was there to say? Then with emotions I shall not try to describe I watched them move on along the trail until they were lost to sight.

6. ONWARD, UPWARD
—AND DOWNWARD

THE TEAM was not yet *quite* out of the twentieth century.

At the end of the second day's march, near the village of Dolal-ghat, they came to the confluence of two of Nepal's major rivers, the Indrawati and the Sun Kosi, and here at trailside stood a uni-formed Nepalese, who handed each member a slip of paper admon-ishing him (in English) not to take pictures of a nearby encamp-ment. The camp was occupied by a group of Communist Chinese engineers and surveyors, engaged in planning a road: a road that would eventually be part of a modern highway across the Himalaya, connecting Lhasa, in Tibet, with Kathmandu.

It was not only U.S. AID and the Peace Corps that were at work in the political cockpit of Nepal.

Then the rivers receded below, as the team climbed the 4000-foot rise on their farther side. At the top came a short level stretch; then a long descent, another valley, another river, another rise; and so it would go for a total of sixteen days. Kathmandu is at an eleva-tion of 4423 feet. The first goal, Namche Bazar, center of the Sherpa country south of Everest, is at 12,400. But the intervening

59

180-odd miles is no steadily inclined ramp. Cutting across the grain of the land, the march was to be an endless up and down, down and up, through the saw-edged world of the Himalayan foot-hills. The expedition on the trail was a 5-mile-long millepede. Or a roller coaster in slow motion.

The daily distance covered ranged from 8 to 15 miles. Each day the start was made soon after daybreak; toward midmorning there was a pause for rest and lunch; and in the early or late afternoon, depending on distance and steepness, the long train straggled into the next night's campsite. The sites had been determined in ad-vance. For though this was remote and primitive country, it was well known to Everesters, and the roster of trailside villages was a familiar litany from the logs of previous expeditions. Up they came out of the waves of distance: Chaubas, Risingo, Manga Deorali, Kirantichap. Yersa, Those, Changma, Sete. Each day was a village, each village a milestone.

For the first four or five days the land roundabout was intensely cultivated. In the subtropical valleys and occasional flatlands were bananas, sugar cane, bamboo and rice paddies, and above them, perched on carved terraces, grew winter wheat and other grains, tiering up to the very tops of the red-earthed hills. Further, this was a well-populated world; for the trail, though only a rough and rocky path, was one of the main turnpikes of eastern Nepal, and there was a constant flow of other travelers. There are few beasts of burden in the country. Men—and women, and children—are their own carriers, and most of the processions that passed were heavily laden. The majority were going to or from a market. But there were others on less worldly missions, such as pilgrimages, Hindu or Buddhist, to one of the holy places of Kathmandu. Occa-sionally, too, there would be a wedding party, consisting of a score or more celebrants, plus a band of horns, drums and cymbals. If it were properly *de rigueur*, the groom would be walking under an umbrella held by an attendant; the bride riding in a palanquin, covered from head to toe in a shroud of red veils.

The weather was fine: a bit warm for hiking (the standard en-semble was boots, or sneakers, shorts and broad-brimmed hat) but clear and golden, and from the high places on the trail could be seen the white wave of the Himalaya shining in the north. There were Ganesh Himal, the Langtang Peaks, Jugal. Farther to the east, Gaurisankar and Menlungtse. No Everest yet. It would remain tantalizingly hidden until the expedition was almost upon it. But what was on show was, for the moment, enough. No less than the generations of Hindus and Buddhists who had followed this trail before them, our men were pilgrims raising their eyes to the Abode of Snow.

On a more mundane level, there was the inevitable start-of-trek problem of sore and blistered feet. And in spite of the tremendous advance preparations there were several logistical contretemps. The burners, mantles and fuel for the Coleman lamps, which were to have done duty as nighttime illumination, showed up in their proper loads—but no lamps. Like most Americans, the team members were preponderantly coffee rather than tea drinkers; but they soon found that, on the march, tea was the more satisfying drink, and there was not nearly enough tea. The smokers, comprising about a third of the team and most of the Sherpas, were dismayed to discover that instead of the expected 60,000 cigarettes there were only 6000 (the Case of the Missing Zero), and any certified addict knows you can't climb a mountain on that small a ration of nicotine. Also there was a toilet paper crisis. For though there was an ample supply, it was at first issued on the basis of one undivided roll a day for all team members and, when urgently needed, was invariably in a pack some mile or two down the trail.

The Ph.D.s, with the help of the M.A.s, finally solved this problem. Sore feet healed and hardened. Tea and cigarettes caught up with the caravan via a special convoy of porters from Kathmandu, which also brought the various items from home that had been delayed in shipment. Overall, the march was soon a smoothly functioning operation, moving up and down, down and up, through the days and the miles.

Not the least of the jobs was that performed by the Sherpa kitchen staff, headed by its senior cook, Danu. Each morning Danu & Company would serve a light, continental-type breakfast between dawn and sunrise; then, leaving camp last, dash ahead to serve a midmorning brunch on the trail; after which, in a second dash, they again caught up with the head of the procession, and by early afternoon were already at work at the next campsite preparing the evening meal. Though there was some overlapping, Sherpas and Americans inclined toward different foods: the former leaning largely to their traditional staples of rice and *tsampa* (roasted barley flour); the latter preferring the contents of cans—of soup, fruit, vegetables, meat, stews. The store of dehydrated and freeze-dried foods would not appear until the team was on the mountain and every ounce of load counted. The army of low-level porters was not fed by the expedition, but provided their own meals, partly from what they themselves carried with them, partly from what they could find in the countryside.

Arrival at each new camp was a complex and spectacular affair, as what had been an empty field or open slope became a swarming acreage of piled-up loads and moving figures. Added to the throngs was usually the total population of the nearest village, looking on in fascination. And the fascination was doubled when, as often happened, many of our men went swimming in an adjacent stream or river; for to the rural Nepalese the sight of persons voluntarily immersing themselves in water was wondrous and inexplicable. Meanwhile the kitchen had been set up. Firewood was collected. In the midst of things, presently, stood a cluster of tents, and in the midst of *these*, looking highly improbable in the primitive surroundings, a gaily colored, garden-partyish folding table and chairs that did duty for tea and dinner. Later, when descriptions of these de luxe accoutrements began to circulate, there was a certain amount of snide comment from hairy-chested outdoorsmen, but AMEE was making no apologies. There would be enough squatting on pointed rocks and lumps of ice farther on in the journey.

Another luxury, on those early hot days, was beer. The official expedition variety came in cans, with familiar stateside labels. But Sherpas and porters picked up their own ration en route, in the form of chang, a milky-looking beverage brewed from rice, barley, or other ingredients; and now and then, from indeterminate sources, there would appear arak—known also as rakshi—the potent schnapps of the Orient. Thanks to this, and perhaps other causes, occasional intraporter fights would develop, a few of them mean and serious. But in general the evening activities were of a happier sort: a spate of laughing, singing and dancing around the hundreds of campfires glowing in the darkness. The team had its own music too: Lute Jerstad and Gil Roberts on the ukulele; a clutch of harmonica virtuosos; impromptu choruses of barbershop balladeers. And sometimes East and West collaborated on a program that ranged from traditional Sherpa dances to the somewhat terrifying spectacle of 6-foot-5 Jim Whittaker doing the twist.

There were the quiet evenings too. Reading (from Shakespeare to Ian Fleming, from the *Bhagavad-Gita* to *Playboy*). Writing letters. Filling in the complex question-and-answer diaries from which sociologist Dick Emerson would assess the composite expedition psyche. And of course talking, talking, talking, of the challenges and problems that lay ahead. Beginning several months before, back in the States, there had been a gradual but definite shifting of opinion among team members as to what should be the expedition's primary objectives, and now this emerged in long and serious discussion. Everest—the top of Everest—was of course, in everyone's mind, still the ultimate goal. But the desire was strong, and growing stronger daily, to try for it not only by the South Col route, which had been used by all previous postwar expeditions, but also by its vast West Ridge, which had never been climbed or even attempted.

Commenting on the discussions in his tape-recorded reports, Norman Dyhrenfurth said at the time: "If we can pull it off [i.e., an ascent of the West Ridge] it would be the biggest possible thing still to be accomplished in Himalayan mountaineering. And it is interesting to see how highly motivated the whole group has become. There is comparatively little interest in Lhotse and Nuptse. The men are aware that when we were raising funds for the expedition the idea of an American "grand slam" of the three peaks had its appeal; but to most of them it means very little. They feel that if we can do Everest by the West Ridge, that would really be *it*. In fact, Tom Hornbein is such an idealist and so enthusiastic about the idea that he would almost be willing to throw everything into a West Ridge attempt, and thus possibly jeopardize success over the conventional Col route.

"Of course I've spoken up very strongly," Norman went on. "I said, this we cannot do. I'm all for making a serious stab at the West Ridge—a thorough reconnaissance to see if it's feasible—and then pushing a line of camps up it, but at the same time establishing camps along the old route. Then possibly we can have the main attempt by the West Ridge, but must still be sure, as a backup, to have a four-man attempt, with support, from the South Col. Only this way can we be certain of success—or at least as certain as one can be on a mountain like Everest. Everyone agreed with that point of view. We have—almost *have*—to have a success. If later on we say, 'We tried the more difficult route of the West Ridge and bogged down,' that will be a very lame excuse for all the people who backed us. So we will try both."

If the West Ridge proved impossible, he felt, there would then not be too much lost. At least AMEE would find that out; in the process it would take pictures of the Tibetan side of Everest (the West Ridge marks the Nepalese-Tibetan border) from a place where no one had ever been before; and the climbers would then come down and join the assault on the South Col side. On the other hand, if the West Ridge "went," there was even the possibility of a traverse—the first not only on Everest but on any peak in the Himalaya—with one team crossing over the top from the West Ridge to the South Col and another making the climb in reverse. It was a feat that was almost too much to hope for, but—

But it was a dazzling prospect: a mountaineer's dream. As the approach march, and the discussions, continued, so did Lhotse and Nuptse continue to fade. And in their place, unknown, still unseen, loomed that West Ridge cleaving the sky.

The days began with a smiling Sherpa face and a steaming cup appearing through a tent flap and a cheerful "Tea, sah'b." (Or "Coffee, sah'b.") And perhaps something should be said here about that word "sahib."

In the semantics of the twentieth century it is a "bad" word. A holdover from the days of the British Raj in India and environs, it carries a connotation of superiority, of a servant-master relationship between addresser and addressee, and is as disliked in the modern East as the words "native" or "Asiatic." The Sherpas, however, are not students of semantics. Sahibs (or, more accurately, sah'bs) is what they have always called their mountaineering employers, and sahibs is what they continue to call them, no matter how much a conscientious equalitarian would prefer it otherwise.

From the beginning Norman was bara sahib, the "big boss." All other team members were sahib—sometimes straight, sometimes with first or last name preceding it—but always sahib. As a result, the men were presently using the name for themselves. "We sahibs did this, and the Sherpas did that," and it will therefore be used here and there in this record, though with none of its old-time implication of superiority. Indeed, in the world of the mountains, feeling superior to a Sherpa is about the ultimate in impossibility.

Many Westerners are under the impression that the word Sherpa means porter, bearer or guide. It does not. It means, in its own language, "man from the east," and the Sherpas are an ethnic sub-group of Tibetan stock who in the unrecorded past migrated from the northern to the southern slopes of the Himalaya and made their home in northeastern Nepal. As already mentioned, some of them subsequently moved on to Darjeeling, in northern India, where, in the 1920's, they first became involved in mountaineering expeditions. For those who remained in their homeland of Solu Khumbu, expeditions did not come until later—with the opening up of Nepal in the 1950's. But by 1963 both branches of Sherpa-dom boasted a cadre of experienced and competent mountain men. Of our own high-climbing group, almost all except the very young-est had been on previous expeditions to Everest, and most had also climbed on other great Himalayan peaks, with some having gone all the way to the top of such giants as Dhaulagiri and Nuptse.

As noted, only four of our men were from Darjeeling—and this was an unfortunate concomitant of the new Asian nationalism. In earlier days a Sherpa was a Sherpa was a Sherpa, like Miss Stein's famous rose, and no one cared about his official political national-ity. But now, according to his habitation, he is also either a Nepa-lese or an Indian, and Nepalese regulations strictly limited our hiring of "foreign" labor. More importantly and regrettably, in human terms, the artificial political barrier was in the process of causing a schism among the Sherpas themselves, and before the expedition was over there was to be some ill-feeling between the Solu Khumbu majority and the Darjeeling minority.

There were other differences among them too. What we usually referred to as "our Sherpas," or *the* Sherpas, were the ones who would accompany the team on the mountain, and these, ranging from Gombu on down, formed a very special elite among their own people: bearers of great reputations, wearers of expedition clothing, knowledgeable at least to a degree in the ways of the Big World. But there were also rank-and-file Sherpas—about 500 of them—who served only as low-level porters and who lived on a far more primitive level. These included men, women and children, and as cameraman Dan Doody described them: "In addition to their 65-pound expedition load they carry their personal gear consisting of extra sweater or jacket; blanket; sack of rice; and for every three or four, a pot and water container. Some have fancy wood and silver cups. Most have worn, tattered clothing but wear ornate jewelry, which is their wealth. Both men and women wear large earrings of silver or jade, along with silver bracelets and rings." In spite of their burdens most were always happy and smiling, and the giggling of the women—called Sherpanis—was the steady obbligato to each day's march. Not a few had babies, perched atop their loads in crude cradles. "When a baby starts to cry," noted Dan, "the mother just gives it a swig of milk from the breast without breaking stride."

The "climbing" Sherpas received a base pay of eight Nepalese rupees (a bit over a dollar) a day, with more for sirdar and assistant sirdar and a rising scale for all who went high on the mountain. In addition, they were supplied with food, clothing and gear. The nonclimbers received six rupees (about 80 cents) daily, with no extras. And so too did the nonclimbing non-Sherpas who formed almost half of our approach march army. These coolies—or, better, porters (for "coolie" is another semantically "bad" word)—were mostly of an ethnic group called Tamangs, dwellers in the central belt of eastern Nepal, and had little likeness to the Sherpas. They were not of Mongoloid but of Indic stock. They were not Buddhist but Hindu. And they had no tradition of mountaineering other than the endless carrying of loads up and down their native hills. All were totally unschooled. Almost all were barefoot and ragged. And most, too, were racked by disease—with an endless file of ailments, mostly tubercular and parasitic, passing before the expedition doctors at daily sick call, while a cacaphony of coughing, hacking and spitting rent the stillness of the nights. The doctors did what they could for them; but it wasn't much. For here was the human debasement of ancient Asia at its most complete, most abject; and it would require not the ministrations of transients but social change, measured in generations, to so much as make a dent in it.

In contrast, Sherpas, no less than Westerners, were almost like men from another world. They too are poor, by our standards, but without misery or degradation. They are tough people; proud, gay, happy people. They called us "sahib," yes—but because they chose to call us sahib. (If they had preferred to, they would have called us "Joe," and grinned as they said it.) When they acted as orderlies or servants, it was not because it was required of them but because they conceived it to be a part of their duties. They were being paid, as all men are paid, for services rendered, but it was not primarily for pay that they were on that march. No less than the Western mountaineers who employed them, they were doing what they wanted to do, what they were born to do. They were not hired help but companions in adventure.

On the eighth day, halfway to Namche Bazar, the procession came to the village of Those. This, the largest settlement along the trail, was in the midst of iron-ore country and, with its forges, possessed the only industrial establishment in northeastern Nepal. "Establishment" is used relatively, for all there was, said Norman, "were a few tiny smithies, with women and children treading the bellows and some old men beating red-hot iron. What they make is strictly for local use, such as plowshares, kukris (curved Nepalese knives) and chain links for bridges." Also, it developed, Those was a lively center of the chang and arak industries, and Sherpas and Tamangs enjoyed a long loud evening.

Then it was the trail again, the long trail, the roller-coaster trail. And along it crept the great slow millepede. In a certain valley it would be at, say, 5000 feet; at the crest of the next ridge, at 7500. Then down it would go to 6000, up to 8000, down to 7000, up to 9000—forever up and down, down and up—but always a little more up; and as the mean altitude changed, so too did the world roundabout. Cane, bananas and rice paddies were now gone. Instead there were high sloping pastures, and in the pastures, instead of cows and water buffalo, there were now big shaggy yaks. Here and there, increasingly, there were stands of forest, with rhododendron and magnolia in lustrous bloom, and high on the hills tall pines and hardwoods. In the valleys it was still warm. With no rain for weeks past, the earth was baked and cracked, and dust rose in clouds from beneath plodding feet. On the ridges, however, it was now noticeably cooler. The snowpeaks to the north loomed closer. Soon the caravan would itself be crossing passes carpeted with snow.

As the world of nature changed, so did the world of man, for the expedition was now leaving the Hindu realm of the valleys and entering the Buddhist realm of the highlands. Sacred *mani* walls and chortens (always pass to the left) lined the trails; prayer flags fluttered on the ridges; and sometimes at night the marchers camped in the courtyards of monasteries, falling asleep to the sound of priestly gongs and horns. They had come to the domain of Gautama the Buddha, of the Four Noble Truths and the Eightfold Path. And it may be permitted a mountaineer, raising his eyes to the snows, to believe that his own path is part of that greater one. The prayer wheels turn. The lips of their holders move in prayer. "*Om mani padme hum.* The jewel is in the lotus." And there was the mountaineer's lotus, white and shining on the horizon, with the jewel waiting within it for him who could reach it.

"How did you feel on top of Everest?" the Sherpa Tenzing was asked when he came down from the mountain. "I felt close to God," he replied. And there are few men who have not felt that closeness as they entered this hidden world above the world. Along the trail, up and down, down and up, there were many hours when the men of AMEE moved quietly in meditation.

Then, inevitably, came the time when meditation was gone. In its place was crisis and action. This was on the eleventh day of the march, beyond the village of Changma, during the crossing of one of the primitive bridges that span Nepal's innumerable mountain rivers. Some of these bridges are built largely of logs, some of bamboo or woven fibers and grasses. This one was of chain links (presumably made in Those), and it had been noted that one of the links at the nearer end of the chain had broken to the point where it was now half open. Using care not to put too much weight on it, most of the procession got across safely and moved on; but it was to be otherwise for some of the rear guard. At this time only Norman and Dan Doody, of the expedition membership, were on the scene, having stayed behind to take moving pictures of what, with swaying bridge and rushing torrent, is always a spectacular procedure. Norman was down on the riverbank shooting upward. Dan was working at the near end of the fragile walkway. Little Ang Dawa, Norman's Sherpa, was close by, warning a gang of porters not to crowd too closely onto the bridge. But they crowded anyway. Eleven of them, with their 65-pound loads moved out onto it at one time. "I was just changing lenses and lining up a shot," said Norman, "when suddenly there was a tremendous crash, tearing noises, metal snapping, people screaming. . . . And the whole bridge collapsed."

Of the eleven men on it—fortunately there were no women or children—three fell directly into the torrent and eight onto the rocks that bounded it on either side. Plunging in, Norman was able to pull out one of those who had gone into the water. The two others, struggling to free themselves from their loads, were carried some 200 yards downstream before they were hauled out by Sherpas who ran after them. Five of those who had hit the rocks lay half-senseless, bleeding and moaning, and "it seemed almost certain," said Norman, "that there were skull fractures, internal injuries, broken arms and legs." Runners were sent racing ahead for the expedition doctors, and presently both they and most of the other team members were back at the bridge. Or what had been the bridge. For an hour the doctors examined, cleaned, treated, bandaged, and astonishingly, gratifyingly, the five who had seemed all but dying came back to life. Two had badly cut heads, one a possible broken bone in his foot, the others no more than severe bruises and abrasions. And in another hour all who had fallen were moving on again under their own power. "Seven of them continued to carry their loads," said Dan Doody. "And those who couldn't were happy to learn that, even without them, they would be paid their six rupees a day. No complaints. No talk of lawsuits or insurance."

On that day AMEE both thanked the fates and took off its hat to its porters.

The next evening, near the village of Junbesi, came an emergency

of a different sort—though again involving the doctors. Throughout
the march they had held sick call each day upon arrival at camp,
not only for team members, Sherpas and porters, but also for people from the countryside roundabout. They had given pills and
injections, pulled teeth, cleaned wounds, performed minor surgery.
But now they were confronted by a case about which, under field
conditions, almost nothing could be done. A terribly burned woman
was carried into camp, her face, arms and upper body charred black,
her eyes peering out as if from a grotesque mask. Six days before,
it was said, she had run into a flaming shed in an attempt to save
a yak—her only worldly wealth—that was stabled there. That she
was still alive was amazing. And it was plain to the doctors that,
with infection well advanced, she would not be alive much longer
unless she could be hospitalized and given the best medical care.
But the nearest full-scale hospital was a ten days' march away, in
Kathmandu.

What to do? Along the trail the expedition had encountered
much serious disease, but it had been largely of the infectious en-
demic sort, for which nothing short of a broad public health campaign would have been effective. Here, on the other hand, was a
single specific case, an individual suffering human being over whom
the expedition had the power of life and death. It was as black
and white as that. In Kathmandu there was a helicopter, used in
the U.S. AID programs, that was available in emergencies—at a
tidy sum, to be sure, but still available. The doctors presented the
case. The team debated it. But it was Norman who, in the end, had
to make the decision.

He made it. AMEE would do what it could. But in back-country
Nepal you don't pick up phones or send telegrams. For the first
time on the trip the expedition radio gear was broken out, and for
a long while, in the darkness, Al Auten and assorted helpers worked
at setting it up. Even a functioning radio, however, did not at once
solve all problems; for at night the ionosphere, off which its messages bounce, moves higher above the earth than during the day,
and strange things happen in the world of beams and kilocycles.
For more hours Al jiggled his dials and repeated his call signals,
but Kathmandu, a mere hundred-or-so miles distant, was unreach-
able. What did come on the air were remote Australia and, on the

fringes, southern Sweden; and it was with an Australian ham operator that Al finally made intelligible contact, asking him to pass on
the message to the American Embassy in Canberra with the request that they relay it back to our embassy in Kathmandu. It is
a small world, perhaps, but sometimes with long lines of communication. And whether the message would complete its circuit,
and the chopper would come, no one knew. As insurance, a runner
was dispatched to Kathmandu with the same message. A note for
the helicopter pilot—if and when—was left with the headman of the
village. Then, the next morning, the expedition continued its
march, and it would be some time before it learned the fate of the
burned Mrs. Pashi Sherpa of Junbesi.

Still the trail flowed on. Still there were the valleys and rivers,
the hills and ridges—and high beyond the ridges the great white
rampart to the north. "After breakfast," wrote Norman, "down to
the stream below Junbesi. Then uphill and around a mountain;
brunch above the next stream; up to the col called Taksindu Ban-
yang and down on the far side through magnolia forest to a beautiful campsite at about 7000 feet near the lamasery of Taksindu."
Beyond this was the village of Karikola, beyond that Puijan, beyond
that Ghat and Phakding. And always between them it was up,
down, down, up. For a while now there were no further major
crises, but an occasional minor one flared up out of nowhere. At
one campsite an irate old Sherpani appeared, claiming that her
property was being trespassed, and stood ready to take on the whole
expedition in tooth-and-nail combat. At another, in the dead of
night, there was a brief but violent ruckus, as thieves of undeter-
mined number and status tried unsuccessfully to make away with
some of the loads. In contrast, there were days that could be
described simply and totally by Xenophon's "they marched so-
and-so many parasangs." And as on that earlier Anabasis there
were to be parasangs aplenty before the march was done.

Day by day, however, the pace was swifter and surer, for blistered
feet and aching legs were now things of the past. The men had
their fair quota of "trots," of wheezing and coughing in the thin-
ning air; and most of them, too, were losing weight. But what was

left of them had hardened and toughened. The smell of mountains was in their nostrils.

AMEE was no longer a list on a sheet of paper; it was a functioning entity—a team, an organism. But it was also a group of nineteen highly various nonregimented non-mass-produced individuals, and each carried with him, along with his pack, the stamp of his own mind and personality. For Norman these were days of comparative relaxation, between the ordeal of organization and the challenge of the mountain. He was at ease, deeply and quietly happy, as he moved on again into this world he loved. Will Siri, on the other hand, was tense, bursting with nervous energy, as if the challenge ahead were already at hand. Though troubled with bursitis in his arm, he carried his full pack on each day's march, and his pace was faster than that of many of the younger men. Tom Hornbein, high apostle of the West Ridge, was forever thinking and planning ahead, working on problems of routes, schedules and logistics with almost mathematical precision. And in Jim Whittaker, striding on through the miles, one could feel the concentrated power of a locomotive. Back home, in Redmond, Washington, through fall and early winter, Big Jim had further hardened his already hard frame by rigorous roadwork and daily swims in the chilly waters of Lake Sammamish. Now on the trail he often did fifty or sixty push-ups at the end of a long day's hike. Furthermore, his intensity of drive was a thing of mind no less than of body. At the psychological testings at the University of California one of the questions asked confidentially of each team member had been whether he thought that he individually would reach the top of Everest. All the others had replied, "perhaps," "it depends," "I hope to," or some variant thereof. Jim Whittaker alone (it was learned later) had said, "Yes, I will."

His longtime climbing partner, Lute Jerstad, wanted the top too—wanted it enormously—but an observer who did not know him would have been hard put to tell it. He was the expedition ukulele player, its balladeer, its ham declaimer of mock heroic verse; as seemingly relaxed as if on a Sunday picnic. And Willi Unsoeld, delivered from his last-minute cliff-hanger with the Peace Corps, was for most of the time no less so. As was well known to his companions, no man on earth could generate a more powerful

VISION

Everest and its plume as seen from above the plains of India. Close beside it, to left and right, are Nuptse and Lhotse. Far to the right is Makalu.

Photograph by Barry C. Bishop, AMEE

THE TEAM IN KATHMANDU

Left to right, front row: Corbet, Auten, Lester, Miller, Breitenbach, Ullman, Dingman, Pownall, Siri, Bishop. *Second row:* Doody, Dyhrenfurth, Jerstad, J. Roberts, G. Roberts, Whittaker, Unsoeld, Emerson, Prather, Hornbein.

WORKOUT ON MOUNT RAINIER

NORMAN G. DYHRENFURTH
Leader

Photograph by Barry C. Bishop, © 1963 NATIONAL GEOGRAPHIC SOCIETY

Photograph by Norman G. Dyhrenfurth, AMEE

ALLEN C. AUTEN

Photograph by Norman G. Dyhrenfurth, AMEE

BARRY C. BISHOP

Photograph by Daniel E. Doody,
© 1963 NATIONAL GEOGRAPHIC SOCIETY

JOHN E. BREITENBACH

Photograph by Lila M. Bishop,
© 1963 NATIONAL GEOGRAPHIC SOCIETY

JAMES BARRY CORBET

Photograph by Norman G. Dyhrenfurth, AMEE

DAVID L. DINGMAN

Photograph by Norman G. Dyhrenfurth, AMEE

DANIEL E. DOODY

Photograph by Norman G. Dyhrenfurth, AMEE

RICHARD M. EMERSON

Photograph by Norman G. Dyhrenfurth, AMEE

THOMAS F. HORNBEIN

Photograph by Norman G. Dyhrenfurth, AMEE

LUTHER G. JERSTAD

Photograph by Norman G. Dyhrenfurth, AMEE

JAMES T. LESTER

Photograph by Norman G. Dyhrenfurth, AMEE

MAYNARD M. MILLER

Photograph by Norman G. Dyhrenfurth, AMEE

RICHARD POWNALL

Photograph by Norman G. Dyhrenfurth, AMEE

BARRY W. PRATHER

Photograph by Norman G. Dyhrenfurth, AMEE

WILLIAM E. SIRI
Deputy Leader

Photograph by Norman G. Dyhrenfurth, AMEE

GILBERT ROBERTS

Photograph by Norman G. Dyhrenfurth, AMEE

JAMES O. M. ROBERTS

Photograph by Barry C. Bishop,,
© 1963 NATIONAL GEOGRAPHIC SOCIETY

CHARLES B. HUESTIS

Photograph courtesy of Hughes Aircraft Company

WILLIAM F. UNSOELD

Photograph by Barry C. Bishop,
© 1963 NATIONAL GEOGRAPHIC SOCIETY

JAMES W. WHITTAKER

Photograph by Norman G. Dyhrenfurth, AMEE

PRABAKHER S. J. B. RANA

Photograph by Norman G. Dyhrenfurth, AMEE

Photograph by Lila M. Bishop,
© 1963 NATIONAL GEOGRAPHIC SOCIETY

JAMES RAMSEY ULLMAN

Ang Dawa

Photograph by Norman G. Dyhrenfurth, AMEE

Girmi Dorje

Photograph by Barry C. Bishop,
© 1964 NATIONAL GEOGRAPHIC SOCIETY

Chotari

Photograph by Norman G. Dyhrenfurth, AMEE

Nawang Gombu

Photograph by Norman G. Dyhrenfurth, AMEE

Phu Dorje

Photograph by Norman G. Dyhrenfurth, AMEE

Tashi

Photograph by Norman G. Dyhrenfurth, AMEE

Anullu

Photograph by Barry C. Bishop,
© 1963 NATIONAL GEOGRAPHIC SOCIETY

THE ARMY ASSEMBLES
Porters at Banepa.

MILLEPEDE
The caravan on the trail.

Photograph by Barry C. Bishop, © 1964 NATIONAL GEOGRAPHIC SOCIETY

TOIL . . . AND REST
(Age and sex variable).

Photograph by Barry C. Bishop, © 1963 NATIONAL GEOGRAPHIC SOCIETY

TRAFFIC JAM
—at every bridge.

ENCAMPMENT
—on a terraced hill.

Photograph by James W. Whittaker, AMEE

ON THE TRAIL

Photograph by Norman G. Dyhrenfurth, AMEE

FUTURE "TIGERS"?

Photograph by Barry C. Bishop, © 1963 NATIONAL GEOGRAPHIC SOCIETY

SHERPANI ON CHAIN BRIDGE

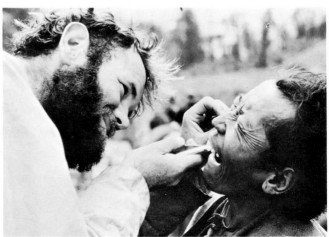

PORTER WITH IDENTIFICATION TAG

Photograph by Barry C. Bishop,
© 1964 NATIONAL GEOGRAPHIC SOCIETY

DR. ROBERTS ATTENDING

Photograph by Gilbert Roberts, AMEE

Photograph by Barry C. Bishop, © 1964 NATIONAL GEOGRAPHIC SOCIETY

FIRST VIEW OF THE GOAL

The crest of Everest (left) barely emerges from behind the Nuptse-Lhotse wall. To the right and in front of it, Lhotse. Far to the right, the spire of Ama Dablam.

SHERPA METROPOLIS

Namche Bazar,
backed by unclimbed peaks.

Photograph by Norman G. Dyhrenfurth, AMEE

THE LAMASERY AT THANGBOCHE

Everest looming
over its shoulder.

Photograph by Norman G. Dyhrenfurth, AMEE

Photograph by Norman G. Dyhrenfurth, AMEE

Toward the Khumbu Glacier

The rectangles in the foreground are the walls of the highest yak pastures.

Base Camp

Photograph by Norman G. Dyhrenfurth, AMEE

AT BASE CAMP

CHOW . . . PLUS ICEFALL

RADIO MAST

DR. DAVE DINGMAN VACCINATING

Photograph by Richard Pownall, AMEE

Threading the Chaos of the Icefall

IN THE ICEFALL

BRIDGING A CREVASSE

COLLECTING SAMPLE OF ICE LAYERS FOR THE GLACIOLOGY PROGRAM

IT WAS A WALL SUCH AS THIS THAT COLLAPSED ON JOHN BREITENBACH

BRIDGE CROSSES BRIDGE

VALLEY OF SILENCE

The Western Cwm, with Lhotse at its head.

ADVANCE BASE

Behind it,
the south face of Everest.

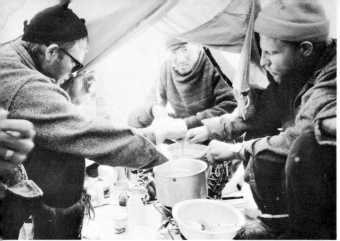

Photograph by Barry C. Bishop, © 1964 NATIONAL GEOGRAPHIC SOCIETY

LIFE AT A.B.

CLOSE QUARTERS

CULTURE

Photograph by James T. Lester, AMEE

Photograph by Barry C. Bishop, © 1963 NATIONAL GEOGRAPHIC SOCIETY

GORAK—AND FRIEND

DAN DOODY
STRICKEN BY
THROMBOPHLEBITIS

Photograph by James T. Lester, AMEE

inner force than Willi when he raised his eyes to a mountain. But—
again seemingly—they were not yet raised. He was the philosopher
of the trail, the peacemaker, the younger elder statesman; and
though he was as keen for the West Ridge as his old friend Tom
Hornbein, he would habitually act as moderator when, as sometimes happened, Ridge versus South Col routes became a subject
of warm debate.

There were the quiet ones: Dick Pownall, majordomo of food
boxes (which was enough to keep any man occupied); Dick Emerson (the sociological listener); Al Auten (who would have full
chance for vocalizing when his radio was set up at Base Camp).
There were the not-so-quiet ones: Barry Bishop (who was everywhere taking pictures); Maynard Miller (everywhere, plus several
other places, doing everything imaginable); and Dan Doody,
cameraman plus comic (who, however, when he forsook lens and
wisecrack for his diary had the sharpest eye on the expedition for
the small details of life along the trail). Jake Breitenbach, Barry
Corbet and Barry Prather, three of the team's "junior" members,
allowed their eyes to stray longingly ahead when they were on the
march, but in camp threw themselves energetically into all manner
of odd jobs and chores. In contrast, Doctors Gil Roberts and Dave
Dingman (also no graybeards) were the team sophisticates: hip,
cool and—in Gil's favorite term—nonjudgmental. But when sick
call came around each evening, or a mishap occurred on the trail,
they were promptly and startlingly transformed into the two most
conscientious workers in Nepal.

Psychologist Jim Lester functioned in his dual role of mountaineering apprentice—his blisters had been the worst of all—and receiver of confidences. (He later paid me the compliment of saying
he wished I had been around to listen to *his* troubles.) And
Colonel Jimmy Roberts carried on equably both with the endless
problems of Sherpas and porters and the new, possibly traumatic,
experience of being the lone Englishman in a pack of Americans.
Not too traumatic, however, one is inclined to think; for Jimmy, a
lifetime bachelor, was a loner by nature. So too, though to a lesser
degree, were one or two others. As always, in a newly formed
group, there tended, at the start of the expedition, to be the "ins"
and the "outs"; and also, in the beginning, there was a certain

amount of cliquishness based on old friendships and associations. This, however, Norman tried hard to dispel. The team members themselves fought against it, and in time were largely successful. Overall, AMEE was a group, not of soloists or "club members," but of friendly, outgoing men; and through the stresses and strains to come they were to put on a fine showing of companionship and teamwork.

Team and Teamwork: This is the endlessly repeated re-repeated shibboleth of every mountain expedition that has ever been. And though the reader may well grow weary of it, it is a price he must pay for his vicarious journey to the heights. (The climbers, it may be added, would pay a far greater one if said T & T were lacking.)

There is a contradiction here, of course. For while mountaineering, in its very essence, is an escape from an overcomplicated, overorganized society, its practitioner, at least on a large expedition, must become in effect an Organization Man. And there are other contradictions too. The mountain way is the way of simplicity, of rapport with the life of nature, but to that life man brings cameras, recorders, radios, oxygen gear, and assorted other products of an advanced technology. It is a renouncement of politics and global strife, of the nationalism that has brought man to the age of megadeath and overkill; yet it is largely in national terms that expeditions are measured and judged. How did the British do? asks the world. How did the Swiss, the Indians, the Chinese do? How, now, will the Americans do? Which are the strong ones and which the weak sisters? The hell with all that, says the true mountaineer who wants no part of jingoistic rivalries. But in the world he lives in he is stuck with his label whether he wants it or not.

Taking nations and nationalism as a fact of life, how did AMEE shape up as compared with the expeditions of other countries? In some respects not so well. In the United States we have nothing to match the long mountaineering tradition of the British; nor did our team possess the similarity of backgrounds (in the case of the British usually Oxford-Cambridge-Sandhurst*) which makes for a homogeneous and tightly knit party. Vis-à-vis most Continental expeditions, we were pretty much amateurs; for in countries like

* As with every generality, there have of course been exceptions—notably the non-Oxford-Cambridge-Sandhurst Edmund Hillary.

France, Germany, Switzerland and Italy, the top climbers are apt
to be full-time professionals, whereas in ours no such specimens
exist. Further, in contrast to teams of almost *all* other nations, ours
was loosely organized and disciplined. Large European climbing
parties—not to mention those of the Asian nations—have operated
largely along at least quasi-military lines. The chain of command
has been rigid. The leader has been leader, with no questions
asked. On AMEE, however—*genus Americanus* being what it is—
Norman had no such absolute authority; nor did he want it. There
were plenty of questions asked. And though this was the only conceivable way in which an American expedition could be conducted,
it was sometimes at the cost of reduced cohesiveness and efficiency.

But there were items on the credit side as well. For one thing
(and for this we are still not making apologies) we were superbly
equipped. For another, the nature of American mountaineering—
involving wild country, long distances and an absence of cheap
labor—is such that our men had had more experience than those of
most other countries in do-it-yourself camping and climbing with
heavy loads. Added to these, as a nonphysical factor, was a tremendous will and desire that in many ways compensated for a lack of
Himalayan experience. Not that the British, Swiss and men of
other nations have lacked driving force; far from it. But it was perhaps heightened for us by the very fact that we were, most of us,
newcomers to earth's highest mountains. We were, though far
from novices, mountaineers who had heretofore had few chances
at earth's greatest prizes. Now, in the Big League at last, we were
resolved to prove to ourselves and the world that we belonged
there.

In some ways, strangely, it was with the Indians and Chinese that
we could best be equated, for they too have been late-comers to the
Himalayan heights. And in the equating process some fascinating
truths begin to appear. For years it was taken for granted that such
an activity as mountaineering was strictly for Westerners; that the
Asian, passive and contemplative, felt no call to such a "cult of
action." But in the twentieth century world this is now, demon-
strably, no longer the case. Further, examining the other side of the
coin, one finds that mountaineering, on the surface so wholly
"Western and activist," is in its essential meaning very close to the

spirit of the ancient Eastern philosophies. "Take action not for its
result but for its own sake," says the *Bhagavad-Gita*. And what is
the climbing of mountains if not action for its own sake? True, on
a mountain one tries for the top. True, too, that on an expedition
such as ours there is a certain amount of "useful" scientific work
carried on. But both these "results" are secondary to the basic
motive, which is the confrontation of man and nature as an end
in itself. The great French mountaineer, Lionel Terray, has called
his book of climbing memoirs *La Conquête de l'Inutile*; and it is a
sound and valid title, for by all pragmatic standards climbing mountains is "useless." That, indeed, is one of its glories: that it needs
no end or justification beyond itself—like a sunset, a symphony, or
like falling in love.

An attempt on Everest is no less a thing of the spirit than of lung
and limb. What a mountaineer brings with him in his mind and
heart is as essential as what he brings in the pack on his back. Many
of the men of AMEE, I am sure, thought back now and then—as
I did—to the eyes on the temples of Kathmandu, watching them,
questioning them, as they set off on their journey. Most of them,
I know, meditated while on the trail on the passing *mani* walls, the
streaming prayer flags, the turning prayer wheels, the words on the
lips of priests and pilgrims: "*Om mani padme hum. Om mani
padme hum.*" *Om* is the sacred word of the Buddhist faith; a
mystical indefinable word, absolute, ultimate, meaning nothing—
and everything. And we too had our *om*.

The place we were going to was known to the West as Mount
Everest, to Tibetans as Chomolungma, to Nepalese as Sagarmatha.
But to the mountaineer, in his deepest heart, it was also *om*.

On the thirteenth day of the march there were spectacular
changes. The expedition had come now to the country of Solu
Khumbu, and, with it, to the Dudh Kosi (or Milky River), a
main arterial stream of eastern Nepal that flows down from near
Everest toward India and the Ganges. Up to here the route had
led almost due east, but at the river it veered off to the north, and
northward it would continue until it reached the mountain. This
was the wildest country yet encountered. For the Dudh Kosi's path
was through deep clefts and winding gorges, and the trail rose and

fell, rose and fell, as it climbed back and forth from the riverbed to the top of the cliffs above. Often, too, it crossed the river, on bridges even shakier than the one near Changma which had collapsed. But the expedition was now on guard. Each time the path dipped down toward a bridge, an advance crew, usually headed by Jake Breitenbach and Barry Corbet, went ahead to examine and, if necessary, improve it; and "policemen" were stationed to make sure that no more than two or three porters ever crossed at one time.

This made for slow going; sometimes it took a whole morning or afternoon for the full column to make a passage. But this was far better than another accident, which here would have been almost surely fatal. For most of the bridges were high above the water, and the water itself was a wild churning of foam and rock.

Above the canyons the forests were larger and denser than before. And though the altitude was higher, they were more tropical in aspect than those previously encountered, for this was a region of greater rainfall. Indeed, the expedition, for the first time, now met with heavy rain. The Kathmandu umbrellas blossomed; the trail became a slippery mire; and at night torrents beat upon the campsite tents, all but drowning out the roar of the Dudh Kosi.

From Dick Pownall's diary: "The porters had a hard time on the last mile today. Downhill: steep, muddy and slippery. Traversed upstream high above the river in a relatively uninhabited region, due to the steepness of terrain. Clouds drifting in and out gave the trail an eerie aspect. Into a deeply forested area, full of ferns and evergreens."

From Dan Doody's: "Eight hours of a long wet day. I noticed a string of porters passing another one who had stopped on the trail, and on coming to him I found it was one of the eleven-year-old boys who are carrying for us. He was not much taller than my waist and was obviously frightened by the muddy slope ahead. I extended my hand, which he firmly grasped with an expression of utter confidence, and he with his 60-pound load and I with my 30 pounds proceeded down the hill. All the while he was confident of the safety I was providing, and I was confident that, should he slip, we'd both go sliding off into nothing."

From Maynard Miller's: "Moved up the river to Puijan, follow-

ing a steeply climbing and descending trail along the east wall of
the Dudh Kosi canyon at elevations ranging from 7000 to 10,000
feet. This brought us to winter snow on the trail. At Puijan, however, we nestled into a dramatic campsite in a magnolia forest, with
weird moss-covered trunks and branches looming in the evening
fog. Here, for the first time on the march, we had a crackling wood
fire, and Noddy (Captain Rana, our Nepalese liaison officer) shot
a Himalayan pheasant in the nearby woods."

That was the fourteenth day. On the fifteenth the going was
much the same, to the villages of Ghat and Phakding. But on the
sixteenth the trail swung off from the Dudh Kosi to climb steeply
to the 12,400-foot elevation of Namche Bazar; at the same time
the rain stopped, the mists cleared; and eyes were no longer on the
river below but on the sky above. Throughout the whole march the
Great Himalaya had been visible from the high places on the trail,
in its gleaming white wave on the northern horizon. But now it was
no longer ahead: it was *over*head: a vast galaxy of peaks—close,
looming, enormous. To the right were the thrusting spires of
Thamserku, Kangtega, Ama Dablam. To the left Taweche, Tso-
latse, with a host of others, all of them summits of 20,000-or-more
feet. Straight ahead, more distant but higher—at over 25,000 feet
for the whole of its sweep—was the vast rock and ice battlement
connecting Lhotse and Nuptse. And beyond this, in turn, still more
distant, still higher—

Yes, there it was. At last.

Approached overland from the south, the King of Mountains is
a shy one. Seen from the air, as we had seen it some three weeks
before, it had been huge, dominant, unrivalled. But for the earth-
bound traveler moving up through Solu Khumbu it remains all but
hidden behind that Lhotse-Nuptse wall. Only its very tip emerges,
trailing its snow plume: a tiny apex—remote, aloof, barely visible.

But there.

7. SHERPALAND

NAMCHE BAZAR, the metropolis of Sherpaland, lies at 12,400 feet on the steep side of a natural amphitheater in the hills. Below it, to the east, is the sounding gorge of the Dudh Kosi. Behind and above it, forming the upper rim of the amphitheater, is a broad gently sloping plateau, and above the rim, more distant but far higher, stands the icy fretwork of the great peaks. Namche has some 140 houses and a population of about 500—no larger than other nearby Sherpa towns such as Khumjung and Thami. But its position on the main south to north trail of Solu Khumbu has made it a famous milestone on the road to Everest.

Both its hillside and its stone houses are dun and bleak. But bleak is the last word that could be applied to its people, who are far livelier, gayer and more prosperous than the Indic-Hindu people of Nepal's lowland valleys. Some of the men wear Western clothing, almost all of it left over from expeditions; others, the classical Tibetan rig of rough yak-hair coat, high boots, and big hats with furry earflaps and bold embroidery. The women's distinguishing garment is a brightly colored striped apron, beneath which they are often incongruously shod in, of all things, tennis sneakers. The broad Mongoloid faces are happy faces. This is the land of the smile, the grin, the guffaw and—for the females—the giggle. And the happiness doubles and trebles when an expedition comes through; for this means novelty, excitement and employment—plus the homecoming of many Sherpas who have been a part of the caravan.

"Throughout the march, in every village," reported Dan Doody, "there had been eyes, eyes, eyes, watching us: some friendly, some dull, some hostile. But here *all* eyes were friendly and smiling." And Spark Schnitzer, AMEE's "camp follower," noted that while Namche "looked drab and monotonous against its stark background of black rock, blinding white glacier and azure sky, its alleys were exotically filled with the lives of man and animal." Wandering through them, he found "Indian and Nepalese border guards loafing at their post; Sherpanis washing clothes and beating them clean under the spout of a bamboo pipeline; an old man combing his waist-long hair in front of his house, while yapping puppies rushed in and out; hundreds of noisy dogs all over town but not a single cat; a huddle of tradespeople exchanging goods, perhaps brought in over wild and lonely distances; goats and yaks, their bells tinkling, separating from their herds and lazily seeking out their home stables; above, huge swarms of Tibetan ravens, whose raucous cries and unrelieved blackness introduced an ominous note in the pastoral scene."

The welcome to the expedition began at the Nepalese-Indian checkpost, where there was a minimum of checking and a maximum of chang distribution. And more welcome-*cum*-chang followed, up and down the street and in Sherpa homes. The latter were all of the same two-story design, with the lower level assigned to yaks and other livestock and the upper, reached by steep ladder-like stairs, to the human tenantry. In almost all cases there was but one all-purpose room, containing a bed or two, low tables, but no chairs. The walls were lined with Tibetan rugs, and against these stood cupboards and shelves holding wooden utensils and brass-bound wooden crocks of rice and wheat. Windows were small, with glazed paper as panes—which served to keep out light as well as cold; and the dimness was abetted by the smoke of cook fires (in the middle of the floor; there were no hearths or chimneys) which hung about in great shrouds until it leisurely seeped out through holes in the roof.

In one such home the expedition sirdar, Passang Phutar, was host to the team members at a dinner of yak soup, yak stew with noodles (the yak gives full service in Sherpaland), plus generous libations of chang. And later, in the gleam of firelight and veils of smoke, there was singing plus chang and dancing plus chang. With the mingled odors of food, drink, smoke and unwashed Sherpadom, there was a certain problem, as one guest put it, of "olfactory survival." But still it was well into the night before the party broke up and the slightly groggy AMEE delegation toiled uphill to the plateau above the town where their camp had been pitched. Even from the most dedicated mountaineers there were no reports as of that evening about the joys of climbing. "I don't know if I felt the chang or the altitude more," Dick Pownall confided to his diary. "But I felt something."

Two nights and a day were spent in Namche Bazar. But they were by no means wholly festive, for, almost simultaneously with the team's arrival, a dark and sinister presence had come onto the scene. The day before, near the village of Phakding, several of the expedition members had noticed that one of the younger low-level porters, a Sherpa boy of thirteen or so, was behaving in strange fashion: moving very slowly along the trail minus a load and with his face almost hidden by a burlap rag. And when they stopped to investigate they found that his face was grossly swollen and covered with pustules. Gil Roberts and Dave Dingman were summoned. Like most American doctors, they had had no direct experience with smallpox. But they knew it when they saw it—and here it was. The boy had been with the baggage train all the way from Kathmandu. For the past three days, it was discovered, his condition had been known to many of the other porters, who had shunned him both on the trail and at the nightly campsites. But no one had reported it to any member of the expedition. Now, of course, he was immediately detached from the party. Under the doctors' supervision, he was put in isolation in a nearby village and given such makeshift treatment as was possible. But he had reached the stage where, in effect, nothing could be done for him, and a few days beyond Namche word reached the expedition that he had died.

Team members and high-climbing Sherpas had all been recently vaccinated—the former at home, the latter in Kathmandu. But the other Sherpas and the Tamangs had no such protection, and how many had been infected (smallpox has a ten- to twelve-day incubation period) no one knew. With the supply of vaccine sent out from Kathmandu our doctors ministered to both porters and Solu Khumbu residents to the number of several hundred. But it was obviously important that immunization be effected on an even wider scale, and to this end the radio was again set up in another effort to reach Kathmandu. This time there was no success, even by a roundabout route. But luckily there was also a radio at the military checkpost at Namche, and through this the word was sent through. In due time vaccine in wholesale dosages was dispatched by the Nepalese headquarters of the World Health Organization, both by air drop and by runner. By then, however, most of the expedition's Tamang porters (all of whom were paid off in Namche Bazar) were on the way back to their lowland homes, and the expedition itself was high in the mountains beyond. Happily, none of the nonvaccinated Sherpas that accompanied it contracted smallpox; and the scattered Tamangs seem at least to have carried no major epidemic along with them. In Solu Khumbu, however, many cases subsequently developed, with an estimated forty deaths, and even greater disaster could well have struck the area, had it not been for the arrival of the additional vaccine. This was administered by our physicians and doctor-members of a team led by Sir Edmund Hillary, which followed AMEE into the Sherpa country some three weeks later, and by the time our own men came down from the heights the disease was at last under control.*

In other aspects of health, too, arrival in Namche was a time of trouble. For no sooner had camp been pitched than Chotari, assistant sirdar to Passang Phutar and a veteran of many climbs, came down with what the doctors diagnosed as acute appendicitis; and at almost the same time they were confronted with an even

* Sir Edmund's 1963 expedition, composed both of British and Americans, was a multipurpose affair. Its principal concern was educational and medical work in the Sherpa communities, but it also (see later) made climbs on two virginal peaks in the Everest area.

more serious case. This was a nineteen-year-old expedition Sherpani, Ang Gyalmu, a cousin of Norman's Sherpa, Ang Dawa, who was tubercular to begin with, and now had developed double pneumonia with a temperature of 105. She was taken to the medical tent and put on oxygen and intravenous feeding, but little hope was held for her recovery. Simultaneously, Chotari was given massive doses of antibiotics, and preparations were made for a field appendectomy. The next day, however, both were, almost miraculously, much better. Ang Gyalmu, now well out of danger, was given over to the care of relatives in Namche; and Chotari soon resumed his normal expedition functions, with no further recurrence of symptoms.

The rain that had fallen in the gorges of the Dudh Kosi had been snow at the higher elevation of Namche. There had been a light white covering over the earth at the time of the team's arrival, and now it was deepened by falls on the two following afternoons. (For weeks and months to come this was to be the basic weather pattern for the expedition: fair and clear mornings, followed by cloud, and often snow, during the latter part of the day.) But on the morning of March 9, still on schedule, the caravan was again on the move. This time the day's objective was the Buddhist monastery of Thangboche, 600 feet higher than Namche and some six miles farther along the trail to Everest.

As noted, Namche was the end of the line for the Tamang porters. Of the original army of 909 carriers, about 400 had been Tamangs; but as the daily consumption of food reduced the total number of loads, some had been sloughed off along the trail, and the number of required bearers was now down to 800-odd. The original low-level Sherpas who had been with the trek since Kathmandu accounted for some 500 of these. Now an additional 300— men, women and youngsters—were hired at Namche, plus five more potentially "high" Sherpas, bringing the number in that category to thirty-seven. And presently the long caravan, like some ancient tribal migration, was again in motion across the face of the land. The trail to the north first led down from Namche's hill site to a point near the confluence of the Dudh Kosi and a tributary stream called the Imja Khola; then up again to the 13,000-foot alpine pasture where stands Thangboche. By noon on this day's march it had started to snow. The fall thickened rapidly, and by the time of arrival the procession was trudging through a foot or more of wintry whiteness.

Though there are possibly other equally beautiful places on earth, you will not hear about them from a man who has been to Thangboche. Roundabout, in staggering array, stand a host of great peaks, so huge, so close and towering, that, in contrast, all other mountains become ranges of molehills. "Landscape is cows," it has been said. "Scenery is when it looks as if it's going to fall down on you." And here was scenery at its ultimate. It did *not* fall, however. The snow fell. In the distance avalanches fell, rumbling and roaring. But the peaks stood up: firm, gigantic, eternal. And their vast unhuman grandeur was heightened by the fact of Thangboche itself; that here at their very threshold, tiny but bold, was one of the last outposts of human habitation. The stone buildings of the lamasery, rising in tiers to a temple crowned by a golden finial, seemed no more than children's building blocks in their pocket of pasture. Human beings were creatures from Lilliput. The wisps of smoke from fires, the sound of drums and horns and gongs, rose from a world in miniature, losing themselves in a cosmos of rock, ice and sky.

But it is not only for its beauty that Thangboche is famous. Together with the Rongbuk Monastery, some thirty miles away on the Tibetan side of Everest, it has been renowned as a center of Lamaistic Buddhism. Now, however, there is no more "togetherness." For Rongbuk, in its religious aspect, has been destroyed by the Communist Chinese; its buildings serve as barracks for frontier-guarding troops; and of the two shrines flanking Chomolungma, Goddess Mother of the World, only Thangboche, in Nepal, remains. Many of the priests at Thangboche were Tibetans, refugees from Rongbuk. In pre-Communist days, the High Lama had been there several times, as well as to Lhasa and to Buddhist centers in Sikkim and northern India. He was an Incarnation Lama, this abbot of Thangboche—meaning that like the Dalai Lamas of Lhasa, he had been selected for his post, after long search, as the spiritual reembodiment of High Lamas of the past. And he was still a young man of about thirty. To the Western mind, of course, there is much smacking of mumbo jumbo in the beliefs and rituals

of Central Asian Lamaism. But the sincerity and piety of Thangboche's leader was unquestionable; and in such a place the trap-
pings of an ancient faith seem to have far more validity than in
the strident twentieth century world of the lowlands.

"Om mani padme hum, om mani padme hum," goes the eternal
chant accompanying the turning prayer wheels. And from the
heights above, if there is no answer, there is no rejection.

Something new, it was at once discovered, had been added to
the monastery in the year just past: a tin-roofed hut of one large
room and four small ones, designed to serve as shelter for expeditions and other passersby. In the heavy snowfall it was a welcome
surprise; and soon it was functioning as AMEE headquarters, with
tents ranged around it for cooking, storage and overflow sleeping.
According to the original plan, there was to have been only an
overnight stop at Thangboche. The team would then move on to
a place called Pheriche, in the high yak pastures near the snout of
the Khumbu Glacier and there spend two weeks or more acclimatizing and doing practice climbs on the nearby peaks. But on the
morning of March 10, with the snow still falling heavily, a change
of schedule was effected. It would have been all but impossible
for laden porters to go higher through the now 2-foot-deep drifts.
Further, the lamasery hut was the last solid and usable shelter on
the trail. So it was decided that this, instead of Pheriche, would be
the site for acclimatization and such. Most of the rank-and-file
porters were sent down to their homes in Namche and nearby
villages, with instructions to return in five days; and meanwhile
sahibs and "high" Sherpas set to work in what was in effect a pre-
Base-Camp base.

This was the earliest in the year that any expedition had been
so close to Everest, and, in the wintry weather, the first step was
the breaking out of all manner of cold-weather clothing. Out, too,
came heavy mountain boots, goggles, ice axes, crampons, and other
gear which would be needed for the hard going ahead; and with
the approach-march food boxes now emptied and discarded, the
first inroads were made on stores labeled Base. As in Kathmandu,
there were items that required persistent digging before coming to
light. And, more seriously, there were some that would have to be
secured from the outside world. One of these was medicines, which

had been used up at a rate far greater than anticipated. Another was down mittens, which were mysteriously in short supply. A third was a new consignment of the wind- and snowproof outer jackets called anoraks, for those at hand were too small to fit over layers of bulky cold-weather clothing. An urgent message for all these to be secured and dispatched as quickly as possible was sent off by runner to now-distant Kathmandu.

At about the same time—and most welcomely—two runners appeared on the reverse course, bearing mail. And for a long silent evening what had been a team became again nineteen separate, and somewhat lonely, individuals, as each withdrew into a private world of home and family. Also with the messenger came word from Sally Dyhrenfurth that the burned woman of Junbesi had, as requested via Australia, been evacuated by helicopter to Kathmandu and was now in the hospital on the way to recovery. Indeed, the mail runner himself had been part of the helicopter story; for he had been a proud, if terrified, passenger on its flight out to Junbesi, and had thus cut his normal trail time by more than half. Since a runner, even when going the whole way afoot, can cover distances at far greater speed than a heavy baggage train, this meant that he had got from Kathmandu to Thangboche in the unheard of time of about four days.

At the lamasery camp the team doctors were still scarcely men of leisure. Fortunately there was no further pneumonia or appendicitis to contend with, but now there came a case of toothache—and the ache belonged to no less a personage than the Incarnation Lama. Every physician in the wilds has to be a jack-of-all-trades, and at the evening sick calls Gil Roberts and Dave Dingman had already several times turned dentist, pulling teeth for Sherpas and Tamangs. But here was a would-be patient of a very special order, and there was some concern that if the treatment did not meet with his approval the expedition might suddenly lose its status as honored guest. An examination of the young man's mouth showed that indeed he had cause for ache: at least four of his teeth were ripe for pulling. Gil and Dave, however, were reluctant to extract. On their first visit they, instead, administered antibiotics and pain killer, only to be told the next day that the High Lama's ache was worse. This time, with a deep breath, they pulled one tooth; not all four that needed pulling, but just one, the farthest gone. They administered more drugs. They hoped for the best, while fearing the worst. But it was the best that eventuated, for, on their next visit the High Lama announced that his pain was gone.

Meanwhile the expedition, too, was having its health problems, though of another sort. All the way up the trail there had been a fair quota of aching bones and muscles, plus diarrhea and other digestive disorders, and to these the increasing altitude and cold now added their own complement. From Thangboche Deputy Leader Will Siri reported: "The vast array of joint disorders, gastro-intestinal disturbances and respiratory infections the team collectively has sponsored are unknown to medical science, and hence untreatable. The wheezing, coughing, blowing, sniffling and squatting are astonishing and chronic." Then, as a more cheerful addendum: "But, despite the runny noses, sore throats and aching bowels, everyone is in the best of spirits."

Granted, mountaineers are a peculiar breed, but Will's statement, unfortunately, was not true of quite everyone. Most of the ailments were of the come-and-go variety. For some of the men, however, they were persistent and serious, and Dick Emerson for one, Dan Doody for another, were to be plagued for the duration by an inability to acclimatize. Norman, too, though he remained basically in good physical shape, began here in Thangboche to suffer an affliction he had known on a previous expedition. In the thin cold air, he developed laryngitis, and through the long weeks to come he was rarely able to speak in more than a hoarse whisper.

Day by day, however, the work of sorting and reorganizing continued. The heavy snowfalls eased off, and up from Namche on a train of yaks came a final batch of supplies that for lack of porterage had temporarily been left behind. Maynard Miller and Barry Prather were busy organizing their scientific gear for work on the glaciers ahead. Will Siri got his physiological lab into working order and pursued his reluctant quarry for blood and urine specimens. A work gang of Sherpas descended to the lower valleys to collect firewood that would be used at Base Camp, logs for the bridging of crevasses in the Icefall, and hundreds of willow wands for the marking of routes. Team members in parties of twos and threes went off on practice climbs on the nearer mountainsides, returning in varying states of euphoria and the opposite.

Said Barry Corbet: "Dick Pownall and I took off up the side of a small peak and discovered bush which puts British Columbia to shame. Rhododendrons! After three hours of hanging upside down in the stuff, we reached timberline and promptly petered out in the deep snow above. Our first defeat. We crawled back to camp highly chastened."

Said Jim Whittaker: "Climbed uphill to ridge, did three sets of twenty-each push-ups, and then back." As a concession, however, he added, "Noticed altitude quite a bit."

Meanwhile attention was increasingly focusing on the details of the "real" climbing ahead. By now everyone was agreed that the attempt on Everest would be a two-pronged affair—by the known South Col route and the unknown West Ridge—and a tremendous amount of work, largely by Willi Unsoeld, Tom Hornbein and Dick Emerson, went into the planning of food-and-equipment logistics for all the various potential combinations of different-sized parties. At the same time the tentative personnel of the Ridge and Col teams was being established, almost entirely on the basis of individual preference. Unsoeld and Hornbein, who from the beginning had been the prime movers of the Ridge project, would of course be in the group to attempt it, and with them would be Bishop, Breitenbach, Corbet, Dingman and Emerson. In the Col platoon would be Dyhrenfurth, Siri, Whittaker, Jerstad, Pownall and Gil Roberts. The support group for both platoons, based in the Western Cwm and including most of the specialists, would consist of Auten, Doody, Lester, Miller, Prather and Jimmy Roberts.

Or such, at least, was the prospectus. In the event, everything would depend on health, weather, climbing problems, and the hundred other imponderables of ascending a great mountain.

There were what might be called "the three worlds of Thangboche." One, growing ever more dim, was the world of below and beyond: existent only in the coming and going of mail and, now and then, on the wings of airwaves. There was still no radio contact with Kathmandu. Before departure, the expedition had set up a schedule whereby the first communication would be on March 20 —still more than a week away; and all efforts, in emergencies or otherwise, to get through earlier had been, and continued to be, futile. More distant broadcasting programs, however, came on in the evenings. From the South, All-India Radio blared of the menace of the "Chinese Dragon," bent on devouring all Asia. From the North, Radio Peking blared back denouncing Nehru and proclaiming "a strengthening of the Himalayan frontier, to protect the fatherland." There, a few miles to the north of Thangboche, *was* the frontier, with the tides of fear and hatred streaming over it. But with a flick of a dial they were gone. The world they came from was gone. The Himalaya stood high, white and silent, as it had through the ages.

There was the world of Thangboche itself; of its outpost monastery; of gongs and horns and prayer wheels and the robed figures of lamas moving meditatively through the snow. On their fifth evening there, the expedition members were invited to dinner by the Incarnation Lama—now recovered from his toothache—and spent the evening in a medieval scene of sooty beams and flickering oil lamps. It was not, however, on the past that the High Lama dwelt, as he spoke in the Sherpa language with Gombu serving as translator. It was on what had happened to Thangboche's brother monasteries under the Communist Chinese; on the plight of the self-exiled Dalai Lama; on what might happen to Buddhism in Nepal when the Chinese had built their road from Lhasa to Kathmandu.

Only the "third world" of the highlands was unconcerned about modern man and his destiny: the Third World—the Third Pole— of the Himalaya itself. And it was for this nonhuman world, with good human perversity, that AMEE had come on its journey. "Lift up thine eyes to the hills," say the Scriptures. And eyes were lifted; minds and hearts were lifted; if not in quest of salvation, then of something almost as good—at least to the eyes and minds and hearts of mountaineers.

Soon the men would be striving to meet the challenge above them with lung and limb. Now they struggled to meet it with word and phrase. Said Unsoeld: "Never were there such fantastic peaks in such profusion!" Said Whittaker: "These are the most beautiful mountains in the world: bathed in moonlight, with silver-rimmed clouds perched like halos on the peaks." Said Miller: "The views are breath-taking, the peaks staggering in their dimensions. Toward evening yesterday the sun broke through and lighted the summits of Everest and Lhotse as if they were aflame. With a great wind whipping plumes of powder snow from their crests, it was a sight to behold. Then as dusk settled into the valleys below Ama Dablam, its spire of ice and rock also burst into a flame-orange alpine glow, all framed in a window outline of up-rushing mists." Said Doody (taking the easy way): "The view is—*too much!*"

There they stood, the enclave of giants: in sunlight and moonlight, in stillness and storm. The tip of Everest, flanked by Lhotse and Nuptse. Roundabout, Taweche, Ama Dablam, Kangtega, Thamserku, and a host of others, named and unnamed: each a cathedral of stone and snow on earth's rooftop; each and all a mountaineer's dream. The Big Three—E, L and N—had seen dreams come true; they had been climbed to the top. But of the lesser ones, mostly in the 21,000- to 23,000-foot range, few had even been attempted. Sir Edmund Hillary's expedition, that was following AMEE in to Solu Khumbu, had announced its intention of trying both Taweche and Kangtega, and in the upshot was to fail narrowly on the first, succeed on the second. Ama Dablam, a 22,494-foot super-Matterhorn that rose close above the Thangboche valley, seemed in its savage sheerness to be the most hopeless of all, a truly unclimbable peak. But seeming is not fact, for it *had* been climbed. Indeed, one of its four conquerors was right there in Thangboche looking up at it, in the person of Barry (The Barrel) Bishop, who had reached its top in 1961 as a member of an earlier Hillary expedition. It had been a feat to be proud of, and Barry may well be excused if he was. But he may further be excused if he grew a bit tired of the name his companions now affixed to the peak, for in his hearing, at least, it was never Ama Dablam: it was the Barrel's phallic symbol.

On March 15, after a five-day layover, the expedition moved on from Thangboche. It was, however, no longer the one continuous column that had marched each day from Kathmandu to Solu Khumbu, but rather a series of echelons spread over the days and miles. Largely because of the still wintry weather, porterage manpower was hard to come by; so it was worked out that, instead of a carrying force of some 800 moving steadily up toward Base Camp, there would be only some 480, of whom most would make two trips between the successive staging points in a back-and-forth ferrying operation. Team members and "high" Sherpas would be strung out along the two-way procession. An advance guard would lead the way and supervise the establishments of camps. Others would be positioned toward the center of things. Bringing up the rear would be Jimmy Roberts, acting as dispatcher and insuring that nothing strayed or was left behind, with liaison officer Noddy Rana and sirdar Passang Phutar as his aides.

The head of the column, it was estimated, should reach the site of Base Camp in four or five days. In eight to ten days the tail should catch up with it, and the whole expedition would be in position at the foot of Everest.

The first day's march began with a downward stretch to the Imja Khola River. Then, crossing a bridge (the next to last of the dozens on the long trail from Kathmandu), it carried gradually across steep hillsides beneath the eastern battlements of Taweche, gaining height until it passed timberline. Beyond it was a realm of long sloping pastures that in late spring and summer would be the grazing grounds for herds of yaks; but now all was still snow-covered and void of life. Here and there were huddles of stone shelters for herders, now also deserted. And at the end of the day's trek came Pheriche, where it had originally been planned to establish an acclimatization camp. At 14,000 feet, Pheriche is one of the high Sherpa "summer" villages. But now, like the countryside around, it was wholly untenanted—a cluster of some twenty stone houses stark and still in a world of snow.

Above Pheriche came the final stretch of pastureland: flat rock-strewn country, with short bushy vegetation pushing up through the white covering. Then even these last shreds of growth were gone. The rocks reared upward, becoming a wilderness of tumbled boulders, and here was the terminal moraine of the Khumbu Glacier. The route wound through and up it, coming out on the Khumbu's western lateral moraine, and this was followed through the miles and hours. On the right was the stream of the glacier itself: at first scarcely visible under the mass of detritus that covered its surface, then slowly emerging in its hummocks and hollows of ancient ice. Here was the inner heartland of the peaks, the frozen artery draining their snow life to the distant lowlands. On all sides were mountains shouldering one another, breaking free, soaring skyward, their summits the highest on earth, had there not been still higher ones hidden behind them.

For Everest and Lhotse had now, for a while, withdrawn. They were concealed behind the mass of Nuptse, rising vast and ice-sheathed to the east of the Khumbu. To the newcomers to this realm it seemed that at any moment the hidden ones must re-appear; indeed, that another hour, or two, or at most three, would bring the caravan to the foot of Everest itself. But they were hav-ing their first lesson in Himalayan dimensions; entering a range beside which Rockies and Sierras, Alps and Andes are mountains in miniature. The hours flowed by. The miles flowed by. And still the Khumbu climbed on toward its invisible source.

There was something else, too, that was strictly invisible. The expedition was now in the domain of what the Himalayan people know as the "yeti" and the world-at-large as the Abominable Snow-man. It had been in this area, on the lower fringes of the Everest massif, that Eric Shipton and other earlier travelers had come across the strange unidentifiable footprints that mystified and in-trigued the world; and the Snowman Expedition of 1958, of which Norman Dyhrenfurth was deputy leader, had done much of its searching hereabouts. The weight of present opinion is that there is no such thing as a Snowman; that the tracks that have been found are merely those of familiar animals enlarged and distorted by melting snow. Some authorities, however, disagree, among them Norman himself, who believes that the yeti (he eschews the word Snowman) is a species of yet-unknown anthropoid ape. In any case, no one—at least no one whose word could be believed—has ever seen the creature. And AMEE was to be no exception. Some members may be said to have been pro-yeti, others anti-yeti, in their beliefs about it. But all agreed that, confronted by the spec-tacle of our advancing army, any specimen in its right mind would have promptly made itself scarce.

At 16,200 feet on the moraine, camp was pitched at a place

called Lobuje, and here most of the team laid over for one to three days while the ferrying of loads continued behind them. It was not, however, a layover for rest, but for more acclimatization through practice climbing—on peaks higher and wilder than those close by Thangboche. Throughout the approach march the team members had carried packs as part of the conditioning program, increasing their weight gradually, until they matched and sometimes exceeded the standard porterload of 60 to 65 pounds. And this sort of carrying, on the present practice climbs, impressed the Sherpas no little. As Barry Corbet put it, on his return from a two-day workout with Tom Hornbein: "Sahibs, at this elevation and stage of acclimatization, are not officially considered 'manpower.' Tom and I, heading across the glacier with 60-pound packs, were quite out of line as far as the Sherpas were concerned. When we returned, they were highly surprised that two sahibs could actually cope for two days and come back not only in one piece but with clean dishes."

There were other benefits, besides the physical, in these forays of twos and threes. To quote Barry further: "Tom and I felt lifted of a huge load to be *alone* for a change. The cumbersome life of a big expedition leaves its mark, and the opportunity to smell nobody's dirty socks but one's own (and Tom's) was very welcome." B.C., however, was not unmindful of his duties as an Organization Man, for he added, "Yet how fine it was to return next evening to camp chairs and The Group!"

The daily weather pattern was quite consistent: fair mornings, cloudy afternoons. And with the clouds there was occasionally snowfall—though nothing like the minor blizzard of Thangboche. In temperature, the ups and downs were enormous, with a range from warm, even hot, at midday to below zero at night. As the going got more rugged, some of the porters quit and descended to the valleys below, necessitating still more back-and-forth ferrying for those who remained. But most provided prime examples of the famed Sherpa hardihood, toting their loads uncomplainingly through the long days and when darkness came, sleeping in the open with no more protection than was afforded by a worn blanket and a hollow scraped out among tumbled boulders.

With the shelter of tents, sahibs and climbing Sherpas had it rather better. After a day's labor there was a hot meal and a sleeping bag. There was talk and planning, reading, diary and letter writing, sometimes a bridge or chess game, or an impromptu musicale with uke and harmonica; and a few even managed such impressive feats as sponge baths and shaving—although beards of varying shape, color and coiffure were now distinctly on the rise. Health remained an in-and-out proposition. For though the team was now beyond the realm of infections and epidemics, the ever-increasing altitude brought its own toll; and headaches, sore throats and nausea were rampant. Another plague of the heights was the phenomenon called Cheyne-Stokes breathing, in which a sleeper would awake gasping and choking, with the sensation that he was sealed in an airtight tomb. There was a suggestion at one time that the name of the whole enterprise be changed to the American Mount Invalid Expedition, but this never quite reached the point of becoming official.

Beyond Lobuje, the goal of the month-long approach march began at last to swing into view. Ahead, to the left of the glacier rose the graceful white pyramid of Everest's westward flanker, 23,442-foot Pumori. Further on, squarely facing the plodding column, were the broad, slightly lower peaks known as Lingtren and Khumbutse, and, to the right—i.e., the east—of these, the white wall of the almost 20,000-foot saddle called the Lho La. This was a notch in the main Himalayan spine, the high frontier between Nepal and Tibet. From its top, forty-two years before, George Mallory and a companion, climbing from the far side, had looked down at the Khumbu and the terrain surrounding it. Seen head on from below, it seemed to be the source, the end, of the glacier. But this was only appearance; for, before reaching it, the ice sheet took a sharp hidden turn to the right and rose steeply into the Khumbu Icefall, the gateway to Everest from this side of the mountain. To the right of it, now towering almost directly above the approaching expedition, were the rock and ice walls of Nuptse. To the left, between the Icefall and Lho La, were the West Shoulder, and above it the West Ridge, of Everest, soaring massively skyward. But until almost the last minute these appeared as extensions of Nuptse rather than as part of another, yet greater peak.

On March 19, with the porters still shuttling behind them, the advance guard made camp in a mountain vale to the west of the glacier, about 17,000 feet high and some 3 miles from the base of the Icefall. The site was known as Gorak Shep and had also been called Lake Camp by previous expeditions because at its center, hemmed in between moraines, lies a long narrow alpine tarn. Or at least it would be a tarn when spring and summer came: a steely sheet of water ringed by rocky terraces of tiny mountain shrubs and flowers. Now it was only a desolate sweep of ice and snow. Here, as at Pheriche and Lobuje, loads were dumped; porters descended for more loads; climbers, arriving in successive groups, rested, acclimatized, and continued their workouts on nearby slopes.

From sundry diaries:

Whittaker: "Broke trail on glacier; came into camp really breathing hard. Then got word Lute, Willi and I will be on first party in Icefall. Hooray!" *Jerstad:* "Beards are getting long and beginning to look 'jungly.' Wash up, but it may be the last time for a while. Jake B. and I are getting used to each other's coughing and groaning at night. We laugh at our misery as we hunch in our bags with coughing fits." *Pownall:* "Food situation difficult now, as three or four boxes must be opened to put together a meal. Will be better at Base Camp, where we'll open everything and shelve it. Take bottle with hot drink into sleeping bag, to keep it from freezing, and nip on it during night." *Doody:* "Nineteen high Sherps moved on up carrying gear. They really look like a team now, as most are wearing the same outfits: black boots, burnt-orange gaiters, green pants, orange anoraks, scarlet hats and goggles." *Corbet:* "Making big strides in acclimatization. Feel strong and eager to move on the mountain. Also increasingly at home with other members of the team and more confident of my reaction to altitude." *Bishop:* "Hiked a bit above Gorak Shep and had dead-on view of the proposed new route on the West Ridge. Said view, I must say, was a little discouraging, but we rationalized by mumbling something about foreshortening."

On the morning of March 21, in warm cloudless weather, the first echelon moved on up the glacier from Gorak Shep. It consisted of Dyhrenfurth, Siri, Unsoeld, Whittaker and Jerstad, plus twenty-three team Sherpas headed by Gombu and Ang Dawa; and its mission was to select and establish the site for Base Camp. Norman wanted to have Base as close as possible to the foot of the Icefall, and they therefore followed the Khumbu along its great bend, moving ever closer to the frozen torrent of Everest's spillway. Up to Gorak Shep, the going had been entirely over rock and scree on the Khumbu's lateral moraine. But now they were on the surface of the glacier itself, moving up slopes of corrugated ice. Around them were a host of "névés penitentes": slender, strangely carved pillars of ice and snow, sometimes forced up from glaciers by pressures below, which were given their name by early European climbers of the Alps who saw in them a likeness to praying figures. To the members of the AMEE they seemed more like a congress of ghosts, especially when seen from Base Camp, thronging the vast ramp of the glacier in the half-light of dawn or dusk. And for this final stretch of the approach to Everest they were soon using the name Phantom Alley, which had been given to it by the Swiss in 1952.

As the advance guard moved closer to the Icefall, it passed the sites of British, Swiss and Indian Base Camps, recognizable by still-remaining debris; and "ten or fifteen minutes beyond the Indian camp," said Norman, "we found a perfect spot for our own. It was right in the middle of the glacier, where it got the full benefit of the sun. There was plenty of dry moraine rock, plenty of level places for tents. This was it, we decided. And at once the loads were dropped, and the Sherpas went to work setting up housekeeping."

After thirty days on the trail—two years and nine months of planning and preparation—AMEE was at the foot of its mountain.

IN MY PERSONAL DISAPPOINTMENT and frustration there was at least one consoling factor: my wife, Marian, had joined me in Kathmandu. A few days after the expedition took off, we flew out to New Delhi for what we intended as a brief visit; but no sooner had we arrived than my bad leg acted up again—this time with thrombophlebitis—and it was a month before I was able to return to Hotel Royal headquarters. In my illness, the consolation was that at least it had not happened on the trail. AMEE on its approach march was sufficiently occupied without having an overage stretcher case on its hands.

The expedition's rear, however, was fortunately not left unguarded. For in Kathmandu, on duty for the duration, was Norman's wife, Sally; and in the aforesaid Royal, Room 29, she ran a combined command post, freight depot, post office, shopping service and—when the pressure was really on—emergency psychiatric clinic.* "I'd been under the delusion," she wrote, "that when the team left I'd have time to spare, catching my breath, writing letters,

* For most of the time there was also another Sally on hand, in the person of Sally Richardson, a U.S. AID Mission wife, who made great contributions of her

97

cultivating health and beauty, and trying to avoid boredom between the arrival of the mail runners. Frankly, Ha!"

For among the other more exotic facts of Kathmandu was the stark and staring one that nothing—repeat, nothing—was ever simple. To begin with, every day on which something simply *had* to be done was a holiday, Hindu or Buddhist, Nepalese or American. The requests that came back from the expedition, for such routine items as cigarettes, windbreakers, medicines, toilet paper, might as well have been for apes and peacocks in terms of the difficulty of finding them. The mail that came in from the team by runner was, by prior arrangement, to go out in pouches of the U.S. Information Service; but changing directives from Washington sometimes left it stranded in Kathmandu for days and weeks at a time. Thanks to the unpredictable weather of the Himalayan foothills, there was an extremely vague relationship between plane schedules and actual flights. And phoning or paying a call to a government official at Singha Durbar was an operation compared to which the climbing of Everest was child's play.

Still, wondrously, things did happen, in their own good time. The Junbesi-to-Australia-to-Kathmandu radio message about the burned Sherpani completed its circuit; the U.S. AID helicopter was secured; the woman was brought in to the United Mission Hospital and eventual recovery.* A few days later came the call for smallpox vaccine, and this too was answered. Unfindable merchandise was finally found. Immovable mail was moved. Undecipherable cablegrams were deciphered.

Kathmandu was many things, but never dull. There was the pageant of the city itself. There was a contretemps a day, a crisis every two days. And between the contretemps and crises, rumors. Ah, what a place was Kathmandu for rumors! The bridge that had

---

time, talents and energies. To her—as to Ambassador Stebbins and staff, Boris Lissanevitch, Lt. Col. William Gresham, U.S. Army, and Father Marshall D. Moran, S.J. (the latter two soon to be introduced)—AMEE owes, and herewith presents, its heartfelt thanks.

* When it was learned around Kathmandu that the expedition had done this, at a cost to itself of some two thousand dollars, there was considerable comment—by no means all of it favorable. In this part of the world life is cheap. What was a burned peasant woman? "It is only the rich Americans showing off," said some. But we were glad we did it.

collapsed on the trail near Sete had carried a dozen men to their deaths. Seven Tamang porters on their way back from Solu Khumbu had perished of exposure in a storm. Encountering small-pox, the expedition had abandoned its climbing plans. And so on, in endless variety. It was well to remind oneself that we were in the land of the people who had invented the Abominable Snowman.*

Then, too, there were the comers and goers. Sir Edmund Hillary and his educational-medical-mountaineering expedition arrived and set out in the wake of AMEE. From the other direction came the Sherpa runners, bearing mail, tidings and redolent odors from up yonder, and then, a day or two later, doubling back to the hinter-land. Down from the hills, too, came "camp follower" Spark Schnitzer, who had hiked in with the team almost to Base Camp and returned lean, sunburned, bright-eyed, and full of tales of the trail. Off whence Spark had come went Barry Bishop's wife, Lila, in company with three old-friend couples, hoping, if things went well, to go *all* the way to Base Camp and then on to Darjeeling. And also off to the mountain, though in far different fashion, went Heinrich Berann, an Austrian artist employed by the National Geographic Society to do a painting of Everest. Chartering the Swiss plane of the International Red Cross, Herr Berann flew to Everest and back between dawn and midmorning; but though he had seen enough of the mountain to knock both eyes out, he had caught no glimpse of AMEE, now tiny and lost in its immensities.

There were other expeditions too, European and Asian, bound for other mountains in the great uplift of Nepal. And the non-mountaineers—government envoys, businessmen, tourists—who appeared from the outer world (it might as well have been outer space), contemplated the wonders and rigors of Kathmandu (with varying emotions) and left when a plane was good and ready to take them. Of these latter, some knew a great deal about AMEE and its venture. Some knew nothing and cared less. One—sex, male; nationality, American; classification, tourist—was somewhere in between, announcing at the Yak and Yeti Bar that he thought it "a great thing that our boys are off climbing the Matterhorn."

The most memorable of commentators, however, was neither

---

* For this statement of a skeptic, apologies are herewith tendered to Norman Dyhrenfurth and his fellow believers.

male, American nor tourist, but a rather grand lady whose husband
was on the staff of the British Embassy in Kathmandu. At a party
at the Hotel Royal she found herself in a group discussing Everest
and the expedition, and at first she seemed puzzled, groping to
catch the drift of the talk. Finally, however, the light dawned—
and with it the assurance that there will positively always be an
England. "Ah yes, of course," she said, "the expedition. You mean
those American chaps who went off with Jimmy Roberts."

Out on the trail, as we have seen, AMEE had been having frustrating experiences with the radio. This was due simply to unfortunate happenstance. There were two expert American ham
operators in Kathmandu: Lt. Col. William Gresham, military attaché at our embassy, and Father Marshall D. Moran, a Jesuit
priest, once of Chicago, now headmaster of Nepal's St. Xavier
School and the longest-term resident Westerner in the country.
Both were immensely interested in the expedition—and were to be
of immense help to it—but during the period of the approach
march they had no way of knowing if and when it would be on
the air. Like good hams anywhere, they were often at their rigs,
fanning the breeze with fellow hams from Albuquerque to Zanzi-
bar—and also trying to reach Al Auten at such times as they
thought he might possibly be operating. But the first prearranged
date set by Al and Colonel Gresham was not until March 20, and
all earlier trial-and-error efforts drew a blank.

Then at last it was the twentieth. It was 5 P.M., the designated
hour. And now, instead of frustration, there was Al, loud and clear
from the Khumbu Glacier. It was a great event, and there were
many "rogers," much give and take of both important messages and
of just plain satisfying gab. During the next few days the sessions
were continued, some in the late afternoon, some early in the morning. And all was still "roger"; all was fine and exciting and satisfying at both ends.

Until seven in the morning of March 25, for this time, when Al
came on the air, his voice was different. "The following message,"
he said, "concerns a fatal accident. . . ."

And then everything was different.

8. GATEWAY

TIME: *The first week of spring.*
PLACE: *Base Camp, 17,800 feet.*

THE MORAINE OF SCATTERED ROCK on which the camp was set was formed by the meeting of the main Khumbu Glacier and a smaller tributary glacier that drained the slopes of Lingtren and Pumori. Below, Phantom Alley, thronged with its icy ghosts, sloped off toward a nether world that had become a phantom too. Above, Everest and Nuptse leapt skyward, and in the cleft dividing them was the Icefall, leading toward the still-hidden world of the heights. Base Camp was in limbo between below and above: on the fringes of both worlds, belonging to neither.

Call it a world of its own, an active, swarming world, a place of endings and beginnings. Through the days following the arrival of the advance guard, the rest of the train followed in platoons and battalions—the millepede pulling its tail up behind it—and what had been an emptiness of rock and ice became a caravansery of tents and high-piled gear and moving, eating, sleeping, working men. During the period when hundreds of porters were still ferry-

101

ing back and forth, there was, to put it mildly, confusion. But this was the end of the line for the "army," and as they dumped their final loads they were paid off, and were soon vanishing down Phantom Alley toward Solu Khumbu. With the departure of the last of them, the population of earth's highest community numbered seventy-two. This comprised the nineteen expedition members, Capt. "Noddy" Rana, our thirty-two original Sherpas, the five additional "high" Sherpas who had been taken on in Solu Khumbu—plus three young kitchen helpers, and twelve "semihigh" porters hired from among the low-level rank and file for extra manpower in the Icefall.

Dan Doody set down a vivid description of Base, once it was a going concern, and I shall not try to go him one better by paraphrasing it. "In the center of things," he reported, "we have two 12' by 12' tents facing each other with awnings united, together forming a combined dining-radio-medical-recreation area. Just outside are the radio antenna and a homemade flagpole, and nearby the mountains of boxes containing food and equipment. At the other end of this supply dump is our kitchen, built by the Sherpas, with walls about 5 feet high constructed of food boxes opening inward to provide well-stocked shelves." ("It looks like a supermarket," was Lute Jerstad's comment.) "The roof is made of four 10' by 12' tarps supported by poles carried up from the valley. A smaller kitchen in which Sherpa food is cooked, three 10' by 10' tents, and a liberal scattering of two- and four-man sleeping tents are roundabout—plus one odd-sized tent off by itself which provides great comfort when nature calls and the wind is blowing. It doesn't have running water, but as it straddles a crevasse about a foot wide, this doesn't seem necessary.

"One other decoration is Maynard Miller's meteorological station, which sits on the high point of the moraine with anemometer cups spinning, wind direction indicator pointing, and a little shelter box on poles holding thermometers and a humidity measuring device. The only thorn in the bush is the constant noise of an engine busily generating electricity to run the radio, recharge batteries, and power various scientific devices.

"At night the temperature drops to zero, give or take 10 degrees. We burrow deep in our down sleeping bags and are aroused in the morning by two delightful words: 'Sah'b, tea.' One has merely to open the tent entrance and there is a brown hand holding a steaming cup. Following the tea, one stays in the sack until about eight, at which time the sun hits the tent, the thermometer jumps 10 degrees, and a whistle blows for breakfast. Then a bit of a struggle, pulling on a wool shirt, down parka, long johns, ski pants, three pairs of socks, and Eiger boots with their felt inner layer and leather outer. And on to the dining tent for cereal, eggs, maybe freeze-dried sausage, canned bread with butter and jelly, and coffee, tea, cocoa or Ovaltine. At about eleven the whistle blows again for bread or cookies with something to drink, and toward one comes lunch, which is a pretty full meal. At four it's tea again, with cookies. (Should you not respond to this whistle, the kitchen boys seek you out at your tent and serve you.) And finally, about five-thirty, comes dinner, possibly a bit bigger than lunch, with soup, meat, potatoes, vegetable, maybe pickles, followed by canned fruit and a variety of drinks. Afterwards, some play cards, some talk, some read or write letters."

Thus, life at the Khumbu-Plaza.

Or one aspect of life. For there were others. And dominating all the rest, poised above Base Camp like a vast white dragon, was Everest's gateway—the Icefall.

AMEE well knew that here, at the outer fringe of the mountain, was one of the most formidable of its defenses: an icy labyrinth a mile and a half in length, rising 2200 feet from base to crest, that presented what was probably the most hazardous stretch of the whole ascent. Higher up, there would of course be problems too: a whole congeries of problems involving routes, weather, altitude, climbing difficulties, and merely keeping alive and moving on the frozen heights. But these could be met, at least in part, by human skill and endurance, preparation and foresight. Here in the Icefall was a concentration of what mountaineers call "objective dangers" —the sort of perils over which mere humans, however cautious, however knowledgeable, can exert little control; which stem entirely from unpredictable caprices of nature. An icefall is exactly what its name implies. It is a thing of ice. It is falling. And though the fall is not ordinarily visible to the eye, as would be the case with water, it is present none the less—and far more menacingly:

an eternal downward flow of colossal mass and power sucked on and on by implacable gravity. Sir John Hunt compared this threshold of Everest to a "gigantic cascade." His expedition gave to its various sections such names as "Hellfire Alley," "Hillary's Horror" and "the Atom Bomb Area," and Hillary, in his own account, called the whole of it "tottering chaos." Filled with twisted towers and gaping canyons, it was an awesome thing, like the debris of a thousand white castles, a hundred white cities, piled one upon another in monstrous wreckage. It was a hateful thing—a destroyed, destroying thing—full of secrets and evil.

Eight expeditions prior to ours had worked their way up through its tortured maze. Towers had toppled around them; crevasses had wrenched open; the whole mass had groaned, trembled, shifted, in its billion-tonned innards. But astonishingly, of all the men who had gone up and down it, in dozens of relays on each expedition, not one had lost his life or even sustained serious injury. This is all the more remarkable in that, even after many passages, there is no such thing as a "set" route through the Icefall; for under the gigantic pressures there is constant change in its structure, and each succeeding party of climbers has had to find a path of its own. Deceptively, there are two routes that *look* easy: a pair of fairly smooth straightaway troughs that border the cascade on each side, close under the walls of Everest and Nuptse. But these are so menaced by avalanches from above that an attempt on them would be little short of suicidal. AMEE, like its predecessors, would have to thread its way through the heart of the labyrinth.

During this stage of the ascent the team would function as a single unit. Though the base of Everest's West Ridge was, in a manner of speaking, close beside the Icefall, it was not in its lower reaches truly a ridge, but rather a huge rampart buttressing the mountain's West Shoulder; and it had long since been decided, after a study of photographs, that, in view of its steepness and the obvious avalanche danger, it would be folly to attempt it from so low down. Rather, it was the plan to try to reach it at a height of about 23,800 feet, roughly halfway between base and summit, where its rise was broken by the broad snow and ice terrace of the Shoulder, and beyond which the ridge continued in a sharp well-defined line. Since the logical way to approach this point appeared to be from the middle of the Western Cwm, the West Ridge and South Col teams would not branch off onto their separate routes until Advance Base was established in the Cwm. And this in turn meant that the whole expedition would move up through the Icefall.

It did *not* mean, however, that the movement, over such terrain, would be an en masse all-at-once affair. First there would have to be advance parties probing the way. Then other parties would follow, marking and improving the route. And finally, when the track was as safe as it could be made, the loads would move up in a long series of relays. Not only in the Icefall but throughout the siege of the mountain, the expedition would be in the process of expansion and contraction, of advance and consolidation: an organism with a head, a middle and a tail, constantly in motion, constantly realigning and regrouping, as it worked its way in multiple echelons toward the heights.

The first group selected by Norman to enter the Icefall consisted of Willi Unsoeld, Jim Whittaker and Lute Jerstad, accompanied by the Sherpas Nawang Gombu, Nima Tenzing and Passang Temba. And here, perhaps, is the place to say a further word about the functions of high Sherpas. Uninformed accounts often refer to them as guides. But they are not guides. They do not select the routes to be followed; they do not lead the way; they are not remotely as versed in the techniques of mountain craft as the sahibs they accompany. On the other hand, many of them are far more than what one understands by the word "porter." They help to cut steps, to fix ropes, to perform all the many maneuvers required on difficult terrain, and on such an assignment as this first foray into the Icefall the carrying of loads is a strictly minor function. As an individual, a Sherpa's status on any given climbing party can vary greatly, depending on age, experience, ability and spirit. Thus Gombu, by virtue of his outstanding qualities, was in effect as much an expedition member as any Westerner on the team. Ang Dawa was not so much Norman's orderly as his assistant and adjutant. In contrast, Passang Phutar, in theory—and pay—the headman of the Sherpas, did not, because of age and acclimatization trouble, ever get as far as Advance Base and, as a consequence, became a minor factor in the expedition.* Once the climbing began, official rank and status became meaningless, and the only criterion was how good each Sherpa was on a mountain.

In spite of its Khumbu-Plaza aspects, the expedition did no dawdling at Base Camp. Indeed, it was on March 22, when Base was barely being set up, that the first reconnoiterers entered the Icefall, working their way slowly, cautiously up through its tumbled wilderness. Simultaneously, Norman, Will Siri and Ang Dawa went up to a vantage point on the lower slopes of the Lho La which commanded a good view of the lower Icefall, and from there, with binoculars and walkie-talkie radio helped the climbers in their search for a route. "In an icefall," said Norman, "you often can't see the forest for the trees. But Will and I, in our position, could survey its overall structure, and we gave our suggestions whenever the others wanted an opinion. They would simply yodel, we would turn on the radio, and then they would say, 'How does it look from there? Is it better to the left or right?' And it worked very well, until finally they moved out of sight in a jumble of seracs and crevasses."

The pioneering went better than anyone had dared hope. "The route proved to be quite straightforward," reported Willi U., "with very little snow and most of the big crevasses bridged by frozen boulders of ice. Lack of acclimatization slowed us up, but in five and a half hours we reached the spot used as a camp by the Indian expeditions, at about 19,300 feet. This, we decided, would be our Icefall dump, so we cached our ice screws, extra rope and unused marking wands and headed back at 3:15 P.M. On the way down we installed two fixed ropes and prospected for better alternatives for certain sections of the route. The worst spot, we felt, was the final ice wall leading up to the plateau on which the dump was located. This was a near-vertical 30-foot pitch on which we placed our upper fixed rope, and it had some nasty blocks balanced above the track which we thought might be removed by chopping. It took us only two hours to slog back to Base."

Ironically, in this world of ice, one of the principal problems had

---

* Passang had not been Norman's and Jimmy Roberts' choice as sirdar, but the nominee of the Himalayan Association, the Sherpa version of a trade union; and it had been deemed best by the expedition to play along with local "politics."

been the heat, which reached 80 to 90 degrees in protected places under the midday sun; and the inevitable high-altitude problem of dehydration was already in full swing. "When we got to camp, we drank about three quarts of fruit juices apiece," said Jim Whittaker, "and still didn't go for nature's call all night." Still and all, it had been a fine day's work. Almost two-thirds of the ill-famed Icefall had been climbed and routed. Though hot at noon and cold at night, the weather was fine and showed no signs of deteriorating. "We were all full of beans for pushing ahead," said Barry Bishop. "We had visions of knocking off our mountain in a big hurry, and everything was going just right."

Man proposes—

On the next morning, March 23, three huge avalanches poured down from the heights around Base Camp: one from Nuptse, one from Everest's West Shoulder, one from the col between Pumori and Lingtren. But the camp—and the Icefall—were well out of their range, and presently a second advance team was moving up in the tracks of the first, to do a "manicure" job of further improving the route to the dump. It consisted of climbers Jake Breitenbach, Dick Pownall and Dr. Gil Roberts, with the Sherpas Ang Pema and Ila Tsering; and working as they went, they followed the wand markers upward through the jungle of towers and chasms.

At about 2 P.M. they found themselves, close below the dump, at the 30-foot ice wall to which the first party had affixed a rope. And they too, as they moved, were secured by their own ropes, with Pownall, Ang Pema and Breitenbach tied together on one and Roberts and Ila Tsering on another. Using the fixed line, Pownall began the ascent of the wall, with Ang Pema following and Breitenbach, the third man in the threesome, waiting his turn in a narrow gully beneath it. Roberts and Ila Tsering were off to the side, some forty feet distant. Then—

"I climbed an ice rib," Dick Pownall reported, "which parallels the ice cliff and is separated from it by about eight feet. I called down to Jake to ask Gil—who was in a good position to see—if there was a better way around this spot; it looked spooky. There was no other way, so we proceeded, and I asked Jake to untie the end of the fixed line so I could use some slack and ice screws to secure it better to the cliff. Just then there was a noise, and every-thing under, around and above us started moving. Since we had been climbing over similar terrain all day without the slightest movement, my first impression was shocked disbelief. My next was the knowledge that I was falling and the thought, "so this is death."

And death it was—though not for Dick Pownall.

Off to the side, Gil Roberts, too, heard the "noise": first a deep ominous rumbling, then a shattering roar, as a section of the ice wall "about the size of two railroad cars one on top of the other" came tumbling down. In the next instant he was caught by the impact and flipped over backward, sliding some thirty or forty feet. But he was not hurt, nor was his rope mate Ila Tsering, and after a loud shout for help in the direction of Base Camp they pushed up to where the other three had vanished in the chaos of ice.

The first they found was Dick, all but buried under the debris. By a stroke of vast luck his head had not been hit, but his chest was pinned by an ice block that at Gil's estimate weighed almost half a ton, and it took ten minutes of hacking with ice axes to free him. Thus far there was no sign of Jake Breitenbach or Ang Pema. But now Gil heard a low moaning from beneath the ice, and digging in the nearby rubble, he and Ila Tsering found the missing Sherpa. He was buried deeper than Dick, legs up, head downward, with his rucksack jammed crazily against the back of his neck; but after another fifteen minutes of chopping he too was freed.

That, however, was the end of the rescuing. For from Ang Pema the rope that joined him to Jake Breitenbach led straight down toward what had once been the narrow gully beneath the ice cliff and was now the very base of the huge mass of toppled wreckage. There was no answer to repeated calls, no movement when the rope was pulled and maneuvered. Nor could any have been ex-pected. Jake was some twenty to thirty feet down under tons of white rubble, and the one consolation to the others—if consolation it can be called—was the obvious fact that death for him had been instantaneous.

Dick Pownall was not seriously injured, but badly bruised and shaken. Ang Pema was worse off, with blood streaming from head wounds and a dislocated shoulder. And all were stunned by the calamity. Still they were able to move slowly down the Icefall, shouting as they went for assistance from Base Camp; and as soon as their voices were heard most of those below hurried up to meet them. Even before the meeting the others were almost sure there had been an accident, for only four instead of five figures could be seen against the ice above. And they could make a good guess, too, as to who was missing, for the descending party made no use of its walkie-talkie, and it was known that Jake Breitenbach had been carrying it. When they encountered the advance group, their worst fears were confirmed. They heard the grim story; then split up to do what they could. Some gave Dick Pownall a helping hand. Jim Whittaker carried the now barely conscious Ang Pema down part of the way; then turned him over to a stretcher team and, with Willi Unsoeld and Lute Jerstad, went on up to the scene of the accident. For an hour, in the fading daylight, they hacked and dug at the debris of what had once been the ice wall, but could accomplish little more than those who had been there when it fell. Jake Breitenbach was gone and lost in the white wilderness, and it would have taken a bulldozer to uncover his grave.

During the next two days there was no movement of men in the Khumbu Icefall. With the expedition no more than on its doorstep, Everest had struck—a life was gone—and at its foot, in the glacier Base Camp, AMEE lay inert, deep in shock, struggling to find its own way back to life and purpose. Fortunately, Ang Pema's injuries were not as serious as they had at first seemed. His shoulder was set, his wounds were stitched and bandaged, and after several days of rest he was all right. Dick Pownall, too, was all right, physically; but his depression was deep, as over and over he relived those terrible few instants on the ice wall, asking himself, agonizingly, unanswerably, "Why was it Jake, not I?" As for Gil Roberts, he had two memories which haunted his days and nights. It had been he who, in the digging out of Ang Pema, had had to cut the rope that joined the Sherpa to Jake; and though the cutting itself had not affected the possibility—or impossibility—of rescue, he could not erase the image of that strand of nylon twisting downward out of sight. Then, a little later, as he and the others stumbled down the Icefall, he had been brought up short by a sound from above

—the sound of what seemed a choked human cry. A moment later he saw what had made it. On a block of ice was the black shape of a gorak, a large crowlike bird that inhabits the fringe world of Everest, and what he had heard was its funereal croaking. But the echo remained, an echo dark and chilling, and it was to be a long time before it faded into stillness.

On the day after the tragedy, March 24, an inquiry was held, examining the circumstances that bore upon it. Eyewitness accounts both of the event itself and of the subsequent rescue efforts were tape-recorded, and an official report was prepared by Norman and transmitted over the radio to Colonel Gresham in Kathmandu—along with a request that Jake's wife and parents be notified before the news was made public. "It was the unanimous opinion of the participants in the inquiry," said the report, "that the accident which took the life of John E. Breitenbach must be considered an Act of God. There was no evidence of poor judgment, negligence or improper procedures. Every effort had been made to minimize the objective hazards along the route, but it is recognized that such dangers cannot be eliminated entirely in mountaineering."*

An Act of God. No one's fault. That was all very well, but Jake was still gone. So suddenly. So—almost casually. "The ice had been still," said Willi Unsoeld. "It gave a wiggle, then was still again." And a life was over. *Why?* Why had it been Jake who was at that exact place at that exact moment? On eight previous expeditions, hundreds of climbers on thousands of individual man-trips had been back and forth through the Icefall without a fatality or even a serious accident. The year before, on the far side of the peak, a group of rash mountaineering novices, Woodrow Wilson Sayre and his companions, had brushed elbows with death a dozen times and come down from Everest alive. Whereas here was Jake, an expert climber in the prime of his career, a member of a skilled, experienced party—

* John Breitenbach's death was the thirteenth that is known to have taken place in the climbing of Everest. Ten men had been lost on the north side of the mountain: the seven Sherpas who were caught in an avalanche in 1922, Mallory and Irvine in 1924, and a lone British climber, Maurice Wilson, in 1934. On the south side, two Sherpas had been killed—one on the Swiss autumn expedition of 1952, one on the Indian expedition of 1962—both by ice avalanches on, or near, the Lhotse Face.

And so on.

The worst part of what had happened was that, in human terms, it had been meaningless. Said Barry Corbet, who had been Jake's business partner in Jackson, Wyoming, and since boyhood his closest friend: "How the hell does eleven years of living in each other's pockets end so insanely?" And then, lashing out in grief and anger: "Stupid goddamned gentleman's sport that kills people in their prime and happiness. . . ."

Barry got drunk that first night. So did Dick Pownall and Gil Roberts. The other members of AMEE lay silently in their tents, trying to sleep, and in the morning came silently out into another day. Again it was a fine day. The peaks gleamed, the Icefall gleamed, in soaring beauty. But now, more than ever, it was a hateful beauty: insensate, cruel, meaningless. All was the same as it had been the day before—as it would be the next day, the next year, the next century—world without end. In terms of this world, nothing had happened. Nothing at all.

To a degree, this seemed to be the attitude of many of the Sherpas as well, and for one of the few times on the expedition there was some trouble with them. "They seemed unable to understand," said Norman, "why we were so upset and disorganized. They couldn't see why we take life so seriously, and there was grumbling among them, particularly the older ones, who said in effect, 'Why are the sahibs making such a fuss?' " Most were ready to go ahead with a normal day's work. One group even picked this particular time to complain about shortages in their own food and clothing, some of which were still on the way up to Base from below; and Norman, with Gombu acting as interpreter, eventually had to give them a dressing down. At the same time he tried to explain to them the present feelings of the team members—"to make them understand," he said, "that we who are of a different background and religion do not for the most part believe in reincarnation, and therefore life and death for us are more important.

"Trying to get this across to a group of Sherpas," he commented, "was not too easy, but it seemed as if Gombu's interpretation of my words did make a certain impression." And to the general indifference there was at least one notable and touching exception. "Jake's personal Sherpa, Nima Tenzing," Dan Doody recorded, "had known Jake for only about five weeks, but on the day after the accident we found Nima in Jake's sleeping bag crying his eyes out. He felt guilty that he had not been along up in the Icefall and was heartbroken at what had happened." Then Dan added: "We have hired the Sherpas for their strong physical capabilities, but into the bargain they have thrown their emotions, their feelings, their hearts." And in general, all were agreed, this was much more the truth of the case than the occasional instances when, by Western standards, they seemed callous and indifferent.

On March 25, two days after the tragedy, the team began to get hold of itself. No climbing was done; the Icefall remained as still as the tomb it now was. But at least the normal activities of camp life were resumed, with loads coming up, gear being sorted and issued, and preparations getting underway for the next upward push. Even more important—for without it all the rest would have been nothing—was the expedition's inner emergence from its state of shock: a putting behind it of a thing that had been done and could not be undone; a reaffirmation of its identity, its function and purpose. "We have started getting our senses together again," Norman wrote of this period, "and once more we are a team instead of a lot of headless miserable individuals." Looking back at what had happened, Willi Unsoeld wrote to his wife, Jolene, in Kathmandu: "Jake was a rare one. Lute and I cried like babies . . . because we loved him . . . but as deaths go, this was a clean-cut kindly one. If Jake could have chosen his final resting place, no improvement could be imagined." Looking both back and forward —his best friend gone, his love of mountains shaken but not broken —Barry Corbet took stock and said quietly: "The one thing that remains to determine if I ever climb again is my ability to push a route over Jake's body in the Icefall."

Barry found the ability, and so did the others. Life—as it must— went on. And the climbing of Everest, too.

Indeed, on the twenty-sixth, Barry, at his own request, was in the first party to re-enter the Icefall. Along with him went Barry Bishop, Dave Dingman, Al Auten and twelve Sherpas, and the detail put in a long day's work clearing out the track, placing additional markers, stringing more fixed ropes, and bridging crevasses with logs and aluminum ladders. Also, they carried up with them several loads of camping gear for deposit at the dump which had been established by the pioneering party four days earlier. They did not, however, spend the night there. Most previous expeditions had found it necessary, or at least expedient, to have an Icefall camp; but Norman had been against this from the beginning, for reasons of safety, and now, after Jake's death, felt more strongly about it than ever. The party therefore descended to Base, and it was from there that almost all subsequent work in the Icefall was launched.*

The next day, with continuing good weather, was a big one. In the lower Icefall, Corbet, Bishop and Gil Roberts did further work on the installation of bridges. Above them, Tom Hornbein and Dick Emerson kept on with the clearing of tracks and the wanding of routes. And out ahead, the lead team of Unsoeld-Whittaker-Jerstad-Gombu was engaged in more pioneering. This time Base to dump took them only two hours, as against five and a half on their first ascent; and above it, though the going was slower, they continued to make good progress, moving steadily toward the 20,000-foot level, where the Icefall at last levels off into the Western Cwm. By noon they were almost there. But it was still an *almost*, for here, at the very top of the steep labyrinth, came the crux of the venture. Confronting them was a vertical cliff of ice about seventy feet tall—more than twice the height of the wall that had collapsed on Jake Breitenbach—and a reconnaissance revealed that there was no route around it. The only way into the Cwm was to tackle it head on.

The tackling took three hours of difficult and precarious climbing: of hacking with ice ax, clawing with crampons, protecting each upward step with a length of rope affixed to ice screws (known in the climbing trade as "coathangers"), so that a lower man holding the end of the rope could belay the top climber above him. Big Jim Whittaker led for the first hour and Willi Unsoeld for the next two—a tremendous performance, no less in endurance than in skill, at some 20,000 feet without oxygen. Lute Jerstad was to have taken over after the second hour, but by that time Willi was so

---

* There were to be occasional times during the expedition when small groups, for one reason or another, spent a night at the dump. But it never took on the dimensions of a true camp.

high and on such delicate stances that it would have been harder
for him to descend than to continue up; so he stayed on in the lead
until he reached the top of the wall. From there he let down a
rope. Lute came up after him, using Jumar ascenders* and foot
slings. And while Jim and Gombu, below, anchored the rope and
prepared the wall for a ladder, the two above moved on into the
Western Cwm.

They did not move far. In a hundred yards or so they came to a
huge crevasse and turned back, roping down the ice wall to rejoin
the others; then, together, the four descended the whole Icefall,
reaching Base Camp at six-thirty after an eleven-hour day. They
were dog-tired but satisfied. The whole expedition was given a lift
in spirit. After a mere four days of actual climbing a route had been
forged through the white monster, and this was at least recompense
of sorts for what it had done to Jake Breitenbach.

Two men up, however, was far from a whole expedition. For
days to come the work in the Icefall went on. Steps in the ice were
cut and recut. Threatening towers and overhangs were chopped
away. The makeshift bridges over crevasses were fitted with pickets
and hand lines to steady laden men crossing over. The section of
track above the dump underwent successive "manicures." And on
the 70-foot summit ice wall there was what amounted to a major
engineering project: the installation of a four-section aluminum
ladder on its lower half and the hanging of a wire ladder from the
top of the wall to meet it. The gateway to Everest would never be
anything but a perilous place, but every effort was made to reduce
its menace at least as much as was possible.

The laying of the Icefall route was done by the ablest and fittest
climbers, and with them they had the pick of the Sherpas. But
meanwhile Base Camp, below them, was scarcely an idle spot. On
March 27, the same day as the breakthrough into the Western
Cwm, the final relay of low-level porters, 140 strong and shepherded
by Jimmy Roberts, trudged up the Khumbu Glacier; and with the
dumping of their loads, all expedition food and gear was at last on
hand. The bearers had put on "a bloody good show," said our one
Briton, Britannically. And that they had, for from Thangboche on
up, manpower had been low, and there had been much double-carry-
ing as well as double-trekking. The record went to a porter who in

* See glossary.

one day had carried a load from Lobuje to Gorak Shep, then a double load from there to Base, and *then*, returning to Gorak Shep, a second more-than-double load, weighing 135 pounds, up the same final stretch. Total: over five official daily man-loads, netting him some four dollars—which was also, by Sherpaland standards, an impressive record.

A few of the loads were for immediate use. Others would remain at Base awaiting the expedition's descent. But the mass of food, tents and equipment that would be needed higher on the mountain was checked and priorities allocated for transportation up the Icefall, with the result that, even while Base was being established, it was simultaneously being disestablished. Meanwhile the team's various specialists were at work in their own fields. Out on the glacier, Maynard Miller and Barry Prather drilled holes in the ice, taking samples of its successive layers and placing stakes for the measuring of movement. Norman Dyhrenfurth and Dan Doody worked at film making. Dick Emerson was busy with his tape recordings, Jim Lester with his interviews and notes, and in one of the 10′ by 10′ tents Will Siri had set up the complex components of his physiological laboratory. According to Will, there was a problem or two that he had not had to cope with back on his home grounds at the University of California. "The tent," he reported, "is a shambles of lab equipment, bottles of urine and tubes of blood; and it's a fearful struggle to get anything done. Most of the time everything in the place, including me, is frozen solid and must be thawed before use—even my ball-point pen, which I have to hold over a candle after writing each sentence. Sleep with four bottles of collodion filters in my bag to keep them warm: good for filters but hard on me. Collecting urine is no problem, but hematology and recording iron turnover (both involving needles) is something else again."

There were other, more general problems, too—and one of them was involved with Will's physiology. For the proper accomplishment of his work he needed not only his blood and urine guinea pigs but also a certain amount of laboratory assistance, and the three expedition doctors seemed to him and Norman the logical ones to be requisitioned. The doctors, however, were less than eager for the assignment. They had, they pointed out (correctly), had a tremendous amount of medical work to do and had done it with great conscientiousness. They were still doing it. But they were not only physicians, they were mountaineers as well; and now they wanted to get about the business of mountaineering—to ascend the Icefall into the Cwm—and not be held at Base in the role of laboratory assistants. It was a typical instance of the classic expedition conflict between climbing and science: the conflict that Norman had tried hard to obviate in his selection of the team. But it was inevitable that it would crop up at some time or other; and here it was.

Nor was the timing fortuitous. Well as things were now going in terms of physical progress, the expedition was still feeling the psychological aftermath of Jake Breitenbach's death. There was still a latent feeling among some of the members that, as Norman put it, "the fun had gone out of the thing. There's a certain attitude of 'let's climb the damn mountain as quickly as possible and get the hell out of here.' " This was in turn involved with the varying points of view about the West Ridge project—with some convinced it should be the team's major project, and others believing it would only hold things up and even reduce the chances of climbing the mountain at all. Happily, there were no major clashes. On the specific matter of lab assistance for Will, it was arranged that the doctors would stagger their climbing schedules so that one would always be available to help him until he himself was ready to move higher on the mountain. As to the optimum speed of ascent, Norman held to a happy medium; and it was agreed that no final decision on the West Ridge could be made this early in the game. AMEE was still—and would continue to be—a basically cohesive and united organism. But to say that there were never disagreements, never stresses and strains, would be as untrue as it was impossible.

Not to be outdone by the sahibs, the Sherpas were presently back in the act as a center of controversy. This time it had to do with sleeping bags. The team members had both outer and inner bags, the Sherpas only outer bags, and even though these were the heavy warm ones—with the sahibs themselves rarely using the others— there was, sure enough, a chorus of protest. For the better part of a day Base Camp became a sort of alfresco courtroom, while assorted "mountain lawyers" (and the Sherpas have some pretty good ones) argued their case and cited precedents from previous expeditions. One of the basic facts, however, was that the expedition simply did not have any extra bags to issue. So in the end— and for the sake of peace—it was decided that a messenger would go down to Solu Khumbu, and that when the next batch of porters came up, carrying Sherpa food, firewood and such, they would also bring along the Sherpas' own sleeping bags (of which there were many, left over from earlier expeditions, stashed about in the villages); and AMEE would pay each man 25 rupees (about $3.25) for supplying his own. As far as Sherpas versus sahibs was concerned, this effected an amicable settlement. There was an unfortunate sidelight, however, in that it had been only the Solu Khumbu Sherpas who had raised the ruckus. The four Darjeeling men—Gombu, Ang Dawa, Passang Temba and Kalden—had felt their complaint was unreasonable, and this further aggravated the already existing friction between the Nepalese majority and the Indian minority.

Apart from general team problems, there were at this time not a few individual ones, physical and otherwise. Dick Emerson continued to have serious acclimatization troubles (weakness, nausea, frequent vomiting), but pushed himself as hard as he could. Dan Doody was having such rough going that most of the time he could not even push, which left Norman with the burden of filming almost all the activity in the Icefall. Gil Roberts and Dick Pownall were still not wholly over the trauma of having been directly involved in the Jake Breitenbach tragedy, with Dick in particular having deep spells of depression. And Norman himself was, at this stage, by no means at the top of his form. For one thing, his laryngitis continued to plague him. ("Trying to be a leader of men without a voice," he croaked into his tape recorder, "is like being a eunuch in a harem.") And for another, he could not wholly shake off the feeling that he, as expedition leader, bore a weight of responsibility for Jake's death. No one else thought so. It is safe to say that even he did not *think* so. But in a situation such as this, thought can be a very pale shadow beside the dominance of emotion. In a letter to Norman, received at Base Camp, Nicholas Clinch, himself the leader of two American Himalayan expeditions (who will appear later in this story), took stock of the matter about as well as it can be done.

"I think I know how you feel about Jake's accident," he wrote.

"The other members of the party have lost a cherished friend. But they are not responsible for the existence of the expedition, and you know you are. . . . You put together the finest group of mountaineers that ever left the United States, and also the best equipped expedition in history. Then there occurs an accident that could not have been prevented by any amount of caution. (You can think of all kinds of ways it could have been avoided now, but they arise from grief and not from reality.) You know this, but you still realize that the only reason the party was there was because you had the vision and put forth the effort to get it there. . . . Unfortunately, Norm, I can't make it easier for you, except to confirm what your mind knows but your heart does not. On high mountains there is no justice, and fortune does not favor the brave. It was not your fault. It happened despite everything you could do."

Such a letter helped. Time helped.

But for a while it wasn't easy.

By now, the reader is probably convinced that he is on an expedition of manic-depressives. If so, he is not too far wrong. All that needs adding is that this would hold for any expedition that ever set out for the mountaintops.

There are, of course, a priori variations in the individuals who compose a team: from introvert to extrovert, from the tight and tense to the calmly phlegmatic. But high in the ranges there are factors that tend to make them all of a piece—or, rather, of pieces. One of these is height itself, the lack of oxygen that affects the mind and spirit no less than body, engendering quirks of personality that were absent or hidden in the lowlands, causing spurts of energy and bouts of lassitude, flights of well-being and plunges of despondency, even when there seems no rational reason for one or another, Beyond this, there often *is* a reason, for the whole process of mountaineering is a continuum of successes and failures, good days and bad days, problems ahead and problems surmounted (or nonsurmounted), on a far more concentrated scale than in the routine of ordinary living. With the one immense moral difference that its end is not violence, the climbing of a great mountain is very much like war—and this goes far deeper than such aspects as strategy, tactics and logistics. Experience, both individual and group, is vastly intensified. Hardship and danger are daily companions. Victory and defeat, reward and punishment, are close, pressing realities. And in the flux of events the spirit soars and sags with vast inconstancy.

Everest was a murderous mountain. And a beckoning mountain. A hateful mountain. And a magic mountain.

Nowhere was the magic more potent than at the top of the Icefall, where the savage wilderness levels off into the Western Cwm. And every member of the expedition, coming up over the huge final cliff, reported that this, for him, was one of the great moments of the ascent. Part of it was the simple physical satisfaction of steepness surmounted and easier going ahead. Part was relief at emergence from an area that, to all, had become a symbol of danger and death. But, beyond these subjective factors, the Cwm in itself was a wondrous place; a place for the forgetting of past troubles and griefs, for the raising of eyes and the lifting of hearts.

In the Icefall there had been no view ahead. All that lay beyond and above it had been shut out by the walls and towers of ice. But now the mountain world leapt up in all its panoply of glory. The Cwm itself was a gently rising corridor of snow and ice, some five miles long, roughly a mile in width, at the very heart of the three-ply mountain massif of Everest and its neighbors. Directly ahead, the corridor rose to meet the west-northwestern wall of Lhotse, and this in turn rose to meet the fangs of rock that were its 27,890-foot summit. To the right ran the great skyline ridge connecting it with Nuptse—now seen from the opposite side to that visible from Solu Khumbu—and from Nuptse smooth fluted ice walls plunged a vertical mile to the floor of the Cwm. To the left, the skyline ridge of Lhotse dipped more sharply, descending to the saddle of the South Col, from which rock and ice again leapt up, this time even higher, to the summit of Everest. And though Everest's ultimate peak was still hidden, all the rest of its southern and western battlements were now revealed in a mass so huge, so tall, as to shut out half the sky. If the Icefall had been the gateway to the mountains, the Western Cwm was their courtyard, sealed in, high and hermetic, by the loftiest walls on earth.

The Swiss, on their expeditions, had given this courtyard a better name than the British. They had called it the Valley of Silence. For here there was no longer the rumbling and crashing of the Icefall, but a stillness so deep, so pervasive, that the sound of a casual voice, the crunch of a boot on snow, seemed almost as if they had been electronically amplified. Sometimes, to be sure, there were more portentous sounds. A wind would penetrate the fastness, moaning or keening. An avalanche would pour in a white tide down the walls of Everest or Nuptse, silent at first, then with a delayed roaring, as the sound waves bridged the gulf of space. But when these had passed it was to leave only a deeper and more total stillness.

On the threshold of this world AMEE set up its Camp I. At first it was positioned on the stretch between the Icefall's topmost cliff and the crevasse at which Jim Whittaker and Lute Jerstad had turned back on their first foray into the Cwm. As soon as bridging materials had been brought up, however, it was moved to the far side of the crevasse, where on a 20,200-foot plateau, there was more room for tents and accumulating stores. The drive, the strength of purpose, of the expedition was now again at full power. It was on March 30 that Camp I was first occupied, and the very next day an advance party consisting of Jim Whittaker, Gil Roberts, Barry Prather and several Sherpas was on its way to site Camp II—or Advance Base—about halfway up the Cwm. The going went well. The weather held. Walkie-talkie communication between the head, middle and tail of the expedition was excellent, and the raised spirits of those in the lead quickly communicated itself down the line.

"I think maybe I'll take a moonlight stroll up to the South Col tonight," Big Jim radioed down on arrival at Camp II with an almost audible grin.

And Norman—buoyed up, the glint back in his eye—was euphoric enough to venture the prediction: "If our health holds up and the weather stays good, it is entirely feasible that we may climb Everest by May 1." To ward off a jinx, however, he verbally crossed his fingers, adding, "I hope I don't have to eat these words. The weather, of course, may decide to give us both barrels just because I said them."

9. *SOUTHSIDE, WESTSIDE*

THE GAME could be called *Who's Where?* (with a subdivision called *What's Where?*) and derives in equal parts from backgammon, musical chairs and the works of Clausewitz. Keeping track of the various components of AMEE, as they worked their way upward during those early days of April is an assignment to tax the resources of an IBM computer.

Not that it was a haphazard procedure; far from it. The movement of men and loads, the forging of routes and establishment of camps, were meticulously scheduled. Thanks to radio communication, through the main set at Base and eleven walkie-talkies, contact between the scattered echelons was perhaps the best ever achieved on a mountaineering expedition. Nevertheless, the daily movement reports, as recorded by the participants, are disturbingly remindful of those math class problems beginning, "If 3½ men walk 7¼ miles in 2 hours, 43 minutes and 13 seconds, then how long . . . etc." And the reader will be spared the details.

Suffice it to say that, with 70-odd—rather than 3½—men moving back and forth, forth and back, between Base Camp and dump,

121

dump and Camp I, Camp I and Advance Base, the lower reaches of Everest's southern and western sides were for a few weeks a busy place.

Lower Base, on the Khumbu Glacier, remained in existence—as it would throughout the expedition. But its depopulation continued day by day, as the loads went up and the advance parties were able to stay at the higher camps; and by the first week in April only a small contingent remained there. One of the rear guard was Jimmy Roberts, who, with Noddy Rana and others assisting, had the essential job of organizing and dispatching the baggage trains. Others were Will Siri and Maynard Miller, at work respectively on their physiology and glaciology. Al Auten was still—a bit restlessly—tied down to the main radio station. Dan Doody continued to fight a grim battle with acclimatization. (In this he was joined for a few days by Dick Emerson, who had gone up to the Cwm with the advance parties but found it necessary to descend to lower altitudes.) And Jim Lester was, at Norman's behest, biding his time until the route through the Icefall was as sound and safe as human effort could make it.

Norman himself, accompanied by the ever-faithful Ang Dawa, spent much time in the Icefall, filming the passage of the pack trains through the white forest of towers, across the bridged crevasses, up the ladders of the summit ice wall. On April 2, 3 and 4, carrying a 58-pound load and filming as he went, he made a three-stage ascent to Advance Base (Camp II), spent a day there to see how things were going, and returned to the lower Base (four hours down, as against three days up) to take care of mail and radio messages and to check with Jimmy Roberts on how the tail-end porterage was going. On the ninth he moved up again—this time to stay high until Everest was climbed. And from soon thereafter until the first general descent early in May, Base was manned only by a skeleton staff, augmented by occasional high climbers down for rest and recuperation (known as R & R).

One who had to remain below much longer than anticipated was Maynard Miller, who on April 5 was the victim of a comparatively minor, but highly frustrating, accident. On return from a day of glaciological work on the Khumbu, he was making his way alone, in almost full darkness, over the tumbled boulders of a moraine, when a big rock toppled, rolled on his right foot, and pinioned him so that he could not move. Luckily his shouts were heard by his assistant, Barry Prather, who was not far away, and hurrying up, Balu* and the one Sherpa who was with him set to work to free Maynard. It took a lot of doing, however; for the rock weighed a ton or more, and even Balu, the expedition strong man, could not move it by the normal methods of pushing and heaving. Mechanically talented—as heretofore noted—he therefore turned *himself* into a mechanical device, inserting a leg into a gap between the pinioning rock and an adjoining one and using it as a lever, while simultaneously he pushed with all his might. At last the rock teetered. It rolled away. Maynard was free, and Balu and the Sherpa helped him back to camp. But it was subsequently discovered that five metatarsal bones in his foot had been fractured, and it was not until after some six weeks of hobbling around Base Camp with the foot tightly strapped that he was able to get up through the Icefall into the Cwm. As for Balu's lever leg, it was black and blue, but that was all. AMEE's twenty-three-year-old "baby" was a tough specimen.

Meanwhile, day after day, up went the loads from Base toward Cwm, and up and down—to fetch more—went Sherpas and sahibs, to the point where the Icefall began to resemble a huge white anthill. On one morning alone a caravan of three climbers and forty Sherpas took off on the 2400-foot ascent from Base to Camp I. The next day eighteen of the Sherpas moved on from I to II, while twenty-two descended to Base. On the third day these went up again, loaded, and the upper contingent came down to meet them at I. And so on, for a week. Into a second week—

Most of the climbers on the way up were now carrying packs of 50 to 75 pounds. In part, this was simply to help get the loads up; in part, a continuation of conditioning; in part, as an example to the Sherpas, some of whom were not above doing a bit of goldbricking when the occasion offered. One, indeed, an exceedingly hip character called Angayle, could be classed as a true "operator," for

* Prather, it may be recalled, had been given the name "Bear" to distinguish him from other Barrys. Now the Sherpas had transposed this to their own word for bear, "Balu," which was the name that stuck.

it was presently discovered that after a week at Base he had done no carrying at all. "He's tall, nice-looking and speaks good English," said Dan Doody, "and his clothes are always so neat Gil Roberts claims he has an iron hidden in his gear. First he said he couldn't climb because he was busy helping the doctors as interpreter at daily sick call. Now that the doctors have moved up, he's started helping Maynard Miller with the strenuous task of painting glacier-movement stakes while listening to music from India on the radio. And at night he's been sleeping in a tent all by himself, while the sahibs sleep two per tent and the other Sherpas three. Everyone's looking forward to getting him up the mountain to give him a taste of what Sherpa work really consists of."

Angayle was the exception, however. Almost all the Sherpas, with at most a little prodding, did a tremendous job—with a smile. And the twelve extra ones who had been hired for pro-tem work in the Icefall proved a useful auxiliary to the thirty-seven "regulars." In age they ran older than the regulars, and their outfits, supplied by themselves, were in striking contrast to the new and glossy expedition issue. "They're a tough looking crew," said Lute Jerstad, "wearing any sort of old boots, pants and sweaters, and carrying loads in baskets or smack on their backs."

To men such as these the Icefall was a day's work, no more, no less. But to one member of AMEE it was the challenge of a lifetime. Jim Lester, be it remembered, was the expedition's one nonmountaineer. Above him at Base loomed the white dragon, the "tottering chaos" of Everest's gateway—no longer a mere latent menace but a proved killer; and it was going to take not only a maximum of lung and limb power for him to get up it but plenty of plain unadulterated guts. Jim did not *have* to go up the Icefall. He could have stayed for the duration at Base Camp and still have been of much service to the expedition. But the service would have been in transport and communications, not in his own field of psychology; for it would have been a bit difficult to function as the confidante and observer of men who had disappeared from his ken up a mountainside. And Jim was determined to do the job he was signed on to do. "I was scared silly," he reported (though one doubts that "silly" was the original word) of the morning of April 9, when he set out up the Icefall with Dick Emerson—who was now ascending for the second time. But scared or no, he kept going. Under the tilting towers; across the catwalks spanning abysses; up the spidery vertical ladders of the final ice wall. To Camp I on one day. To Advance Base on another. And though he himself was perhaps too done in at the time to care one way or another, his fellow Everesters were proud of him.

Norman went back up for the second time on the same day as Jim and Dick, and Will Siri, complete with laboratory gear, had gone a few days before. Dan Doody made it up—with a tremendous effort. Al Auten, released from the radio, headed for Advance Base, while "Balu" Prather (also an expert ham) stayed below to spell him, as well as to help the incapacitated Maynard Miller in his work on the glacier. With most of the loads past the Icefall, Jimmy Roberts had transferred himself to Camp I to supervise the next stage of the carry. And now the special Icefall porters, having been paid off, went down the Khumbu toward their villages, leaving Miller, Prather, Captain Noddy Rana and a few of the older Sherpas as the only inhabitants of Base Camp. Noddy would have very much liked to go higher. And he was well qualified to, for he had had much expedition experience, including an ascent in person to the summit of Annapurna IV. With Jimmy Roberts moving on, however, it was essential that he remain at Base to manage the "ground floor" level of the transport system. And here he did a first-rate job during the remainder of the expedition.

Camp I, at the entrance of the Cwm, was after the first few days largely a baggage depot, with two large tents and five smaller ones serving as board and lodging quarters for passers-through. And beyond it the newly blazed trail wound off up the long slope toward Advance Base. On this stretch there was none of the steepness of the Icefall, no menace from crumbling walls and towers; but it was far from straightway going, for the upper glacier was seamed with huge lateral crevasses. Sometimes these could be outflanked by a long zigzag to right or left. In other cases they extended for the whole width of the Cwm and, as with the Icefall crevasses, had to be bridged by logs, which were then furbished with pickets and handrails. The depth of some of the chasms was enormous. The eye could follow them down 200 feet or more along cliffs of sheer blue ice, and beyond this were still greater depths screened by snow bridges or the curving of the walls.

Falling from one of the bridges was not recommended.

The crevasses were mostly in the lower part of the Cwm. Higher up, progress consisted of a long uninterrupted grind. "We slogged on over little snowbump after little snowbump for what seemed an eternity," said Lute Jerstad, "until I began to feel like a Rainier client on a bad day." Yet if one could keep his thoughts off the discomforts of the flesh, it was a slog with rich rewards, a passage through a world of transcendent majesty and beauty. Ahead was Lhotse, to the left Everest, to the right Nuptse, and the Cwm was an enchanted avenue piercing the very heart of the trinity. In the brightness of the mornings black rock and blue-white ice soared up in preternatural clarity and stillness. In the afternoons clouds came, and with them often snow, and then the clarity was gone but the stillness deeper than ever. Plodding, bent over beneath their packs, goggled and hooded faces dusted with snow, the men of AMEE moved like files of ghosts up the Valley of Silence.

Advance Base, or Camp II, was established about halfway along the Cwm, toward its left-hand side, at a height of 21,350 feet. And here, in the very belly of Everest, rose what was to be expedition headquarters and nerve center during the days of siege that lay ahead.* Like the lower Base, it was a big installation, able to shelter and feed all sahibs and Sherpas simultaneously. But it was minus the stir and confusion of the low-level porters coming and going, and certain of the expedition's bulkier items, such as the main radio set, had been left below. Another difference from Base was that the tents here were not pitched on rock, for there was no rock in the Cwm—only ice and snow. They were, however, grouped in a hollow that gave protection from the wind, and the mountain walls round-about served as a second and higher screen. It was a good site, a good camp, all agreed. And though 1000 feet higher than the top of Mount McKinley, the highest point of North America, it was to prove a snug expedition home for weeks to come.

---

* Its location was almost identical to that of the British Expedition of 1953. Their Advance Base, however, had been numerically Camp IV; for they had had both Base Camp and Camp I on the Khumbu Glacier, Camp II in the Icefall, and Camp III at the entrance of the Cwm.

As on the lower levels, life was sometimes good, sometimes not so good. Those who were suffering serious acclimatization problems had, of course, an even worse time of it at this higher elevation. ("Weak and nauseated," Dick Emerson reported, even after his trip down to Base for R. & R. "Started off the day losing my breakfast," said Dan Doody. "Then set up camera and almost fainted. Aside from that, a swell day.") On the other hand, those who were going strong felt even stronger—in spirit if not always in body—as they came nearer to the challenge of the heights; and as early as April 3, while most of the expedition was still strung out along the Icefall and lower Cwm, two reconnaissance teams were already pushing out above Advance Base in two different directions.

Note the *two different*. For here at the center of the Cwm was the bifurcation point of the routes by which it was hoped Everest could be climbed, and from Advance Base on up, the South Col team and the West Ridge team would function as almost separate entities. The line of attack for the first would be over known terrain; up the rest of the Cwm to the foot of the Lhotse Face; up and across the face to the Col; thence onto Everest's southeast summit ridge. For the second, however, every step of the way beginning at a point a few hundred yards beyond A.B., would be a step never taken before; and the initial problem was to see if the West Ridge could even be reached. From the middle of the Cwm to the West Shoulder, which was the first objective, the vertical rise was about 2400 feet, almost all of it a steeply slanting wilderness of ice and snow, with only a few black rocks emerging here and there from the whiteness.

Willi Unsoeld and Barry Bishop were the first to enter this terra incognita. Probing and zigzagging, they pushed up long slopes, surmounted ice cliffs with the aid of ax, rope and crampon, and in what the Barrel described as "a delightful day" reached a point about 1000 feet above Advance Base. What was "delightful" to two expert climbers testing their skills would, however, be a different cup of tea for files of laden Sherpas, and on the descent, therefore, the climbers searched for easier routes over, under and around the steeper cliffs and, to their satisfaction, found them. That was on April 3. On April 5, after a day of rest, Barry went up again— this time with Tom Hornbein—and following the easier route, they presently passed the previous high point and climbed on farther. "First," said Barry, "we traversed almost horizontally across a steep ice slope (on which we subsequently put many fixed ropes), and then, about halfway between the Cwm and the shoulder, turned right and faced straight uphill. Here was a broad channeled slope, mostly with snow but with rock outcrops near the top, at an angle varying between 35 and 45 degrees. We chugged up it for three hours and at 3:30 in the afternoon reached the West Shoulder of Everest at about 23,500 feet." The shoulder was broad and rounded, and they were not yet at its top, where it met the crest of the West Ridge. Also, they found no suitable campsite—and even if there had been one, they had nothing with them to establish a camp. By evening, therefore, they were back at Advance Base. But it was highly gratifying that they had got as high as they did after a mere two days of reconnaissance.

Meanwhile the South Col team—or South Collars, as they came to be known—were off on their own tangent. On their first day, Jim Whittaker, Lute Jerstad and Gombu slogged on up the Cwm and, in spite of wind, cold and altitude trouble (for they had ascended almost a vertical mile from lower Base in the past few days), reached a point on the lower Lhotse Face at a height of 22,900 feet. Like the West Ridgers, they spent the next day at Advance Base resting and organizing, and then on the fifth moved back up again to establish Camp III. Other than Gombu, who ranked as a team member and not a porter, there were no Sherpas along; the whole force was still busy ferrying up the Icefall and lower Cwm. But the original three were now augmented by Dick Pownall and Gil Roberts, and all carried 40- to 50-pound loads of food, tentage, climbing gear and oxygen. Gil, who was now having acclimatization trouble, was unable to make it the whole way and returned to A.B., with Lute taking over his pack to make a double load. Dick had his problems too. "I'd never felt such complete fatigue," he said; "I was just rubber all over." But he had nevertheless staged a remarkable comeback from the depression and lassitude that had engulfed him after the disaster in the Icefall, and continued on with the rest. It was to be these four—Whittaker, Jerstad, Gombu and Pownall—who would spearhead the advance not only to Camp III but all the way up the Lhotse Face to the South Col.

Camp III was positioned on a glacial terrace of the lower Face beneath an outthrusting ice cliff that seemed to provide good protection from possible avalanches on the slopes above. And on April 7, after another rest day at Advance Base, Big Jim and Gombu, with the Sherpas Nima Dorje and Ang Nuru, went up and slept there. From the beginning of the expedition it had been the hope of Jim and Lute that, as old friends, they could work together as a pair throughout the climbing. But it was decided that since they, with their Rainier guiding background, were the two most experienced ice climbers, it would give the Col teams better balance if they split up; Jim pairing with Gombu and Lute with Dick. The latter two, therefore, spent the seventh at A.B., with Lute disappointed and champing restlessly at the bit. But whatever lift his spirit needed was more than supplied by the afternoon's radio contact with Barry Prather at lower Base. A message had just come in from Kathmandu, Balu reported, that Lute's wife, Paula, in Gig Harbor, Washington, had on April 4 given birth to a baby girl. There were no cigars available for distribution. (One dreads to contemplate the collective digestive consequences if there had been.) But there was an unusually high decibel content that evening in the Valley of Silence, and Lute's thoughts were rather more on Gig Harbor than whether he was, for the moment, at one camp or another.

The next morning, in any case, the new father and Dick moved up to III. Simultaneously, in spite of bitter cold and strong winds, Jim and Gombu began the pioneering of the higher slopes of Lhotse. At first they tried to follow the 1962 Indian route, which still bore vestiges of rope and other gear; but with the changes a year had wrought in the snow and ice, it soon proved "no go," and from then on, with Jim leading, they worked out their own route. It was hard going. Twice, as he probed and scraped upward, Jim came to sheer walls in which he had to fix ice screws to hold himself —"while Gombu, belaying me below," he said, "looked as if he thought I'd peel off any minute and pull us both down." But in the end he got up them, Gombu came after, and together they reached a height of about 24,000 feet before stopping and turning back. Jim had hoped to go higher; almost 1000 feet higher, in fact, to the level where it was planned to install Camp IV. But even with the help of oxygen—which was now, at III and above, being used for the first time—the going had been hard and exhausting.* And the descent, it developed, was to be little easier. "We came down very slowly," said Jim, "running out of marking wands and getting lost en route; then as a final indignity got down into a basin we didn't belong in and had to climb *up* out of it. Really bushed." When they reached III, however, there was at least the welcome sight of Lute and Dick, with tea and supper already prepared, and together the four dug into their bags for the night. "What a powerhouse!" was Lute's comment when he heard of Jim's doings on the ice walls. But Jim, for the moment at least, was feeling anything but.

The next day was his and Gombu's turn for rest, while Lute and Dick went up the Face. Jim had felt that part of his trouble had perhaps been due to insufficient oxygen intake (of a maximum 4-liter-per-minute flow he had used only 2), and the second team therefore started off on a flow of 3. They had not gone far, however, when they discovered that the regulator of Dick's apparatus was leaking, and not wanting to risk running out higher up, they turned down to 2 liters and later to 1. Following the route already blazed, they improved it as they went; cutting deeper steps in the ice, stringing fixed lines, inserting aluminum pickets that, in difficult places, would be used either for hand and footholds or for the securing of ropes. At one point they found the going so tricky that it took them two hours to gain 200 feet. And at another Dick had his first fall in a climbing career of almost twenty years, when one of his crampons came off and he was suddenly spun from his steps on a steep slope of ice. It was not a bad one, however, for Lute, who was higher on the slope, was able to hold him on belay before he had gone far, and Dick himself even managed to grab the crampon as he fell—after which came a hard struggle, on his precarious stance, to get it back on. Then up they went again. To

---

* Each oxygen cylinder weighed 13 pounds when full (10 pounds when empty) and was good for four hours when set at the highest rate of flow. On the upper mountain the climbers carried, for current use, either one or two cylinders, depending on the altitude and the prospective length of the day's work. And both sahibs and Sherpas often also carried unused cylinders for the stocking of the high camps.

Jim and Gombu's highest point. To a few hundred feet above it. But they, like their predecessors, fell short of the 24,900-foot mark, which was the planned height for Camp IV. By evening they were back at Advance Base, and the following day preparations were under way for the next stage in the assault.

On the far side of the Cwm, in their own steep white domain, the West Ridgers were now also gaining momentum. But they had their problems as well, and prime among them was manpower. Later on, as the overall campaign strategy developed, this was to be principally a matter of Sherpas. But at the present stage the serious shortage was in climbers, for of the original seven who were to have made up the team, only four were now available. Jake Breitenbach was gone. Dick Emerson, after a few days at Advance Base, had become so ill that he had had to descend again to lower Base for R & R, and Barry Corbet, though not so badly off as Dick, had as yet not acclimatized enough to go higher than the Cwm. This left Willi Unsoeld, Tom Hornbein, Barry Bishop and Dave Dingman. And though they would have preferred to have more than a four-some for the coming tilt with the unknown, they were soon, like the South Collars, up and at it.

On April 7 Tom and Barry, with seven Sherpas who had been pried loose from the lower carries, moved up to the point some 1000 feet above Advance Base which had been the high point of the first day's reconnaissance, and there pitched an intermediate camp that was to be known as the West Ridge dump. With the loads delivered, the Sherpas returned to A.B., but Tom and Barry stayed there; and the next morning up came Willi and Dave, accompanied by the same Sherpas with more loads. It had been the plan to go still farther that day—indeed to establish Camp 3W (meaning 3-West) on or near Everest's West Shoulder. But the rising wind was deemed too high for laden men on the slopes above, and so the Sherpas, with insufficient tentage for them at the dump, went down once again and climbed up for the third time on the morning of the ninth. On this day the weather was better. With Sherpas and sahibs alike carrying heavy loads, the eleven-man caravan, following the route taken by Tom and Barry four days earlier, moved across the ice traverse, ascended the channeled slope above, and passing the previous high point at the shoulder, went on to a height of about 23,800 feet.

Here, on a gentle slope just below the crest of the West Ridge, a level platform was dug in the snow and on it was pitched a single 4-man tent, the nucleus of 3W. The Sherpas, led by two Solu Khumbu men, Girmi Dorje and Tashi,* had over a three-day period done a tremendous job, and now, for the final time on the operation, they descended to the Cwm, leaving the four climbers in their lofty eyrie. The next day, for the first time, the West Ridgers would be climbing with oxygen, and that night, also for the first time, they used it as they lay in their sleeping bags. This was to be the general practice from now on in the camps, both on Ridge and Col routes, above Advance Base, for the oxygen was helpful not only for falling and staying asleep but, even more importantly, for the maintenance of blood circulation and bodily warmth. One cylinder with twin tubes attached was shared by two men, with the flow set at a rate of 1 or 2 liters a minute, and instead of the heavier and more complicated "climbing mask" each user wore a hospital-type "sleeping mask" of lightweight polyethylene. While the beneficial effects were self-evident, so too, however, were certain problems. "For the masks," said Barry Bishop, "were like flexible aquariums, gathering so much moisture during the night that we felt we were drowning in them. Nevertheless, Dave Dingman and I continued to use them during the reconnaissance; but Willi Unsoeld and Tom Hornbein discarded them in favor of just sticking the hoses into their mouths and pretending they were getting oxygen after they fell asleep."

During the next three days the West Ridgers probed persistently upward, returning to 3W each night for supper and sleep. The objective was now a site for Camp 4W, and the logical spot seemed to be a place on the ridge, at about 25,000 feet, where the core rock of Everest breaks loose from its overlying snow and ice and soars upward in a final 4000-foot summit pyramid. But as things developed, it took some doing to reach it. On the first day they

* Girmi Dorje was Bishop's "personal" Sherpa, having been with him throughout the Hilliary scientific and mountaineering expedition of 1960–61. Tashi was notable in that he was in his middle fifties, the oldest active participant in AMEE; and even more notable was the fact that during the past few years he had reached the summits of two major Himalayan peaks, Nuptse and Annapurna IV.

climbed 300 feet up the snow slopes and presently stood—the first of all men—on the crest of the West Ridge. Even as they reached it, however, wind-driven clouds closed in around them, and they could see neither the way ahead nor the stupendous view to the north that they knew now lay before and beneath them. "On a reconnaissance," said Barry, "you're supposed to see what you're doing, and we couldn't see a bloody thing." So back they went to 3W.

The following day the weather was better, with only tatters of cloud, and when they again reached the ridge there was the expected view in all its glory. Far out, stretching endlessly to the horizon, lay the brown rolling plateau of Tibet. Closer and seen at a steep angle, thousands of feet below, were the northern skirts of Everest, the huge white iceflows of the Rongbuk Glacier and its tributaries; and beyond the glaciers, some fifteen miles distant and barely discernible through binoculars, was what had once been the Rongbuk Monastery and was now a Chinese weather station and garrison for troops. To the left, on the Chinese-Nepalese frontier, was first the dip of the Lho La saddle, then the peaks of Khumbutse and Lingtren, and beyond them Gyachung Kang and 26,750-foot Cho Oyu, the seventh highest mountain in the world. To the right, near and monstrous, was the last vertical mile of the highest of all mountains, its rock and ice cleaving the sky. And beneath it, slanting off from the West Ridge in a vast rampart, the north Face of Everest swept on toward the east. This, beginning with the North Col and the Northeast Ridge at its far end, had been the route of the early British expeditions to the mountain— of Mallory and Irvine, Norton and Somervell, Smythe and Shipton and Tilman, and the whole company of the Everesters of old— and the four Americans gazed at it with many memories and silent awe. Then, turning, they looked down into the deep white gash of the Western Cwm and across at the Lhotse Face, on which they knew their own companions were now climbing toward the South Col. They were the first ever to see these historic sides of the mountain simultaneously—as they were the first to challenge the unknown third side that lay between them.

From the point where they reached the ridge, the climbers moved higher: first directly up the ridge along a sharp snow crest; then, when the going got too steep, out onto the tilt of the North Face. Here, as they had known they would, they found themselves on downsloping slabs, for the layers of sedimentary rock of which Everest is built slant downward from south to north, and on the northern side the surface structure resembles that of a steeply angled shingle roof. A covering of light snow and patches of iron-hard ice made the already treacherous going no easier. But proceeding on two ropes—Willi and Tom on one, Barry and Dave on the other—they kept going up and slantwise across the face, until Willi and Tom, out ahead, managed to work their way back to the ridge at a height of about 24,400 feet. It had been the plan to go still higher, if possible, to the base of the summit pyramid rocks several hundred feet above. But now, again, clouds moved in. Rocks and ridge, North Face and Western Cwm, everything beyond a radius of a few yards around them, disappeared, and there was nothing for it but to make their way slowly, gropingly, back to 3W.

Another morning, another setting out.

Thus it was, on the West Ridge, on the Lhotse Face, day after day. And though the specific climbing problems varied, from route to route, from one pitch to the next within each route, the overall pattern was the same.

For a start, there was the struggle of simply getting up, of unzipping the sleeping bags, of piling more clothes on over the already large amount worn while sleeping. Half-numb hands fumbled with the opening of cans, the lighting of pressure stoves, the heating of food and liquids. The water, to begin with, was not water but either ice or granulated snow and even when after an endless wait it came to a boil, it was, at these altitudes, not hot but merely tepid. Breakfast over, there was the lacing of boots, the pulling on of still more clothing, the readying of oxygen apparatus, the laborious tying of crampon bindings—the last, despite cold and wind, always an outdoor procedure, lest the sharp crampon spikes rip the floor of the tent. Finally came roping up, the slinging on of packs and oxygen bottles, the adjustment of masks and regulators, the hefting of axes, by which time an average of two hours had passed and breath was coming as hard as after two hours of climbing.

Then—up, up, up. The kick-kick-kick of boots in steep snow.

The whack-whack-whack of the ax in steep ice, where steps cannot be kicked, and then the careful scraping to make the steps clean. Ahead, presently, looms a wall, a bulge, a sharp corner to be turned, and now the leader climbs up alone, moving a few feet, sometimes only a few inches, at a time, pausing for seconds, or minutes, to plan his next move—then making the move, digging in with ax and crampons, using his assorted "hardware" of pitons, carabiners, pickets, and ice screws to provide holds, stances and protection. Through the carabiner, or snap ring, anchored to the ice by screw or piton, the rope goes down to his companion, placed (hopefully) in a secure position, with the rope belayed around him so that he can hold the leader in case of a slip. Now and then, as has been seen, there *is* a slip. But thank God, no fall. The belay holds; the loosened crampon is refastened—with bare hands that grow quickly cold. For another ten, or twenty, or thirty minutes the hard going continues, and then the slope eases off. Now the leader belays while his rope mate comes up after him. For a while it is again kick-kick-kick, then whack-whack-whack, and with each stroke of the ax the ice particles rise in fountains, glittering like diamonds in the crystal air.

Under the midday sun it grows warm, even hot, and laboring bodies are sweating. Anoraks and outer sweaters are pulled off— and no sooner are they stowed in the packs than the sun vanishes in the clouds and the sweat congeals in bone-clenching cold. The wind rises: in a hum, a moan, a wail, a roar. Then it dies, and the only sound between earth and sky is the crunch of boots and the slow rhythmic hiss of oxygen masks. It is past noon now, but no one is hungry. It is thirst that is rising, raging. But the water in the canteens is frozen, and the snow and ice that is everywhere around is so hard, so dry, that it will scarcely melt in the mouth.

Kick-kick. Whack-whack. Until arms are aching. Back and legs are aching. Then another wall or bulge or corner appears ahead. How long will it take to get up it? What time is it? How far have they come?

On every day's climb—except those on which the goal is an already established camp—there comes a time of decision; the decision of when to turn back. Most of mind and body yearns for the turning, for the surcease from struggle, for the bliss of downhill. But, strangely, there is a part of both that wants still to go on; to see what is beyond that next wall or bulge or corner; to push up another fifty feet, a hundred, two hundred until—what? Until it is dark? Until one sits down, lies down, in the snow and that is that? No. The turn is made. The way leads down. Down the kicked steps, the cut steps, around the corners, over the walls and bulges; and the going is easier now, blessedly easier—but also more dangerous—for gravity is pulling, pulling; and legs are tired, body and eyes and brain are tired, and it is cloudy and darkening, perhaps it is snowing, and the new snow fills the well-kicked, well-cut steps. The mountain is an enemy now: an evil thing: the thing that killed Jake Breitenbach and is waiting to kill again. The slope leads on and on. The steps lead on and on. There will be no end to them: not in this world, not in this life—And then there is an end. There is the camp, thank God. (Yes, again thank God.) They can see it. They are almost there. They *are* there. They are in the tent. The ordeal is over.

And then, within an hour, they are wondering what there was to give thanks for. For the ordeal here is worse. The tent is a shambles of air mattresses, sleeping bags, oxygen gear, clothing, cooking utensils, food, and soon half the food is spilled in a welter of bumping shoulders and elbows and knees and outsized boots. No one wants solid food anyway—even now. The gorge rises at it; and it is only because of the knowledge that one *must* eat that tins and packets are opened (and spilled), the stove is tended, and a stew or a hash, beef or sausages or tuna, is forced down. What is wanted, more than ever, are liquids—tea, juices, soups, by the quart, by the gallon—and even when a gallon is consumed the body is still so dehydrated that there is no need for urination. Until one is at last zipped in a sleeping bag, and then, of course, the need is immediate and great. Three choices are available. There is a plastic urinal that can be used in the bag—and spilled. There is a hole in the flooring of the tent, specially designed for this purpose—but it is covered over by food boxes, clothing, oxygen bottles and a sleeping companion. There is outdoors—where it is 20 below, the wind is wailing, and a false step will mean a 2000-foot plunge to extinction.

Back in the sack, the Everester simultaneously breathes his life-giving oxygen and half-suffocates in his aquarium mask. His layers of socks are stiff and cruddy, his back aches, and, in spite of a sleep-

Photograph by Barry C. Bishop © 1963 NATIONAL GEOGRAPHIC SOCIETY

CHALLENGE

Approaching the Geneva Spur. Behind it is the South Col; beyond,
the summit pyramid.

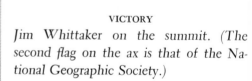

VICTORY

Jim Whittaker on the summit. (The second flag on the ax is that of the National Geographic Society.)

Photograph by Nawang Gombu
© 1963 NATIONAL GEOGRAPHIC SOCIETY

TRINITY

The vast massif of Everest-Lhotse-Nuptse viewed from the slopes of Pumori, above Base Camp. (See endpapers for routes and camps.)

MAN PROPOSES
The upper West Ridge and
part of the North Face, as seen
from between Camps 3W and
4W.

Photograph by Barry C. Bishop © 1963 NATIONAL GEOGRAPHIC SOCIETY

SUMMIT RIDGE

Lute Jerstad approaching Camp VI.

STILL THERE

The flag on the summit, as seen by Jerstad and Bishop on May 22. (see overleaf).

GULFS OF SPACE

Sherpas descending from Camp VI toward the South Col. Beyond them, the Lhotse Ridge, in shadow. In the distance, Makalu, in sunlight (facing page 137).

ing pill, there is no sleep. "What am I doing here?" he wonders.
"What in the name of God have I got myself into? I am out of my
mind and need mental therapy." But the nearest brain technician,
in the person of Jim Lester, is a few thousand feet down the mountain at Advance Base. Then at last sleep comes. Eventually morning
comes. And he is up and at it again. He is in the chaos of the tent;
in the cold outside. He is climbing again: through the wind, up the
steepness, on the snow and ice. His legs protest, his lungs protest,
his mind, or what is left of it, protests. But—and here is the wonder
of it all—in his misery he is not miserable. Something beyond leg
and lung and mind is functioning deep within him, pushing him
on, answering once and for all the questions—"What am I doing
here? What have I got myself into?"—that he has asked himself
during the night just past.

The answer is simple. He is a mountaineer. He is climbing Mount
Everest. And he would rather be climbing Everest than anything
else in the world.

It was on the twelfth of April, their eighth day of active reconnaissance, that the West Ridgers made their big push. This time
there were only three of them in the party, with Dingman, who
was not feeling well, remaining behind at Camp 3W. But Unsoeld,
Hornbein and Bishop got an early start and by midmorning, in fine
weather, were standing for the third time on the crest of the ridge.
Another hour or so brought them to Willi and Tom's previous high
point of about 24,400 feet, and from there they moved up toward
their thus far elusive goal—the rocks at the base of Everest's summit pyramid, where they hoped eventually to establish their next
camp.

As before, however, their advance was not straight up. For the
ridgeline was still forbiddingly steep and narrow, and veering off
from it, they again traversed obliquely upward across the North
Face. Though they did not yet know it, this was to be their route
not only for that day but for almost the whole remaining ascent
of the mountain. "What we really climbed," said Willi Unsoeld
later, "was not the West Ridge itself but the West Buttress beneath it, on the northern side." And as a consequence, for nearly
all the while, the Western Cwm and Lhotse Face were hidden

from view—with only the skyline of the ridge above on the right, and to the left, at the foot of the mountain, the glaciers and plains of Tibet stretching out into distance. Indeed, on this side of the ridge, the climbers were themselves in Tibet: i.e., in Communist China. But neither the Passport Division of the U.S. State Department nor the Chinese border patrol at Rongbuk bothered to come up the mountain to say to them nay.*

The going was still of the "shingle roof" variety, with the slabs at an angle of 35 to 40 degrees. And the mixed snow and ice that plastered them to a depth of an inch or two made for added difficulties, in that crampons were needed to keep from slipping but at the same time were forever catching their prongs in the underlying rock. The threesome was of course traveling all on one rope. Sometimes the three could move simultaneously; at other times two would have to stop and belay while the third moved over particularly steep or slick pitches. But in general their progress was steady. The weather held. Toward midafternoon their altimeter showed that they were passing the 25,000-foot mark, and at four o'clock, after angling back up to the ridge, they found themselves at their objective—the long sought point, at 25,100, where the ridge rose up into the rock of Everest's vast capstone.

It was a great moment. Again the view was open to both sides of the mountain, but now even more spectacularly than before—with the Cwm a white abyss far below, the Lhotse-Nuptse ridge at the same level as themselves, and even the summit of Nuptse only a little higher than the point at which they stood. Also, and more practically, there was no need for further concern about a likely spot for Camp 4W; for here was a perfect one, a broad level platform of snow, big enough for several tents, at the very base of the upthrusting rock. "It was a fairy-tale campsite," said Tom Hornbein. "The most idyllic campsite I have ever seen," said Barry Bishop.

* This foray across the Nepalese-Chinese frontier was, however, grist for the wildest of all the wild rumors that eventually found its way to the world below. *Rumor:* High on the North Face the climbers had been intercepted by Chinese guards and ordered to go back. *Fact:* On the return trip, near Dolalghat, virtually in Kathmandu's suburbs, two team members visited the camp of the Chinese road-surveying team that was at work there and were told to go away. The discrepancy of a mere two months in time, 200 miles in distance, and 20,000-plus feet in altitude made no matter at all to the flourishing Nepalese grapevine.

Then all eyes went upward; and if what they saw there could not be called idyllic, it was at least not without hope for the future. The rock of the summit pyramid was, like almost all of Everest's rock, rotten, and therefore dangerous for climbing. But threaded through it, like a pattern of arteries and veins, was a vast network of snow-filled gullies, or couloirs, leading up, úp, up, as far as the eye could see. It could not see all the way; the top of the mountain was screened by cliffs bulging out against the sky. But what *was* visible—though huge and savage—appeared at least not totally impossible. One or another of the couloirs might well be made to "go." High up in their maze Camp 5W could then be pitched, ideally at a height of some 26,500 feet. Still higher would come 6W, as near to 28,000 as it could possibly be placed. And from there—

But all that was for later. First 4W must be established where they now were, stocked with the food and tentage and oxygen that would be needed both there and higher up. On reconnaissance the West Ridgers were traveling light, and all they had with them that could be left at their highest point were a few lengths of rope, a few pitons and ice screws, to mark the spot. For a while longer they looked up; peering, estimating, studying the future. Then, if not in jubilation, at least with deep and tingling hope, they descended that evening to Camp 3W, and the next day to Advance Base in the Cwm.

On the Lhotse Face, too, during these days, things were scarcely at a standstill. On the morning of April 11 the first big load-carrying caravan went from Advance Base to Camp III, consisting of the usual spearhead of Whittaker-Gombu and Jerstad-Pownall, plus Will Siri (taking time off from his lab), Barry Corbet (conditioning himself for the West Ridge) and fifteen Sherpas. Through the afternoon, work was done on the lower part of the Lhotse Face and a new route established that was easier and safer than the old. Then, the next day, there was another large carry to the head of the Cwm—this time with Norman participating—and still more work on the steep ice above. All previous expeditions had had two camps on the upper Lhotse Face, between the Cwm and the South Col; but Norman did not think this necessary; he believed one was enough, provided it was placed good and high, as near to 25,000 feet as possible. A likely site had been picked long before; after careful study of the Face through binoculars. But both the Whittaker-Gombu and Jerstad-Pownall climbs of April 8 and 9 had fallen short of their mark, and now, several days later, Camp IV was still no more than a tentative X on a map. Big Jim—who was scarcely the patient type—felt it was now high time it became something more than that. At Camp III, on the evening of the twelfth, he wrote in his diary, "Tomorrow, if the weather's all right, we're going to put in IV, or else."

There was no *else*. The next morning was clear and windless, and up he went with Gombu and the Sherpas Girmi Dorje (recently down from the West Ridge) and Passang Temba.* Following the new and improved route up the slopes of ice, they took only two hours to gain the highest point previously reached, and from there worked steadily higher, chopping the inevitable steps and installing fixed ropes. Presently they came to the ruins of two tents, which proved to be relics of one of the Swiss expeditions, and the Sherpas were in favor of making this the end of the line. But Jim was unwilling to stop short of the set objective. They went on. And at about noon, at a height of 24,900 feet, they came to a tall serac, or ice tower, which had been noted through glasses from the Cwm and marked with that tentative X. Up near the serac, as had been hoped, was a reasonably level and sheltered ledge. The loads were dumped. A tent was pitched. Camp IV had come into being. After an hour there, the four men descended, stringing more ropes as they went, and reached III in the late afternoon. "Feel we've licked the last real climbing problem," said Big Jim that evening— a bit too optimistically. But at least it had been a day of achievement and satisfaction.

The next day was Easter Sunday, the day after that Income Tax Day. But neither rabbits nor Internal Revenue Agents made an appearance.

What did appear at Camp III on the fourteenth (Easter) was

* There were two Passang Tembas on the expedition (as well as two Angcherrings and two Nima Tenzings): one from Darjeeling and one from the village of Lukla in Solu Khumbu. This was the P.T. from Lukla.

still another caravan of load-carrying climbers and Sherpas, and when they had finished their work the establishment at the foot of the Lhotse Face boasted two 4-man tents, several 2-man tents, and a formidable stock of food and gear. Heading this contingent —while Jim and Gombu went down to Advance Base for rest— were Lute Jerstad and Dick Pownall, and with them came Gil Roberts and Al Auten, in the cause of still more "manicuring" on the lower Face. For the first time since Thangboche it snowed all day, but not heavily enough to halt operations. This time, sahibs and Sherpas alike dug in at III for the night. Supper, Dick Pownall recorded, consisted of sausage, nut bread, canned pineapple and tea, and when it came time for the sleeping bags it was, in the interests of conservation, without oxygen. "Couldn't sleep worth a damn," said Dick, "what with gulping for air and mental turmoil." But in the morning he and Lute were ready for the trek up to IV.

This was no reconnaissance but a carry in force, and seven Sherpas went with them on the 2000-foot ascent. "With all the new snow," said Lute, "the steps cut by Jim and Gombu had just about disappeared, and we had to chop and clear hundreds of them all over again." But thanks to the labors of the past week there was now some 1600 feet of fixed line festooning the ice slopes, and this was of huge help to the laden column. The Sherpas, indeed, were enthusiastically impressed by the route—except for the redoubtable Tashi, whose fifty-six years had proved no deterrent to a quick switch from West Ridge to Lhotse Face. "This Mickey Mouse climb," was the verdict of Tashi, who had been on the Lhotse route on previous expeditions and found it too tame for his rugged tastes. Later he switched back to the West Ridge, but for the time being he made do with Mickey Mouse. The procession plodded on. Like all team members when climbing above Camp III, Lute and Dick were using oxygen, breathing it at a rate of 3 liters per minute. The Sherpas were without oxygen and would remain so on all carries until the beginning of the actual summit assault. But the physical demands of the ascent were about equalized by the fact that the latter were moving from one prepared step to the next, whereas the sahibs were out in front hacking and scraping them. For most of the way, on this day, Lute was in the number one position.

"Then my arms gave out," he said. "I just couldn't swing the ax any more." So Dick took over for the remaining few hundred feet to Camp IV.

At IV, the food boxes and gear were stacked. Two larger tents were set beside the small one that Jim and Gombu had pitched. Then, in the late afternoon, five of the Sherpas turned and began the descent toward III, leaving Lute, Dick, and two Sherpas— Chotari and Nima Tenzing*—to spend the night. During the late stages of the climb Dick's left foot had gone numb and cold, but sustained massaging by himself and Lute restored it to normal— or what passes for normal on Everest—and in their tent it was warmer and more comfortable than on many nights in lower camps. Throughout the day it had been largely cloudy, with gusts of wind and occasional flurries of snow. But now, as darkness came, it was clear and utterly still. The roof of the tent seemed almost to scrape against the stars.

After a good night's sleep, this time on oxygen, Lute and Dick hoped for an early morning's start. But at almost 25,000 feet intentions are one thing, the sluggishness of body and mind another, and though they were awake at first light it was 10:30 before they and the two Sherpas were organized and on their way. The schedule for the day called only for reconnaissance and the putting in of a route about halfway to the South Col; for no one on AMEE had yet been higher than Camp IV, and it was known that the terrain from there to the Col would involve a considerable amount of laborious "manicuring." The vertical height to be gained was not great: about 1300 feet from IV to the Col, as against 2000 feet from III to IV. But this would be well made up for by the linear distance involved; for at IV the straight-on ascent of the Lhotse Face was at an end, and what came next was a long diagonal traverse toward the dip between Lhotse and Everest. On the way the route would pass over two of the salient and most famous features of the Lhotse-Everest complex. One was known as the Yellow Band, a stratum of

* Chotari, it will be remembered, was the expedition's assistant sirdar, who had suffered the acute but transient appendicitis attack in Namche Bazar. Of the two Nima Tenzings, this was the one who had originally been assigned to Jake Breitenbach and who had shown such grief when Jake was killed.

tawny beetling rock, clearly visible from below, that cuts horizontally across the upper reaches of the whole mountain massif.* The other, to which the Swiss had given the name of the Geneva Spur, was a second more localized outcropping of rock that formed a rugged bastion guarding the entrance to the South Col. Both were scalable. The Swiss, British and Indians had all breached their defenses. But, as with the Icefall, there was no such thing as an established route, and AMEE would have to find its own way.

The first stretch out of camp took the four men over one of the most dangerous areas on the mountain. This was a great trough of ice known as the Lhotse Couloir, a natural chute for anything falling from above, and it had been here, the year before, that a Sherpa with the second Indian expedition had been killed by an avalanche of ice. Hacking steps and stringing rope—for the going was steep and slippery—Lute, Dick, Chotari and Nima Tenzing got across as quickly as possible. (Nothing fell.) And in another few minutes they were at grips with the Yellow Band.

From Lute's logbook: ". . . find a foot of snow on sheer water ice; hard and slippery, with rock underneath. Put in anchor for a fixed rope and chop bucket steps across it. Ice so hard I can't twist a screw or pound a picket in, so I just keep chopping and drag the 200-foot fixed line with me. When it comes to the end, we get three turns around a rock and anchor it. Next stages the same: dragging fixed line, looking for place to anchor. Get a small picket halfway in and use it. Then we run out our total 450 feet of rope and can't find any place to tie it. Dick goes out ahead of where the rope will reach and finds he can get a 4-foot picket in. Nothing to do but use it, and since the fixed rope won't reach we cut our climbing rope in half and tie it on.

"We'd figured the whole thing would take thirty minutes," he said. "And it took two hours." To which Dick added: "Our big mistake was not having rock pitons to hammer in under the ice. Just one or two would have made the job a breeze."

As it was, it had been something else again. By the time they had passed the Yellow Band it was early afternoon. The sky had

---

* The main mass of Everest and its adjoining peaks is limestone. The Yellow Band is a layer of schist: specifically a calc schist.

turned gray, and dark clouds were massed behind the ridge of Nuptse to the west. Both the time and the weather spoke for a return to Camp IV; and besides, their assignment for the day was only to reconnoitre and prepare a route across the Band. But—there are times when two and two don't add up to four. There are other subtler factors in man's inner arithmetic that make him say yes to this and no to that. In spite of the labors just past and their 40-pound loads, Lute and Dick were still feeling strong. They had enough oxygen left to continue on a 3-liter flow, and Chotari and Nima Tenzing, though without oxygen and also carrying 40 pounds, had shown no signs of tiring. The climbers looked at their watches. They looked at each other. They looked down the mountain, then up the mountain. And they went up.

Above the Yellow Band they came first to another snow couloir. Then they were at the cliffs of the Geneva Spur; and though from below, it appeared steep and savage, it was freer of ice and snow than the lower outcrop of rock, and they were able to scramble up without serious difficulties. By design, they kept bearing to their right, aiming toward a snow dome that marked the top of the spur toward the Lhotse side. For though this would involve extra climbing, bringing them out at a point some 200 feet above the South Col—from which they would then have to descend—most previous expeditions had considered this route the safest and easiest. Looking back after a bit, however, they saw that the two Sherpas had other ideas. Instead of following along, they had cut off to the left on the lower part of the spur, taking the most direct line toward the entrance to the South Col. And it proved a good choice. When Lute and Dick came out on the top of their snow dome, they saw that Chotari and Nima Tenzing had already reached the goal.

Lute and Dick came down to join them. There were grins, handshakes, slapping of backs, for, as with the West Ridgers when they reached the base of Everest's summit pyramid, this was a great moment in the siege of the mountain. Most especially it was great in the aspect of timing—this being by far the earliest in the season at which any expedition had ever gained the South Col. It had not been until May 21 that the British, in their victorious 1953 ascent, had climbed to this 26,200-foot jumping-off place for Everest's summit. The Swiss and the Indians had also not reached it until late in May. For AMEE, however, the date was April 16; and whereas the others, from here on, had been confronted by a touch-and-go race with the monsoon, there were now still six weeks of potentially good weather remaining for the assault on the final 2828 feet.

The rocky windswept plateau of the South Col had been called the most desolate place on earth. It has also been called the world's highest junkyard, and roundabout, as the four men surveyed it, lay the abandoned debris of the six previous expeditions that had been there—oxygen cylinders, empty food cans, scraps of gear and clothing, and skeletal tent poles swaying and creaking in the gale. Along with their other accomplishments, Sherpas are among the ablest and most dedicated of scroungers, and, digging in the remains of an Indian tent, Chotari, who ranked *primus inter pares*, emerged triumphantly with three pairs of unused woolen socks. By way of keeping the balance a few items were cached in a marked and protected place: a moving picture camera, several tins of film, a small miscellany of climbing gear ("we shall return"). But there was not much lingering, for the afternoon was getting on, the wind was rising, and it was bitterly cold.

The descent of the Geneva Spur was by the Sherpa route. (They had won the scouting honors for the day.) Then it was down, down, down over the Yellow Band, across the Lhotse Couloir, to Camp IV—and still down, in fading light, over the slopes and walls of ice to near the head of the Cwm. Here, at Camp III, Chotari and Nima Tenzing stopped for the night, but Lute and Dick continued on into the darkness, negotiating the upper Cwm with the help of headlamps. "The stars were out," said Lute. "It was beautiful. And I felt so good I found myself reciting poetry—until I ran out of breath."

It was 9:15 when they reached Advance Base, after a continuous descent of almost 5000 feet. Norman, who had issued the instructions to them to go no higher than the Yellow Band, had been of a mind to make a few remarks on the subject when they returned. "But now," he said, "I didn't have the heart to bawl them out." They were too happy.

And so was everyone else.

"9N1ME. CALLING 9N1ME. This is 9N1DD—9N1DD—calling 9N1ME—9N1ME. This is 9N1DD calling, with 9N1MM standing by."*

Spring is the dry season in Nepal. Although the sky was clear, the mountains to the north were usually hidden behind veils of dust. But through the veils, each afternoon at five o'clock, a voice came down from the Khumbu Glacier into Colonel Bill Gresham's radio shack in Kathmandu. Sometimes the voice was Al Auten's; sometimes it was Barry Prather's; now and then it was Dan Doody's or Maynard Miller's. "9N1DD. Calling 9N1DD, with 9N1MM on the side. This is 9N1ME—9N1ME. One two three four five. Five four three two one. Can you read me? Can you read me? Over." Occasionally we could not read, because of electrical storms or other interference. But usually the voice from the Khumbu was loud and clear.

* 9N1 is the call signal for all radios in Nepal. ME, the expedition's own call letters, stood for *Mount Everest*. DD, Colonel Gresham's letters, stood, less formally, for *Donald Duck*, and MM, Father Moran's letters, stood for *Mickey Mouse*.

146

Father Moran listened in on his set at St. Xavier School. In his own shack, Bill Gresham of course presided at the controls, with a varying number of others sitting in on the sessions. Sally Dyhrenfurth, Sally Richardson, Willi Unsoeld's wife, Jolene, and my own wife, Marian, were, along with myself, the regulars. ("Good God, there's Ullman with his harem again," came the not infrequent plaint from the womanless heights.) Ambassador and Mrs Stebbins often dropped by, as did Bob Bates of the Peace Corps and other Embassy people. Sometimes Base Camp was frustratingly shy of information as to what was happening "up the hill." More often it had the latest news and passed it on. And on a few memorable occasions we were able, by what the hams called a "duplex operation" on the Base radio, to talk directly to the walkie-talkies at Advance Base or above. It was an exciting exercise of the imagination to try to visualize the speakers in their snow-and-ice world 18,000 to 20,000 feet above our heads.

On occasion, we feared that the altitude had really got them. Norman, after inquiring about the expedition bank balance, asked that a dozen blank checks be sent in with the next runner. (Was it to pay ransom to Communist Chinese or for salary to an Abominable Snowman?) Maynard Miller wanted the address of a Hong Kong tailor. Jim Lester was worried about a package of neckties from Calcutta. But in contrast there were times when the air crackled with suspense and drama. On April 17, in particular, there were a few moments of chilling tension when Al Auten said quietly, "I have an official expedition announcement," and all thoughts went back to the message of Jake Breitenbach's death. But this time the announcement was that Lute Jerstad and Dick Pownall had, the day before, reached the South Col, and chill turned to joy in Bill Gresham's shack.

We too had our messages to give: some routine, some otherwise. The happiest was the news of Lute Jerstad's baby daughter. The saddest was the word that Barry Prather's brother-in-law had gone down on April 10 with the submarine "Thresher." By happenstance, Balu himself was operating the Base Camp radio when this message arrived in Kathmandu. So we kept silence at the time, sending the word up by the next pair of runners to leave for the mountain.

The time record for upgoing runners (other than the one who was partly helicoptered) was twelve days. For downcomers it was eight. And with each arrival came masses of material that composed the log of AMEE. There were rolls of still and moving picture film, by the dozen and score, that were sent on for processing to the *National Geographic* in Washington. There were tape recordings by Norman and others that were first listened to on our own recorder at the Hotel Royal and later transcribed for the record. There were diary-letters to wives, families and friends, many of which I was authorized to read before forwarding and which added up to a rich multifaceted portrait of the expedition in action. Indeed, thanks to all that I was getting, I was presently so far along in my notes and newsletters that I had to warn the team over the radio that, unless they kept moving up briskly, I might reach Everest's summit before them.

In mid-April we were waiting from day to day to hear of the arrival at Base Camp of Lila Bishop and her trekking companions. And meanwhile, in to Kathmandu came two others also heading for Base, in the persons of Charles Huestis, AMEE treasurer, and old Himalayan hand (though aged only thirty) Nicholas Clinch. Chuck and Nick had but limited time at their disposal. Their plan was to charter the U.S. AID helicopter for a flight to Namche Bazar; then to hike in to Base for a visit, hike back to Namche, and return by chopper to Kathmandu—all in a matter of some ten days. Before they were through, however, they were both to learn that plans rarely jibe with the Facts of Kathmandu, or Nepal, and were to provide AMEE with some lively rear-echelon drama.

In the first place, it was a week before the helicopter was available. In the second place, even then, it could take just one of them at a time, for they had with them a mass of supplementary equipment that the expedition had requested, and it could carry a payload of only some 450 pounds. It was decided that Nick would fly in first, and he did—taking off one morning at dawn. Since it was a mere 1½-hour flight to Namche (as against the sixteen days it took the expedition), the plane was to be back in some three hours and would then take Chuck in, either later that day or the next morning, depending on weather. But the hours passed and there was no sign of it. The whole day passed, then the next morning and the whole of that day, with no sign of it, and the atmosphere grew steadily grimmer at AMEE's base in Kathmandu. Obviously the plane was down somewhere in the wild country to the east, and for all we knew, Nick and the pilot had been killed. The first obvious step was to get the Namche Bazar government checkpost on the radio to see if the chopper had arrived there, but—as was SOP for Nepal—their radio was out of order. As the next step, Chuck, on the third day, chartered the small Red Cross plane that had earlier flown Heinrich Berann out to Everest and set off to see what, if anything, could be found.

What eventuated was, happily, not tragedy; merely utter confusion. At a village called Giri, about halfway to Namche, was one of the very few airstrips in rural Nepal, and close beside it, downed but not smashed, was the missing helicopter. The Red Cross plane landed and was greeted by the chopper's pilot, who reported that he had delivered Nick to Namche on schedule, but had had engine trouble on the return flight and had made a forced descent at Giri. At least he and Nick were both all right. But—there was Nick at Namche, with no way of knowing why Chuck had not appeared and increasingly concerned that *he* had been in a crash. As the only way of getting word to him, we told the story on the radio to AMEE Base Camp, asking them to send a messenger down to Namche; and this was done—though by the time the message arrived Nick had already been sweating it out for a week. In the end, he finally went on to Base. But poor Chuck, who had also come halfway around the world just to get there, never made it at all. By the time the helicopter was brought back to Kathmandu and put in shape for further flights, he was already overdue back at Hughes Aircraft in California, and the only look he was to get at Everest was from the DC-3 that flew him out toward Calcutta and home.

With all this going on, there was time, on the Kathmandu-Khumbu radio sessions, for little else but "Where's Clinch? Where's Huestis?" But presently it was recalled that, on the far side of Base, there was a group of men engaged in climbing a mountain, and 9N1DD was again asking, "Where's Norman? Where are the South Collars? The West Ridgers? Where are Lute, Willi, Tom, Gombu, and the assorted Jims, Dicks and Barrys?" Back in Bill Gresham's shack we knew that May 1 or thereabouts was now the target date for the summit, and day by day over the airwaves hope and tension increased.

10. GORAKVILLE

AMEE WAS INVOLVED in the climbing of Everest. But it was also involved in *living* on Everest. At Advance Base, a thousand feet higher than the highest point in North America, life—as elsewhere —comprised a number of things.

Among them—

Tents: Growing ever more cluttered and messier. Among the expedition's more exotic equipment were a half-dozen brooms (known to the Sherpas as "haysticks") which were occasionally put to use in an orgy of good housekeeping. But the wind usually managed to blow the debris back into the tent—preferably into the sweeper's face.

Sleeping bags: Growing riper and riper. Putting them out to air was tantamount to issuing a formal invitation to a gale or a blizzard.

Food: Too controversial a subject to be discussed.

Department of Sanitation: Consisting of two holes in the glacier —one close to the kitchen tent, serving as garbage pit; the other, farther off behind an ice hummock, as latrine. Both were the scene of nonscheduled activities, as for instance: (1) Hollow, ominous

150

noises were presently heard roundabout the latrine, and it was feared that they were coming from a hidden crevasse preparing to swallow both facility and users. Investigation disclosed, however, that the sound was only the brushing of the wind over surface crusts of ice and snow. (2) One morning, while the premises were occupied by Will Siri and two Sherpas, an enormous ice avalanche came down from the walls of Nuptse, hurling chips and shards almost the whole way across the Cwm. The Sherpas, with much heaving and zipping, made a dash for shelter; but Will maintained both his position and his dignity, and the flying ice obligingly fell short of him. (3) On another morning, Dan Doody, who was still feeling weak and lethargic, was given a Dexedrine tablet by Dr. Gil Roberts—and the effect was spectacular. Within a half-hour Dan had decided that the existing garbage pit was not adequate; seizing a shovel, he set about rectifying the situation; and by the end of the day, after hours of labor in a snowstorm, he had dug a new hole in the glacier, 8 feet long, 6 feet wide and 4 feet deep. (Whereupon—the Dexedrine having done its duty—he collapsed back into the sack.)

Reading: There were Everest and other mountaineering books on hand. There was poetry, drama, biography, history and fiction (of which the favorite was Durrell's *Alexandria Quartet*). For the Ph.D.s there was *Mad* Magazine and—as a surprise—a batch of girlie magazines, which had been used as stuffing for the food and equipment boxes by a public-spirited professional packer in Seattle. In a more specialized category, there was a much admired notice for posting from the Office of Naval Research which stipulated that, as a recipient of its funds, AMEE must practice no racial discrimination and observe a forty-hour week.

Recreation: In the Cwm it was too cold for ukulele strumming, but there were still harmonicas (with due care in the meeting of lips and metal). There were cards, chess, dominoes (with the Sherpa Urkien soon becoming undisputed domino champion). For a few die-hard sahibs and most of the Sherpas, there was smoking. (Some of the latter would soon be smoking even at the South Col and above, pushing aside their oxygen masks for a blissful drag on a cigarette.) And as a special treat for the Sherpas, there was Lute Jerstad's beanie copter. A beanie copter, it should be explained to readers of limited cultural background, is a device consisting of a skullcap, a small plastic rotor atop the cap, and a string which, when pulled, causes the rotor to revolve and the cap to take off into the air. As a candidate for a Ph.D. in dramatic arts, Lute considered such an item an essential part of his equipment, and if the response of his Sherpa audience could be taken as a norm, he can look forward to a sensational career behind the footlights. Roars of delight and approval rent the air whenever his beanie copter zoomed up through the Valley of Silence.

Goraks: These birds had been in evidence now and then at Base Camp and in the Icefall; but the Cwm, of all places, was their favorite domicile, and a colony of them shared Advance Base with the expedition for the whole time that it existed. They were big, black, dishevelled and ugly. They squawked—"gaaaw-rak, gaaaw-rak"—in hoarse sepulchral voices. They were so awkward and flew so badly that they had to take off downhill. Where they slept, or what they ate when no expedition was present, was a dark mystery,* but their saw-edged beaks were tough enough to cut through heavy cardboard food boxes, and they would obviously have been glad to share the climbers' tents if they had been allowed to. With a pro-gorak and an anti-gorak faction on the team, they were soon almost as controversial a subject as food. "Black unholy monsters," was the verdict of Lute Jerstad, of the antis, throwing whatever was handy at them with vigor and venom. But Gil Roberts, of the pros, found them, if not holy, at least likable, and when he caught Lute throwing things reminded him warningly of the fate of the Ancient Mariner. Somewhere in the middle of the road was Dan Doody, who, on a day when the climbing of Everest seemed not the most rational of human pursuits, brooded: "Here they live with another bunch of misfits, oddballs, or whatever one wants to call mountaineers."†

Whatever one *does* want to call them, these mountaineers were soon to have problems on their minds unconnected with goraks. The period of April 10 to 16 had, both on the South Col route and

* Except to Maynard Miller, who reported that the normal gorak diet consists of enormous quantities of minute snow fleas—which, in turn, live on microscopic organic matter found in the snow.

† Actually, the gorak is a type of raven (Corvuscorax *tibetanus*)—and Edgar Allan Poe would have felt right at home with him.

the West Ridge, been a time of high achievement and spirit; but now, perhaps inevitably, it was followed by a sustained "low."

One contributing cause was the weather, which, though it generated no major storm, fell into a pattern of almost daily onslaughts of wind and snow that made effective progress increasingly difficult. Another was the grim facts of logistics, for the lead climbers, like the assault troops of a swiftly advancing army, had, for the time, outrun their supply lines. Both the South Col and the 25,100-foot mark on the West Ridge had been reached in remarkably short order. But reaching them in light reconnaissances was one thing, placing well-stocked camps there quite another. And now there was little for the climbers to do but wait—and wait— while the Sherpas, during the breaks in the weather, moved slowly up with their loads over the prepared routes.

Also, this was the time for certain basic strategic decisions and the decisions did not, and indeed could not, please everyone. Willi Unsoeld and Tom Hornbein, the two prime movers of the West Ridge venture, had come down to Advance Base full of enthusiasm for their project and eager—as were the South Collars—to be given ample manpower for the establishment of their chain of camps. Tom, on the basis of carefully calculated logistics, was convinced that the Col and Ridge assaults could be mounted simultaneously without damaging either's chance for success. Willi, though conceding that the two-prong attempt "would spread even an army like ours pretty thin," still felt that it would not be *too* thin; that the double climb could be pulled off. But Norman— with Deputy Leader Will Siri in agreement—thought otherwise. To him, as to Willi and Tom, the climbing of the West Ridge represented a great challenge, a great adventure. But he believed that the expedition's first obligation, both to its backers and to itself, was to reach the top of Everest *by whatever route;* that the known Col route offered the best chance of success; and that a simultaneous double attempt might—just might—result in the mountain's not being climbed at all. It was therefore his conviction that, for the time being at least, the Col team must have priority, particularly in the assignment of Sherpas to get food and gear to the high camps.

Turning conviction into decision was perhaps the hardest job of any Norman had to face as Bara Sahib of the expedition. For the West Ridgers, and particularly Tom Hornbein, were not the sort of men to give in without a struggle. Both he and Willi had been on previous Himalayan ventures. Both prided themselves, justifiably, not only on their physical abilities as climbers but on their knowledge of mountaineering strategy and tactics. And in the tents at Advance Base there were long, sometimes heated discussions as Tom persistently pushed the West Ridge cause. Those who agreed with him thought him an idealist, the champion of pioneering and adventure as against the easy road of cheap success. Those who disagreed were not above calling him a fanatic who put his personal preferences and purposes above the common goal. In any case, his dedication was total. He fought what was to him the good fight with every ounce of his 140 pounds. And it was far from easy for Norman to have to say in the end, "No, the West Ridge must wait."

As an added setback, the West Ridgers were at this time in the process of losing some of the manpower they already had. Dr. Dave Dingman had had hard going in the final days of the reconnaissance and decided that the Ridge was not for him. Barry Bishop, knowing that the National Geographic Society wanted the best possible photographic coverage of the climb, switched over to the South Collars, since with them he would have the better chance for the summit. Dick Emerson was not yet in good enough shape to get above Advance Base. Barry Corbet, on the other hand, now seemed ready to go, but with Unsoeld and Hornbein, this added up to only a skeleton team of three climbers—plus, at most, the half-dozen or so Sherpas who would now be available to them.

Norman well understood their feeling of frustration and, aware that they were three of the best climbers on the expedition, offered them prominent places on the South Col team. There was more discussion, during which, according to Willi Unsoeld, "we came awfully close to tossing in our chips and joining the stampede." But their final decision was to stick with the Ridge. "Our chances for the summit are tremendously decreased," Willi said, "but surely mountaineering is more than a matter of summits—even when the summit is that of Everest."

From the overall point of view—in terms of expedition goals and a leader's responsibility—it is hard to see how Norman can be faulted for his decision, at this stage, to throw the weight of the assault at the South Col route. But one must, at the same time, salute the embattled West Ridgers. Theirs was the very essence of the spirit of "pure" mountaineering: that it is not so much the summit that matters as the fight for the summit; not the victory but the game itself.

What came to be known as "the big buildup" to the Col began immediately after the first reconnaissance team reached it on April 16 and continued for ten days. Even now, after almost a month on the mountain, not everything that was destined for the high camps had yet reached Advance Base; porter trains were still coming up through the Icefall and lower Cwm. But at least enough loads were on hand for the concentration of effort to be moved upward, and from now on there would be more Sherpas working above A.B. than below it. As throughout the expedition, there were day-to-day changes in the assignments and whereabouts of the various men (following the pattern of the Clausewitz-backgammon-musical chairs syndrome), but a specific nose count as of April 21 fairly represents the general distribution. Of the thirty-seven "regular" Sherpas, there were, on this day, ten working in the Icefall, six between Camp I and Advance Base, one at A.B. (Danu the cook), three on the West Ridge approach, four between A.B. and Camp III, on the Col route, and thirteen higher on the Col route, moving up the Lhotse Face. From Base Camp to Col, between the bottom and top of this moving ladder, there was a vertical distance of 8400 feet.

For the team members, this was a period of comparative inactivity. The West Ridgers, in their now attenuated state, did what they could on the lower part of their route. Several of the South Collars kept a hand in by helping on the carries from Advance Base to Camp III. But none went higher than III, for now, according to plan, they were hoarding their resources for the summit push soon to come. This included Gombu, Ang Dawa and Barry Bishop's Sherpa, Girmi Dorje, who were ranked as assault team members, and the getting of loads up the Lhotse Face to the Col was therefore accomplished entirely by the rank-and-file Sherpas. For operational purposes they were divided into two platoons, one of seven men and one of six, which shuttled back and forth, up and down, each spending alternate nights at Camps III and IV.

Heading Group A was the expedition's assistant sirdar, Chotari, who down below had often been something of a problem (from his record of drinking and politicking Jimmy Roberts had dubbed him "the Sherpa Irishman"), but who now, with every step higher, seemed to gain in competence and responsibility. In charge of Group B was Phu Dorje, a tough old campaigner who in another milieu would have been wearing sergeant's stripes as his badge of office.*

At the Lhotse Face altitude of 23,000 to 26,000 feet the average man-load was 40 pounds, including the usual miscellany of food, tents, stoves, climbing gear—and of course oxygen. But the Sherpas still did not use oxygen themselves; nor would they until the time came for the summit assaults. In this phase of the expedition, more than any other, there was manifest the physiological differences between Himalayan hillmen and Western lowlanders, for it is highly doubtful if any of AMEE's members could, without oxygen, have done this killing labor. The Sherpas, however, simply took it in stride. They set no speed records. They had their ailments and complaints. But they delivered the goods without breaking down; then descended and went up again, delivering more. Years ago, the early British climbers of Everest bestowed a prestigious name upon their top-level Sherpas. The name was "Tigers." And here was another generation of Tigers putting on a performance that no other men in the world could have matched.

Even a Tiger, however, is not *quite* a superman. On the Lhotse Face, this was a period of bitter cold, high winds and almost inevitable afternoon snowstorms, with consequent delays in the pre-set schedule. Twice the weather turned so bad that a carrying team had to hole up for two nights and a day at Camp IV; and on the first try for the Col itself, Phu Dorje & Company encountered a gale just past the Yellow Band and, depositing their loads there, retreated to IV. The next day, April 22, however, Chotari and his crew went all the way, and AMEE made its first appreciable contribution to "the world's highest junkyard." Two days later Phu

---

* In earlier days of Himalayan climbing Sherpas were rarely, if ever, permitted to make high carries without an escort of team members. By 1963, however, their general level of climbing competence was so good that, once a route had been prepared, unescorted carries were routine; and on AMEE the all-Sherpa parties performed in first-rate fashion.

Dorje's platoon made it. And by the twenty-sixth there were a total of seventeen loads on the Col, with fifteen more needed to supply the summit assault. These, it had been decided, would not go up in an exclusively Sherpa carry, but with the combined sahib-Sherpa task force that would make the try for the top.

Meanwhile the West Ridgers were perforce at work on a more limited scale, with the goal of stocking their Camp 3W, at 23,800 feet near Everest's West Shoulder. The first step was to get loads up to the dump that had been established on the snow and ice slopes above Advance Base, and this was accomplished largely by Willi Unsoeld and Tom Hornbein, with the help of the few Sherpas they could beg, borrow or steal. Beyond this, the plan was, if possible, to make use of one or more of the three winches—two motor-driven, one hand-operated—that had been tried out on Mount Rainier and brought along as part of the expedition's more experimental equipment. Originally it had been hoped that the winches might also be used on the South Col route; but the surface of the Lhotse Face had proved so rough and broken that, had the winch-hauled loaded sleds been used, they would have constantly been in danger of overturning. On the slopes leading to the West Ridge, however, the texture was smoother. The sledding might well be possible. And besides, with the shortage of manpower, there was, for the time being no alternative. It was either winch and sled or nothing.

Two stations were therefore set up along the route. The upper one, the site for the winch, was a few hundred feet below Camp 3W. The lower one was at the dump, at which considerable gear had by now accumulated; and successive changes in its location, necessitated by the conformation of the slopes above, resulted in there eventually being three separate depots, known respectively— not to mention confusingly—as the Old Dump, the New Dump and the New New Dump. (None of which, to make it *more* confusing, are to be confused with the dump in the Icefall.) With a vertical distance of some 2000 feet between bottom and top of the double ropeway, and the motor winches capable of hauling almost 500 pounds of deadweight, a formidable number of man-load hours could be saved when and if a winch was operative.

It was a large *when and if*, however, for Himalayan heights are even harder on mechanical equipment than on human organisms, and there was to be a long fierce struggle before the first laden sled made an upward journey. To begin with, there was the West Ridgers' current shortage in membership, for, as noted, Barry Bishop and Dave Dingman had withdrawn from the team, and they had now, with the still ailing Dick Emerson, descended to Base Camp for R & R. Of the original group, this left Willi Unsoeld, Tom Hornbein and Barry Corbet. And now they picked up one additional member in Al Auten, who had recently come up from lower Base, while Barry Prather went down to spell him at the main radio set. Auten was mechanically talented and therefore seemed a good bet for work with the winches. Corbet was eager to go high for the first time. So these two went to work on the prospective ropeway, while Unsoeld and Hornbein, with their few Sherpas, continued to carry loads from Advance Base to the dumps.

From Corbet's logbook: "*1st day:* Up from A.B. with borrowed Sherpas, carrying loads to 3W. Tough 11-hour day. Only two Sherpas stay with us. . . . *2nd day:* Dig winch site. Then take cable hundreds of feet down to dump, put skis together into a sled, place loads and self on sled and give signal for up. Slowly, about 8 feet per minute, sled jerks its way up 30-degree slope—then dies. After interminable wait Al finally calls down that winch starter is broken. Climb back up. . . . *3rd day:* Fight to compress huge coil spring which controls starter rewind. Time after time Al and I get four hands on it, pushing and poking to make it lie flat, and every time, out it comes like a jack-in-the-box. All this in below-zero temperature and high wind, with snow tearing by in a ground blizzard. . . . *4th day:* Two Sherpas go down. Put engine back together, and a completely different part of starter mechanism breaks. Go halfway down to dump to meet Willi and Tom bringing us food, fuel and second motor winch, and carry them back up. . . . *5th day:* Terrific wind and cold. Snow blows into delicate fuel mixture of alcohol, castor oil, nitro-methynal, and eventually ice, clogging all parts and enraging operator. Neither winch works. . . . *6th day:* Winches won't start. Al and I down to Advance Base. Goddam."

A few days later, he added:

"The loaded sled still hangs as a sad memento 500 feet below the winch site. Dick Emerson up from Base Camp again, feeling better, and will go up to try hand winch. Now my turn to go down for R & R—mainly to repair my broken psyche."

Other psyches, too, were having their troubles at this time. Particularly was this the case for the South Col team at Advance Base, where day followed day in drab monotony and, in terms of personal activity, the expedition seemed almost to have ground to a halt. Helping out with the carries to Camp III was little more than "made work," designed to keep bodies active and boredom at bay. The real job, during this phase of the climb, was being done by the Sherpas up on the Lhotse Face, and there was a glumly recurrent, though scarcely realistic, vision of their going on all the way to the top of the mountain while the sahibs cooled heels and behinds in the Western Cwm. THIRTEEN SHERPAS REACH SUMMIT OF EVEREST; AMERICANS GREET THEM ON DESCENT WITH CHEERS AND HOT TEA would be a fine message to send out to Kathmandu and the world beyond.

The ones who had it least badly during this period were those who, for one reason or another, descended to Base Camp on the Khumbu Glacier. Some went primarily for R & R. Others were on specific missions, such as Barry Prather, to take over the radio from Al Auten, and Dr. Dave Dingman, to have a professional look at Maynard Miller's injured foot. But for all there was a salutary effect: in the change of scene, in movement and action, in the restorative effect, physical and mental, of at least a few days at lower altitude.

Best and most special of all was Barry Bishop's downward mission; for this was the time when his wife Lila and her fellow trekkers were due at Base, and "the Barrel," by happy happenstance, found himself between West Ridge and Col Route assignments and was thus able to descend to meet her. In fact, he descended farther than Base—all the way to Lobuje, almost 2000 feet below it, where Lila and companions were camping on their upward trip. And for the next five days, there and at Base, the Bishops enjoyed what it is safe to say was the highest reunion in matrimonial history. For the romantically minded, however, Barry's

comment on their altitudinous togetherness perhaps leaves something to be desired. "I must say, sleeping at 16,000 feet with lungs
full of air certainly differed from former nights some 7000 higher,"
was his total report on their first night at Lobuje. And Lila later
confided that, while there was pleasure and joy in the reunion,
there was also a great strangeness. "It was—" she paused, thinking,
feeling "—as if Barry just wasn't there," she said. "As if, somehow,
we weren't there. Only the mountain was there." The answer
would seem to be that a man at grips with Everest has little left
for anything else—however meaningful and precious that *anything*
may be.

An exception was perhaps to be found in the expedition's scientists and specialists, who had the advantage of absorption in their
various jobs. (And these jobs, of course, were in their varying ways
part and parcel of the Everest enterprise.) Maynard Miller, still
hobbling and unable to get up into the Cwm, was nevertheless
able to do much glaciological work down at Base Camp. Barry
Prather, moving up and down between bases in the triple role of
Maynard's assistant, second-string radio operator and all-around
Mr. Fixit, was probably the busiest man on the expedition. Psychologist Jim Lester, dug in at Advance Base, had his hands—and
notebooks—full, meeting with the other men in private sessions,
recording hopes, fears, ambitions, dreams and gripes.* Sociologist
Dick Emerson, though fighting a grim acclimatization battle of his
own, conscientiously kept the team at work on his specially prepared question-and-answer diaries, and often tuned in with the tape
recorder on group discussions and walkie-talkie interchanges to
catch the interplay—and sometimes interconflict—of personalities.
Physiologist Will Siri had moved his laboratory tent from Khumbu
to Cwm and was continuing his blood and urine analyses at its
higher altitude. Also, he was conducting a series of exercise tests to
record fluctuations in pulse rate and blood pressure; and out of
them, among other findings, came at least a partial explanation of
why the Sherpas could go higher than the team members without
benefit of oxygen. Subjected to a test involving quick steppings up
and down on a box in the lab tent, the Sherpas showed no appreci-

---

* Hopes, fears, ambitions and gripes were, not unnaturally, almost all focused on
Everest. But not the dreams. Here the favored subject matters were warm sunlit
beaches and—for as yet unexplained reasons—girls with red hair.

able change, physiologically, from "before" to "after." But sahibs, the ordeal completed, had a strong inclination to collapse into the sack.

Indeed, at this stage of operations, everyone at Advance Base was spending a good deal of time in tent and sleeping bag. Will reported that "our main problem here isn't frostbite or exhaustion; it's bed sores." And Lute Jerstad commented: "We spend so much time horizontal that the ice under the tents melts away and we sleep with our heads high and our rumps in a hole." Partly this was because of the continuing wind and snowstorms, which made a sleeping bag both the most comfortable and most rational place to be. But also it was a sign that, both physically and mentally, things were beginning to stretch out a bit thin. In terms of overall timing there was no cause for worry; for there were ample food and supplies, and the team was well ahead both of its own schedule and those of previous Everest expeditions. But waiting, anywhere, is a strain. Waiting, at 21,350 feet, can become almost intolerable. And the strain was showing on those of the team who had now been at Advance Base or higher for three weeks and more, without a descent to the lower Base for R & R. For the human body, sustained living at great heights is simultaneously a fight *for* acclimatization and *against* deterioration. And now, for most of the men, deterioration—of blood and muscle, cell and corpuscle, body and spirit—was beginning to get the upper hand. Several had lost between 20 and 30 pounds. Appetites were gone. Nerves were frayed. Night after night, and during storm after storm, the temperature would drop well below zero, and there was nothing to do but huddle in tent and sleeping bag. Then the sun would come out; the ice and snow world blazed with blinding light; and in the dead warm windless calm the camp was wrapped in lassitude and apathy.

These were AMEE's dog days. Or, more aptly, gorak days, for the big black ugly birds were ubiquitous: pecking away at food boxes, waddling in and out of tents, eyeing their co-habitants of lofty Gorakville with beady questioning stares. Their tangle-winged efforts at flying seemed almost a deliberate parody of the expedition's climbing frustrations, and their endless, mindless squawking was an obbligato of futility. Letters and diary entries of this period were filled with "depressed," "bored to death," "going nuts," "can't take it much longer." Self-descriptions ranged from "rib cages with boots" to "inmates of Dachau and Buchenwald." About the best that could be obtained in philosophical detachment was Lute Jerstad's comment at the end of a comprehensive listing of complaints and miseries. "What the hell," was Lute's resigned dictum, "nuts like us ask for it."

In the midst of the general Cwm fever came a sudden happening that was far worse than "depressing" or "boring." After his long siege of weakness and semi-illness, Dan Doody had at last seemed to be acclimatizing. On April 17, following several unsuccessful attempts, he had managed to make it from Advance Base to Camp III and return, and had now hopefully begun to look forward to going even farther. On the morning of the twenty-first, however, he awoke with acute pain in his right leg, and examination by Dr. Gil Roberts showed that he had suffered an attack of thrombophlebitis. This condition, involving the formation of a clot in the bloodstream, is a not uncommon and extremely serious ailment of high-altitude living, in which the blood manufactures so many red cells it cannot carry oxygen and therefore tends to coagulate; and if Dan's clot broke away from his leg and traveled toward his heart or lungs, it would more likely than not be the end for him. Thrombophlebitis, with tragic consequences, had occurred on earlier Himalayan expeditions, and not only Gil but the whole team knew the stories well. Dan himself knew them. "If I'm unlucky and the clot travels," he wrote, still true to his diary, on the day he was stricken, "I'll be joining Jake—up here forever. Gil has the needed medicines. But when your time's up, it's up."

Dan's time, happily, wasn't. Gil bedded him down and moved into his tent with him. He put him on oxygen and an intravenous anticoagulant. And Dan's clot, staying put, gradually dissolved. His hopes of going higher, of reaching South Col or summit and performing his full function as expedition cameraman, were smashed for good and all. But after ten days of treatment and total rest he was at least out of danger, and was subsequently able to descend to Base Camp under his own power. As on so many occasions, before and after, AMEE—and Dan—had cause to give thanks for its doctors.

That was for later, however. At the time, up in Gorakville, no one knew whether Dan would live or die, and the possibility that the expedition might suffer a second fatality cast an even deeper shadow over already gloomy spirits.* It was not only the sick man —who could not yet be moved—who so desperately needed the balm of lower altitudes. "Ideally," said Norman, "we should all go down to Base Camp to recuperate for a few days, and then come up again; but the summit assault is so imminent that it is now too late, unless we get a radio weather report that we are going to have a major storm." Then, too, there were the Sherpa carrying teams high on the Lhotse Face, who of course could not be abandoned. All that remained was to watch through binoculars as the tiny dots moved on the white slopes high above; to root them on toward their South Col destination; to return to tent and sleeping bag when cloud and snow moved in and they were blotted from sight.

A tentative assault team had long ago been selected. It consisted —to no one's surprise—of Jim Whittaker, Nawang Gombu, Dick Pownall and Lute Jerstad; and it was planned that it would function in units of two, as it had during the pioneering of the route to the Col. During the days of waiting, however, Norman grew ever more convinced that this first try for the top must be as strong as expedition resources could possibly make it, with the result that now, as finally lined up, it had been greatly expanded. Instead of two teams of two, there were to be two teams of four. On successive days, exactly twenty-four hours apart, the two foursomes, each with a train of Sherpas, would move on up the mountain: from Advance Base to Camp III, from III to IV, from IV to a new Camp V, on the Col. Continuing up from V, the first unit, still accompanied by carrying Sherpas, would follow Everest's Southeast Ridge and establish a topmost camp, Number VI, as near to 28,000 feet as it could. The Sherpas would then go down.† The climbers, after spending the night at VI, would on the next day

---

* It was exactly at this time, too, that word reached Advance Base by radio that Nick Clinch was missing on his helicopter flight from Kathmandu to Namche Bazar. Nick was a close friend of many of the team members, and several days were to pass before the news came that he was safe.

† Throughout the expedition, as has been seen, there was the tricky question of when, and when not, was a Sherpa a Sherpa. Answer: In organizational terms a Sherpa was not a Sherpa when functioning as a full-fledged member of a climbing party.

make their bid for the top, returning that evening to the South Col. Meanwhile, a day behind them—weather permitting—the second unit would move up to VI and repeat the same process. In the two waves of attack, no less than eight men would be pushing toward the top of the mountain.

In the revised and enlarged roster, the first team would consist of Whittaker, Gombu, Norman Dyhrenfurth, and Ang Dawa; the second of Jerstad, Pownall, Barry Bishop and Barry's Sherpa, Girmi Dorje. Nor were these all who would soon be ascending. Following a day after the second team would come a final two-man unit of Dave Dingman and Barry Prather, also accompanied by Sherpas. Their goal, however, would not be Everest but Lhotse (for Lhotse had not been wholly forgotten), and they would branch off toward it from Camp V on the Col. If they could make the top, it would be a fine second feather in the expedition's cap. If not, they would return to the Col as support for the other teams, and then Jim Whittaker and Lute Jerstad, descending from Everest, would—if they had enough gas left—make a second try for Lohtse. All that would be missing on the heights, said an AMEE wag, was a cop to direct traffic.

The surprise member of the first summit party was of course Norman himself. Everest—the climbing of Everest—had been his lifelong dream, but he had neither wanted nor expected to be in the climbing spearhead. Aged almost forty-five, and bearing the manifold responsibilities of expedition leader, he had no desire to push himself to the front, preferring to leave the first try for the summit to younger, and presumably stronger, men. Now, however, an unforseeable situation had developed. In terms of AMEE's commitments and its potential future solvency, it was of the utmost importance that moving pictures of the climb be taken as high as was humanly possible; and it was to this end that Dan Doody had been brought along as high-level cameraman. But Dan was now totally *hors de combat*. Norman was the only other professional cameraman on the expedition. Through a simple process of subtraction and addition—and a far from simple process of thought, emotion and decision—he thus became a summit climber, committed to go as far as he could.

Similarly, Barry Bishop's inclusion in the team was, at least in part, connected with photography; in his case, stills for the *National Geographic*. Indeed, it had been specifically for a better chance at the top that he had withdrawn from the West Ridge contingent, and, along with his professional skills, he was a strong and ambitious climber. As for the Sherpas (functioning as non-Sherpas): Gombu had all along been ranked as a top summit prospect; Ang Dawa and Girmi Dorje were logical nominees both as excellent climbers and longtime companion-assistants to Norman and Barry. Jimmy Roberts pointed out that this selection would probably cause resentment among the other Sherpas, for Gombu and Ang Dawa were both from Darjeeling, with only Girmi representing the Solu Khumbu majority. But Norman was convinced that these three were the sound and reasonable choices and refused to defer to political pressures. What mattered was that, of the eight men going for the top, five would be Americans and three Sherpas (of whatever stripe), and this blend seemed to him—as to all team members—exactly as it should be. For though the two breeds came from worlds as far apart as is possible on earth, here on their mountain they were bound together, as on their ropes, by the bonds of shared venture, shared danger. In life, in the facing of death, they were companions and brothers, and it was in that relationship and no other that, God willing, they should stand together at last on earth's summit.

Other than the potential Sherpa rumblings, there were no resentments at the selection of the teams. The West Ridgers had been given the chance of switching over to the Col route—and had declined. Of the others, Dan Doody and Maynard Miller were incapacitated, and Maynard, along with Jimmy Roberts and Jim Lester, had not, in any case, been a prime summit candidate. Gil Roberts was at this time having his turn at bad altitude trouble and realized he was not up to still higher going. And for different reasons Will Siri knew that he too was destined for the Cwm and no farther. Indeed, of all the expedition members, Will had undergone the most notable psychological changes during the course of the venture. On the approach march, as noted, he had been driving, ambitious, and self-demanding, with Everest's summit, or at least its upper reaches, very much in his mind and heart. On the mountain itself, however, things became gradually different. He had no notable physical difficulties; he made the Icefall in fine form; his acclimatization problems were rather less than average. Yet change there was, for in the process of ascent Will had come to the realization that he could not simultaneously be a top climber and do justice to the vast amount of scientific work to which he was committed—and when the moment arrived for decision, it was science that came first. By the time he was established at Advance Base, his inner conflict had been resolved, and with it had gone the taut restlessness it had engendered. His decision made, he sacrificed his chance to go to the Col as a support team member, and was content to call the Cwm his ceiling, to work with dedication at his physiology, to confer and plan with Norman in his capacity as Deputy Leader. He had made his peace both with Everest and with himself.

As individuals, therefore, no expedition members felt that they had been slighted. But for the West Ridgers as a group the expansion of the Col campaign had come as still another blow to hopes and plans. The more climbers on the Col route, the more food, gear and oxygen they would need. The more food, gear and oxygen, the more Sherpas would be needed to carry them. And the consequence was that, until this first summit drive was over, the West Ridge enterprise would lose most of the few Sherpas it had, leaving it with insufficient resources to stage even a token advance. In terms of the world at large, it was scarcely a unique experience. In every organization that ever was—be it a government, an army, an institution, a business—there are times when one subdivision feels itself being shortchanged to the advantage of another. Yet even at sea level such a situation is sure to generate heat, and at 21,000-feet-plus, in a group of highly motivated men with worn bodies and ragged nerves, it could very easily become explosive. Fortunately it did not—quite. Tom Hornbein, who from the beginning had been the apostle of simultaneous and equal efforts by both routes, protested strongly and fervently. ("So they can call me a fanatic. I speak for what I believe.") Willi Unsoeld protested too. Barry Corbet and Dick Emerson, though less vocal, were with them. But in the end all recognized that Norman, as team leader and the ultimate bearer of responsibility, must also be the ultimate maker of decisions. And Norman, for his part, pointed out that, though he had no desire to be arbitrary or dictatorial, this was the only way in which the expedition could be run. He was not, he reiterated, against the West Ridge enterprise. On the contrary, he agreed that it was as alluring and exciting a challenge as could be imagined in mountaineering. But first things must come first. Then, as soon as the South Col assault was over—

Yes, as soon as—

But when would that be?

After the seemingly eternal waiting, April 25 had been set as U- (for up) Day; but when it came, storm came with it, and *up* was obviously out of the question. On the Lhotse Face, the Sherpas with their loads for the Col were holed in at Camps III and IV. At Advance Base, the climbing teams huddled in their tents. "Snowing and blowing like hell," said Jim Whittaker, "and it looks as if it would keep up forever." "The worst day yet," said Dick Pownall. "How many days can one stay here and still maintain the strength and energy to climb?"

The next day was not quite so bad, but bad enough. Up on the Face, the Sherpas at IV made a try for the Col, but encountered deep snowdrifts and turned back. The Sherpas at III and the sahibs at A.B. stayed put, while morale dropped to a new low. During the afternoon Norman called a meeting in the big mess tent, and it was decided that on the following day there would *have* to be movement, one way or the other. If the weather cleared, it would be up. If it did not, it would be down—all the way to Base Camp. "If we stay here any longer," Norman said, "we'll never make it. We'll be too deteriorated, too far gone." And physiologist Will Siri was even more emphatic in his opinion that, if the ordeal continued, it might well spell doom for the whole expedition.

The men returned to their tents. Dan Doody (who had not left his tent) lay for the sixth day immobile in his sleeping bag. The others crawled into their bags; tried to read, to sleep—and waited. Toward evening they crawled out again, returned to the mess tent, struggled to force food down into their skinny bodies. The wind howled. The goraks pecked and croaked. Back in the sack, the men tried to sleep—and waited.

In the morning the wind was down. The sun beamed in splendor.

11. THE MAYPOLE

"YIPPEEEE!"

The Himalayan cowboy was Lute Jerstad, his mount was the Sherpa Chotari, and together they pranced about Advance Base with Lute brandishing an ice ax. As a member of the second echelon, he wasn't even leaving that day. But one day didn't matter. The sun shone. The assault was on. Though Lute, with Chotari's cooperation, was the only equestrian, that morning of April 27 was a great one for everybody in camp. As if by the wave of a wand, the depression, dissension and lethargy of the past two weeks were swept away in a tide of energy and joy.

Since it was only a three-hour slog to Camp III, the first team did not leave until after lunch. During the morning clothes were changed, rucksacks were packed, and though every superfluous ounce was carefully eliminated, the loads averaged 45 to 55 pounds per man. Norman's gear leaned heavily toward moving picture equipment. And to Jim Whittaker's pack, affixed to its frame with bright orange tape, something new had been added: a 4-foot aluminum stake, ordinarily used as a rappel picket, but now bearing a tightly furled 3′ by 4′ American flag. The flag would not be unfurled until—

But the men were not talking of that. Thinking, yes. But not talking. Indeed, as the time for departure came, the camp grew quiet. The shouting and horseplay had ended. Here at last was U-Day, U-Hour—the countdown had reached zero—and many things, of one sort and another, could happen before those who were now leaving returned. Backs were slapped, hands were shaken; then slowly the column began to move. There was more than a foot of fresh snow beyond camp in the upper reaches of the Cwm, which would mean fairly strenuous trail-breaking for whoever went first; and there was a bit of nonheroic backing and filling, Jim Whittaker reported, as to who would have the dubious honor of leading. "The Sherps kept waiting for me to leave," he said, "and managed to outwait me waiting for them." So Big Jim, roped to Gombu, went ahead. Norman and Ang Dawa followed. And after them trudged a file of thirteen Sherpas. If plans held, all thirteen would go with the team up the Lhotse Face to the Col; eight would go on from the Col to help establish Camp VI; and beyond that Jim and Gombu, Norman and Ang Dawa, would be on their own.

The trek up to Camp III was, as always, made without oxygen. (And, also as always, said Norman, "that final glacial slope up to the tents was a killer.") But that night the climbing team slept on a light flow, with plastic masks, and also used it the next day at a 3-liter-per-minute rate, on the climb up the Lhotse Face to Camp IV. On this second day, April 28, the weather continued fine; but here, as below, there was much new snow, and Jim and Gombu, still leading the way, had to kick thousands of steps and, on the steeper pitches, uncover the fixed ropes that were now buried in drifts. Norman, with Ang Dawa assisting, alternated between climbing and filming—the latter a no less laborious assignment than that of Jim and Gombu, involving heavy load-carrying, the finding of stances, the setting up of tripod and camera, all on a precipitous slope at a height of 23,000 to almost 25,000 feet. During the course of it, incidentally, Norman was setting a personal record of his own. His previous top in climbing altitude had been a camp on this same Lhotse Face during the International Himalayan Expedition of 1955, and every step he took beyond its site—about halfway along in the day's ascent—was a step higher than he had ever been before.

The thirteen carrying Sherpas (as distinguished from the now non-

Sherpa Gombu and Ang Dawa) were still climbing without oxygen, but were old timers on the route and, with one exception,
were doing well. The exception was young Ang Norbu, the eldest
son of the expedition sirdar, Passang Phutar; and son, like father
(who never got to Advance Base) was apparently allergic to Everest, for soon after leaving Camp III he complained of feeling ill
and dropped out of the procession. This meant that his load had
to be distributed among the remaining twelve. But dropouts, with
resultant heavier burdens, are expected occurrences in high Himalayan climbing, and the others took it in stride. By midafternoon,
in a light snowfall, the column came up around the tall ice tower
at 24,900 feet, which Jim Whittaker and Gombu had first reached
fifteen days before, and a few moments later were at Camp IV.
What had once been an empty shelf of ice was now a huddle of
three 4-man tents and two 2-man tents, pitched by the Sherpa
teams on their earlier carries; and soon all were crowded with men,
gear, food and butane stoves. While the Sherpas prepared the
evening meal, Norman and Jim unlimbered their walkie-talkie, reported their arrival to listeners below, and learned that the second
assault team of Jerstad, Pownall, Bishop and Girmi Dorje, with
four carrying Sherpas, had, as scheduled, come up from Advance
Base to Camp III.

So far, so good.

But that night came the first contretemps in what was presently
to become the expedition's thorniest and most controversial aspect:
the use, conservation—and/or nonconservation—of oxygen. The
regulator on Norman's apparatus sprang a leak. Instead of going to
his lungs, part of the gas passing from cylinder to mask seeped out
into the air with a depressing hiss, and there were neither effective
tools at hand to fix it nor spare regulators for replacement. Ang
Dawa, whose devotion to his Bara Sah'b was total, immediately
insisted on exchanging regulators. But Norman said no; Ang Dawa,
no less than he, would soon be going all out to reach Everest's
summit and must also have a dependable oxygen flow. The exchange should be with one of the Sherpas who would be going no
higher than Camp VI. Gombu was brought into the discussion
and, going to the other Sherpas, asked that one of them give up
his own regulator for the faulty one. But in spite of the fact that

none was using oxygen that night, all refused. Norman was convinced that the refusal was directed not so much at himself as at Gombu and Ang Dawa, in still another manifestation of the Solu Khumbu versus Darjeeling feud, and his impulse was to go to the Sherpa tents and settle the matter himself. With his gravelly laryngitic voice, however, he could speak in no more than a highly unauthoritative whisper. So, for the time being, he refrained from forcing the issue, and Ang Dawa spent the night and the next day with the leaking oxygen gear.

Another probable—and understandable—reason for the Sherpas' recalcitrance was that, on this next day, they were to be using oxygen for the first time. Or at least some of them. The four who would carry only to the Col and then descend would, as on earlier carries, climb without it. But the eight who would go on to establish Camp VI had been issued their gear and had it explained to them, and the day of the ascent from Camp IV to Col had been designated as the time when they would begin to use it. The masks, tubes and cylinders were, to them, not merely items with a practical purpose. They were status symbols, differentiating the super-Tigers from the lesser ones, and no one wanted a second-class status symbol. On the morning of the twenty-ninth, therefore, the argument was not reopened. Ang Dawa kept the leaking regulator. Packs were hoisted, oxygen turned on, and the day's climb began.

Again the weather was fine, and during the first part of the ascent there were no problems. As before, Big Jim and Gombu led the way, clearing fresh snow from the steps and uncovering the fixed ropes that had been strung by Lute Jerstad and Dick Pownall on their pioneer climb to the Col. Norman, roped together with Ang Dawa and the Sherpa Passang Temba (one of the four without oxygen), followed along behind, filming the column as it crossed the icy chute of the Lhotse Couloir and approached the stony outcrop of the Yellow Band. Here, on the rotten rock with its plastering of snow, the going grew harder. Axes could not dig in, and crampon prongs caught on the rough footing, sometimes tearing the whole crampon loose from a boot. ("My own came off three times," said Norman, "but good old patient Ang Dawa was always there to help me get them back on.") After the Yellow Band came a long slog up the slope of a snow bowl, and above this the more solid but steeper crags of the Geneva spur. At this point the weather began to deteriorate rapidly, with clouds covering the sun, the beginning of snowfall, and wind that grew stronger and stronger as the climbers neared the South Col. Never in Everest's history had an expedition encountered quiet windless conditions at this "most desolate place on earth," and the assault teams of AMEE were to be no exception.

Taking the shortcut blazed by Chotari and Nima Tenzing on the first reconnaissance climb, Jim, Gombu, and the vanguard of the Sherpas reached the Col about midafternoon. Then, picking their way through the debris of old camps, they came to the site where the earlier Sherpa carriers had dumped their loads and set about pitching their own Camp V. No one had yet spent a night here. Tents still had to be set up, and for an hour or more, in the gale, there was a struggle with flying guy lines and billowing fabrics. During the process, one half-pitched tent was hit by so strong a gust that it broke loose and somersaulted away; but eventually it was caught and pinioned. And presently, to the ghost world of old abandoned habitations there had been added a new and living one: three low aluminum-ribbed four-man tents hunched together in lonely companionship in the desolation of rock and ice.

Meanwhile, Jim sent two Sherpas back down onto the Geneva Spur to help Norman, Ang Dawa and Passang Temba, who were still struggling up with their loads of photographic equipment. When the tents were pitched and secure, the four Sherpas who were to go no farther began their descent to Camp IV. Then the remaining twelve men dug in for the night, with Norman, Jim, Gombu, and Ang Dawa sharing one tent and the eight Sherpas distributed in the two others. Almost immediately, the oxygen hassle of the previous night was resumed; for Norman had now decided that both he and Ang Dawa *must* have properly function-ing regulators for the highest climbing, and this time he sent in-terpreter Gombu to the Sherpa tents not with a request, but with a direct order, that an exchange of apparatus be effected. In the end, one of the best of the men, Ang Nyima, complied. That crisis was settled. But simultaneously another developed, when it was discovered that for the twelve men at the camp there were only eleven sleeping bags. Again the Sherpas were in the driver's seat—

meaning, more literally, in eight of the bags—and possession, in the Himalaya as elsewhere, being eleven points of the law, they stayed there, leaving the "sahib tent" with the mathematical problem of three bags and four bodies. Once more it was Ang Dawa who, at his own insistence, made the sacrifice: sleeping without a bag and, swathed in double layers of clothing, wedging himself as tightly as possible between Big Jim and Gombu. But this time he at least had a nonleaking oxygen rig, and with four men piled so closely together he did not suffer from cold.

Before all this, of course, there had been the labor of preparing the evening meal. Of readying stoves, melting ice into water, opening packets and cans with half-frozen fingers—with, finally, the ordeal of eating, the reward of drinking. Then within the tents, as night came, there was darkness and stillness: three tiny pockets of stillness, five miles high in the substratosphere, engulfed and lost in the winds of space.

April 30—

In the morning, on the Col, the winds still howled. The tents flapped and trembled. But again the decision was *up*, and presently twelve masked and laden figures were moving on across the bleak wilderness of ice and stone. Behind them, the summit crags of Lhotse loomed like dark ruined castles in the scudding sky. Ahead —"a mountain on top of a mountain"—rose the last 2828 feet of Everest.

At Camp IV on the Lhotse Face, the second team was also making ready and setting out. The previous day's climbing, up from III, had gone well—with Lute Jerstad and Dick Pownall, who knew the route, leading, followed by Barry Bishop, Girmi Dorje and four other Sherpas. In the evening they had been unable to get the higher team on the radio. (Indeed, on this first summit assault none of the walkie-talkies functioned above Camp IV.) But during the afternoon they had seen them moving up over the Yellow Band; they knew the Col had been occupied, and now it was their turn to move up after. As in every group, each climber, according to his own temperament, behaved a little differently from the others. Waiting for the take-off, Dick was quiet and controlled. Lute moved about, restless, impatient. Barry secured his crampon straps with measured, almost dramatic deliberation. Then he was ready. The Sherpas were ready. Packs were slung, oxygen turned on—and they were on their way.

From Camp III, at the foot of the Lhotse Face, Dave Dingman and Barry Prather, with three Sherpas, were on their way to IV. Above them, high on the Face, was the steep ice couloir that had been the Swiss route to Lhotse's summit in 1956. But whether they would have a chance at it themselves or merely act as support for the two Everest echelons would be determined by what happened during the next two days higher up.

At Advance Base, on this day, there were only Gil Roberts, Jim Lester, Dan Doody, and a handful of the oldest and youngest Sherpas. "Danu the cook," wrote diarist Dan, "gave his usual breakfast signal by banging a pot with a ladle. A tall skinny figure crawled out of his smelly sleeping bag, where he had lain for a week, with his body heat melting a hip hole 8 inches deep in the ice beneath the tent floor. After dressing slowly, he got to his feet with the aid of tent poles, and standing, he felt like a newborn colt with long shaky legs. Then he walked, very carefully, past a stretcher (brought up from Base to carry him down) to the mess tent. . . ." As if to celebrate the occasion, one of the pressure stoves exploded. But Danu was unconcerned. He only laughed. And Dan laughed too, because he now knew that he was not going to die.

On the white slopes directly above Advance Base a skeleton force of West Ridgers was still doggedly at work. After their ordeal with the motor winch and ropeway, Barry Corbet and Al Auten had gone down to the lower Base for R & R, and Willi Unsoeld and Tom Hornbein had taken their place. Then it became Willi and Tom's turn to go down, and Barry came up again—this time with Dick Emerson, who was at last winning his long battle for acclimatization. As helpers they had four Sherpas, only two of whom were really functioning, and the endless labor on the transportation route continued: from Advance Base to the three dumps, from the dumps up to Camp 3W near Everest's West Shoulder. By the last day of April they had given up on the motor winch and were working with the hand winch—a killing labor at such an altitude, and thus far not a fruitful one. From Dick's notes:

"Winching again, with one of us at each end of the cable. Sled heads for big pit in ice. Try to divert it by running cable around ax, but pressure hurls ax 100 yards through the air with sled going on into pit." So it went. With another try. And another.

At Base Camp, down on the Khumbu Glacier, Maynard Miller was still hobbling about on his broken foot. Will Siri and Jimmy Roberts were down. Al Auten was again at the main radio rig, trying to make contact with the high climbing teams, but from the South Col and above there was only static and silence.

In the Icefall, the lower-level Sherpas, under the direction of Jimmy R. and Noddy Rana, were still on their eternal treadmill, packing loads up through the labyrinth. Ang Pema, the Sherpa who had barely escaped with his life in the accident that killed Jake Breitenbach, had since his recovery continued working in the Icefall; but now, in a second accident, he fell into a crevasse and was saved only by the rope that bound him to his companions. With this, Ang Pema decided he had had enough Icefall and asked that he be transferred to a higher station, where things might go better for him and certainly could go no worse.

In the Western Cwm, Willi Unsoeld and Tom Hornbein moved down toward the Icefall on their way to R & R at Base Camp. "We watched the play of light and shadow," said Willi, "over the endless march of crevasse lips near the mouth of the Cwm." The shadows were blue. And they too were blue; for it was hard to be going down when they knew that behind them, on the heights, others were going up toward the distant goal. They were convinced they had done right in declining the invitation to be members of the South Col team. They still believed that the West Ridge was the greatest of challenges and adventures. Yet— "Yet," said Willi, "there is a magic about the summit that makes it hard to turn one's back to it at almost the moment of its attainment; a moment so symbolic of the conquest by the best elements of the human spirit over the dross of laziness, timidity and selfishness." And it was therefore silently, a little glumly, that the philosopher-mountaineer and the anesthesiologist-mountaineer slogged on down. At Base Camp there was at least better breathing and fresh eggs and goat meat brought up from Solu Khumbu. They went on making their plans. They bided their time.

—While more than 8000 feet above them, on the South Col, twelve men moved on toward "the mountain on top of a mountain."

The bugaboo of oxygen problems, however, moved right on with them. Indeed, on this morning of April 30, it struck at the first assault team with what might be called a triple whammy. First, it was discovered that many of the bottles, including those not in use, had lost much of their pressure because of the cold and altitude. Second, the Sherpas, who were not supposed to sleep on oxygen —only to climb with it—had, it developed, used up some nine bottles during the night. And third, Ang Nyima, who had exchanged regulators with Ang Dawa the previous evening, turned out to be not quite the gold-plated hero he had seemed. Having spent the night with the faulty gadget, he had had all he wanted of it; in the morning he had somehow talked Ang Dawa into a re-exchange; and the first Norman knew about it was after the Sherpas had already taken off from Camp V (for he and Ang Dawa had, as usual, stayed behind taking pictures) and it was too late to affect a re-re-exchange. "I then tried to fix the thing," said Norman. "Taking the screw mount off Ang Dawa's regulator, I replaced it with one from my oxygen mask repair kit. I tightened every screw on his apparatus and taped up the place where the gas seemed to escape. But all to no avail—it still kept right on with its damnable hissing."

So, hiss and all, they went on after the others.

Except for the strong bitter wind, the going at first was not difficult. To begin with, there was the flat boulder-strewn plateau of the Col and then a glacial slope angling gently upward. At the head of the slope, however, the ascent grew steeper. The route— first pioneered by Raymond Lambert and Tenzing on the first Swiss expedition of 1952; later followed by the British, the Swiss of 1956 and the two Indian expeditions—led up a long narrow couloir that rose steeply toward the skyline of Everest's Southeast Ridge. The ridge itself was almost invisible behind veils of streaming windblown snow; but now and then there were clear glimpses of Jim Whittaker, Gombu and the Sherpas climbing the upper reaches of the couloir.

As Norman and Ang Dawa neared the couloir, Norman felt a tug on the rope. Turning, he saw that the breathing bladder of Ang Dawa's oxygen apparatus was no longer inflating and deflating, which meant that the cylinder was empty. "So I cramponed down to him," Norman said, "and disconnected the tube and regulator from that bottle. Taking the bottle from his rucksack, I threw it off down the slope, and then I connected the regulator—that damned bad one, unfortunately—to his second full bottle." At least Ang Dawa was now again getting *some* oxygen. And as a small bonus, the discarded cylinder reduced by one-tenth their combined load-weight (of oxygen, extra clothing, climbing and photographic gear) of some 130 pounds.

In any case, Ang Dawa went on all right. Norman went on all right. "In fact, at this stage," he commented, "I was feeling good. This day, for the first time since leaving Advance Base, I was sure that I could get to the Southeast Ridge and on up to the highest camp. There was no certainty in my mind that I could go higher. But in the past I had had doubts if I could even reach the Col— and here I was above it, at the ripe old age of almost forty-five."

As they climbed still higher, however, that "ripe old age" began to make itself felt. Near the top of the couloir there was a traverse across steep ice and snow that required careful belaying with rope and ax; and beyond that, on the outcrop beneath the ridge, there was the same sort of treacherous footing, on rotten rock and plastered snow, as they had encountered the day before on the Yellow Band. Feet slipped and tripped. Catching on rock, Norman's left crampon came loose no less than four times, and each time it had to be laboriously retied. "By the time we reached the ridge," said Norman, "I was pretty well done in." He and Ang Dawa rested—went on again—rested—went on again. "Up ahead, we could see that Jim, Gombu and the Sherpas had stopped and were preparing a camp. It seemed fairly close. But it took us hours to get there. . . ."

The others had come up more quickly and easily—if "easily" is a word that can ever be used for movement on Everest's heights. At any rate, they moved steadily. The wind was strong, but not overpowering. The cold was bitter, but not unendurable. Reaching the ridge, they had followed it upward, now on its crest, now to its left a bit below it, slogging on through a mixed footing of rock and snow. By early afternoon they were a thousand feet above the South Col—at 27,200 feet, then higher—but, as through the whole of the ascent from Base Camp, the top of Everest was still hidden from view. Above, the ridge culminated, or seemed to, in a white point in the sky. But this was not the true summit. It was the South Summit, 28,750 feet high. The ultimate peak would not be visible until on the next day, God willing, someone came up over the subpeak and went on from there.

Even this close to earth's last outpost there were human relics. Out of the waste of rock and snow emerged the remnants of the highest Indian camp, the highest Swiss camp, tiny clusters of rusted tent poles, torn fabric, empty and abandoned oxygen bottles. The top British camp (their Camp IX), from which Hillary and Tenzing had gone on to their victory, had been even higher than these —at almost 27,900 feet upon the Southeast Ridge—and it had been Norman's hope to place his own final tents at roughly the same altitude. But this was not to be. A short distance beyond the Swiss camp, at about 27,450 feet, the Sherpas decided that they were now higher than any previous camp, and accordingly dropped their loads. Gombu, at the time, was also under the impression that they had somehow passed the British Camp IX without seeing it; and Jim Whittaker had no reason to question their opinion. Only Norman was aware, from his close study of the 1953 ascent, that this site was still a good deal farther up the ridge. But since he was still struggling uphill a few hundred feet below the advance party, it was the Sherpas, not he, who had the last word on Camp VI.

There was no such thing as a level place on the ridge, and it took the ten men two hours to carve out a platform and pitch two 2-man tents side by side. One was on snow, one on rock, and both were anchored as securely as possible by ropes, pitons and such heavy objects as were available. Everyone worked without oxygen. The cylinders were stacked nearby in the snow, and when the tents were up and it was time for the Sherpas to go down, Jim expected them to leave not only the full ones they had brought up but also the now partly filled ones from which they had breathed on the ascent. Indeed, this had been a part of the basic plan: that the Sherpas would descend from VI without oxygen, leaving the whole supply for the first and second assault teams. But when the time came the Sherpas were having none of it. Even at 27,450 feet, they had plenty of breath left for argument. On the Swiss expedition of 1956, they pointed out, the porters had gone down from the highest camp using oxygen—and if this was all right with the Swiss, why not with the Americans? Jim and Gombu did their futile best to persuade them. When they saw it was a lost cause, they pleaded that at least one set with a good regulator be left, so that Ang Dawa would not have to climb the next day with a leaking valve. And at last, as on the previous night at the Col, one hero emerged: this time the Sherpa Dawa Tenzing. Indeed, he was a rather more bona fide one than Ang Nyima, in that, once he had turned over his apparatus, he did not subsequently take it back. But the others were not to be moved. Up they had come on oxygen, down they would go on it, and that was that.

By now it is perhaps apparent that the Sherpas are a very special breed, not only as mountaineers but as men. And nowhere could this be better illustrated than in the hassle at Camp VI. They love to argue; they are dedicated to what they conceive to be their rights. But at one and the same time they are trustworthy, loyal, helpful, and just about everything else in the boy scout catalog— and, most of all, they are good-natured. There was no sullenness or rancor in their waging of the oxygen battle. They argued, they made their point, they won it, and in the next moment they were grinning, shaking hands, wishing Jim and Gombu the best of luck. Then they took off down the ridge, and after a while came to Norman and Ang Dawa, who were still plodding upward. "I was horrified," said Norman, "when I saw that seven out of the eight of them were still wearing masks and carrying bottles." But he too was unable to persuade them to give them up. There were more grins, more handshakes, a warm "good luck, Bara Sah'b!"—and down they went to the South Col.

As Norman trudged on, it was not exactly through the happiest moments he had known on the mountain. He was tired almost to exhaustion. Seven precious cylinders of oxygen were on their way down, instead of up, the ridge. And as he approached the camp he realized it was lower by some hundreds of feet than he had hoped and planned it would be. On his arrival, however, he did not make an issue of this. With the Sherpas gone, nothing could be done about it; and besides, he had strength for little more than to crawl into one of the tents and lie sucking the breath of life from his own oxygen rig. "Later, when I had come to a bit," he said, "I did considerable worrying about the comparatively low position of the camp." But there was still no way to change worry into action. And on the credit side, there was at least the fact that the day's carry, by twelve men, had been by far the largest to a top camp in all of Everest's history.

At VI now, the daylight waned. The wind grew stronger, the cold deeper. Again there was the long procedure of melting snow, tending a cooker, preparing food and drink, more laborious than ever now that the Sherpas were gone and at an altitude at which even the slightest effort caused a gasping for breath. As always, in the men's dehydrated condition, it was liquids, not solids, that were most wanted and needed. They drank juices. They drank boiling, but lukewarm, coffee and tea. They struggled to unfreeze, and finally ate, some canned peaches. Then they settled in for the night —Norman sharing a tent with Ang Dawa and Jim with Gombu, for the two big sahibs together could scarcely have fitted into one of the tiny shelters. Norman took a sleeping pill, set his oxygen flow, and managed to doze fitfully, but toward the middle of the night his cylinder ran out and left him panting convulsively. "Then with cold hands," he said, "you try to dig out another bottle, with the fingers of your hands sticking to the frosted metal. You have to turn on your flashlight, disconnect your breathing hose from the regulator, put the regulator on the new bottle, connect the hose, then set the flow at 1 liter a minute and wait for the breathing bladder to fill with oxygen. When all that's done, you turn off the flashlight and try to find sleep again—with another pill."*

During the early hours of darkness the wind had dropped and it was fairly calm. The hope and prayer was that it would stay that

* Most, though not all, of the team members had to take barbiturates for sleep during much of their time on the mountain.

way. But it did not. Later, the wind rose again; lightning streaked the sky; the tents swayed and trembled in the tides of night.

May 1—
In the morning, Everest's first conqueror, Sir Edmund Hillary, looked up at the mountain from his camp at the base of neighboring Taweche. Never, he said, had he seen its snow plume boiling more wildly, nor more impossible conditions for a try for the top. At Advance Base in the Western Cwm, Dan Doody wrote in his diary, "Expect all above are staying put for the day."

Both Sir Edmund and Dan, however, were later to have a surprise. For there was no staying put that day on the summit slopes of Everest.

At first light Jim Whittaker and Gombu were astir in their tent. From within they could feel the cold and hear the roar of the gale, but when they peered out they saw that the sky, above the driven veils of surface snow, was clear and almost cloudless. "It was not the weather we had hoped for," said Jim, "but we had climbed in worse, and we decided to go on up and make our try." Even in their sleeping bags they had been wearing much of their clothing, but now they put on everything else they had that could be fitted over their frames and still allow them to move. When Jim left the tent, he had on his feet three pairs of woolen socks and stockings, heavy climbing boots and, over these, nylon overboots that came almost to his knees.* Covering his body he had, in successive layers, thermal cotton-wool underwear, a turtle-neck T-shirt, down underwear, a wool shirt, wool climbing pants, a pair of down-filled pants, a down jacket, a waterproofed parka and a down parka. For his hands he had cotton gloves, wool mittens and leather and canvas shells—which he later changed for down mittens. Protecting his head was the light helmet of his oxygen rig, a wool pullover toque, the hood of the waterproofed parka and the fur-trimmed hood of the down parka. Over his face went big skiing goggles and his oxygen mask. Onto his back went a pack containing two full oxygen bottles, rope, other climbing gear, a camera, a canteen, a bit of food and some extra clothing, to a total of about 45 pounds.

---

* What were called "overboots" were actually not boots at all, but simply nylon coverings designed to keep snow out of the climbing boots.

Outside, with already cold fingers, he laced his crampons on over his boots. He tied on his end of a climbing rope. He hefted his ice ax. And he was ready. Gombu, similarly clothed and accoutered, was ready. It was 6:15 A.M. The sun was up. The wind howled.

Norman and Ang Dawa were still in their tent, not yet ready to leave; and it was decided that Jim and Gombu would go ahead on their own, for their pace, in any case, would be faster than that of the other two. Following after, Norman, with Ang Dawa's help, would try to film them through telescopic lenses higher up on the peak.

The two lead men started off, and in the beginning, as Jim reported it, "moved fairly rapidly up from camp; first traversing the slopes to the left of the ridge; then cutting back up to the ridge-line and following it toward the point where it steepens into the rise to the South Summit." The wind buffeted them. Worse, it half blinded them, carrying snow that coated their goggles and sifted in at the sides onto their eyelids and lashes. Even when they removed the goggles to wipe them—and this was dangerous, because of possible resultant snow blindness—they could see little beyond the white slant of the ridge. Off to the south of them, beyond the notch of the Col, was Lhotse; to the southeast, a mere 12 miles distant, was Makalu; but even the vast masses of earth's fourth and fifth highest mountains were only occasionally visible in bits and pieces through the driving spume. Soon they were higher than Makalu's summit—then higher than Lhotse's—but only their altimeter told them so. Only the altimeter and their plodding feet told them that they were getting closer, ever closer, to the highest summit of all.

The snow on the ridge was deep. Taking turns in the lead, Jim and Gombu had to kick steps all the way. But at least the snow was of a consistency that they *could* kick; only at rare intervals did it become so hard that they had to cut steps with their axes. As they went, they kept looking for the remains of the highest British camp —the famous Hillary-Tenzing camp of 1953, which they now knew to be well above their own Camp VI. (It had been close beside the ridge and, if still there, would be visible even through the pall of snow.) But they found no sign of it. Unlike the Swiss and Indian camps lower down, it had apparently blown away, to its last remnants. They climbed on. A few steps. A pause for rest. Another few steps. Another pause. And at about eight o'clock they reached the point where the ridge steepens toward the South Summit.

Here they decided that, to lighten their loads, they would each dump one of their two cylinders of oxygen. They discarded the partly used ones, leaving them in a conspicuous place where they could find and retrieve them on the descent, then attached their regulators to the full cylinders and moved on again. As through most of the climb, there was rock on their left and snow on their right, both falling off into abysses below. And at the bottom of the right-hand abyss, some two miles down, lay the Kangshung Glacier, in Tibet. Like the West Ridge, the Southeast Ridge was the border-line between Tibet and Nepal, but, unlike the West Ridge climbers, Jim and Gombu got no more than a foot, or part of a foot, into Chinese territory. "A very delicate margin had to be maintained here," said Jim. "If we got too far out on the snow, it would almost surely avalanche, carrying us down with it, while the rock on the other side made for hard going with our crampons. So we stayed between the two, working back and forth, zigzagging, taking to the rock when it was necessary and hitting the edge of the snow when the rock became too steep."

Progress was now much slower than before. There were pauses not only for rest but for protective belaying over the steeper pitches. During this stage Big Jim stayed in the lead, using a 3-liter flow of oxygen, carefully testing each step, each stance, before he used it.

Kick, kick. Pause. Kick, kick.

Below, Norman and Ang Dawa had left Camp VI at about 7:15, and now they too were inching upward, bent almost double in the tide of wind and snow. With Norman's photographic gear—movie camera, two still cameras, tripod and film—added to oxygen bottles and other items, their loads were heavier than Jim's and Gombu's: more than 50 pounds apiece. And with such a burden, and in such weather, Norman had no illusion about making the top of Everest. His best hope was to reach the South Summit, at 28,750 feet, and from there to film the others on the summit ridge beyond. Even this, however, would depend on an easing of the wind and driven snow; and as the minutes, and then the hours, dragged by, there was no indication of this happening. The snow had blown so quickly into the tracks made by Jim and Gombu that Norman, who was leading, had to break trail all over again. "My back-pack," he said, "grew heavier and heavier, and I was taking three or four breaths for every step. I counted my steps, and after every twenty I rested. Then after every ten. . . ."

Came a tug on the rope, and turning, he had to clean out his snow-filled goggles before he could see Ang Dawa gesturing. Even with the sound regulator he was now using, Ang Dawa's first oxygen bottle was used up, and, as he had on the previous day, Norman descended to him and hooked up his breathing hose to the second bottle. Then they went on again. They came, after a while, to a small snow shoulder where the ridge leveled off before beginning its steep climb to the South Summit. And here Norman's first oxygen bottle gave out. Taking it from his pack, he threw it off the right—the snowy—side of the ridge and watched it vanish into the mist on its 2-mile journey toward the Kangshung Glacier: a gift for the honorable Comrades of Peking and Lhasa. He hooked into his second bottle. Then he turned to his companion and said "Ang Dawa, this is it."

The little Sherpa wanted to go on. "But I explained to him," said Norman "—though I didn't use such fancy language—that this was the point of no return. If we went on, we would run out of oxygen about halfway between the South Summit and the Main Summit, and that would be that: we would never get down alive. Also, we couldn't reach the Main Summit, so we wouldn't even be dead heroes on the top of Everest." In the prevailing conditions it would have been fruitless to struggle on even to the South Summit for photographic purposes. In the shroud of blowing snow, the Main Summit, Jim and Gombu, anything beyond the range of a few yards, would be as invisible to a camera's lens as to the human eye. It would be a matter simply of packing the killing loads up— then down again.

Through a brief rift in the shroud they had a glimpse of Lhotse. Its crest was 27,890 feet high, and they were clearly above it: about 28,200 feet was a fair estimate. Well—the goal was still 800 feet above. The dream of Norman's lifetime was not going to be realized. But at least he had climbed 4,000 feet higher than he had ever in his life been before. He was at the highest point on earth ever reached by a man of his age or by the leader of an expedition.

"Well, Ang Dawa—"

Ang Dawa, a bare 5 feet tall, but with every inch indomitable, was not yet quite convinced. He pointed. "Up go, Bara Sah'b?" he asked.

Norman shook his head. "No, Ang Dawa," he said. "Down go." And slowly, gropingly, down they went.

That was at 11:30 in the morning. At almost exactly the same moment Jim Whittaker and Nawang Gombu came up the steep slant of the ridge and stood on Everest's South Summit. Some 300 feet below it, Gombu's sharp eyes had spied a small green object lying on a patch of reddish rock, and picking it up, he had put it in his parka pocket. It was a metal typewriter-ribbon box. Inside it were a Catholic rosary and a medallion of Pope John XXIII that had been given to the 1962 Indian Expedition by Father Marshall Moran of Kathmandu, and the top Indian climbers had left it to mark the highest point of their ascent. All this, however, was not learned until later. At the time, Gombu simply shoved the box into his pocket. He and Jim had other things on their minds as they pushed on to the South Summit and stood looking at what lay beyond.

It was a scene which only eight men had ever looked upon before. First there had been Hillary, Charles Evans, Tom Bourdillon and Tenzing, of the 1953 British Expedition. Three years after them there had been four Swiss: Jürg Marmet, Ernst Schmied, Adolf Reist and Hansrudolf von Gunten. But for Jim at least, who had repeatedly studied it in photographs, it was as familiar as the slopes of his own Mount Rainier. Familiar—yet at the same time unfamiliar, at the same time strange and alien; for there is always a difference between picture and reality, and always a difference in the eyes that see them. The vertical distance from South Summit to *the* summit was only 278 feet. "But the climb," said Jim, "looked longer than I'd expected. It looked steeper than I'd expected." For five minutes he and Gombu rested, their goggled eyes moving up the ridge.

They had been later in reaching the South Summit than they had hoped to be, and they had used up a fair part of their second bottles of oxygen. It was still deathly cold. The wind still roared. But visibility was better than it had been lower down, with only a concentrated snow cloud blowing away to the east. In any case, there was little debating of pros and cons. The two men were committed. "I will," Jim Whittaker had said back home, when he had been asked if he would climb to Everest's summit. And now the time had come. "I will go where you have gone," Gombu had told Tenzing before he left his home in Darjeeling. The time had come for him too.

From the South Summit the ridge broke downward almost vertically for about 30 feet, and they descended cautiously. Then, from a small snow saddle, it rose again, and they followed it up. As before, they hewed close to a line where rock on the left met snow on the right; but this time they were even more careful not to venture far onto the snow, for they knew that here, on Everest's final heights, the snow projected from the mountain wall in great cornices that could crumble without warning beneath their feet. Jim led a pitch, belayed, and Gombu followed. Jim led another pitch, belayed, and Gombu followed. And in the process history, in a fashion, was repeating itself, for, as with Hillary and Tenzing ten years earlier, here again were a Man of the West and a Man of the East climbing together to the summit of the world. To whatever God, Christian or Buddhist, who may have been watching, they must have presented a strange contrast—these two dots inching upward—for one dot, Big Jim, was, at 6 foot 5, the tallest man on the expedition, and the other, Gombu, was more than a foot shorter. But in what it took to keep going they shared and shared alike.

Joined by their length of nylon rope, they were as alone as two men can be on earth's surface. Yet at the same time they were not alone, for, in all but the physical, palpable sense, other men were there with them. Hillary and Tenzing were surely there. The four Swiss were there. And not only these who had preceded them in their path, but many others as well. The old Everesters, from Mallory onward, who had first dreamed the dream and blazed the way; the later Everesters—British, Swiss, Indian—who had tried and triumphed and tried and failed: all who had struggled and aspired on the mountain were there beside them, and none knew better than Jim and Gombu what they owed to those who had gone before. They knew, too, what they owed to their own fellow climbers, American and Sherpa, now strung out down the mountain beneath them, and to the vast amount of labor, dedication and sacrifice that had put them where they now were. Norman, though now descending the ridge a thousand feet below, was none the less there with them. The second assault team, now at the South Col awaiting their own chance, was there. The West Ridgers, also waiting, were there. The men at Advance Base and Base Camp were there. Above all, Jake Breitenbach was there, climbing beside them.

As now they approached the goal they came to "Hillary's Chimney," a near-vertical wall angling up between rock and snow cornice on which he and Tenzing had had their final great struggle. But apparently the years had wrought changes in its structure, for now, mercifully, it presented no major obstacle. Jim first worked his way up the snow, taking great care not to move too far out on the cornice; then he cut back to the rock, clambered to a small platform above; and Gombu, without difficulty, came after. Beyond the platform, the slope eased off. There was still the rock on the left, the snow on the right, and still they followed the line between them. But there was no steepness now; only humps and hummocks, each just a little higher than the one before it; and there were ten of them, fifteen, twenty—rising, rising. Some were of rock, some of snow, some a mixture of both. Then there was no more mixture, no more rock, but only snow; only a rounded white dome curving slightly above them. Jim, in the lead, stopped and waited for Gombu to come up to him. "You first," he said. "No, you," said Gombu. Then, the dome being wide enough, they walked side by side to its top. Beyond, everything fell away. And there they were.

Jim speaking: "I slapped Gombu on the back. We hugged each other. I dug my ice ax in and slung my pack over it. It was very windy, very cold, and my fingers and toes were numb." (At that time—exactly 1 P.M.—a thermometer on the South Col registered 20 degrees below zero, and a fair estimate is that it was 30-below on the summit.)

Then:

May Day used to be the day of Maypoles. Then the Comrades took it over. Now, happily, it was back to Maypoles again: specifically the 4-foot aluminum stake with American flag attached that Big Jim had carried up from Advance Base, and that now he detached from his pack frame and planted on Everest's crest. The wind tore at stake and flag, but they held. And soon Jim's camera was out and he and Gombu were taking pictures of them; of each other holding other smaller flags—of the United States, of Nepal, of India, of the National Geographic Society, of Gombu's Himalayan Institute of Mountaineering, in Darjeeling; and of Gombu holding a *kata*, the traditional "friendship scarf" of the Buddhist faith, that had been given him by his uncle, Tenzing, to take to precisely where he had it now. Then came a long wheeling view of the world roundabout: of the summits of Makalu, Lhotse, Nuptse and the host of other giants, now all far below; of rock and ice walls plunging to glaciers, of glaciers plunging to valleys; of the brown distances to the north that were the Tibetan plateau and the dim miles to the south that were the plains of India. Ironically for Norman, now far below, panoramic moving picture photography would have been possible from the summit, for, though the wind still raged, the mountaintop pierced above the snow veils of the slopes beneath it. To north, south and west all was clear and brilliant. Only to the northeast was Jim and Gombu's view obscured—by Everest's own great snow plume boiling away in the west wind from beneath their feet.

There remained one more thing: that hypothetical bust of Mao Tse Tung that the Chinese Everest Expedition may or may not have left on the summit in 1960. There was no sign of it—nor, barring a miracle, could there have been. For if the Chinese (assuming they got there) had placed it on the surface of the snow dome, it would long since have been buried or blown away; and if they had buried it themselves, buried it would remain forever. Conceivably, it could have been cached among the highest rocks on the northeastern side of the peak, which would have been the Chinese route of ascent. But Jim and Gombu had better uses for their remaining strength than to go down and look. In those altitudinous moments they were not worrying about Mao. They were worrying about the wind and the cold, about numb hands and feet, and, most of all, about the fact that right there on earth's pinnacle *they had run out of oxygen.*

In leaving their two partly used cylinders below the South Summit, they had estimated that they could get to the Main Summit and back—descending on a reduced flow—on one full bottle apiece. But their judgment had been faulty. They were out *now*, on top. After twenty minutes there, very slowly, very warily, they began their oxygenless descent.*

Only a short way down came the first of three crises. As on the ascent, they were following the ridgeline where rock (now on their right) met snow (now on their left); but at one point, with Gombu ahead and Jim second on the rope, the snow beneath their feet trembled and shifted, and in the next horrifying instant a whole section of the cornice between them dissolved and fell away. The first stop in its fall would be the Kangshung Glacier, more than two miles straight down. And Jim reported, "We hopped fast to the right."

The second crisis, of a rather different genre, occurred at the small snow saddle before the ridge's rise to the South Summit, when Jim, to his consternation, felt—and heeded—what was undoubtedly the highest call of nature in mountaineering history. And the third came a few minutes later on the 30-foot ascent to the South Summit. Until this point the going had been all down, and though without oxygen and in a still-howling wind, they had moved along fairly well. But now, even for 30 feet, the uphill climb was killing, and besides, Jim was already gasping from his just-completed struggle with layers of trousers and underwear. On this pitch Gombu was still going first, and presently reached the top of the rise. Jim was coming after, when suddenly the rope leading up toward Gombu fouled on the top of his pack, pulling him over backward; and in the next moment Jim found himself sprawled upside down with the rope biting into his midriff. He shouted, but in the

---

* Though not for the official record, there is a story Jim likes to tell about one other, and somewhat putative, occurrence on the summit. To wit—

Questioner: What did you do when you got to the top and looked around you?

Jim: I said, "My God—"

Questioner: What then?

Jim: A voice from below answered, "Ye-e-e-s?"

gale Gombu could not hear him. Then, with a mighty effort with ax and crampons, he righted himself and battled on to the South Summit at a rate of about twenty breaths per step. Once there, he could do nothing for several minutes but lie prone in the snow, trying to rekindle the strength and will to go on.

This, he said later, was the worst point in the climb. He and Gombu had now been two hours at around 29,000 feet without oxygen, and their hypoxic condition was obviously getting serious. Further, they had gone the whole day without a drink—for their canteens had frozen—and their bodies were drained by dehydration. For the first time in that day's great doings, Jim began to doubt that they would get down alive.

Get down they did; but not until after a continuing ordeal on the steep section of ridge beneath the South Summit. "Here," said Jim, "we crept very *very* slowly, belaying each other, moving one at a time, moving perhaps half our rope's length and then stopping to fight for breath; doing nothing but breathing for three or four minutes, then creeping on together until we were in position for the next belay, after which it was one at a time again. . . ." After an eternity or two, however, they were past the worst of the steepness. They were at the almost level platform on the ridge where, on the ascent, they had left their two other oxygen bottles, and now came the best of all the rests, as they hooked them up to their masks and sucked in the breath of life at its fullest flow. Then, still on oxygen, down they went again—down, down, down—their crampons catching on the rock, their heels kicking endlessly into the snow, making new steps to replace the old ones that the storm had obliterated. The worst was over, however. In the late afternoon Camp VI at last became visible; it moved slowly nearer; and at 5:45, staggering with weariness, they reached the tents where Norman and Ang Dawa were awaiting them with hot food and drink. All they had the strength for was to make a soundless sign of victory. "All I could do," said Norman, "was croak my congratulations."

Later, however, he had something to add. It was "miraculous," he said, that Jim and Gombu had made the top on that day of wild wind and bitter cold. Indeed, it was "superhuman." For his part, thinking it over later, Big Jim Whittaker took a rather different point of view. How did he feel on top? he was asked. "Not expansive, not sublime," he said. "I felt like a frail human being."

Frail or mighty, human or superhuman, the big man from the West and the small man from the East had come down from their Maypole with a shining victory.

IN KATHMANDU, thanks to the radio, we had known for some time that May 1 was Target Date. We knew that during those last days of April the assault teams were close to the summit. No less than on the mountain, tension was building up at the Hotel Royal, and we had no oxygen, only scotch and martinis, to sustain us.

In the beginning, the world press—and especially the American—had shown small interest in AMEE,* but now, as the word of impending climax got around, the situation changed drastically. The corps of Kathmandu journalists beat a daily path to the Royal. Correspondents for the wire services flew in from India and points beyond. The demand to attend the daily radio sessions at Colonel Bill Gresham's shack was so great that we soon had to exclude all the press and substitute post-radio briefings at the Royal. As before, the 5 P.M. regulars *chez* Bill were Sally Dyhrenfurth, Sally Richardson, Jolene Unsoeld and myself (my own wife, Marian, having by

* To this, there was one notable exception, in the person of Miss Elizabeth Hawley, an American newspaperwoman who was the Nepalese representative for both *Time*, Inc. and Reuters. Miss Hawley was keenly interested in the expedition from beginning to end. She was also, on many occasions, extremely helpful to it, and AMEE herewith presents its thanks.

192

now left for the Great Outside). Father Moran listened in on his own set. Ambassador and Mrs. Stebbins were now almost daily visitors, and other members of the American community were invited when and if they could be squeezed into the shack.

"9N1ME. Calling 9N1ME. This is 9N1DD—9N1 Donald Duck —calling 9N1 Mount Everest, calling 9N1 Mount Everest—" Each day we sat before Bill's dials and tubes as if in the magic of a darkened theater waiting for the curtain to rise.

On April 29 Al Auten had word for us that the first assault team had reached the Col. On April 30 that it had reached Camp VI, and that Sherpas descending to Advance Base had reported VI as "high, much high." That night—as if provided by a thoughtful stage director—there was thunder and lightning over Kathmandu.

Then it was May 1. It was 5 P.M.

"9N1ME—this is 9N1DD—"

"We have a problem," said Al Auten.

"What?"

"Well, we have a batch of fresh eggs here, brought up by Sherpas. The boys think it would be nice to make some mayonnaise, but nobody knows how. Could one of the ladies there help us?"

One of the ladies could. Bill Gresham's wife, Juanita, was in the shack on that day of days, and she took over the microphone.

"Do you have any oil?" she asked.

"Yes," said Al.

"Not machine oil."

"No."

"I mean salad oil."

"Yes."

"Well," said Juanita, "first you mix the oil into the eggs; not all at once but very slowly, drop by drop, so the eggs will absorb it. Have you got that?"

"Yes, drop by drop," said Al.

What seemed like an hour later the Fanny Farmer Program was over. Then—

"Any news on your end?" Al inquired.

Yes, there was news on our end. Willi and Jolene Unsoeld's four children were in the shack that day with their mother, and they had glad tidings for their father, who was now at Base Camp. Willi then came on the air and was given them. The Unsoeld cat had had kittens.

"Wonderful!" said Willi. "How are they?"

"Fine."

"Where are they?"

"In the bathtub."

Another hour (or two, or three) later, AMEE's rear-echelon historian managed to get hold of the microphone. There were rumors around, he said, that there were some men out there trying to climb a mountain.

The rumors, said Al Auten, were correct.

"And what, please, did they do today?"

"We don't know."

"You've had no word?"

No, Base had had no word. Advance Base had had no word. The weather up above was bad. There had probably been no movement. But no one knew.

Then it was May 2. It was 5 P.M.

Still, no one knew. Al, however, would again be speaking to Advance Base at 6 P.M., and he hoped that by then there would be some word. Please God, yes. (There was no talk today of mayonnaise and bathtubs.) But if so, how could we in Kathmandu find out without waiting another agonizing twenty-four hours? 9N1ME and 9N1DD could not reach each other after dark. The only way in which post-sunset contact could be made would be—possibly— through some distant ham operator, and Al Auten and Bill Gresham agreed that they would try their luck between 7:00 and 7:30. Also, all of us knew that some of the press was now listening in to these conversations on other radios, and we did not want anyone scoring "beats" on us. If there was big news from AMEE, we wanted AMEE and no one else to be the first to make it known to the world. So Al and Bill therefore devised a simple code (taking care to conceal the key from any present listeners) which—if It had happened—would give us the word but be meaningless to others. Bill was not overly confident that they would be able to make contact through the roundabout circuit, for the burned Sherpani message had been a one-in-a-hundred success. But he felt it was worth the try, and it was arranged that, if the long shot materialized, he would phone me immediately at the Hotel Royal.

There was a goodly predinner crowd that evening in the Yak and Yeti Bar. I had told the press that there might, just possibly might, be an interesting announcement forthcoming by eight o'clock, and they were swarming over the premises. Like Bill, I was not optimistic about the possibilities, and tried—with no success— to focus my thoughts on other matters. At 7:40, however, the Royal's reception clerk appeared. I was wanted on the phone, he said. Taking as many deep breaths as Jim Whittaker on the South Summit, I went to the phone.

Bill Gresham's voice was studiedly casual. "I've been gabbing with a ham called Ian Wollen in Ceylon," he said. "He'd been talking to 9N1ME and had a message for us.*

There was a pause. "The message," said Bill, "is that *two mail runners left at 1300 hours May one.* Repeat: *two mail runners left at 1300 hours May one.*"

First I went upstairs and kissed Sally Dyhrenfurth. During the rest of the evening I kissed anyone who would let me.

On May 3 at 5 P.M. we had it officially. "One American and one Sherpa member of the expedition reached the summit of Mount Everest at 1 P.M., Nepal time, May 1." There followed a few details about wind and cold, the stake and the flags. But no names. Nor did this last come as a surprise, for on April 26, after a parley with Base Camp, I had made the following announcement to the press:

"It has been decided by a vote of expedition members that during the final phases of the first assault the names of the high climbers will not be publicly announced. It is the hope of the expedition that not merely two, but perhaps several, team members will reach the summit, and it believes that those who happen to be first should not be publicized and glorified at the expense of the others. Announcement of all—if any—who reach the top of Everest, by whatever route, will be made when the summit attempts are concluded."

This was a matter on which most of the team felt strongly—and especially Norman, who a few days earlier had croaked over the

---

* At the time Mr. Wollen had no idea the message meant anything but what it said. Later, however, he was told—and warmly thanked for his remote assistance.

radio: "This is a team effort all the way, and I'm damned if the world is just going to hear about one or two heroes." But making the decision was one thing. Making it stick, after the fact, was quite another. For now, at last, AMEE was in the public eye, and everyone wanted to know *all* about it. Congratulations were pouring in from everywhere. But questions were pouring in also, and *the* question was who? *who?* WHO? The pressure from the press was tremendous. Families and friends back home joined in. Ambassador Stebbins felt that, for many reasons, it was inadvisable to withhold the names. And it was soon manifest that, inadvisable or not, it was impossible, for in an incredibly short time rumors were flickering down the grapevine about "a Darjeeling Sherpa and a big sahib called Jim." If the subsequent summit assaults had followed the first by a few days, the admirable wishes of the team could have been fulfilled. But as things were developing on the mountain, it was to be not a matter of days but of weeks, and in the world of twentieth century communications secrets simply cannot be kept that long. If AMEE did not announce the names of the top climbers, the press would soon have them anyhow, and we would have been in the position of having either to deny the truth or to, in effect, plead the Fifth Amendment.

Up on the heights and sealed off from the pressures, the team took some convincing. But of necessity, it was accomplished at last. "All right, we give in," Norman said on May 9, adding a few choice expletives. And the names of Jim Whittaker and Nawang Gombu were made known to the world.

One postscript remains to be added to the communications saga, to the effect that sorely harried Nick Clinch arrived at Base Camp precisely on the red-letter day of May 1. That evening he presumably learned how to make mayonnaise, but because of his long delay at Namche Bazar waiting for Chuck Huestis and the helicopter, he was able to stay for only a night and a day, and left without knowing that Everest had been climbed. He finally heard about it on the evening of the third, back in Namche, from someone who had heard it from a member of Sir Edmund Hillary's expedition, who had heard it on the radio from India.

12. *SECOND BREATH*

AT CAMP VI on Everest's summit ridge, on that evening of May 1, Norman Dyhrenfurth and Jim Whittaker had things on their minds other than publicity and press relations. One of them was, quite simply, survival.

When Hillary and Tenzing had come down from the top ten years before, they had, on the same day, descended all the way to the South Col. But with Jim and Gombu not reaching VI until almost 6 P.M., it was now too late for that, and these two, together with Norman and Ang Dawa, dug in for a second night at 27,450 feet. First there was drink and food (in that sequence and order of importance): vast quantities of tea, bouillon and juice; smaller rations of dried beef and canned peaches. There was the struggle to strip off layers of outer clothing, to crawl into sleeping bags, to get the night flow of oxygen going from the few partially filled cylinders that remained to them. Outside, the stars were brilliant. But the wind still poured over the white ridge and through the gulfs of blackness on either side.

The walkie-talkie was unable to make contact with the South Col camp or any others below. There was no way of telling the rest

197

of the team either that the summit had been reached or that the
four top men were going to spend the night at VI, and all that
could be hoped was that the rest were patiently biding their time.
Just as darkness was closing in, there had been a few bad moments
when they heard what was unmistakably the sound of shouting
from below. "Oh my God!" Norman had thought. "The men on
the Col figured we'd be moving down and are coming up to take
our place." This would have caused a desperate situation, with four
more bodies trying to squeeze into the two tiny tents. But luckily
it was not the case; the voices, it soon became apparent, were
coming all the way from the Col, whence the second team was
calling up trying to learn what had happened. Gombu, the only
one with enough lung power left, shouted back, and though—it was
learned later—his words could not be heard, his voice carried. At
least those below now knew that the summit team was still alive.
And the summit team knew that the others were not coming, and
that there would be no nighttime housing crisis on the Southeast
Ridge.

The black hours crept past. Again the four men slept fitfully,
bodies aching with tiredness, lungs sucking in oxygen through
plastic masks. But by midnight the precious gas was almost gone.
Of the bottles that had been brought up to Camp VI, just one
remained that was about a third full; and since it would have
served only one man for a fraction of the descent to the Col, it was
decided to leave it for what little use it might be to later parties.
There was a cup of lukewarm jello for breakfast, followed by the
slow-motion ordeal of dressing. Then the descent began—with Jim
and Gombu again going first, for Jim had suffered from cold feet
during the night and was anxious to get to lower altitudes as quickly
as possible. The weather was not quite so savage as on the previous
day, and Norman was able to film their departure and then take
both still and moving picture shots of the world around and beneath: of nearby Nuptse, Lhotse, Makalu, Chomolönzo, and, far
to the east, mighty Kangchenjunga. This done, he and Ang Dawa
zipped up the two tents, anchoring them as tightly as possible with
rope and empty oxygen cylinders. And then they in turn started
down.

They went slowly. Very slowly. The strain of the six days since departure from Advance Base had taken its cumulative toll, and even downgrade going was, without oxygen, an almost killing grind. Norman's balance was bad. His and Ang Dawa's feet slipped and stumbled on the loose snow-plastered rocks. And many times they had to stop to rest. As the morning wore on, the sky, which had been clear to begin with, clouded over, and tides of fog flowed over the ridge, obscuring the South Col and the figures of Jim and Gombu, now far below them. Eventually they reached the point where the route veered off from the ridge into the snow couloir cutting down toward the Col; and in the couloir, slowly, cautiously, they stumped and kicked downward. "By now we were so tired," said Norman, "that when the fog moved in we simply stopped; we sat down and waited. Then when it lifted a little and we could see the Col and the tents there, we went on again."

Slowly—Slowly—

There were not only tents on the Col. There were men too. And they had now been there for almost two full days.

The second assault team of Lute Jerstad, Dick Pownall, Barry Bishop and Girmi Dorje had left Advance Base on April 28 and, following a day after the first team, had moved up the Western Cwm, up the Lhotse Face, to Camp V on the Col. For Lute and Dick, it was the second visit to this "most desolate place on earth." For Barry, its attainment made him, at the time, the most widely traveled man on the expedition, for he had already been to 25,100 feet on the West Ridge, and now here he was at 26,200 on another side of the mountain. Four carrying Sherpas had accompanied the climbers on the three-day ascent. At the Col camp they dumped their loads and headed back down, leaving Lute, Dick, Barry and Girmi to make their second-wave bid for the summit.

No sooner had they dug in, however, than they suffered a rude jolt of surprise—and again, as with the first team, the deliverer of the jolt was oxygen. Or rather, the lack of it. Besides what they had brought up themselves, they had expected to find twelve to fifteen full cylinders waiting for them at the Col, but what they found instead was only four full ones and more than two dozen empties. A search through the debris of the old British, Swiss and Indian camps netted one more full usable bottle; but that was all. The

only hope was that the first assault team had carried up to Camp
VI a great deal more oxygen than they themselves would need for
their summit try. And this seemed a slim hope indeed. During
the night they held their consumption of their own supply to a
minimum, but even a minimum was more than they could well
afford.

On the morning of May 1 the wind was pouring over the camp
in a battering gale, and the summit pyramid of the mountain was
all but obliterated in swirling snow. Efforts to reach Camp VI by
walkie-talkie were fruitless; but the men on the Col, like those
further below, decided that the top climbers must be staying put
for the day—and therefore stayed put too. At about 11:30 A.M.
they had the first indication that they had not been right, when,
through a break in the scud, they saw two dots on the Southeast
Ridge slowly descending toward Camp VI. Actually, these were
Norman and Ang Dawa returning from their highest point beneath the South Summit; but the watchers on the Col assumed it
was Jim and Gombu and, in view of the early hour, reasoned that
they were retreating from an unsuccessful summit try. After that,
the hours dragged by. The four men alternated between huddling
in their tents for warmth and scrounging—unsuccessfully—about
the Col "junkyard" for more usable oxygen. And then, toward five
in the afternoon, in now clearer weather, they saw a sight that
astonished them and brought a lift to their hearts. Again two
descending dots were visible on the Southeast Ridge, but this time
far higher than before—well above the location of Camp VI. And
now they knew they had been wrong in the morning: that the
first two dots had been Norman and Ang Dawa, that *these* two
were Jim and Gombu, and that, on the evidence of their height
and the hour, they had made an all-out try for the summit.

That they had come very close was obvious. But whether they
had reached the ultimate goal there was no way of telling. In any
case, the second team had been right in its decision not to go up
to Camp VI, for it was now certain that Norman, Jim & Company
would be spending a second night there, and at least there would
not be eight men up yonder struggling for shelter in two 2-man
tents. When dusk came, they shouted upward, hoping they could
learn what happened. But, as with the men above, they could hear

THREE TO MAKE READY

Photograph by Barry C. Bishop, © 1964 NATIONAL GEOGRAPHIC SOCIETY

TOM HORNBEIN CONDUCTS OXYGEN SEMINAR FOR SHERPAS

Photograph by Norman G. Dyhrenfurth, AMEE

LACING ON CRAMPONS

WHITTAKER AND GOMBU LEAVING ADVANCE BASE FOR FIRST SUMMIT ASSAULT

Photograph by Barry C. Bishop, © 1963 NATIONAL GEOGRAPHIC SOCIETY

Photograph by Norman G. Dyhrenfurth, AMEE

THE LHOTSE FACE

(see endpapers for route and camps)

Photograph by James W. Whittaker, AMEE

CAMP III

–low on the Face.

CAMP IV

—with Lhotse-Nuptse Ridge behind it.

Photograph by Norman G. Dyhrenfurth, AMEE

Photograph by Norman G. Dyhrenfurth, AAEE

SUNSET WORLD FROM CAMP IV

Cwm, Icefall and Khumbu Glacier are beneath the clouds in the foreground. The pyramid in the middle distance is Pumori; and beyond is
Cho Oyu. To the right is Gyachung Kang and in the right foreground

Photograph by Richard Pownall, AMEE

THE LONG PULL

Coming up over the Geneva Spur.

READY FOR THE HEIGHTS

Dick Pownall at Camp IV.

Photograph by Barry C. Bishop, © 1964 NATIONAL GEOGRAPHIC SOCIETY

"HIGHEST JUNKYARD IN THE WORLD"

Empty oxygen bottles abandoned by previous expeditions on the South Col.

Photograph by Barry C. Bishop, © 1963 NATIONAL GEOGRAPHIC SOCIETY

Photograph by Luther G. Jerstad, AM

SOUTH SUMMIT FROM SOUTH COL

Southeast Ridge on right. The main summit is hidden behind the South Peak. The site of the bivouac of May 22–23 is slightly below the ridgeline on the far right.

ADVANCE BASE AND WEST RIDGE

The route blazed to the ridge slants upward from right to left across the mountainside.

Photograph by Maynard M. Miller, AMEE

Photograph by William F. Unsoeld, AMEE

RECONNAISSANCE

Bishop and Dingman on the West Ridge approach.

MASSES AND MIDGES

A column of Sherpas moves up toward the West Ridge.

Photograph by William F. Unsoeld, AMEE

WHITE WILDERNESS

–between Cwm and West Ridge.

CAMP 3W

Beyond it, the West Shoulder–and Tibet.

Photograph by Allen C. Auten, AMEE

Photograph by William F. Unsoeld, AMEE

ACROSS THE VOID

View from Camp 3W toward the summit pyramid. The route of the
South Col climbers slants up behind the righthand ridge toward the
south and main summits.

HIGH LOGISTICS

One of the ski-sleds hauled by winch on the West Ridge route. To the
left is Everest's summit, to the right, Lhotse: both from angles never
seen before.

Photograph by William F. Unsoeld, AMEE

WEST RIDGE CORNICE

–between 3W and 4W.

WEST RIDGE PAUSE

Unsoeld and Hornbein with gear, en route to 4W.

Photograph by Barry C. Bishop, © 1963 NATIONAL GEOGRAPHIC SOCIETY

Photograph by Norman G. Dyhrenfurth, AAEE

HIGH ON THE COL ROUTE

Whittaker and Gombu at Camp VI, with Makalu in the background.

Earth's Highest Rampart

Lhotse and the ridge leading toward Nuptse, seen from Camp VI. The white plateau on the lower left is the South Col, some 1500 feet below.

NAWANG GOMBU
ON THE SUMMIT

WHITTAKER AND GOMBU
BACK AT THE COL

—AND AT ADVANCE BASE

answering shouts but no words, and when they turned in for the night they still did not know if Everest had, or had not, been climbed.

Another morning came: the morning of May 2. And if the previous day had been the expedition's Day of Triumph, this was to be its Day of Disappointment—at least for this second assault team of Jerstad, Pownall, Bishop and Girmi Dorje. The weather was still wild, but rather less so than before, and the four made their preparations to go on up to Camp VI. After two nights and a day on the Col, however, their oxygen situation was worse than ever. With what they had themselves, plus what little might be left at VI, it was glumly obvious that a four-man try for the summit, as originally planned, was now out of the question. The best that could be hoped for was a two-man attempt, with the other two helping in the carry up to the highest camp and then returning to the Col to remain there in support. The decision as to which two would do what could have been a thorny one, but Dick Pownall saw to it that it wasn't. Dick had made a remarkable recovery, both physically and psychically, from his involvement in the Jake Breitenbach tragedy. He had twice reached the South Col. But now the effects of all he had been through had begun to tell; he knew that the drive that had carried him this far was weakening; and he therefore, on his own, relinquished his role as a candidate for the summit. If a try for the top proved possible at all, it would be Lute and Barry who would make it. Dick and Girmi Dorje would back them up.

All this, however, was to be purely theoretical.

For within a half hour of setting out, at 10 A.M., they met Jim Whittaker and Gombu descending from Camp VI, and that was as high as their foray was to take them. The first moment of meeting was one of excitement and joy, for with it came the news of the previous day's victory. But close on its heels came the realization that they would have to return to Camp V. Jim and Gombu were desperately tired. They needed food, drink and, above all, oxygen, of which they had had none during their descent from VI; and, from Jim's account of the situation, it was plain that Norman's need would be even greater, when he and Ang Dawa got down to the Col. The second team therefore turned around and went back to V with Jim and Gombu. They ministered to them. They waited for Norman and Ang Dawa. And one and one-half hours later they saw two figures emerging slowly from the couloir onto the plateau of the Col and went out to meet them.

It was none too soon. "Norman was delirious," said Lute, who was the first to reach them. "He kept calling me 'Dave.' He collapsed in my arms, saying 'I'm at the end of my rope,' and we stretched him out on the snow and gave him oxygen right there." Ang Dawa, too, was exhausted. Both men's faces were blue from hypoxia, and they were barely able, with the others' help, to stagger down to Camp V. They were put into tents and given warm drinks, and they sucked in oxygen with the need of men who had been drowning in space.

In an hour they were better. The color and texture of life had returned to their faces. But Norman was still far from able to take care of himself. Jim, Gombu and Ang Dawa were almost done in. On top of this, they had confirmed the second team's fears that there was virtually no oxygen left at Camp VI. And to add the finishing touch, the weather, which during the morning had shown signs of improving, was now worsening again into gale and ground blizzard. In any case, fair or storm, oxygen or no oxygen, the compelling fact was that the summit team, and Norman in particular, had to be got down that day to lower and safer altitudes. "We knew that our own summit hopes were finished," said Lute. Then added doggedly "—for the time being."

Norman protested. He said he and Ang Dawa would remain at the Col in support, without oxygen, while the second team went up and Jim and Gombu went down. But to everyone but himself this was clearly out of the question, and presently the eight men made ready for the long descent. As before, Jim and Gombu went first, with Dick Pownall roped up with them. Barry Bishop and Girmi Dorje followed with Ang Dawa. And last came a two-man rope of Lute and Norman. Mindful of future assaults, they left much of their gear on the Col, including tents, food, stoves, fuel, and the few full bottles of oxygen that were on hand. But Barry and Lute still carried loads of about 60 pounds each, consisting largely of Norman's photographic equipment. Only Norman used oxygen on the way down, breathing at a light flow from one of the partly used cylinders.

The way led to the western rim of the Col, then over the steep flanks of the Geneva spur; and here Norman and Lute suddenly found themselves face to face with Dr. Dave Dingman and two Sherpas. Dave and Barry (Balu) Prather, it will be recalled, had, with three Sherpas, formed the third wave in the series of assault teams and had left Advance Base on April 29, a day behind the second team. Their purpose had been the dual one of giving support to those above them and also, if all went well, of branching off from the Col-to-Everest route and making an attempt on neighboring Lhotse. But all had already *not* gone well; for on the previous morning of May 1, when Dave and Barry were to have climbed from Camp IV to the Col, Barry had felt poorly, and Dave plus two of the Sherpas had started off without him to deliver oxygen to Camp V. They had not gone far, however. In the atrocious weather the Sherpas had presently refused to go on, and Dave had had to return with them to IV, in what seemed still another setback. As it developed, however, it was a bit of great good fortune —as was the fact that Dave was a physician—for on the return to IV he found Barry in alarmingly worse condition, with a pulse rate of 140 (after resting all day) and much difficulty in breathing. Diagnosing the ailment as pulmonary edema, Dave immediately put him on oxygen and administered intravenous and intramuscular injections. (Not the least of the performances of AMEE's doctors was that they carried both their wits and kits with them as high as they went.) As a result, Barry's serious symptoms soon disappeared, and what could well have been a second expedition tragedy became, in terms of critical illness, no more than a one-day crisis.*

All hopes for Lhotse, however, were now of course at an end. Barry could go no higher. Indeed, in spite of his youth and enormous strength, he was to be allowed to do no more high climbing during the rest of the expedition. But the very next morning, May 2, he was able to go down to Advance Base, escorted by two Sherpas who were passing through Camp IV on their descent from

* "It was a close thing, though," said Dr. Gil Roberts, discussing the matter later. "If Dave had gone on to the Col—" He left the sentence hanging.

the South Col. And though the trip took him seven and one-half hours—more than twice the usual time—he was able to make it under his own power. Meanwhile Dave returned to the struggle of performing his job as support of the teams above and again started up the higher slopes of the Lhotse Face with the Sherpas Pemba Tenzing and Nima Tenzing (of Pangboche). Reaching the high point of the previous day's attempt, they retrieved the five full bottles of oxygen they had cached there and continued up over the Yellow Band toward the Geneva spur. Suddenly they became aware of another group on the Face, descending by a slightly different route and already below them. But they were close enough so that Dave could recognize them as Jim Whittaker, Gombu and Dick Pownall, and through an exchange of shouts he learned that the summit had been reached and that the other members of the first two assault teams were also on the way down from the Col. Further, he found out that at least part of the reason for the second team's descent was a shortage of oxygen above; and he therefore pushed on with the two Sherpas as fast as he could, in the hope that, with the extra supply he was bringing, Lute Jerstad, Barry Bishop and Girmi Dorje might after all make a try for the summit, while he and his Sherpas brought Norman and Ang Dawa down.

It was not to be, however—as he discovered a little later when he met the other descending climbers on the Geneva Spur. For the die had been cast. The second team, no less than the first, was now almost done in. And with only four and a fraction usable oxygen bottles left above, the additional five that Dave was bringing would still not raise the figure to the needed total. Now that Barry Prather was out of the picture, there was no point in Dave's going up alone with his Sherpas. Once again the oxygen they were carrying was cached on the mountainside—this time a few hundred feet higher than on the previous day. And now the whole of the three assault teams were on their way down.

Down—Down—

The going was painfully slow. Dave had given dexedrine tablets to Norman, Lute and Barry Bishop, but still their legs were rubbery, their energy low, their reactions sluggish, and time and again there were slips on the loose snow and rotten rock. Once

Barry peeled off altogether and began falling, but was held on the rope by Ang Dawa. Once Lute, who was behind Norman on another rope, lost his footing and began to slide, but caught himself so quickly by jamming his ax into the snow that Norman was not aware of what had happened until he turned and saw Lute picking himself up. By the grace of God, plus skill and care, there were no serious accidents. In time, they reached Camp IV. Jim Whittaker, Gombu and Dick Pownall had already passed through it, having decided to go all the way down to Advance Base in one day; and after a brief rest, most of the others followed after. The first group got to A.B. at 5:30 in the evening, the second at eight at night, threading the crevasses of the upper Cwm by the light of the moon. Waiting for them was a joyful welcome, hot drinks, all the food they could eat—and, as a special treat, their first chance in almost a week to contribute to Will Siri's blood and urine collection. Surely, in the long history of "before-and-afters," there can have been few more notable "afters" than those presented by Jim and Gombu.

Norman spent that night of May 2 at Camp IV with Dave Dingman and three Sherpas. From here on downward their walkie-talkie worked, and in the morning they were asked by Gil Roberts at Advance Base if they needed help for the rest of the descent. They answered no, they would make it on their own, and continued down the Lhotse Face to Camp III. But Gil came up anyhow, meeting them at III with assorted refreshments and his medical kit, for he was concerned about Norman's possible condition. Happily, it was now all right. Once below 25,000 feet, Norman's strength, worn perilously thin by his week-long ordeal, had returned almost miraculously. And now, with his unneeded medical escort, plus Sherpas, he slogged on down to Advance Base, to be greeted by Danu the cook with a broad grin and a shout of "Bara Sah'b—tea party!"

That there happened to be rum in the tea was of course strictly for medicinal purposes. "Boy, did it burn going down!" said the Bara Sahib. "But boy, did it feel good just the same!"

Few others were still left at the headquarters in the Cwm. For now a general withdrawal was in progress down the whole sweep of the mountain, all the way to Base Camp on the Khumbu

Glacier. The other members of the assault teams—except of course
for ever-faithful Ang Dawa—had set off that morning for the
descent of the lower Cwm and Icefall. Of the West Ridge group,
Willi Unsoeld, Tom Hornbein and Al Auten had gone down, leaving only Barry Corbet and Dick Emerson on the high slopes, fighting the battle of the winches. Will Siri and Jimmy Roberts were
down. Even the two convalescents, Barry Prather and Dan Doody,
had descended, proceeding shakily but safely, helped by stronger
companions. With Norman and Dave Dingman preparing to follow the next day, only four team members would, for a while, be
left on the mountain: Corbet and Emerson on the West Ridge
slopes and Gil Roberts and Jim Lester at Advance Base. With each
pair there would be a small contingent of Sherpas—and as an extra
bonus, Gil and Jim would have the goraks.

Everest was no antagonist to permit a mass descent without a
farewell salute. With fine perversity, however, it was directed not
at those who had trespassed on its heights but at a group of
Sherpas doing a routine porterage job on the lower stretches of the
West Ridge route. There were now three small tents pitched at
one of the dumps near the foot of the winch-and-cable lift, and
on the morning of May 3 the four men who were established there
(Corbet and Emerson were at Camp 3W above) heard the sound
of an avalanche coming down on them. Fortunately it was an
avalanche of—by Himalayan standards—modest proportions; two
of the four managed to dodge out of the way. But the other two,
Passang Temba of Darjeeling and Urkien (the domino champion)
were not able to get out of their tent in time, and tent, Sherpas
and all went tumbling down the slope in a white torrent of snow.
Luck was with them. The tent was not buried deeply, nor was it
carried out over a sheer drop, and Passang and Urkien crawled out
unharmed after a somersaulting ride of a few hundred feet. But
the tent and one of the two others were damaged beyond repair,
and much camping and climbing gear was carried away and lost. As
result, the four now-homeless Sherpas had to make their way down
the steep, treacherous slopes without benefit of rope, axes and
crampons. But make it they did, arriving at Advance Base soon
after Norman, Dave & Company came in from the Lhotse Face.

Being Sherpas, they of course grinned as they told their story.

The next morning, the last large caravan, led by Norman and Dave, moved off down the Cwm and the Icefall, following those that had gone before; and with its arrival at Base Camp in mid-afternoon, most of the expedition was together at the foot of the mountain. There had been great changes in the Khumbu region during the month since it had last been fully occupied. For here spring had now come to the high Himalaya; in the troughs of the glacier the once iron-hard ice had dissolved into streams of running water; and to the high climbers, now at a mere 17,800 feet, it seemed almost as if they had come to a seaside resort. Victory had been won, and it was sweet, and the sun was shining. But, 11,000 feet up, it was also shining on Everest's summit ridge—and to the members of the second assault team that was not so sweet. For, happy though they were at the Whittaker-Gombu triumph, they could not but realize that, on this very day, they themselves would have been up there, if . . . if . . . if. . . .

For most expeditions this would have been the end. But not for AMEE 1963. In spite of one tragic death and two disabling ill-nesses, it was still strong in manpower. It had before it almost a month of potentially good climbing weather before the coming of the monsoon storms. It had ample food and supplies. The one marginal item—and a hugely important one—was oxygen, which had been used in far greater quantities than anticipated on the first summit push; but it was felt that with careful planning and rationing the team could make do with what was left.

Above all, vis-à-vis the mountain, there was still desire. The West Ridge platoon, comprising several of the best and most dedicated climbers on the expedition, had not yet had its chance. Some who had gone so high on the Col route, only to have the prize snatched away, were burning for another try. And further, the master plan of the expedition had all along been geared to the ambition of putting more than two men on top of Everest. The British had done that ten years before. The Swiss had put four men there, plus two on Lhotse. Lung, limb and the Lord willing, AMEE wanted not merely to repeat, or less-than-repeat, what others had done, but to add something of its own.

First, however, there were other matters to occupy the attention:

the simple facts of being even temporarily down off the mountain; of breathing breathable air, eating eatable food; of wallowing in the sybaritic luxuries of R & R at the Khumbu Plaza. Considering the rigors of the campaign just ended, the team was in fair physical condition. Will Siri's scales showed that a total of about a quarter of a ton in weight had been lost by the eighteen sahibs since setting out from Kathmandu; but what was left of them was for the most part hard and fit, and the wheezing and coughing, headaches and nausea of the early days were now largely a thing of the past. Jim Whittaker, on his summit push, had acquired a windburned, superficially frostbitten face. But his oxygen mask had saved him from worse, and a ring of frost blisters on his wrists, where his gloves had separated from his parka sleeves, was also not serious. Norman, though still unable to muster more than a croak from his laryngitic throat, was otherwise soon over the effects of his ordeal. Dick Emerson, who had suffered protracted acclimatization miseries, seemed at last to be rounding into shape and was looking forward to taking off with his West Ridge companions. Maynard Miller, his broken foot now almost healed, was planning soon to go up to Advance Base to pursue his glaciological work in the Cwm. And Dan Doody and Barry Prather, though they would remain at Base and below for the rest of the expedition, were at least out from under the shadow and on the way back to health and strength.

From assorted diaries—

Dyhrenfurth: "Clean up, shave, and try to become a human being again."

Whittaker: "Resting. Drinking all kinds of juice, coffee, tea, cocoa. Soaking toes in warm water. Lie out in sun with shirt off for fifteen minutes. What bliss!"

Jerstad: "Eat and eat. Fresh eggs and mutton."

Doody: "Photography. Haircuts."

Pownall: "Sleep fine. Weather fine. Lazy day. Feel almost human again."

Bishop: "R & R the order of the day. Rest and Recuperation— plus Recouping and Regrouping."

Not the least of the daily features were the 5 P.M. radio talks with Kathmandu, during which congratulatory messages from all over the world were read by the rear echelon in Colonel Bill Gresham's shack. And as a fitting climax, on May 7, came Norman's forty-fifth birthday. On that evening, in celebration, liquid refreshments were broken out, and this time, for a change, *not* for the purpose of combatting dehydration. There was singing. The ukulele and harmonicas were unlimbered. Lute recited from his store of ballads. And one should have been—though it wasn't—"*The Ballad of Johnnie Armstrong*," who once sang:

> *. . . Fight on, my merry men all;*
> *I am a little hurt, but I am not slain;*
> *I will lay me down for to bleed awhile,*
> *Then I'll rise and fight with you again.*

It was not all cakes and ale, beer and skittles. For though the bleeding was of another sort than Johnnie Armstrong's, there were wounds none the less. At Base, between the accomplished victory and the new confrontation to come, there was a delicate oscillating balance between relaxation and tension. As no one needed psychologist Jim Lester or sociologist Dick Emerson to tell him, this was "a group of highly motivated men under severe and prolonged stress"—and even among the amenities of the Khumbu Plaza, the stress sometimes showed.

One unhappy aftermath of the Whittaker-Gombu triumph was the reception Gombu received from his fellow Sherpas. Or, more accurately, the lack of reception; for here the resentment of Solu Khumbu versus Darjeeling showed itself at its plainest, and far from being lionized by his own people, Gombu was virtually ignored. This attitude was in turn resented, on Gombu's behalf, by the team members, but a Westerner had no more influence in intra-Sherpa hostility than would a New England Yankee in a feud between Hatfields and McCoys.

Another touchy subject was that of the announcement, or non-announcement, of the names of the summit climbers, and this grew in intensity as, day by day, the pressure mounted over the radio. As heretofore noted, the team, in the cause of "no heroes," had voted that no names would be given until all summit attempts were concluded. Norman, in particular, felt strongly about it. Even

Jim Whittaker, who was human enough not to have minded recognition for his feat, said, "This is probably the best policy for the good of the team, and I concur." If this was a brave stand, however, it was also, as demonstrated, an untenable one; and after several days of mounting pressure and argument over the radio, the team reluctantly gave in.

Finally, and most seriously, there was The Great Oxygen Debate. There was no denying the bald and galling fact that on the first summit campaign oxygen logistics had gone wrong, and that, largely because of it, the second assault team had been denied its chance at the top. But about the how and why of the going wrong there was, at the time, much disagreement. In the beginning, it was Norman's feeling that Tom Hornbein, the expedition's oxygen planner, had underestimated the team's needs, and that the 216 bottles on hand were not enough for the job. Further, he believed that too much oxygen had been kept in reserve for the coming West Ridge venture, with a resultant shortage for the Col Route climbers. Tom and his supporters felt, on the contrary, that the allocations had been fair; also that the overall quantity was ample and that the trouble had stemmed from its mis- and over-use. The logistic planning, Tom declared, had been based on the two primary needs of climbing oxygen and sleeping oxygen, but that, quite reasonably, no provision had been made for "sitting oxygen"— meaning that which was consumed while team members and Sherpas were awake but immobile at high camps. Norman took exception to the "quite reasonably," claiming that men living for days at more than 26,000 feet needed *some* oxygen when neither climbing nor sleeping. Tom took exception to his exception. And so it went for several days—with that "severe and prolonged stress" adding its not inconsiderable mite to long and sometimes heated arguments.

In the long view, taken later, it was agreed that several factors had contributed to the situation. To begin with, the oxygen requirement had been figured out, back home, on the basis of the original Everest-Lhotse-Nuptse project, with the West Ridge not yet firmly in the picture; and even though three mountains were involved, less oxygen would have been needed than for Everest alone, by two routes.* In regard to operations on the climb itself, it seemed plain in retrospect that mask-and-bottle breathing should not have begun as low as Camp III at the head of the Cwm, and that a stronger line should have been taken in advance as to when the carrying Sherpas should, and should not, make use of it—in which the "should" would certainly not have included sleeping at the South Col or making descents from high camps. As for "sitting oxygen," it remained a moot subject, largely because the need or non-need of it varied greatly from man to man. Tom Hornbein himself and several others managed almost entirely without it while on the upper reaches of the mountain. But all four members of the first summit assault team used it at Camps V and VI, and there were some who, deprived of it, would probably have become critically debilitated—among them, not illogically, forty-five-year-old Norman. The contingency that Dan Doody would break down and that Norman would take his place as high-level cameraman was one that could scarcely have been foreseen; nor could Norman, once he went up, have been expected to let himself die of anoxia at Camps V and VI, with the breath of life ready at hand.

To such problems of human variability there are probably no hard and fast answers. And there were none, to be sure, during those early May days at Base Camp. The controversy simmered, bubbled, then faded away. The strident voice of the radio, carrying the questions and demands of the world below, faded away. As before, there was only the world above. Only the mountain was there —*still there*. And again eyes were lifted.

Not everyone was to be actively involved in the second siege. For those who had already gone to the top, and for some who had come close to it, the campaign—at least in terms of high climbing —was over. Jim Whittaker and Gombu, Norman and Ang Dawa would henceforward remain at Base, and so too would Dick Pownall, whose part in the Icefall accident and subsequent two trips to the South Col had, in his own words, "taken a hell of a lot of poop out of me." Will Siri, after a month above 21,000 feet, was

* The climbing of Lhotse from the Western Cwm is, as has been indicated, not a separate and distinct ascent from that of Everest, but rather a branching off in route at high level. And for Nuptse, with a summit lower than Everest's South Col, oxygen would not have been used at all.

down for good too, and continuing his scientific work at the lower altitude of the Khumbu. Remaining at Advance Base with Jim Lester after the others had descended, Gil Roberts had hoped to be at least a support member in the next Col Route attempt. But he too was one of those who had spent long weeks in the Cwm without descent for R & R (indeed, longer than anyone else), and at last, on May 11, realizing that he had deteriorated too far to be of further use up high, he reluctantly descended with Jim to stay at Base until the end. With the convalescents—Barry Prather and Dan Doody added—this made a total of eight team members for whom front-line duty was ended.

The West Ridge team would remain as it had now been constituted for several weeks, composed of Willi Unsoeld, Tom Hornbein, Barry Corbet, Dick Emerson and Al Auten. Two summit assault teams of two men each were planned for this route, with Tom and Willi as the first, Barry and Dick as the second, and Al as high support man for them both. On the Col Route, this time, there would be only two climbers specifically designated as a summit party, in the persons of Barry Bishop and Lute Jerstad, both back for a second try. But Dave Dingman, Jimmy Roberts and Barry's Sherpa, Girmi Dorje, would, acting as their support, go as high as they could. Maynard Miller, soon to go up the Icefall for the first time, would be at Advance Base as mid-level support for both operations.

At last the West Ridgers were no longer to be the poor relations. Among the Sherpas, no less than the sahibs, there had been attrition during the first phase of the campaign, and there were some who were obviously no longer fit for high climbing. But their ranks were by no means decimated, and the ridge team would be amply provided with both quantity and quality of helpers. It would be the Col team that this time would be operating on a close-to-marginal level—at least in comparison to the small army of the first assault. Jerstad, Bishop, and possibly Dingman and Girmi Dorje, were the only summit candidates left. Oxygen, butane and other supplies would, even for a small group, have to be carefully rationed. And the schedule of advance, once set, would have to be adhered to as rigidly as possible. For the long-planned, never-attempted climb of Lhotse there was now simply not enough manpower or materiel still available; it was relegated, along with Nuptse, to the discard list. But in the mountaineer's lexicon, the climbing of Everest by two different routes would be worth a dozen Lhotses and Nuptses.

The beau ideal was to pull off the climbs simultaneously; to coordinate the ascents so that the two summit tries would be made on the same day and that, if they were successful, the West Ridgers would descend with the South Collars down the Col side of the mountain, in the first traverse not only of Everest but of any Himalayan peak. The problems in accomplishing such a feat would be enormous. "The chance of the two teams meeting on the top," said Norman realistically, "is one in a thousand." But the excitement of even trying for such a consummation was worth all the effort that could be put into it.

Timing and planning were immensely complex. Level by level, camp by camp, the mountain was surveyed logistically to determine what food, oxygen and other supplies had been left at the various way stations and what still had to be brought up along with the climbers. Insofar as possible, a day-by-day schedule of advance was worked out, plus a schedule for radio contacts—between the two teams, Advance Base and lower Base—so that everyone would know what everyone else was doing and all movements could be carefully dovetailed. Except for weather, the Col team knew what they would find on their route all the way to the summit. The West Ridgers, on the other hand, knew their route only up to 25,100 feet, and the going beyond would be, to put it mildly, experimental. Further, there were no already established high camps on the ridge, as there were on the Col route, for materiel had thus far been carried only to the various dumps above Advance Base and to Camp 3W near the West Shoulder. Camp 4W, at the foot of the summit pyramid, was still merely a selected site, with nothing yet on hand there; and above it would have to be still two higher stations—not yet sited, let alone stocked—to correspond with the Col camp and Camp VI on the old route. Even with its *nouveau riche* status, the West Ridge platoon would need more time for its operation than the Col group, and the schedule was drawn up to take this into consideration.

Interestingly—and perhaps at first sight with seeming illogic—the first dates designated were those for the evacuation of Base

Camp (May 22) and arrival in Kathmandu (June 6). But this was essential, for logistically everything had to be figured backward from the time when the climbers would, and must, come down from the mountain. With this as a yardstick, the eighteenth was tentatively set as the summit target date for both teams, and all planning would be coordinated to try to effect a simultaneous arrival. If things went well—that thousand-to-one "well"—the West Ridgers would then effect their first-ever traverse and descend on the far side of the peak with the Col team. If, however, the "well" was only partial and the Ridge climbers reached the summit alone, they would then go down by the same route they had ascended. "In such an event," Norman declared strongly, "a traverse is absolutely out of the question." For by the time they were at the top, it would probably be late in the day; they would obviously be tired; and a descent without guidance down a route unknown to them would be dangerous in the extreme.

So the discussions went at Base Camp: detail by detail, contingency by contingency. And simultaneously the climbers prepared to move up.

There were both similarities and differences in the attitudes of the two teams. Each was composed of men whose experience thus far on the mountain had been largely frustrating: the West Ridgers because they had been held back by lack of Sherpa carriers; the South Collars because they had already labored so hard and climbed so high, only to be deprived of their chance at the summit by a series of events over which they had no control. For Lute Jerstad, Barry Bishop and Dave Dingman, it required—apart from physical prowess—an enormous amount of will and desire to drive them back again up that huge mountain they had so recently descended. Both in the flesh and the spirit, theirs was a rallying of last resources, a dogged resolve to make one more supreme effort. On the other hand, the West Ridge team, though it had worked hard and gone fairly high, had not yet been called on truly to use its resources or show what it could do, and in the process of what Tom Hornbein called "spinning our wheels," it had by now developed a tremendous head of steam. The melancholy blue of frustration, the vacuum of inactivity, had now at last been dispelled. "All energy is being sucked together for the final sustained effort," Willi Unsoeld wrote to his wife, Jolene, on the day before he and Tom were to take off from Base for the heights. "From tomorrow on there will be no letup in our drive; and on this drive are concentrated all our planning powers, imagination, physical sources, and incidental dreams and passing fancies."

As of the first week in May, Barry Corbet and Dick Emerson were already up on the white slopes with the winches. Al Auten with a group of Sherpas had headed up with still another winch. And on the sixth Willi and Tom followed after, "It's a terrific job they've set themselves, and they know it," Norman said on the evening of the day they left Base Camp. "But with their ability and drive and almost fanatical dedication, I have a feeling that they're going to make it."

Then on May 12, the day appointed in the double-barreled timetable, Lute Jerstad and Barry Bishop, in their turn, began the long push upward. Like Johnnie Armstrong, they had risen to fight again.

13. *SUN AND STORM*

Spring had come not only to the valleys but to the heights as well. Under the warming sun avalanches plunged with increasing frequency down the mountainsides, and in the Icefall labyrinth of towers and chasms chaos had been compounded by thawing and melting. The Icefall maintenance crew, under the direction of the veteran Sherpa Annulu had, however, done its work well, and the route, though far different from before, was still passable. On May 6 Willi Unsoeld and Tom Hornbein made their way up to Camp I without incident and, indeed, were going so well that they went on to Advance Base the same day.

There they were greeted both by the goraks and by their fellow West Ridgers—Barry Corbet, Dick Emerson and Al Auten—who had gone up before them and were now down from several days' work on the slopes above. All the materiel for their assault had at last been cleared out of A.B. The winches were more or less operative. But most of the loads were still distributed at the various dumps, and the first task was to get them all to Camp 3W near Everest's West Shoulder. Willi and Al went first, with seven Sherpas; the others followed in stages with more Sherpas, and from May 8 through 13 all efforts were concentrated on winching and carrying. There were still problems, to be sure. One stemmed from the avalanche that had swept away the tents at one of the dump sites, with the result that there was now no habitable shelter between Advance Base and Camp 3W. And another was two days of foul weather. "On the ninth," said Tom Hornbein, "it snowed continuously, and we were fearful of sending anyone out on the slopes because of the hazard of more avalanches. Then on the eleventh came one of those terribly windy days, with a lenticular cap seething over the summit of Everest, and there was no possibility of setting foot outside a tent."

On the other days, however, the campaign moved on steadily. Porters plodded upward. Winches sputtered and groaned—but worked—and loads came creaking up at the end of the cables. Indeed, at this stage of operations, two winches were being used simultaneously: the hand-operated one on the lower stretch between the "New" and "New New" Dumps, and one of the motor winches between "New New" and a point about a fifteen-minute climb below 3W. Of a total of forty-two upgoing loads, twelve were hauled on sled by the winches, including two cargoes of eighteen oxygen bottles each, weighing a total of almost a quarter of a ton. By the thirteenth everything had reached 3W, at the 23,800-foot level ("we never thought we'd see the day," said Barry Corbet), and from now on this would be the base for still higher operations.

Meanwhile the South Col team was first waiting at Base Camp, then moving up to Advance Base in the Cwm. As its spearhead there were Lute Jerstad and Barry Bishop, and following after in support were Dave Dingman and Girmi Dorje. Gil Roberts and Jim Lester, who had remained at Advance Base during the mass descent, had now gone down to lower Base. But up to replace them came Jimmy Roberts, who hoped to go as high as the South Col with Dave and Girmi, and Maynard Miller, who would dig in at A.B.

According to the timetable, Lute and Barry were to move on toward the higher camps on May 14. But this was not to be. For though things had on the whole gone well with the West Ridgers, they had suffered delays because of the two days of storm and now

sent down radio word that they could not meet the original schedule. Their target date for the summit was therefore deferred by
Norman from the eighteenth to the twenty-first. Since it was the
essence of the two-pronged assault that the tries for the top be
simultaneous, this also meant a three-day postponement for the
South Collars; and this in turn meant the same postponement in
leaving Advance Base, for once they did so, they were committed,
because of oxygen and other shortages, to an upward progress of a
camp a day. Eager to be up and at it, Lute, Barry & Company were
not happy about the delay. To rub it in, the days of storm were
now followed by a period of ideal climbing weather. But they had
no choice but to remain at Advance Base, champing at the bit,
while the West Ridgers still struggled into position for the final
take-off.

At least it was a struggle that was now bearing fruit. For on the
fourteenth, the day after the last of their loads had reached Camp
3W, the Ridgers were again in motion, with Willi Unsoeld leading
a file of thirteen Sherpas up to the West Shoulder, onto the ridge
itself, and up across the West Buttress on its farther side. Two of
the Sherpas—both of whom had, a short while before, carried to
Camp VI on the Col route—were not able to make a full day's
carry. But Willi and the others kept going and dumped their loads
at the site of 4W, at 25,100 feet, which had first—and last—been
reached, by Willi, Tom Hornbein and Barry Bishop a month and
two days before. That evening Willi and Sherpas returned to 3W.
The next day he, Tom and Sherpas went up with more loads. And
this time, with the Sherpas again descending, the two sahibs spent
the first night at 4W. "It was a beautiful night," Tom reported,
"and a tremendously wonderful feeling to have finally, after all
this time, established a tent at the site we had picked a whole
month before. It must, we thought, be the most beautiful spot in
the whole Himalaya: on a fine flat platform just where the snow
ridge meets the rock of the summit pyramid—but at the same time
at the edge of everything—overlooking the South Face and the
Cwm, looking straight across almost at the summit of Nuptse, up
at Lhotse; on the other side, across the North Face of Everest,
down to the Rongbuk Glacier, on out into Tibet. . . ."

On this day, May 15, Al Auten was working at 3W, and Barry
Corbet and Dick Emerson, who had been briefly down at Advance

Base, started up again for the umpteenth time. Their schedule was
to reach 3W that evening, proceed on the next day to 4W, and on
the seventeenth to carry out a high reconnaissance for the siting
of 5W. But as so often with plans of mice, men and mountaineers,
things went agley—specifically with Dick's innards, which, after a
period of good behavior, had now gone wrong again, draining his
strength with diarrhea and nausea. With the tents gone from the
dump site, there was no longer a place to break the journey from
Advance Base to 3W; it was presently apparent, as he struggled
up, that he could not make the whole distance in one day; and
leaving Barry to continue, he reluctantly turned back to descend
to the Cwm. More than reluctantly. Desolately. "For I knew," he
said later, "that if the West Ridge was going to move at all, it was
going to be in the next few days, and if I missed out now it would
be forever."

Barry went on to 3W. The next day he, Al Auten and eight
Sherpas climbed up to 4W. And meanwhile, Willi and Tom, the
high men on the ladder, moved up above 4W to investigate what
lay beyond. A month before, with Barry Bishop, they had surveyed
the upper reaches of the mountain and decided that, as below, the
most promising route lay not on the ridgeline itself but on the
slopes to the left of it—on what they called the West Buttress,
leading out onto Everest's North Face. Here, threading the downsloping slabs of rock, was a network of snow-lined gullies or
couloirs, several of which looked from a distance as if they would
"go." But no one had yet actually had a try at them, and each
step that Willi and Tom would take would be over terrain where
no man had ever trod. On this particular day, they did not intend
to go far. According to plan, the main reconnaissance upward
would be undertaken the next day by Barry Corbet and Dick
Emerson, who were due to arrive at 4W that evening. Also, the
weather had taken a turn for the worse, with a blustery wind and
scudding clouds, and it was about noon before they set out from
camp. What they had in mind was no more than "a reconnaissance
for a reconnaissance."

On their earlier visit to the site of 4W they had given names to
various of the features of the mountain above, and now they started
off by following a transverse gully which they had called the Diagonal Ditch. Above it, at intervals, other gullies furrowed the

rock, leading straight up the mountainside, and of these, a large long one which they had named Hornbein's Couloir seemed to offer the best key to the heights. But it was a considerable distance even to its base, and as of that day they had no particular thought of reaching it. "As we moved up the Diagonal Ditch, however," said Tom, "we had no difficulties, and after working across a couple of rocky spurs and small couloirs we suddenly found ourselves open to the North Face, with snowfields extending before us clear up to the base of Hornbein's Couloir. The temptation, in spite of the questionable weather, was too great to resist. So we dumped our fixed rope and extra pitons at the top of the Diagonal Ditch and headed up, on a 2- to 3-liter oxygen flow, reaching the foot of the couloir at about 3:30 P.M. There we sat for about half an hour, looking down at the Rongbuk and East Rongbuk Glaciers; then up the couloir some four or five hundred feet, at which point it turned and we could see no more, but only ponder on what was around the corner."

They had climbed some 1100 feet above 4W and were at a height of 26,200—exactly equal to that of the South Col on the other route. It was somewhere around this point, or a little higher, that their Camp 5W should be pitched, but a brief survey revealed no reasonably level and protected spot. As for 6W: that would be high up around the bend in Hornbein's Couloir, and there would be no telling until men had climbed there. Even with no campsites leaping into view, however, the day's exploration had been far from disappointing; for the Diagonal Ditch had proved an excellent route, and what could be seen of the couloir above seemed to present no major obstacles. At four o'clock Willi and Tom began their descent. In spite of steadily strengthening wind and poor visibility, they reached 4W at six, in time for the daily scheduled radio contact with Base and Advance Base. And waiting for them there were Barry Corbet, Al Auten and four of the eight Sherpas (the other four had gone down) who had come up with them that day from 3W.

But no Dick Emerson—

Down at Advance Base, after he had had to turn back from his attempted ascent with Barry, Dick had spent the previous evening stuffing himself with protein and otherwise doing all he could do to build up strength and banish nausea.* The results were not spectacular, and the next morning he was still well under par. But if the flesh was weak, his spirit was something else again, and after breakfast he was off for another try—this time alone, for he could find no available unassigned Sherpa to accompany him. Solitary climbing, as he well knew, was strictly against expedition policy,† but he knew too that, if he were to catch up with his West Ridge companions, it must be now or never. He did not overestimate himself. Aware that he might not be able to reach Camp 3W in one day's climbing, he had carefully considered the problems of an enforced night out. And it was well he had. For after a long day's pull, late afternoon found him still on the icy slopes about a third of the way short of his goal, and here he realized that he could climb no farther.

As Dick tells it:

"This meant that I had a choice. Even though I was two-thirds of the way up, I could turn back—or I could plan on a bivouac. And after weighing the alternatives as thoroughly as I could, I chose the bivouac, for two reasons. For one thing, I felt I was equipped to handle it; and for the other, a descent would mean withdrawing from the entire climb. When I say I was equipped to handle it, this was based on three things: (1) While I didn't have a sleeping bag, I did have an air mattress and plenty of clothing; (2) I knew the location of a crevasse at the nearby New New Dump—a crevasse I had already been down in for the purpose of untangling winching cable; and (3) I knew that at the dump were two or three bottles of oxygen that had not yet been moved up to 3W. My reasoning was that with oxygen to sleep on and the crevasse as protection I would be reasonably safe from frostbite. So I trudged on to the dump, concerned only about the possible worry of the men down at Advance Base, who were in a position to follow most of my progress and would now not know what my situation was.

* Along with, and as a result of, his acclimatization troubles, Dick was also the prime weight loser of the expedition, with a beginning-to-end decrease of no less than 48 pounds.

† Indeed, Norman, when he heard on the radio that Dick had had to give up his attempted ascent with Barry Corbet, radioed back to Maynard Miller at Advance Base that Dick be instructed to descend to Base Camp. But by this time he was already on his way up again.

"At just about dark I reached the dump and, locating the oxygen bottles, took two of them into the crevasse with me—about 30 feet down—where I spent the next two hours getting myself arranged. Not having a light, I had to do everything by feel. This involved, first, shoveling snow with my ice ax so as to clog up the lower portion of the crevasse sufficiently to give me a place to bed down. Then came adjustment of the oxygen mask, regulator and such, without being able to see them: taking my hands out of my gloves for very short intervals, working with the apparatus, putting hands back into gloves to warm them, etc. At last I had myself ready and arranged. But no sooner was this accomplished than a wind developed. This must have been around 10 P.M. The wind was blowing across the mountain slope parallel to the crevasse, and consequently the crevasse gave me little protection. On the contrary, it was a catch-all for the great quantities of snow being blown horizontally across the slopes and dumped in on me, and soon I was thoroughly buried—which at least protected me from the wind. I took off my crampons, and curled up on my mattress, breathing oxygen at a 1-liter flow while the snow blew in over me, and whether I should have or not, I spent a rather comfortable night.

"The next morning at daybreak, however, the wind was even stronger, and so much snow was blowing in on me in great drifts that it almost blocked out the light. As a result I climbed out of the crevasse rather anxiously; but once out, I discovered that the sky was blue, the weather basically good, except for the high wind sweeping across the mountain face and rolling the snow before it. So I started up. When the wind was at full force, however, it was almost impossible to climb against, and I could move only between gusts. During gusts I had to drive my ax in all the way and hold myself by literally clinging to it. Once, even while I was doing this, the wind suddenly changed direction, caught me off balance, and knocked me sideways off my feet, blowing so powerfully that I sailed horizontally, instead of downward, across a 30-degree slope."

Dick caught himself, however, by plunging his ax into snow and ice. Regaining the lost ground, he struggled on, and at about ten o'clock, still in a gale, he arrived at Camp 3W. Later in the day, to his surprise, his fellow West Ridgers appeared there too, descending from 4W. And he learned that his own adventure had been mild compared with what had happened above.

For the storm of that previous night which Dick Emerson had weathered out in his crevasse had been the worst of all the storms that AMEE encountered on its mountain. It was a "high" storm. Down at Base Camp that night, Dick Pownall reported, "we had hardly any wind, but there was a constant roar above—like the sound of a jet."* And in that roar the men at 4W had been all but swept from the peak.

Indeed, six of them *were* swept from it—though not, by the grace of God, all the way.

There were three tents at Camp 4W on that night of May 16: the one small one, in which Tom Hornbein and Willi Unsoeld were now spending their second night, and two larger newly pitched ones, joined together at their entrances, in which were Barry Corbet, Al Auten and the four Sherpas who had that day come up and stayed with them. Outside, the wind was howling. But they were snug in their shelters, and spirits were high, for apart from Dick Emerson's troubles everything was now at last going well. "After supper," said Barry, "we sang songs and were really carried away with our *hubris*." Then all crept into sleeping bags, turned on the night oxygen flow, and fell asleep.

Hubris was to have its usual classic consequence, however—no less for Everesters than for ancient Greeks. For a few hours later, at about midnight, Barry and Al, in their part of the two joined tents, awoke to a wild fury of blowing and realized to their horror that the tents had begun to slide downward. All they could do for the moment was to dig their fingers into the flooring, trying to claw a hold into the snow beneath; but it had not the slightest effect. The sliding continued. Then, suddenly, it was no longer a

---

* Strangely, there was something else jetlike overhead on that very night—but far swifter than a jet and far higher than a "high" storm. This was the space capsule of Astronaut L. Gordon Cooper, which passed over the Everest area three times during its journey of twenty-one orbits and twenty-four hours. The members of AMEE who were at Base Camp knew of the flight through broadcasts by All India Radio, but no one saw it or knew at exactly what times it was overhead. In any case, the men on the mountain presumably had enough on their minds without adding an astronaut. But to us in Kathmandu there was fascination in this momentary juxtaposition of what might be called inner and outer spacemen.

sliding but a rolling. The tents were of a design with external tubular frames; and on these frames the two of them, still lashed together, now tumbled over and over, with everything inside—men, sleeping bags, food, clothing, climbing gear—tumbling with them. In the black confusion, there was no way of telling in which direction they were going. If it was to the south, it would in a matter of seconds be the end for them, for here the mountain walls fell away almost vertically 4000 feet down into the Western Cwm. If it was to the north, they at least had a chance; for though on this side the drop was some 6000 feet, down to the glaciers of Tibet, the gradient was easier and there would be no free fall. When after a moment or two they were still rolling, not plummeting, they knew they were on the north side. Yet all they could do was pray. At a caprice of the wind, or of the conformation of the mountainside, the bouncing, somersaulting tents could go straight to the base of the mountain, and the only difference from a fall to the south would be slow instead of instantaneous death. But the caprice was otherwise. Everest was primed to strike but not to kill. About one hundred vertical feet and perhaps fifty linear yards below Camp 4W there was a shelf, a shallow trough, in the mountainside. And here the tents came to rest in a chaos of torn canvas, jutting poles, scattered gear, and dazed struggling men.

A quick stocktaking revealed that, amazingly, no one had been hurt. "Al and I were all right. The four Sherpas were all right," said Barry. "But things were in quite a shambles, with the tent floor now overhead and the main body of the tent fabric under and around us." With the gale still roaring in 100-mile-an-hour gusts, it was obvious that the lesser of the possible evils was for most of the men to stay where they were, serving as ballast to keep the tents from blowing even farther down the mountain. So it was Al alone who crawled out of them, emerging through a rent in the fabric. "In the dark and with the wind blowing a ground blizzard across the tents," he said, "I at first couldn't see anything. But Barry rummaged around in the wreckage, found a flashlight, and handed it out to me. Beaming it around, I determined that we probably weren't going to take off again—at least not immediately. But things needed a lot of anchoring, and I got to work; meanwhile the others passed out my down parka, which I was badly

needing, and my outer boots, which I pulled over my down boots."
With the rest doing what they could from inside, Al pinioned down
some of the ruin. Then, realizing that more help was needed, he
battled his way up the slope, without oxygen, to where the Unsoeld-Hornbein tent still stood at its original site.

Through the howl of the storm, Willi and Tom had heard
nothing of what was happening until Al, snow-rimed and gasping,
appeared to tell them. But now, putting on their outer clothing,
they went down with him to the wreck. In the witches' cauldron
of night and gale there was no possible way of restoring true order.
The best that could be done was to bind the remains of the two
tents together with lengths of rope and to run other ropes up to
belay points above to provide further anchorage. Then Willi, Tom
and Al crept back up to the original campsite, where Al squeezed
into the tiny tent with the others; meanwhile Barry and the
Sherpas, still serving as ballast, weathered out the rest of the night
in the wreckage below. They were shaken, stunned, battered—but
at least still alive.

In the morning the storm was raging on. In the upper tent, Tom,
who was lying on the windward side, could feel his body, in its
sleeping bag, being lifted into the air by the gusts that drove in
under the flooring, and to make things worse, the wind had un-
zipped the zipper of the tent entrance and was seeping in at an
alarming rate. Soon the three men were clinging to the aluminum
frames to keep their whole habitation from taking off, but even
though they succeeded, it was, in the process, said Tom, "being
beaten and smashed to a residual pulp." At about eight o'clock, in
spite of the frenzy around them, Willi was able to make walkie-
talkie contact with Base Camp (during which he carefully under-
stated their plight, for there was nothing anyone could do to help
them). And, fantastic though it may seem, it was through Base
that the upper three had their first word that morning of Barry
and the four Sherpas in the ruins below. For Barry was on the
air with another walkie-talkie at the same time—managing it by
poking its antenna up through the urinating hole of his upside-
down shelter.

In the upper tent there followed another period of waiting and
holding on, in the hope that the wind would slacken. But if any-

thing, it blew still more fiercely. After a while three of the Sherpas came up from below, announcing that they were getting out and descending to 3W ("not a bad idea," said Tom); and soon after Barry appeared with the fourth Sherpa, the fifty-six-year-old Tashi. Now everyone was preparing for evacuation. Al left the tent briefly to search for his pack, which had blown away. Inside, Tom and Barry were struggling to assemble gear, and Willi was again on the radio with Base Camp, announcing their imminent descent. At which moment there was a heaving and snapping of guy ropes, and the tent, like the others on the previous night, began to slide ominously over the snow. "I was nearest the entrance," said Tom. "I dove for it and got half out, with my legs wrapped into the vestibule, and there, right before me, was a rappel picket lying on the snow. I picked it up, jammed it into the snow, and hung onto it in the manner of a self-arrest, managing to stop not only myself but the tent from blowing and sliding on down the slope. Barry crawled out after me and began piling boxes of food and oxygen bottles on the tent, to collapse it, and Willi crawled out behind him, still talking calmly on the radio."

Between earth and sky, however, that was the only calmness, as what came to be known as The Great Rout of May 17 now continued. With the last of the tents down, there was no choice for anyone but to descend to 3W—if it could be done—but first a detour had to be made down to the two blown-away tents to retrieve several ice axes that had been left there to pinion them. During this operation the wind reached the height of its savagery, whipping the mass of ruined tentage around and trying to blow everything and everyone off the mountain. "Willi, stretched out flat on the snow," said Tom, "was literally lifted off it by the wind blowing underneath him, picking him up and just transporting him." And the rest held themselves only by lying prone with their axes jammed into the slope.

Finally they were able to get moving again. In the vicinity of 4W they were at an open gap in the West Ridge, but after descending a little they came into its lee, and though the wind was still wild it was not quite so bad as before. At all events, they managed to stumble on down, and in midafternoon they came at last to 3W, to be greeted by Dick Emerson, who earlier in the day had arrived there on his upward journey. The pleasure of reunion, however, was far outweighed by exhaustion—and even more by depression. For while all were alive and unharmed, the mountain had struck what seemed a mortal blow, both in delay of their schedule and in loss of materiel. Three tents had been destroyed. Several sleeping bags, mattresses, oxygen masks, and packs containing personal gear had blown into eternity.* Whether replacements for even the most critical items could be brought up quickly—or enough Sherpas could be mustered for subsequent carries—appeared at the time highly dubious. After their weeks of frustrated waiting, and then their rapid high-hearted push toward the heights, it looked as if the gallant band of West Ridgers had drawn their last short straw.

Everest is nothing if not schizophrenic. For a night and a day it had been demoniac. Now it smiled and beamed. But whether sun and stillness could undo what the storm had done still remained to be seen.

On the morning after their rout, the West Ridgers, at Camp 3W, took stock of their situation. It was obvious to all that their chances for the summit, problematical at best, were now thin indeed, and there was no little urge, after the beating they had taken, to call it a day and descend to Base Camp. It was an urge that was not answered, however, for there was another that was even stronger—the urge that had brought these men across the world to confront the greatest of mountains—and abetting it, rekindling it, goading the others on, was the implacable will and dedication of Tom Hornbein.

During the night he had formulated a plan, and now he presented it. To begin with, there were the negatives: a critical shortage of time, caused by their setback from 4W to 3W; and a renewed shortage of manpower, for their roster of Sherpas, which a few days before had added up to a formidable task force, was now drastically depleted. Most of the carriers, having served in the first Col route campaign, had been a bit the worse for wear even at the

---

* Among Barry Corbet's lost possessions was a wallet containing all the money he had brought with him to Nepal. Just why he was carrying money with him up the West Ridge of Everest is something that no one, including Barry, has been able to explain.

start of the West Ridge push. But now, after the storm, almost all had definitively "had it"; there were only three of them at 3W able and willing to go high again—and five was the absolute minimum needed to mount even the sketchiest recouping operation. True, two new men could probably be procured from below. But it would take them time to get up. It would take time to reoccupy 4W. And even with five Sherpas, it would be manifestly impossible, in the face of dwindling time and supplies, to carry out the original plan of going on from there to site and stock two still higher camps large enough to accommodate two 2-man summit teams. What, then, *could* be done? Well, said Tom, the single and sole possibility was to cut the program in half. Instead of two camps above 4W, there would be only one. Instead of two summit teams, there would be only one. Granted, the chance of success on such a shoestring would be almost nil. It would really, said Tom, be more of a gesture than anything else—"a gesture of putting in one more small camp just as high as we can get it, and then climbing beyond it as high as we can; in effect, probably just reconnoitering a route for some future expedition." But at least it would be better than giving up now and calling it quits. They would at least be making one last desperate bid to go as high as they could.

The others agreed with him. The "gesture" should be made. On the radio they discussed their situation and plans with Norman at Base Camp, and it was arranged that two new Sherpas would be sent up to them from Advance Base, carrying tents and other materiel to replace what had been lost at Camp 4W. But this could not be until the next day—May 19. The return to 4W would therefore be on the twentieth and the push to the higher camp on the twenty-first (if there were no more storms), meaning that the summit target date, if it could still be called that, would again have to be postponed—to the twenty-second. The much-discussed summit rendezvous with the South Col team, a slim prospect to begin with, was now so remote a possibility as to be almost past consideration. But, for what little it was worth, the timing there was still all right; for the Collars, who had been scheduled to leave Advance Base on the seventeenth, had themselves been delayed— though not blitzed—by the storm, and by taking off today, the eighteenth, would, at the expected pace of a camp a day, also be in a position for their summit bid on the twenty-second.

One further decision remained for the West Ridgers. When they were still thinking in terms of four men going for the top, it had been understood that Unsoeld and Hornbein would constitute the first team and Corbet and Emerson the second. But now that only one pair would be going above the highest camp, whom should it consist of? Two of the team were almost automatically eliminated. Al Auten had done some fine climbing and shown great endurance, but from the beginning he had been considered a support member, not a summit candidate. And Dick Emerson, though he *had* been a candidate, and had waged a valiant struggle against his physical ailments, was still obviously not as strong as the others. With Barry Corbet, however, the situation was very different. In spite of early acclimatization problems, plus the shock and grief of losing his closest friend, Jake Breitenbach, he had taken to the mountain in magnificent stride. He was generally considered the best rock climber on the expedition. And there was little question that, though he had been paired with Dick in the original second assault team, he was the mountaineering equal of first-teamers Willi and Tom. If Barry had been another man—a pushing, self-centered, out-for-himself man—there might have been a problem, a discussion, even a choosing by lot. But he was not remotely the sort for that, and quickly, decisively, he settled the matter himself. Willi and Tom were the prime movers of the whole West Ridge enterprise. They were a perfectly matched pair. They had been designated as the first summit team. And such they would remain. Barry, giving up whatever claims he had, would, with Al and Dick, serve as their support, helping to put their top camp as high as it could possibly be placed.

That settled, the five men dug in at 3W—waiting, resting, gathering strength for what was to come. The rest of the day passed, and the night, and the next morning. And on that afternoon of May 19 the two new Sherpas arrived on schedule from below.

Down at Base Camp there was waiting too. The wait was longer. And in many ways it was psychologically harder, for while the men up on the mountain still had challenge and struggle ahead, those below had, as active participants, finished the campaign. There was satisfaction in victory attained, hope for further victories to come; but blended with them was the inevitable letdown of after the fact. Before turning back from the foot of Everest to Kathmandu, "camp follower" Spark Schnitzer had noted in his diary: "In my heart, happiness and sadness are strangely mingled, and I feel keenly how much more rewarding it is to travel toward a goal than to reach it; for the attainment lasts but a moment." Now the no longer active members of AMEE were experiencing this in full measure. What had once been single-minded concentration on the mountain was increasingly diluted by thoughts of exodus and home.

In purely personal terms, of course, the inward climate varied from man to man. Jim Whittaker, who had said, "I will climb Everest," had climbed it: mission accomplished. Norman, in reaching more than 28,000 feet, and Jim Lester, in attaining Advance Base, had, on different levels, accomplished all they could conceivably have hoped for. Will Siri, who had originally been aiming for the South Col or higher, had sacrificed his climbing ambitions to his scientific work; but the choice had been deliberate and he was philosophically content with it. For some of the rest, on the other hand, there had been deep frustration and disappointment. For Dick Pownall, for one, who had twice reached the Col, only to realize on his second descent that he "had had the course." For Gil Roberts, who in the performance of his medical duties, had spent longer than anyone else in the Western Cwm, with the result that he had now deteriorated too far to go higher. For Dan Doody and Barry Prather, who, just as the heights seemed in reach for them, had been stricken by illness. As should be abundantly clear by now, it was not only in theory but in fact that AMEE was a *team*, and there was not a man on it who was primarily motivated by dreams of personal "glory." But those who fell short of the goals they had set themselves would have been less—or more— than human if they had not felt the sting.

There was a difference too, at this stage, in the degree of "function" that was left for the various men. Norman, though his high-climbing was over, was still expedition leader, with manifold responsibilities; the radio reports from the Col and West Ridge teams called constantly for new assessments and decisions; and, on the side, he was occupied with motion picture filming. As deputy leader, Will Siri was likewise involved in overall strategy, and was, besides, still deeply involved in his physiology. For most of the team, however, the days passed slowly, with little to do. There was picture taking. There was sunbathing, reading, diaries, the radio, and occasionally skiing—with pratfalls—on the Khumbu Glacier. But mostly there was waiting.

And waiting—

With the postponement of the summit target date came also a deferral of the evacuation date, from May 22 to 25; and Chotari, the assistant sirdar of the Sherpas, was sent down to the Solu Khumbu villages to round up the porters who would then be needed to move the expedition out from Base Camp. The estimate of the needed manpower was 275, as against the 909 carriers who had set out in February from Kathmandu—the differential, of course, stemming from all that had been consumed or would be left behind on the mountain.

Meanwhile, as part of the glaciological program, a small group would leave Base several days before the main party, bound for the Mingbo Glacier, in the vicinity of Thangboche, where certain types of work could be better accomplished than on the precipitous skirts of Everest. Maynard Miller himself was now up in the Cwm, and would remain there until the high climbers descended; but his assistant, Barry Prather, was now well enough for such an exploit, and he would be accompanied by Dick Pownall, Gombu, and a squad of supporting Sherpas. The schedule was aligned so that they would meet the main body of the expedition on its way out at either Thangboche or Namche Bazar, and all would then proceed together toward Kathmandu, with ETA now set for June 9.

Such matters were important but scarcely dramatic. The excitement at Base during these days came from the vicarious sharing of adventures higher up—and particularly those of the West Ridgers as they gave battle to the storm at Camp 4W. Willi Unsoeld was, as noted, talking to Base on the radio on the morning of May 17, at the very moment when 4W's last still-standing shelter

seemed about to take off, and suddenly his listeners below heard
him interrupt himself to shout: "Tom—Barry, get out! The tent's
going!" For most, it was a moment of damp palms and thumping
hearts. But it would have taken more than a storm—whether he
himself were in it or not—to shake the monumental calm of Balu
Prather, who was operating the Base radio. "Real fine, Willi, real
fine," he replied soothingly over the airwaves; then added what was
to become an expedition classic: "Do you want me to give you the
weather report now?"

Willi's answer, if any, to that one was lost in the roar of the
wind. But later (to everyone's relief) he was again on the air,
from 3W, this time with no roar. And subsequently plans were
discussed for the Ridgers' revised and curtailed assault, with the
final one-day postponement of their highest push. On May 22, it
was arranged, the Base radio would be kept manned for the whole
of the day. Norman and a few others would meanwhile go up the
slopes of Pumori, on the far side of the Khumbu Glacier, from
which, if the weather was fair, a clear view could be had of the
upper reaches of the West Ridge and its North Face buttress.
What they would see was, to put it mildly, problematical. But
they would be watching—waiting—watching—

Four days earlier, on May 18, came the long-awaited U-Day at
Advance Base, with Lute Jerstad, Barry Bishop and the Sherpas
Pemba Tenzing, Nima Tenzing (of Pangboche) and Kalden moving through the upper Cwm toward Camp III and beyond. The
next day, on the planned twenty-four-hours-apart schedule, Dave
Dingman, with the Sherpas Girmi Dorje and Nima Dorje, followed after. At A.B. there remained, as planned, Maynard Miller,
and, as a result of his own last-minute decision, Jimmy Roberts.
Jimmy, AMEE's one Englishman and its Himalayan veteran of
veterans, would dearly have loved a try at the South Col; indeed,
he had been preparing for it throughout the siege of the mountain
and, though the team's oldest active member (one year Norman's
senior), was in excellent trim. But here again logistics played its
villain's role, in the shortage of oxygen and other material; and
Jimmy, like Will Siri and Barry Corbet, became one of the expedition's "sacrificers," relinquishing his chance to go high in

favor of younger men who would presumably make a stronger team.

Arriving at Camp III, Lute, Barry and their Sherpas found the tents there partly buried in an ice avalanche that had fallen from the Lhotse Face (though the site was theoretically safe from such slides). But they were able, with a good deal of labor, to dig them out, and on the nineteenth moved on up the Face toward Camp IV. Here too there was plenty of work to be done, for though the weather was now fine, the storm of a few days past had wreaked its havoc conscientiously—"giving us the job," said Lute, "of practically putting in the whole route again: rechopping all the filled-up steps and digging out the fixed ropes that were buried in 2 to 3 feet of snow." At IV there was more of same: no ice avalanche this time, but huge drifts of snow that required long shovel work before the tents were habitable. And the next day still more, as they dug, scraped and clawed their way across the Lhotse Couloir, then up the Yellow Band and Geneva Spur. "The Sherpas," Lute reported later, "were just fantastic, carrying about 70 pounds each without oxygen." And the sahibs, one gathers, were themselves scarcely having a rest day, for though their loads were somewhat lighter and they were breathing oxygen, it was they who did the clearing and securing of the route. Near the top of the Geneva Spur, they added to their loads as well—to the tune of 26 pounds each; for here they came upon the bottles of oxygen that had been cached by Dave Dingman on the descent from the first summit campaign, and Lute and Barry each hoisted two of them for the remainder of the climb to the South Col.

Then they came to the Col—Lute for the third time, Barry for the second—eighteen days after their Day of Disappointment, when they had had to turn back from their first bid for the top. And for a few bad moments it appeared that the disappointment might repeat itself all over again. Throughout the ascent they had worried about what the recent storm winds might have done to the tents on the exposed flats of "the most desolate place on earth"; and now, as they came up onto the plateau, it seemed at first that their worst fears were realized, for they could see no sign of them. They themselves were carrying no tents. Without a camp on the Col, they were done, finished. And they were almost in despair, until they came up over a low rolling ridge that they had not noticed before and found the tents hidden behind it. "Barry spotted them first," said Lute, "and started leaping up and down." (Quite a feat at that altitude, even with oxygen.) "And we knew we were in business."

There was to be more worry, however, before the day was ended; for soon after they had occupied the camp, the Sherpa Kalden became ill, with considerable pain and labored breathing, and for a time it appeared that he might be a serious case. After what had happened to Barry Prather, pulmonary edema was much on everyone's mind, and Kalden's symptoms indicated that he might be suffering either from that or pneumonia. On their walkie-talkie, Lute and Barry Bishop tried to raise Dr. Dave Dingman at the camp just below them—without success. But they were subsequently able to reach Dr. Gil Roberts at Base Camp, and from him received long-distance diagnosis and instructions. Penicillin was produced from the medical kit and administered to Kalden both orally and by injection, and presently, to their enormous relief, his condition took a strong turn for the better.

Night came. A night, as always on the Col, of wind and cold. But there was no all-out gale or storm; in the morning the weather was fine; and soon the little caravan was moving on toward Camp VI. Kalden, of course, was not in shape to go higher. But he was well enough to be left alone at V until the other two Sherpas returned that evening, and the loads that had to be carried higher were not so great that four men could not manage them. Pemba Tenzing and Nima Tenzing each carried three oxygen bottles, breathing from one. Lute and Barry, trying to conserve their strength, carried only one each, which they were currently using; but the next day, on their summit try, they would take over the four full ones that the Sherpas now had on their backs.

The sun was bright, the wind negligible. Everest was smiling. But the smile was a hard one, a smile of ice-sheathed glittering snow, and almost every step of the way up the couloir toward the Southeast Ridge of the summit pyramid had to be hacked out with axes. Still, slowly but surely, height was gained. The Col dropped away below. The ridge drew nearer. They were on the ridge. They were stumping up the line of rock and snow between two oceans of space, and ahead they could see the two tiny blobs that were the tents of Camp VI.

Across one of the airy oceans, beyond snow slope and gulf and precipice, the West Ridge team was now also again in motion. On the previous day, May 20, they had climbed back from 3W to 4W and, with the help of their skeleton crew of Sherpas, set up a new camp on the wreckage of the old. And on the twenty-first, while the South Collars were pushing up to Camp VI, they launched what must surely be ranked as one of the great one-day feats of mountaineering history. On difficult and unknown terrain on a great peak, the usual order of events is, first, a reconnaissance and trail-blazing, second, a series of load-carryings to establish a higher camp, and third—if all has gone well in the first two stages—the actual occupation of that camp. But on the West Ridge there was no longer time for such a program, and all three operations were performed simultaneously.

Ten men were involved: the whole West Ridge team of Unsoeld, Hornbein, Corbet, Auten and Emerson, and their five Sherpas, Ang Dorje, Ila Tsering, Tenzing Nindra, Passang Tendi and Tenzing Gyalsto. Of the Sherpas only Ang Dorje was an experienced veteran. The rest were young untried men who, until now, had done little or no high climbing. "All good Sherpas down sick. Only bad Sherpas up here," said the youthful Ila Tsering, grinning at the West Ridgers. Then, hoisting their loads, he and his brethren proceeded to write their own bright chapter in the book of Tiger achievements.

Not all the day's climb was on virgin mountainside. In the beginning it was along the Diagonal Ditch, leading up and across the North Face, which had been pioneered by Willi Unsoeld and Tom Hornbein five days before, and this was followed for about three hours to Willi and Tom's high point—the base of Hornbein's Couloir, at 26,200 feet. The team moved in three echelons. First went Barry Corbet and Al Auten, the reconnoiterers of the operation, who would try to forge a way up the couloir and find a site for Camp 5W. They were followed, some time later, by the Sherpas, carrying the materiel to stock the camp. And finally came Willi and Tom, who would occupy the camp, and who, like Barry and Lute on the far side of the mountain, were traveling as light as possible to conserve strength for the next day. Third on the rope with Willi and Tom was Dick Emerson; but Dick, at this stage, was only "along for the ride." Thanks to an immense output of effort—and his night in the crevasse—he had made Camp 3W. Subsequently he had made 4W and was now climbing up even beyond it. But he was well aware that he would reach his ceiling before the airy heights of 5W and, on this day, was limiting his ambitions to going on with his old friends as far as he could.

In their three groups of two, five and three, the climbers moved on: largely following the snow of the Diagonal Ditch; occasionally, when it became necessary, veering off onto the tilted slabs of the bare rock face; then cutting up over the snow slopes to the base of Hornbein's Couloir. When Willi, Tom and Dick reached this point, Barry and Al were already far above it—two tiny creeping dots high up on the steep ribbon of snow. The Sherpas, however, were there, waiting and resting, and here the three sahibs stopped and rested too. This was the end of the line for Dick Emerson. "It was evident," he said, "that the summit team should pick up speed and get themselves up the couloir into their high camp as quickly as possible. Also that I was holding them back somewhat. So here I said a fond and rather tearful farewell to Willi and Tom."

Alone, he settled himself to wait on the vast wilderness of the mountainside until the return of Barry, Al and the Sherpas later in the day. Whether he would see Willi and Tom the next day, back at 4W, neither he nor they had any way of knowing. They might return by this route, having scored either a wide miss, a close miss or, just possibly, a direct hit. They might, if a miracle happened, not return, but cross over the summit and descend with the South Collars on the far side of the mountain. Or they might not return because—

No. Not that.

Then Dick was alone with his thoughts. Soon Willi, Tom and the Sherpas were also dots on the ribbon of snow, high above.

And the dots crept on. The angle of ascent in the couloir was between 35 and 40 degrees; the snow was hard and glazed; and up ahead, Barry and Al had to cut a stairway of thousands of steps. Behind them, Willi, Tom, and the Sherpas, with no steps to cut, moved at a faster pace, slowly closing the gap between them. But they did not close it altogether, and through midday and early afternoon the two parties moved up several hundred feet apart, advancing higher and higher toward Everest's citadel. On either side of their narrow gully were the smooth downsloping slabs of the North Face. Overhead, however, about a thousand feet above the base of the couloir, the smoothness stopped, and the walls containing it bulged out in rugged looming cliffs. This was the Yellow Band—the same stratum of tawny schist that, cutting through the whole massif of the Everest group, also shows itself on the Lhotse Face, along the South Col route. But on Lhotse the Band is at around the 25,000-foot level. Here on the north of Everest its lower margin is above 27,200 feet. Through the hours, nine masked and roped men moved slowly toward it: nearer—nearer—

Kick-kick-kick. Whack-whack-whack. On two sides of the mountain, on North Face and Southeast Ridge, feet shuffled upward, axes rose and fell.

"Climbing a great mountain," Norman Dyhrenfurth had said in an interview before the expedition took off, "is one-tenth beauty and nine-tenths hell."

This was part of the hell.

Millions have been through hell on earth: in wars, famines, pestilences, and the many other disasters to which man is heir. But in most cases it has been unwanted, unsolicited, uncontrollable hell. Here on Everest was hell self-imposed.

We are back to the old question: the original, eternal, blank-faced, unanswerable question: *Why?* Every mountaineer has been asked it. Perhaps the reader of this story is asking it. The eyes on the temples of Kathmandu had asked it as the expedition passed through on its journey. The climbers themselves asked it as they lived and struggled on their mountain, inching up to the very limits of human endurance. *Why?*

It is easier to reply with negatives than with positives. The Chinese, on their climb of three years before, had declared that "we thought of Comrade Mao, took strength, and moved onward and upward"; but such sentiment would not do for AMEE. With due respect to our Chief Executive, and due allowance for the politics of the various team members, it is highly doubtful if anyone was climbing Everest for the President of the United States. Even allowing for the flag on Jim Whittaker's Maypole, conventional patriotism had little part in the venture, and, on that high roof in the sky, Washington and Moscow, cold war and warm war, the alarums and excursions of jangling nationalism, were so remote as to be unimaginable. "Everest is too great to belong to anyone. It is for all men," Tenzing Norgay had said. And the mountaineer's answer must be, now and always, "Amen."

Kick-kick-kick. Whack-whack-whack.

As for the other non-motives—

Obviously these men were not climbing for money. (Indeed, many had jeopardized jobs or delayed careers in joining the expedition.) They were not climbing for fame (for in the United States at least, mountaineers do not rate such kudos as crooners or quarterbacks). They were not climbing for families or loved ones. (On the contrary, the five-months'-long absence from home put no little strain on several marriages.) Pending psychologist Jim Lester's definitive report, it is safe to say that they were not full-time masochists (one had only to watch them eat to know that) and that the lure of the mountain was involved neither with death wish nor phallic symbol. Even the concept of *conquest*, beloved of headline writers and book titlers, was only a small part of their motivation, for each and every one of them knew, with Lionel Terray, that on a mountain there is only *"la conquête de l'inutile"*; knew, with George Leigh-Mallory, that to his question, "Have we vanquished an enemy?" there was only one answer—"None but ourselves."

On the two teams went: up the ridge, up the couloir.

Kick-kick-kick. Whack-whack-whack.

Mountaineering has been defined as many things: as a sport, an art, a science, an exploration, an adventure. And it is all of these— plus a response to challenge: a challenge not only physical but to the deepest recesses of the spirit. The members of AMEE were no regimented robots. The very essence of their venture was that they were in it voluntarily; not as conscripts, not because of objective pressures, but as freely and highly motivated individuals. Men like Norman Dyhrenfurth, Willi Unsoeld, Tom Hornbein,

Lute Jerstad, and Barry Bishop—indeed the whole pack and parcel of them—had not been produced by automated machinery like German Nazis or Chinese Communists. Each had his own personal response to the sport, art, science, exploration, adventure—and challenge—of climbing Everest. Each brought to it, and would take from it, something specially and privately unique to his own mind and heart.

For all, however, the challenge and response were *there*. No less than the mountain was *there*. All, perforce, had to face it with the "up and at it" of men of action. But mingled with this was far more than one might expect in a group of steak- and milk-fed young Americans of Buddhism's mystic and reverent *om*. Everest was not merely an adventure of the body but of mind and soul. It was an exercise not only in struggle but in awareness: a heightening of human experience; an extension, beyond the demands of normal living, of man's scope and capabilities.

These were not fanatics or monomaniacs. They knew that their world, their normal lives, still existed, and had full expectation that —with the exception of Jake Breitenbach—they would soon be returning to them. From Base Camp, before setting out for this final push, Willi Unsoeld had written to his wife Jolene of the enormous intensity of will and energy that was needed for the job ahead. But then he had added: "In the midst of such all-consuming concentration, though, is the dim awareness of the background provided by you, Jo, and the kids and the Peace Corps job and the years that lie ahead for us. The foreground of the all-out effort on the mountain gives depth and richness to this background; but without the background the mountain would lose all perspective, becoming a mere comet burst whose light fails to illumine the life that follows. . . ."

Kick-kick-kick. Whack-whack-whack.

The life that follows, however—would follow. This was the time of the comet burst. The time of the mountain: all consuming.

"Our present world," the English writer-mountaineer Frederic Harrison has written, "is a world of remarkable civilization, but it is not very natural and not very happy. We need yet some snatches of the life of youth . . . to draw sometimes great draughts of simplicity and beauty. We need sometimes that poetry should not be droned into our ears but flashed into our senses. And man, with all his knowledge and his pride, needs sometimes to know nothing and to feel nothing, but that he is a marvellous atom in a marvellous world."

The men of Everest had their knowledge and their pride. It had got them where they were. But now it was gone, lost, meaningless, for they had climbed past it into a life where meanings and values are different. They had climbed past Norman's "nine-tenths hell" into the one-tenth that lay above and beyond it. And if ever there have been marvellous atoms in a marvellous world, it was these atoms, these dots of flesh and breath, stumping upward on the two sides of earth's rooftop.

Kick-kick-kick. Whack-whack-whack.

14. MAYPOLE REVISITED

AT ABOUT TWO in the afternoon the kicking and whacking ended for Barry Corbet and Al Auten, leading the climb up Hornbein's Couloir on the North Face. They had reached the lower margin of the Yellow Band, at a height of about 27,250 feet, and there on the wall of the couloir, buttressed by rock, was a small platform of snow that might just conceivably hold a single 2-man tent. Ideally, they would have liked to go higher. If the original plan for a Camp 5W and a 6W had held, the first of them would have been down near the base of the couloir, the second several hundred feet above their present point. But there was to be no second. A high 5W would be it. Almost 1800 vertical feet remained to the summit—a forbidding distance at such altitudes and over totally unknown terrain. But there was nothing for it. Willi Unsoeld, Tom Hornbein and the five Sherpas, laboring up the couloir, were some two hours behind them, and as it was, it would be a close thing for Barry and Al to get the Sherpas and themselves down to 4W before dark.

They waited. At four the second echelon arrived and dumped its loads, and almost immediately Barry, Al and the Sherpas made

241

ready for the descent. "Good-bye. Good climbing. We'll be seeing you." But where and when no one knew. Neither then nor afterward did Barry Corbet speak of it, but that moment of turning back must have been for him one of almost unbearable poignancy; for of all the men on the expedition none more richly deserved a chance at the top. There was no alternative, however. His job was done. Al Auten's job was done—and magnificently—for, as radio specialist and communications officer, he had not been expected to be one of the truly high climbers. The Sherpas job was done. And let their names be repeated—Ang Dorje, Ila Tsering, Tenzing Nindra, Passang Tendi, Tenzing Gyalsto—for they too had done themselves proud. No one knew better than Willi Unsoeld and Tom Hornbein, taking their leave from them, that if it had not been for what these, their companions, had done that day, there would have been no tomorrow—whatever the outcome.

The seven receded below. The two remained. And for more than an hour they hacked and shoveled, enlarging and leveling the tiny platform that was Camp 5W. Then came the no less arduous job of pitching a tent, with a stiff wind pouring down the mountainside, trying its best to dislodge both tent and pitchers. "We finally got it up," said Tom, "at a rather eerie sloping angle, with about a foot and a half of its outer side hanging over the edge of the platform. This bulge we ultimately filled up with our reindeer boots, to give us some false sense of security. We anchored the tent's upper guy ropes with a piton driven about a half an inch into the rock of the Yellow Band and pinioned the rest with our ice axes, our oxygen bottles and some prayer."

Inside it at last, they prepared supper; and, unlike many of the high climbers, they had appetites, downing a meal of bouillon, chicken-noodle soup, shrimp with curry and tomato sauce, and— to quote Tom—"a few other odds and ends." Then it was into the sleeping bags, almost fully dressed (except for the boots doing service as tent stuffing), together with their two recently used small stoves, to warm them, and two bottles of water, to be kept freezeproof during the night. At about eight o'clock Willi fell asleep, breathing oxygen at a 1-liter flow. But Tom remained awake for another hour, writing his diary and a letter to his wife; and—ever the scientist, at whatever altitude—he noted that "I consciously did it without using oxygen, to record the nature of my handwriting."

Then he too slept. Outside, the wind rose and howled. The tent trembled and teetered on its flimsy perch. But inside, both men slept warmly and well until four in the morning, when their oxygen ran out and, waking, they began to prepare breakfast. They hoped, though they could not know, that on the other side of the mountain, some 200 feet higher than themselves, two other men were also stirring in a tent in the darkness, waiting for daylight.

They were.

Lute Jerstad and Barry Bishop, with the Sherpas Pemba Tenzing and Nima Tenzing, had reached Camp VI on the Southeast Ridge in the early afternoon of the previous day. Pemba and Nima, their loads delivered, had then turned to go back to the South Col, and the summit pair, like Willi and Tom, set themselves to the labor of digging in. Unlike the others, they did not have to start from scratch. The two tents from the first assault were still there. But they were drifted over with snow, partly torn and half-collapsed, and it took them almost until dark to put the less battered of the two into shape for occupancy.

Then they too were inside, out of the night and the wind. But it was with none of the snug euphoria that had rewarded Willi and Tom. Both, of course, were tired. But Barry, it was soon apparent, was more than tired; even at rest, he was having great difficulty in breathing, and soon it appeared that he might be becoming seriously ill. With Lute's help he got his oxygen going, and it helped a little—but not much. "He still couldn't breathe properly lying down," said Lute. "So he'd try sitting up, and that was no good. Then lying on his stomach, and that was no good." Meanwhile Lute was trying to get some water prepared, but nothing went right there either. "I got some water made," he said, "and we kicked it over, and I made some more, and the stove ran out, and all sorts of things happened. We just couldn't get anything to eat. For a while we couldn't even get any liquid. Then finally we got some soup made and drank some water." But Barry, instead of getting better, was getting worse: shifting and turning constantly, but unable to find a position in which he could relax and rest.

"Lute, I think I'm going mad," he muttered suddenly, through clenched teeth.

Later, recalling the experience, he said: "It wasn't just breathing that was bothering me. I was fighting a terrifying claustrophobia and had to suppress a wild desire to break out of the cluttered tent. Also, my sense of balance was muddled. Lying flat, I felt as if I were at an absurd and sickening angle, and nausea wrenched my stomach. Only by bracing myself semi-upright could I keep some semblance of equilibrium."

He increased the flow of oxygen into his sleeping mask from 1 to 2 liters per minute. Again there was slight relief—but only slight —and as the hours dragged past he was able neither to lie down nor sit up, but only to maintain a cramped position halfway between. In both his and Lute's minds was the grim unspoken thought that in the morning he might be unable to go on up—or even down. But they could only wait and see. And hope. Having done all he could to help, Lute, at Barry's urging, took a sleeping pill and dozed fitfully; and finally Barry too, still on 2 liters of oxygen, managed to close his eyes and sleep.

At 4:30 in the morning Lute was up and stirring, trying again to prepare some food for their empty stomachs. Soon after, Barry awoke—and was feeling better. Though still weak, he was at least not nauseated and disoriented, and he too began to get ready for the day ahead. Their troubles, however, were far from over. For a few minutes later, as Lute was attaching a fresh butane cylinder to one of the two stoves he was using, there was a sudden great whoosh and a burst of flame filled the tent. Both men's beards and eyebrows were singed. Barry's plastic oxygen mask was consumed in one blinding second. And in the next, with the fire still burning, the little tent was filled with acrid white smoke.

Said Barry: "Panic gripped us. Lute struggled toward the zippered entrance, and I tried to smother the flames with my sleeping bag; but my legs were still inside it and I could get no leverage. Meanwhile the fire was feeding on the air in the tent, soon exhausting it, and our lungs were aching. I was groping desperately for a knife to cut through the tent wall, when Lute managed to tear open the zipper and literally dived outside. His momentum was so great that he almost pitched down the steep slope toward the South Col. I was on his heels. We snatched the flaming stove from the tent, doused it in the snow, and soon the fire had died in the thin air." The tent and most of its contents were all right; they did not go up in flames. But the spasm of violent action was almost more than the two men could take, and for several minutes they sagged, gasping and choking, on their hands and knees in the snow. "When at last we crawled back into the tent," said Barry, "we said nothing to each other, but we shared the same thought. The omens were bad, all bad."

Their hope for an early start was gone. Hampered both by their own weakness and the shambles in the tent, they needed almost three hours to prepare a bit of liquid breakfast and get themselves ready for take-off. The delay, following on top of everything else, seemed at the time an almost insuperable setback to their chances of success. As happened so many times on the mountain, mischance was eventually, through the workings of fate, to prove a godsend. But they were not to learn this until many hours later.

Finally, at eight o'clock, they were on their way. At least the weather was fine, the sun was brilliant, and compared with the gale on the Whittaker-Gombu ascent, the wind was no more than a zephyr. Before them the Southeast Ridge climbed up in a white arc into the flawless blue of the sky.

What was left to them in strength and endurance was perhaps not much. But they were going to give all they had.

On that morning of May 22, some 1250 feet below, Dave Dingman and the Sherpas Girmi Dorje and Nima Dorje were setting out from the South Col. Hewing to schedule, they had come up from camp to camp a day behind Lute and Barry, and now they were headed for VI in support of them—as well as of Willi Unsoeld and Tom Hornbein, if the West Ridgers were able to make their traverse across the top of the mountain. Thus far, things had gone excellently for them. Dave was climbing strongly, and both Sherpas were doing well too, each carrying four bottles of oxygen without using any himself, either while climbing or at the Col. According to plan, Nima was to have gone only this far; but he had volunteered to go higher, and so all three were now moving on toward the highest camp. Even at their present height they used oxygen sparingly. For Dave and Girmi now had high hope that they would be not only a support team, but would, on the next day, have their own chance at the summit; and the brightness of that chance would depend largely on how much oxygen they had left—on that, and of course on what happened this day to the climbers up higher. Soon after leaving the Col, they had a glimpse of two tiny figures moving up the Southeast Ridge high above them. But beyond this they would see and know nothing for a while to come.

On the far side of the mountain, the West Ridge support team of Barry Corbet, Al Auten, Dick Emerson and their five Sherpas were waiting at Camp 4W. The previous afternoon, after taking leave from Willi and Tom at 5W, Barry and Al had themselves engineered one of the prime climbing feats of the expedition in getting themselves and the largely inexperienced Sherpas down the steep slant of Hornbein's Couloir. In contrast to the Lhotse Face operation, there had here been no time on the ascent for the installation of fixed ropes; so now they devised one with Barry as the live "fixing point"—anchoring a long line at the top with his ax, while Al, leading, and the Sherpas, following, descended hand over hand—then descending himself and repeating the process, over and over, until they had negotiated the 1000-odd vertical feet (2100 linear feet by the rope's measurement) to the couloir's base. There they had picked up the waiting Dick Emerson. They had reached 4W shortly after dark. And this next day, the twenty-second, they were to spend—as Barry put it—"worrying and not knowing anything." If Willi and Tom came down the way they had gone up, they would still be "support." If not, their only remaining function would be to get themselves and their Sherpas down the mountain.

At Advance Base, in the Cwm, Jimmy Roberts and Maynard Miller waited, watched, and stood by their walkie-talkie. A.B. was not in line of sight or hearing for the West Ridge summit pair, now off on the North Face; but it was possible that they might see or hear the top men on the Col route. During the morning Maynard did some surveying of the Cwm with his theodolite, but this

was not the day for all-out glaciology. He and Jimmy kept returning to binoculars and radio: searching, listening.

At Base Camp there were now only six team members left.
Barry Prather and Dick Pownall, with Gombu and a few other
Sherpas, had departed the previous day for their trip to the
Mingbo Glacier, leaving Norman, Will Siri, Jim Whittaker, Gil
Roberts, Dan Doody and Jim Lester encamped at the foot of the
mountain, together with liaison officer Captain Noddy Rana and
a larger number of Sherpas. On the twenty-second, Big Jim volunteered to stay in camp, monitoring the radio and keeping it "live"
all day for any messages from above. And meanwhile Norman and
the others climbed up, as planned, to the 20,000-foot level on the
slopes of Pumori, to keep vigil with binoculars and telephoto lenses.
They kept it through the morning, through noon, into the early
afternoon. But they saw no movement. Only rock, snow and sky.

There *was* movement, however: on both sides of the mountain.

Indeed, West Ridgers Unsoeld and Hornbein, with no fire to
delay them, had started at seven o'clock, an hour earlier than
South Collars Jerstad and Bishop. But in terms of the goal this
could scarcely be called a headstart; for they had farther to go, their
angle of ascent was steeper, and every foot of the way would be on
terra incognita. Behind them they left the little tent that was
Camp 5W, and in it their sleeping bags, air mattresses and most of
their food—hoping never to see them again. With them they took
only their climbing gear, two full oxygen bottles apiece, and a few
other assorted items of essential equipment, adding up to loads of
about 40 pounds each. Though they had been through no such
preclimbing ordeal as Lute and Barry, they were, however, not to
be altogether fortune's favorites; for they were presently to find
that, of their two oxygen rigs, one—Willi's—had a slight leak and
the other—Tom's—a regulator that did not accurately record the
flow of gas.

For the first part of the way they were still in Hornbein's Couloir,
cutting straight up through the rock of the Yellow Band. At an
average the gully was 10 to 12 feet wide and was filled with loose
granular snow; on the unstable footing, tilted at a 45-degree angle,
they had to move one at a time, kicking and cutting steps and

zigzagging from wall to wall. At one point the rock on either side nudged in, narrowing their funnel to a slot that they could barely squeeze through. Then it opened up again. But the unrelenting steepness remained, and nowhere was there a place level enough to sit down and rest.

Over their shoulders and beneath their feet they could see, far below, the glaciers and plains of Tibet sweeping down and off into distance. Indeed, they themselves were *in* Tibet—and had been, ever since they moved out onto the North Face. But still no one appeared to point out that their passports were no longer valid; and for all purposes, practical and imaginary, they were more nearly on a province of the moon than within the political borders of an earthly nation. On all that mighty mountainside there was only one bond to the world of men, and that was a thing not of the present but the past. Off to the east, between the Rongbuk and East Rongbuk Glaciers, was Everest's North Col, the 23,000-foot snow saddle by which the early British expeditions of the twenties and thirties had reached the upper flanks of the peak. Above it rose the slant of the Northeast Ridge; and still higher, not far from Hornbein's Couloir but hidden by its containing walls, were the two routes by which the British had almost gained the summit. One was the long line of the eastern summit ridge, marked by two steep rocky rises known as the First and Second Steps, and it had been on the First Step, at about 27,500 feet, that George Mallory and Andrew Irvine, of the 1924 party, had last been seen from below. The other, known as the Great Couloir, was, like Hornbein's Couloir, a vertical trough high on the North Face, paralleling it several hundred yards to the east; and here, at about 28,000 feet, had been the turning-back place for Colonel E. F. Norton in 1924 and Frank S. Smythe in 1933. The West Ridgers' route and the old British routes did not converge. All the way up, Willi and Tom would be blazing their own trail. But nevertheless, on this side of the mountain, they were on historic—for mountaineers, even hallowed—ground. And as with the South Collars on the far side of the peak, the shades of their predecessors climbed with them.

Kick-kick. Whack-whack. An hour passed. A second. A third. Above, the couloir, with its ribbon of snow, seemed to lead on endlessly into the sky.

Throughout this part of the ascent Willi was first on the rope, and so he would continue to be for most of the day's climbing. But this did not mean that the team was composed of a stronger and a weaker member. Over the years, Willi and Tom had climbed many times together; in strength and endurance, skill and determination, they were an ideally matched pair; and it had been both their own hope and the long-standing expedition plan that they would be the Number One West Ridge summit team.* During the long siege on the mountain neither had had serious acclimatization problems. (Indeed, the only ailment between them had been, for Willi, an annoying case of hemorrhoids, which he called his "Achilles anus.") And though like all the climbers, they had lost weight, it was not so drastically as some of the others. Tom, to be sure, was from the beginning the smallest team member. Now at 5 foot 7 and a mere 125 pounds, he was more of Sherpa than of American dimensions, and one might well have thought that a small puff of breeze could blow him away. But even the wildest winds of Everest were not to accomplish that, and he was living proof that a man— even a non-Sherpa—does not need the physique of a Big Jim Whittaker to climb to the top of the world.

During this early stage of the final day's push, however, Tom was for the first time having considerable altitude trouble. "As I climbed up the couloir behind Willi," he said, "I found myself reaching his stances almost entirely out of breath, very exhausted, and a little puzzled as to why." Later he discovered the reason: his faulty oxygen regulator was giving him less than 2 liters per minute, although it was set for 3. But at the time he could only wonder unhappily about what had suddenly gone wrong with him.

Nevertheless, they continued their slow steady grind: kicking, chopping, moving one at a time and belaying each other against slips in the steep unstable snow. And at last, after four hours of climbing—and some 500 feet gained above 5W—there was a change in the couloir. It was not, however, a change for the better. They were still moving up through the zone of the Yellow Band; but whereas until now the rock had merely formed the walls of their

---

* With a total of nine children between them (Tom—five, Willi—four), they could also well have been called AMEE's Paterfamilias Team; and the hopes, fears —and perhaps destinies—of a lot of family were moving with them up their mountain.

gully, it now closed in to form its surface as well, and what had thus far been a steep but straightforward slog was now about to become an exercise in highly technical climbing. "It was apparent," said Tom, "that we were going to have some very messy going on downsloping rotten slabs. And to make it worse, the covering of snow was no better than the rock. Of a floury consistency, it would slide off under your weight, cascading down on the man below."

Here, for the first time, Tom took the lead, trying one alternative after another, slowly moving from one precarious stance to the next in a concentrated effort that lasted almost an hour. The vertical height of the pitch was some 60 feet, and finally he had negotiated all but the last ten of them. At this point, there being no further hand- or footholds, he tried, and at last managed, to drive a large piton into the crumbling rock overhead. But beyond it was a short bit of absolutely vertical slab, and after his exhausting maneuvers—and with his insufficient flow of oxygen—he was unable to surmount it. Descending, he stood again at the foot of the pitch, fighting for strength and air. Together, he and Willi studied the wall above, foot by foot, almost inch by inch. In the hope that they would find a likelier route, they then moved out of the couloir, traversing onto the open North Face, scouting upward. But here the prospects were even worse. *The* route—if any—was the one they had been trying. So they returned to the couloir and had at the vertical wall again. This time Willi took the lead, working his way up to Tom's highest point, and at last, using Tom's piton, moving beyond it. For the topmost part of the pitch he had to take off his mittens and climb barehanded, clawing and worming his way up almost holdless surface, affixing still another piton into the rotten rock. But in the end he came up over it. Tom came up after him. At a height of almost 28,000 feet, they had accomplished the most difficult stretch of climbing that the expedition encountered anywhere on the mountain.

Above, the couloir widened again. Its surface was again of snow, and, though steep, it was no longer vertical. For another few hundred feet they were once more kicking, hacking, zigzagging. And then the couloir ended. The Yellow Band ended. The bristling band of tawny rotten rock was at last, mercifully, beneath them, and ahead the mountainside opened out in a sweep of firmer gray rock and broad bands of tilted snow. At this point they were at about 28,200 feet, with the summit of Everest no more than 800 or so above their heads.

By now, however, it was three in the afternoon. And where *was* the summit? The rock and snow ahead did not converge into a visible apex, but swept in a great featureless mass across half their field of vision, and whether the proper route was to the right, to the left, or straight ahead, they had no way of telling. They had finally come to the first place on the whole day's ascent where they were able to sit down; and pausing to rest, they tried to reach Base Camp on their walkie-talkie. They were successful. Jim Whittaker answered, and wanted, of course, to know where they were. They told him, in general, but added that they were puzzled as to how to go on. From more than 10,000 feet below, Jim could not help them with that, but he raised the question of whether they should go on at all. It was now midafternoon, he pointed out, and at the rate they were going—

Willi and Tom had been fully conscious of that. "We're thinking it over," they told Jim. And now, with the radio turned off, they were faced with making what could well be the decision of their lives—or deaths. It was obvious that, even if they found the right route and had easier going ahead, they would not reach the summit much before darkness; and no less obvious that, when and if they reached it, there would be no summit meeting with the South Col team. With the bulk of the mountain intervening, they could not make radio contact with Jerstad and Bishop to find out where they were. But it was as good as certain that, if they were to make the top that day, it would be long before Willi and Tom could get there—indeed, Jerstad and Bishop would probably be there already—and they surely could not be expected to wait for hours on that most exposed point of all earth's surface. According to the basic plan of the two-pronged ascent, the West Ridge team would cross over the summit and descend by the South Col route *only* if the Col team met them on the summit and was thus in a position to lead them down. Meaning that, if they hewed to the plan, they would descend by the route they had come up, whether they reached the summit or not.

But—

There was a rather pointed *but*: Was such a descent possible? Coming up the long couloir had been hard enough. Going down it would be, if not harder, surely far more dangerous; for descent is always more hazardous than ascent, and, besides this, the snow in the gully, loose and treacherous to begin with, had been growing ever more unstable through the warmth of the day. "All in all," said Tom, "it was a most revolting prospect." And making it more so was the vertical rock pitch, which would be even worse; for the only moderately safe way of negotiating it would be through the roping-down technique of a rappel, and there were no sound projecting points anywhere on which to anchor a rope for such a maneuver.

Thus the pros and the cons of going on or retreating. Plus one pro for going on that was stronger than all the others combined. As Tom put it: "It was the old onwards and upwards; a total rejection of turning back; a total detachment from everything else in the world. Only Everest *was there*. Only the summit above us, beckoning."

"It was not reasoning but desire that moved us," said Willi. "We had committed ourselves." And for body and mind and heart—when all the rest had been added and subtracted—these were the great driving forces: desire and commitment.

Besides, the weather was good. Not too cold. Not too windy.

They called Jim back on the radio.

"We're going on," they told him.

Earlier in the day, through the hours of the morning, Lute Jerstad and Barry Bishop, on the far side of the mountain, had toiled up the incline of the Southeast Ridge. In the beginning, following the advice of Jim Whittaker and Gombu, they avoided the actual crest of the ridge, moving instead along the left-hand slope just below it on a surface of broken rock flecked with ice and snow. Lute was first on the rope, and he climbed very slowly; for both men were still shaken by the experience of their breakfast fire, and Barry, in addition, was still feeling the effects of his ordeal of the previous night. After an hour or so they were off the rock and onto snow. Before them they could see the bootprints of their predecessors, still clear after three weeks of wind and weather. But most of them had partially filled up and iced over, so that they were useless as stances, and for all but a few steps Lute had to blaze his own trail. Indeed, though the first climbers, in the gale of May 1, had had it worse with the weather, the second team was, throughout the climb, to have harder going underfoot. Jim and Gombu, Norman and Ang Dawa had climbed in snow of a consistency in which most steps could be kicked, with few strokes of the ax. For Lute and Barry the snow was ice-hard and it was whack-whack-whack for almost all the way.

At about eleven o'clock, after three hours of climbing, they worked their way back onto the ridge and from there peered down the all-but-vertical walls of its far side to Tibet's Kangshung Glacier, 2 miles below. And now, for a while, Barry took over the lead, as for some three or four hundred yards they followed a knife edge of snow. Often they paused—sometimes simply to rest, sometimes both to rest and take pictures; for Barry, in his National Geographic Society capacity, was the expedition's professional still photographer, and Lute, after a brief course in cinematography, had been entrusted by Norman with taking moving pictures as high as was humanly possible. Unlike the West Ridgers, however, they were without a walkie-talkie. Having had no luck with their instrument since surmounting the Lhotse Face two days before, they had left it behind them at Camp VI, and throughout the day they would have no contact with the world below.

As they climbed on, the wind rose—not to gale force, but enough so that they were thoroughly aware of it, particularly since it kept pushing them in the direction of the Kangshung precipice. With Lute again leading, they therefore kept as much as possible to the windward side of the ridge, following, as had Whittaker and Gombu, the dividing line between rock and snow. As Barry put it, "We were trying to enjoy the best of two very tricky worlds."

Soon the ridge steepened. They had reached the stretch in which it flares abruptly upward toward Everest's South Summit, and here it took them two and one-half hours to gain a mere 200 vertical feet. At a rocky outcrop which offered a place to sit they stopped for ten minutes and ate the only food they were to have that day —a quarter of a candy bar apiece. Then they struggled on. A while later, at 28,500 feet, 250 feet below the South Summit, Barry's first oxygen bottle ran out, and Lute, checking his, found that it too was almost empty. So hooking into their second bottles, they discarded the used ones, and for a moment revelled in the 13-pound lightening of each of their loads. The moment was brief, however, "for in the next instant," said Barry, "I tripped over one of the bottles at my feet and flew out into space. Instinctively I twisted in mid-air. Hitting the slope face down I clawed at the snow with hands and feet and managed to stop, and at the same time I saw Lute beside me, holding me tight with his right hand. He had jumped out after me, flipped on his belly, and grabbed. We crawled back up to the ledge and lay there for a long moment."

Then they were climbing again. "I felt spent, dull," said Barry. "One step . . . six long breaths . . . another step . . . again six breaths. Each pace required almost half a minute. My entire body ached."

But the South Summit was drawing slowly closer. They were almost there. Then they *were* there. At two o'clock they stood on its 28,750-foot crest, 500 feet higher than any other mountain on earth, leaning into a 60-mile-an-hour wind and peering up at the one bit of our planet that rises still higher. "It loomed above us," said Barry, "in crazy snow-scarred grandeur." And as with Jim and Gombu, it seemed steeper and more forbidding than they had expected; so, to conserve their now dwindling supply of oxygen, they turned their regulators down from a flow of 3 to 2 liters a minute. Perhaps this was part of the cause of what happened next. There is no way of telling. While actually on the mountain, all the members of the summit teams were convinced that their minds were clear and rational. It was only later, in reviewing their actions, that they realized how disoriented and befuddled they had often been from lack of oxygen.

In any case, Lute looked down the 30-foot near-vertical drop at the far side of the South Summit, did not like what he saw, and veered suddenly off to the left, down a slope that led directly away from the route they should have followed. Afterward, the best he could do in explanation was that "I was a little spooked, I guess, by that steep pitch. I thought that this couldn't possibly be the way, and I don't know whatever possessed me, but all at once I took off down to the side. I saw some rocks below. I must have thought I saw some footprints. But anyhow I went 75 feet down, while Barry looked after me, thinking I was crazy. Then I got to the end of the rope and realized I had made a foolish mistake, and had to grind my way back up those 75 feet—which, at that elevation, was kind of tough."

Back on the South Summit, he got his proper bearings. Going first, with Barry following, he carefully descended the snow cliff that dropped down to the saddle at the foot of the final ridge. Then they were ascending again. A half-hour passed. And an hour. Coming to the slot between rock and snow that is known as Hillary's Chimney, they climbed it, as had Jim and Gombu, without undue difficulty. And beyond it the last of the steepness fell away and they were out on the snow of the gently sloping summit ridge. Here, as almost all the way up, there was rock on their left, snow on their right—snow which they knew projected out in great cornices above a sea of space. At its inner margin, close by the rock, the footprints of their predecessors were still visible: the improbable spoor of man in a world man never made.

Now two new dots were moving where two other dots had moved three weeks before. They were not, however, a big and a small dot, but a pair of about the same size—nearer Gombu's size than Big Jim Whittaker's—for though Lute and Barry were bigger than Sherpas, bigger than wispy Tom Hornbein, they were among the smaller men on the expedition. Lute was normally a lithe 5 foot 8 and 155 pounds; Barry ("the Barrel") a stocky 5 foot 7 and 165 pounds. But there was nothing stocky about the Barrel now. Both he and Lute had lost about 20 pounds in their enormous efforts on the mountain, and they were haggard, emaciated, depleted. Moving up the last reaches of Everest, each was—as Big Jim had described himself—a fragile human being.

Although the slope was gentle, they moved even more slowly than before. Now it was one step, seven breaths—one step, seven breaths—lifting a foot, placing it—lifting, placing. Their feet were no longer made of flesh and blood, but of lead. Their bodies were things they were dragging with them: amorphous yet aching. Behind their goggles, their eyes were glazed with weariness and by the gleaming unearthly brilliance of snow and sky. "But if we had to crawl the rest of the way on hands and knees," said Barry Bishop, "we were going to get there."

Mostly he climbed with head down, but at intervals he raised it. Off to the right he saw the long line of cornices, and now, ahead, the old footprints angled off toward it, and there was a break in the prints, a jagged gap in the snow, which he knew must be the place where a cornice had fallen away between Jim and Gombu on their descent. But he did not look at it long, for at almost the same instant there was something else ahead. The rope joining him to Lute, 75 feet in front, had gone slack. Lute had stopped and raised his arm. Slowly, very slowly, Barry came up to him. And now they were together. They were side by side, looking up at the snowy ridge. And ahead there was a white hummock, and another, and another—but that was not all, as it had been for Jim and Gombu—for there above there was a final hummock, a dome, a white crest in the sky to which something had been added; and it was something that brought a lift to their hearts and tears to their eyes.

It is clear by now, one hopes, that mountaineers, in the practice of their calling, are not jingoistic flag wavers; that it is a fundamental of their creed that earth's great mountains and the climbing of such mountains should rise above the worldly demarcations of state and nation. But Lute Jerstad and Barry Bishop may well be forgiven by even the staunchest proponent of One World if, in that moment, they were very consciously, very proudly American. For Big Jim Whittaker had done his work well. After three weeks his aluminum Maypole still stood firm and tall. And from it— wrapped once or twice around the pole, but not ripped and shredded, only slightly tattered along its edges—Old Glory streamed out above the summit of the world.

Almost a month earlier, Lute, looking up at Everest, had written in his diary: "Comes a moment of truth when I feel like a little boy humbled before this huge mountain, knowing I am in the wrong place." But now—humble or proud, wrong place or right place—there he was, he and Barry, on its top. It was 3:30 in the afternoon, when, arm in arm, they stepped up together. They embraced, but they did not speak. On the metal stake beneath the flag Gombu's *kata* scarf, given him by his uncle Tenzing, was still tied securely, and roundabout, frozen into earth's summit, were his bootprints and the larger ones of Big Jim. The wind was stronger than on the slopes below, and for a while Lute and Barry sat resting, hunching against it, gazing out on a world that was clear and dazzling on all sides. On arrival they had turned off their oxygen. And now, still without oxygen, they set about the task of taking pictures—many pictures—for in the gale of May 1 Jim and Gombu had been able to do very little photography. Working slowly and carefully, in agonized concentration lest his numbed mind and fingers betray him, Barry, with his still camera, made a series of shots around the full circle of the horizon. Lute, ramming his ice ax into the snow and anchoring his small movie camera to its head, also made a 360-degree swing, as he recorded the first motion pictures ever taken on Everest's summit. During this work, both removed their shells and mittens from their hands, retaining only their inner nylon gloves, and their fingers froze rapidly in the handling of the metal instruments.

Jim and Gombu had spent twenty minutes on top. Barry and Lute spent forty-five. Their picture making done, they looked around them: out across mountaintops into miles of space; at their own mountaintop, falling away on all sides beneath them. As had been the case with the first summiteers, they saw no sign of Mao Tse Tung. More important—there was no sign, down the West Ridge or North Face, of Willi Unsoeld or Tom Hornbein. They waited until four o'clock—until 4:15—but there was still no Willi, no Tom. And with the sun sloping toward the west above the ridges of Nuptse, they made ready to descend. Lute had brought along pictures of his family to leave on the summit, but he forgot to dig them out of his parka pocket. He had also brought a New Testament, given him by his parents, that he had intended to leave there, but now he decided it would be the better for having been to Everest—and back.

Turning up their oxygen, they started down.

In the waning afternoon, on the other side of the mountain, Willi and Tom were still out of sight of—and from—the summit, but they knew it was no longer far above them. They had come up at last out of Hornbein's Couloir. They had talked on the radio to

Jim Whittaker. They had made their decision. And now, after a brief rest, they were again moving upward.

For a while they were still confused in their bearings: as to whether the summit was to the right or left or straight ahead. But at least they were past the crumbling schist of the Yellow Band, back on Everest's usual gray limestone, on which the going was better. And as they climbed, the bulge of the Band fell away beneath them, allowing them to see past it to the glaciers below, and thus to orient themselves as to their own position on the peak. Beyond the stretch of rock above the couloir was a great sloping snowfield that led up to the final pyramid of the North Face, and at 4:30 they reached its lower edge at a height of about 28,400 feet. Here Willi's first oxygen bottle, with its slight leak, gave out, and abandoning it, he switched to his second, which seemed to function properly. Tom was still on his first bottle, and though, with his faulty regulator, he could never tell precisely how much oxygen he was getting, he was feeling better and climbing more strongly than earlier in the day.

The summit, they now knew, was almost directly overhead; but as the snow steepened before them they soon had to decide on a tack over rock to either right or left. The route they had tentatively selected through binoculars from below was the left-hand one, leading toward the northeast of the summit—which would have brought them to the top by what would have been the route of the old British Everesters, if the British had gone all the way. "But now," said Tom, "we felt that our best hope was to traverse to the right, back over to the West Ridge, and to try to get onto some snow there to continue the ascent." So they diagonaled upward, stopping en route for a quick and late lunch of kippered snacks. The weather, which until now had been almost ideal, began to blast them with stronger winds as they neared the ridge; and presently, to their dismay, they struck a stretch of rock even more unstable than that of the Yellow Band. But at last they gained the ridgeline, and for the first time since leaving Camp 4W the day before were able to look across it toward Lhotse and Nuptse—now both far below them—and down almost vertical walls to the Western Cwm and Advance Base. "It was," said Tom with fine understatement, "a rather impressive drop."

It was five o'clock. And only now, after ten hours of use, did Tom's first oxygen bottle give out. Like Willi before him, he hooked into his second, noting with gratitude the 13-pound decrease in weight of the load on his pack. In spite of the dizzying height and their enormous expenditure of energy, both men were feeling strong and fit, with none of the miseries of lung and limb that had beset Lute Jerstad and Barry Bishop during their ascent. "In fact, the going began to be a wonderful pleasure," said Tom. "I felt almost as though we were on a climb in the Rockies."

With Willi still leading, they followed the West Ridge upward, with the North Face and the miles of Tibet on their left, and on the right the precipice and the deep white chasm of the Cwm. For a time they were on snow. But soon a sheer knife edge of rock sprang up before them, and here they were forced to stop and remove their crampons and overboots before working their way along its sheer flank by a series of tiny cracks and holds. For a distance of four rope lengths they crept up one at a time, each securing the other by belays from such stances as they could find. Then they were past the rock. They were again on snow, replacing overboots and crampons. As they moved on, the wind grew steadily in strength, for they were truly high now—higher than Everest's South Summit, off to the right—and all that remained was a ridge slanting on, with two other ridges converging on it from northeast and southeast.

It was six o'clock; then 6:15. The sun was low. And it was in the sun's red rays, streaming across earth's rooftop, that they saw what the others had seen before them. The pole. The flag. The flag stiff and streaming in the winds of space. Said Tom: "Willi, up ahead, waited, and I joined him, and we hugged each other, full of unspoken thoughts and feelings—almost unfelt feelings in a way, at that time and place." The flag was perhaps 40 feet away when it came into view. Then with each step, as they moved on, it was closer. Approached from the west, the very tip of Everest is more dramatic than as seen from the south. It was not a final hump in a line of humps, but an entity in itself: a peak, an apex. And now, after almost twelve hours of climbing—after weeks and months on the mountain, months and years of planning before reaching the mountain—Willi Unsoeld and Tom Hornbein, side by side, stepped up to that apex and stood beside the flagpole. They were the eleventh and twelfth men ever to stand on top of Everest.* They were the fifth and sixth of the expedition of which they were members. But they were the only ones ever to reach it by a route other than that of Lhotse Face and South Col, and theirs was one of the great "firsts" of mountaineering history.

The sun was setting now. The wind was bitter. And in the deepening cold and grayness they spent only some fifteen minutes on their perch in the sky. Like the others, they took pictures—though only stills, and not so many as Barry Bishop. They left a few mementos, including a crucifix which Willi wrapped into Gombu's *kata*, and two prayer flags given them by their Sherpas—which seemed a good balance for an expedition that was part Buddhist, part Christian. In the snow around them they saw both the old bootprints of Jim Whittaker and Gombu and fresh prints, which they knew must be those of Lute and Barry. They knew, too, that the other pair must have been here hours before them and that they would have to descend the unknown Southeast Ridge on their own. But there was no question in their minds but that this was what they were going to do. Back on the North Face, at the top of the couloir, they had made their decision. They had made their commitment. Not only had they been the first to climb Everest by a new route; now—though the hoped-for, thousand-to-one, summit rendezvous had not materialized—they would be the first to attempt its traverse from one side to another.

They had turned their oxygen off. Now they turned it on again. The first thing was to get as far down as they could before night closed in.

Throughout the day, at Advance Base, Maynard Miller and Jimmy Roberts had scanned the heights and kept their radio open. At about 5:30 Maynard thought he saw, close beneath the South Summit, a "nubbin" that had not been there before; and using his binoculars, he found that there was not one nubbin but two, and that they were moving slowly downward. One speck was green, one was yellow, and though he could not be sure, he assumed—correctly —that they were Bishop and Jerstad descending from the summit.

---

* We are here following the lead of most mountaineering authorities and discounting the Chinese claim of placing three men on the summit.

But he was concerned because they seemed to be off to the West of the Southeast Ridge, which was their proper route.

Then they were lost to sight. An hour passed; another half hour —and it was growing dark—when, electrifyingly, the radio came alive with Willi Unsoeld's voice. He and Tom had just come off the summit, he said. They were a few feet below it. They were about to descend the Southeast Ridge.

His voice faded in the crackle of static and the howl of the wind.

"Roger! Roger!" Maynard called back into space.

Then Willi's voice came through again. Faintly; very faintly. And it seemed to the incredulous Maynard that what he was hearing from up there was poetry.

It was. Willi was speaking lines of Robert Frost's. He was saying,

> "*. . . I have promises to keep,*
> *And miles to go before we sleep,*
> *And miles to go before we sleep . . ."**

---

* The "promises" were to his wife Jolene that Everest would be his last "big mountain." Ever the gentleman, even at 29,000 feet, Willi then changed Frost's "I sleep" to "we sleep," so as to include his companion Tom.

"9N1ME. CALLING 9N1ME. This is 9N1DD—9N1 Donald Duck—calling 9N1ME—9N1 Mount Everest—"

But now there was no 9N1MM (for Mickey Mouse) standing by. For Colonel Bill Gresham, proprietor of DD, and his wife Juanita had taken off on a long-planned holiday trip to Europe, and MM's proprietor, Father Moran, had moved into Bill's shack during his absence to operate his more powerful set. Every day, sometimes two or even three times a day, the Kathmandu faithful gathered about him there to hear the latest word from the mountain.

As things moved toward climax—the final climax—the press was again avid for expedition news, and I now held my post-radio briefings on the Gresham lawn instead of at the Hotel Royal, to save the newspapermen five minutes in their race to the cable office. The American wire service representatives based in India, who had left Kathmandu after the first reaching of the summit, had now returned for the final inning. The National Geographic Society, AMEE's major sponsor, had three representatives on the scene in various capacities, and these were soon to be joined by others.

262

Earlier in the month Nick Clinch had at last returned by errant helicopter from his visit to Base Camp and followed Chuck Huestis home to California. But Lila Bishop, back from her trek, was now in Kathmandu, where she would stay until the expedition returned, and was a regular at the radio shack along with Sally Dyhrenfurth, Sally Richardson, Jolene Unsoeld and myself. With new summit attempts impending, Ambassador and Mrs. Stebbins were again frequent visitors; and knowing that their Deputy Director, Willi Unsoeld, was one of the high men on the mountain, Peace Corps corpsmen took to thronging the premises until they swelled at the seams.

This time there was no attempt at secrecy as to who was who and doing what. Everyone knew that it was Willi and Tom Hornbein, Lute Jerstad and Barry Bishop who would be going for the top; and while this served to make most interested parties, and particularly the press, happy, it was scarcely the easiest thing for Lila and Jolene. Indeed, the tension on them was tremendous, as the target dates were announced, reannounced, and then inexorably drew nearer.

May 20: "Barry and Lute have moved up to the South Col," said Dan Doody, who was now operating the Base Camp radio. "Dave Dingman and Girmi Dorje are at Camp IV. The West Ridgers are moving up from 3W to 4W."

May 21: "Barry and Lute have moved up to Camp VI. The West Ridgers have left 4W to set up 5W as high as they can on the North Face, and Willi and Tom will spend the night there."

Then it was May 22. It was 5 P.M.

"9N1ME, this is 9N1DD. What news?"

"No news."

"Nothing?"

"Almost nothing. Willi and Tom talked to Big Jim on the radio a while ago. We know they're high. We'd guess that Barry and Lute are high too."

"No word from them?"

"No."

Father Moran and Dan arranged that they would try to make contact that night through an intermediate ham, but there was no such luck as there had previously been through Ceylon. Father

Moran succeeded in reaching an operator in South Korea who was eager to help, but Korea was unable to get through to 9N1ME.

On the twenty-third we were back in the shack at nine in the morning. And this time there was both contact *and* news. Willi Unsoeld and Tom Hornbein had reached the top of Everest the evening before. Willi had talked to Maynard Miller at Advance Base on their walkie-talkie, and Maynard in turn had talked to Base.

Marvelous! Tremendous! But what about Barry and Lute?

There had been no word from them.*

And where were Willi and Tom?

No one knew.

There had been no further word from them?

No, not from anyone.

Another contact was set for 1 P.M. Four hours that seemed four days to most of us, and must have seemed four years to Lila Bishop and Jolene Unsoeld. For Lila there was nothing, a blank nothing. Jolene at least knew that her husband had reached the top, but that is scarcely the type of news to which wives give first priority. In terms of where they were, and *how* they were, both men—all four men—had been swallowed up by the gulfs of space.

We waited.

At 1 P.M. we were on the air again.

And there was still no more news. We would call again at five.

Back at the Hotel Royal I had lunch with Jolene and Lila. It was a quiet meal, but not a dreary one. Throughout it, people appeared and reappeared with questions, encouragement, good wishes, and the two girls answered and smiled and said thank you. If their husbands could have seen and heard, they would have been proud of them.

Then it was 5 P.M. There in the shack were Lila and Jolene and Jolene's four children and the rest of us. And again Father Moran was working the dials.

"9N1ME. Calling 9N1ME. . . ."

---

* The Unsoeld-Hornbein radio message, combined with the silence from Bishop and Jerstad, resulted in false early press reports that the West Ridgers had reached the summit before the South Col team.

15. "... BEFORE WE SLEEP"

NOT MORE THAN 50 feet below the summit, Lute and Barry's rope had gone askew. The wind, blasting from the west, blew it out in a taut crescent over the snow cornices that were now on their left; and as Lute, going first, descended a curving dip in the ridge, it dropped onto the cornice, caught on its edge, and hooked itself in.

"I shouted into the 70-mile gusts," said Barry, "but Lute heard nothing, and the fouled rope between us began to draw me toward the edge. I dived onto the snow and wriggled out on the cornice, trying to free the rope. My face was just above the snow. But my weight was too much. A section of the cornice at my chest gave way, and I had a sudden hair-raising view of the Kangshung Glacier 10,000 feet below. Scrambling back, I noticed that Lute's continuing forward movement was causing the rope to cut ever deeper into the snow; so I undid the knot that secured it to my waist. It whipped up and away across the whiteness, and unroped, I paralleled its route. I waited until the end of the rope, like a frozen snake, slithered free of the cornice, and then I retied it to my waist. Elapsed time: less than a minute. Not until I told him back in Kathmandu did Lute know what had happened."

They moved on down.

But slowly. Almost as slowly as on the ascent. For they were very nearly done in. Rallying what was left of strength and concentration, they inched their way down Hillary's Chimney, down the other steep pitches that followed, and at the base of the summit ridge collapsed onto the ice-coated rocks for a short breather. Thus far they had been using a frugal 1-liter flow of oxygen—at least theoretically. But now Lute, who had been having an even harder time than Barry, discovered that a string had become fouled around the breathing bladder of his apparatus and that he had been getting no gas at all.

He ripped the string away. For the 30-foot vertical push up to the South Summit, they allowed themselves the luxury of a 2-liter flow; then, as the descent continued, cut back again to 1, for by now their supply was almost gone. "We stumbled and staggered and crawled," said Lute, "for what seemed like generations of time." As if hypoxia and exhaustion were not enough, they were both now having trouble with their vision, and Lute in particular found himself half-blinded, both by the wind seeping in through his goggle frames and by the aftereffects of the singeing his eyes had suffered in that morning's breakfast fire. Several times they wandered off the proper course. (It was at one of these times that Maynard Miller, at Advance Base, saw them off to the west of the ridge.) Each time they eventually regained their bearings. But each time it was harder, for now the sun was gone and dusk was closing in.

"We began to wonder," said Lute, "if we would make it."

They had left the summit at 4:15. At a little before eight they were at about 28,400 feet—a descent of a mere 600 feet in more than three and one-half hours—and Camp VI was still almost a thousand feet below.

As Barry told it—

"The last of the light reflects wanly off the snow. The sky is cold, moonless, black. Our feet gro· colder as we lurch down the mountain.

"I stop abruptly. Is it the wind?

"'Hellooooo . . . Hellooooo. . . .'

"From somewhere the sound echoes across the mountain, eerie in the enveloping darkness.

"Lute stops too. We listen intently.

" 'Hellooooo . . . Hellooooo. . . .'

"On Everest the wind speaks with many voices. It rises, it falls, it thunders. Sometimes it is the remote night cry of a sick child. But it is always the wind.

"Then we hear still another 'Hellooooo. . . .' and this time it is unmistakably human.

"Could it be Dave Dingman and Girmi Dorje, our support party, searching for us out of Camp VI? No. The wind drops, and in the sudden stillness the cries have a bell-like clarity. They are floating down from above.

"*Above!*"

Leaving the summit, Willi Unsoeld and Tom Hornbein were a little over two hours behind Barry and Lute. This meant that daylight began to fade even while they were on the summit ridge. But they were able to follow the footprints leading down before them; kept clear of the cornices; and negotiating Hillary's Chimney without trouble, reached the South Summit in forty-five minutes. Both West Ridgers were in notably better shape than the South Col pair. But of the two, Willi, who had led almost all the day's ascent, was the more tired, and he therefore still went first on the rope, with Tom in the more demanding belaying position behind. On a steep pitch below Hillary's Chimney Tom had a bad few moments when he banged his one remaining oxygen bottle against a rock, with a resultant loud hissing and the chilling fear that he had lost his valve. After a bit of desperate gasping, however, he discovered that it was only the regulator that had been loosened, and upon tightening it, he was able to move again more normally.

From the South Summit they had a brief glimpse of Advance Base, down in the Western Cwm—so remote that it might have been in another world, on another planet. Then it was gone, and there was only the icy spine of the ridge falling away before them, while twilight thickened into dusk, and dusk into night. Now they too were going slowly: stumbling, groping. Repeatedly they lost the tracks they were following, in darkness or in outcroppings of rock. At one point they stopped and conferred, weighing the dangers of continuing against those of halting where they were for the night. But the decision was to go on, and veering off the ridge, they stumped on down one of its buttressing snow slopes. The wind was not inordinately strong, but it kept slapping at them, first from one direction, then another, making it difficult to keep balance. The footprints and ice-ax holes they were trying to follow kept appearing—and disappearing. They had a flashlight which they used to search for them, but its beam was weak and fading rapidly; and presently they cut their 120-foot rope in half, so that they could be closer together and have better coordination of movement.

They began to shout and yodel, hoping to raise a reply from Dave Dingman, who, according to schedule, should now be at Camp VI. And after a time—almost incredibly in that vast wilderness—answering shouts came back from below. At first the voices were faint; no more than distant hoots in the blackness. It was eight o'clock—eight-thirty—nine o'clock, as their groping crawl still continued. But then finally the gap was lessened to a point where back-and-forth words could be understood. Tom and Willi called down to those below to turn on a flashlight to guide them, but the answer came back that the others had no light. The best that could be done was for the West Ridgers to keep their own weak beam going, so that their invisible teammates could at least know roughly where they were and shout instructions as to the proper route. "This way—come on," came encouragement from below. And then, at the moment that Willi fell into a crevasse up to his armpits: "That's right—come on—you're doing fine!"

Another half hour dragged on. It was after 9:30. Then at last came the great moment when dark figures loomed against the snow, and a few minutes later the men who on that day had climbed Mount Everest were no longer two teams of two but one team of four. At first, however, Willi and Tom did not know who it was they were meeting. They assumed that the two masked and muffled shapes were Dave Dingman and Girmi Dorje, and it was not until they had embraced and pounded one another's backs that they asked "Who are you? Who are you?" and discovered that they were with Lute Jerstad and Barry Bishop.

They were, of course, astonished. They had assumed that by now Lute and Barry would be down at Camp VI, or even at Camp V on the South Col; not waiting for them at some 28,400 feet on the open ridge. And here was where the unforeseeable bad, plus good,

luck of Lute and Barry's early-morning fire played its part, for had
it not been for the fire and the consequent delay in starting their
day's climb, they *would*, by the time Willi and Tom began shouting, have been back at VI, and at such a distance, inside a tent,
probably unable to hear them. Thanks only to the fire, they had been
late enough, hence high enough, to hear. They had stopped their
descent at the point where the shouts first reached them. And for
the next two hours they had stayed there, propped on their ice
axes, shuffling their freezing feet, doing what they could to help
Willi and Tom in their descent.

In theory it would be the South Collars who would now lead the
West Ridgers down the rest of the way. But this was to be only
partly the case, for Lute and Barry were closer to exhaustion than
the others. Indeed, Barry at first declared that he was physically
unable to move on at all, and it took the strong insistence of the
others, plus an immense effort of his own will, to get him started.
With all joined on one rope, Tom went first, with Lute a few feet
behind him trying to point out the way, and Willi, farther back,
giving Barry such encouragement and help as he could. As before,
when they were two separate teams, progress was no more than a
crawl. Lute's vision was now hopelessly blurred, and even those
whose eyes were all right could see almost nothing in the black
moonless night. The ridge was a spectral tightrope between the
gulfs of darkness. A false step anywhere, by anyone, could mean a
slip, a slide, a fall—and extinction.

Could, but did not quite. For at one point Lute *did* slip and
slide, off toward the precipice of the Kangshung Face. But he did
not fall. He was held by the rope joining him to the others. And
peering, groping, zigzagging, they struggled on down. The West
Ridgers' feeble flashlight gave its last flicker and died. One by one,
their oxygen bottles ran out, until all four were finished and discarded. And still the ridge plunged down, down, down, with no
easing and no end.

An hour passed. And a second hour. By midnight they were
below the knife-edged section of the ridge, but here, though the
exposure was less, the route became even harder to follow in a
jumble of mixed snow and rock. Lute and Barry knew that, along
about here, there was a sharp turnoff leading down to the lower

ridge and Camp VI. But they knew too that the chances of pin-pointing it were small, and that if they made a wrong turn it might be the end for them all. They were still at a height of more than 28,000 feet. Even if they could find the right way, it would take them hours to reach the camp's level of 27,450. Barry, by now, could scarcely stand, let alone climb; the others were not much better off; and at 12:30 A.M., by almost unspoken agreement, they halted and made a decision.

Some 25 feet below the ridgeline they found a fairly level out-cropping of rock in the slope of snow. They settled down on it. And they waited for morning.

At Base Camp, word had been received from Maynard Miller six hours before that Willi and Tom had reached the summit and were about to begin the descent by the Col Route. But of where they were now—and of what had happened to Lute and Barry—there was no inkling.

At Advance Base, Maynard and Jimmy Roberts also knew no more than what had come over the walkie-talkie.

At Camp 4W, on the West Ridge, Barry Corbet, Al Auten and Dick Emerson knew even less than that. In the late afternoon they had heard from Base that Willi and Tom were going for the summit and planned to traverse it. But their radio had not picked up the relay of their subsequent message from the top, and they were totally in the dark as to what was going on above them.

At Camp VI, on the Southeast Ridge, Dave Dingman was, in different fashion, having almost as bad a time as the summit climb-ers themselves. With Girmi Dorje and Nima Dorje, he had arrived there early the previous afternoon, and an assessment of their oxygen situation showed that, if all went well higher up, there would be enough on hand for him and Girmi to make their own try for the top the next day. As the hours wore on toward evening, however, he became concerned about the nonreturn of Lute and Barry; and by seven o'clock, when the sun set, concern had grown into all-out alarm. Girmi, because of his long and close association with Barry, was no less upset, as the two grappled with the problem of what should, and could, be done.

In the early darkness they took turns beaming their single flash-

light up the ridge, but like Tom and Willi's, it was half frozen and
would emit only brief feeble flickers. Frustrated, they went back
into the tents. "And then at about nine," said Dave, "I thought I
heart faint shouting in the darkness above us. I went into the
Sherpas' tent and spoke to Girmi, and he thought it was only the
wind. But back in my own tent, listening and straining, I still
heard the sounds from above, and after a while I was absolutely
sure they were human voices. Going outside again, I started shouting back and tried to use what was left of our flashlight to signal
upward. But this got no apparent result; so I roused Girmi again
and told him the two of us were going up ourselves."

It was about ten when they started off. Dave carried one oxygen
cylinder, from which he breathed a 2-liter flow. But Girmi, though
he carried two cylinders, performed the remarkable feat of climbing with no oxygen at all, so that there would be a full supply left
for the men above, when and if they found them. Their route of
ascent was along the western slope of the ridge, for it was from this
direction that Dave believed the shouts had come; and for an hour
and more they toiled on, gaining some two or three hundred vertical feet. "Here we reached the area," Dave said, "from which I was
sure the voices had been coming. I took off my oxygen mask and
gave many long shouts, and Girmi shouted too, and we waited, but
to our great distress there was no answer. My worst fears, I thought,
were being realized: that the men above, surely out of oxygen by
now, and in total darkness, had either fallen or had already taken
a wrong route past Camp VI and were lost."

Again he and Girmi shouted, loud and long, but there was still
no answer. By now, in the inky night and cold, Dave was becoming
worried about their own safety, and slowly, reluctantly, they descended to camp. Through the rest of the night Dave sat in his
tent—listening, dozing, reawakening and listening. Now and then
he thought he could hear voices again. But he was not sure.

Twice before in mountaineering history, men had spent a night
out near the summits of great Himalayan peaks and lived to tell the
tale. In 1953 it was done by the Austrian climber Hermann Buhl
on the descent from his solo climb to the top of Nanga Parbat, in
Kashmir; and in 1954 it was again done by the Alpine guide Walter

Bonatti and a Pakistani porter named Mahdi during the course of the successful Italian ascent of K2. Buhl's bivouac was at some 26,000 feet, Bonatti's and Mahdi's a few hundred feet higher. Now four men down from the summit of Everest were enduring the experience at 28,000 feet. They had no tent, no sleeping bags, no food, no drink, no oxygen. All they had were the clothes they wore, their ropes and axes, and their now almost empty packs.

On their little eyrie of rock, Willi Unsoeld and Tom Hornbein huddled close together. A few feet off, Lute Jerstad and Barry Bishop made the second pair. "By this time," said Barry, "we had both slipped into a stupefied fatigue.* My feet, which while I was still moving had been growing colder to the point of agony, had now lost all feeling, and the tips of my fingers were following them into numbness. We curled up in our down jackets as best we could. Then after a while I was lying dazedly on my back, with my feet propped up like two antennae, wondering—almost too weary to care—how badly they were damaged. I tried to wiggle my toes, but felt nothing. Then, knowing it was hopeless, I gave up the effort and sank into a fitful sleep."

Lute, on the other hand did not—or thinks he did not—sleep at all. He hugged himself; he dug hands into armpits; he kept moving his toes and knocking his feet together for hour after hour. "As grimly as I had vowed to reach the summit," he said, "I now felt an indescribable savage drive to live through that night. Nothing was going to turn our victory into defeat. . . ."

Of the four of them, only Tom was lucid enough—or had enough energy—to remove his crampons, which, with their steel spikes, were prime conductors of cold. And later Willi, in a typical Willi action, removed Tom's boots and warmed his stockinged feet by drawing them under his clothing and holding them against his bare stomach. At this time Tom's feet still had sensation and were paining him. But when he suggested to Willi that he would now reciprocate the foot-warming, Willi said no, it was not necessary; his feet were all right. His awareness was so dulled that he did not realize that they were frozen numb. Even Tom, who was less far

* Barry and Lute, and to a lesser extent Willi and Tom, were by this time so exhausted and hypoxic that they later had much difficulty in recalling the details of their night in bivouac. While telling their story, they had often to supplement and correct one another, in an effort to set the record straight.

gone than the others, could not think clearly enough to realize that this must be the case. Willi, Lute and Barry kept their crampons on, their feet exposed. The most they did was scrape and clink them on the icy rock.

The hours passed. The night crept on. In a whole year's cycle of Everest nights there are no more than a handful in which unsheltered men at 28,000 feet could conceivably live to see the morning. But this was one of them. The mountain was kind. God was merciful. The temperature hovered at 18 degrees below zero; but sheer cold, however bitter, is not so fierce an enemy as cold with wind behind it—and in the early hours of darkness the wind had dropped. There was only an occasional vagrant gust; then stillness. Utter stillness. On the roof of earth's highest mountain such a thing was a miracle. And the miracle had been granted.

Beyond the stillness hung the frozen stars. Far, far to the south, beyond the blackness of Lhotse and Makalu, heat lightning flared and faded above the plains of India. It was three o'clock. Two men stirred and two others lay like stones. It was four o'clock. Two men dozed and two men stared at the sky. Then it was almost five, and all were staring at the sky. At still another miracle: the miracle of a new day. Above, the stars were receding, fading. But around them the world was emerging: slowly, slowly. Rock was no longer black but gray. Snow was no longer gray but white. Above and below, the ridge took shape; beyond, and around them, other mountains took shape; all that had been gone and lost returned.

The four men were silent, watching.

And God said, "Let there be light"; and there was light.

And still they watched and waited, while a day was born.

Color seeped into the grayness and whiteness. First in the east; then everywhere. A tide of pink and gold flooded the host of earth's highest peaks and poured down their flanks to the glaciers and valleys. There was no wisp of wind, of any sound or movement. The luminous miles spread away in such stillness, such clarity, that it seemed not merely the dawn of a day but of the world itself. Never in his life, said photographer Barry Bishop, had he seen a sight that so demanded to be recorded in its full panoply of grandeur. But his hands were too numb to change the film in his camera.

Now the sun was up. It streamed across the earth and upon the four men huddled close beneath earth's summit. It touched their faces and eyes. It penetrated through their layers of clothing to blood, bone and spirit. Though it had been light now for some time, they had deliberately waited for sunrise and its life-giving warmth. And now they rose too. They were *able* to rise. Their bodies were stiff, their minds dulled, their eyes bleared. For all but Tom Hornbein, their feet were unsentient stumps at the end of their legs. But still they could rise. They could move. They could even make a few wry jokes. "What's for breakfast?" "Who's got a new razor blade?"

Struggling with sticklike fingers, Tom got his crampons back on. The others slung on packs and shuffled about. Then they tied into their ropes, in their original pairings of Lute and Barry, Tom and Willi, and at six o'clock, after five and a half hours on their perch in the sky, they were ready to go. Tom and Willi went first, following the now visible tracks in the snow. Lute and Barry followed a few moments after. Lute could barely see through his wind- and fire-burned eyes, and one of Barry's had now also fogged over. "We moved as much by feel as by sight," he said. But move they did.

Down—down—

At 5:30, in the first dawnlight, Dave Dingman and Girmi Dorje had started up again from Camp VI. Each carried two bottles of oxygen, breathing from one of them, and both were still physically in good shape; but all thought of a summit attempt on their own part was now a thing of the past. They were now not a summit team. They were a rescue team—if there was anyone left to rescue—and as long as daylight and strength held out, they would search the upper mountain for Lute and Barry. That Willi and Tom might also be up there, on *this* side of the peak, did not occur to them.

Partly they followed their own route of the previous night, partly the upward tracks of Lute and Barry, which were now plain to the eye in the light of morning. And in an hour or more of climbing they again gained a few hundred feet. Then again, as on the night before, they took off their masks and shouted. "And, lo and behold," said Dave, "about 100 feet ahead of us two figures slowly staggered to their feet." His excitement was so great that he virtually dashed up toward them, leaving him with no breath to speak when he arrived. And he was rendered even more speechless when he realized that the two men were not Lute and Barry but Willi and Tom. "I was so astonished, so absolutely dumfounded," he said, "that the significance of their being there didn't dawn on me for another half hour; that it meant they had made their traverse of Everest."

Willi and Tom told him that the other two were following a bit behind them. When Dave offered them oxygen they said that no, they could get to Camp VI without it; Lute and Barry's need would be greater. And after Dave had pointed out the way, they continued their descent. Meanwhile Dave and Girmi continued on. They gained another hundred feet or so. Once more they shouted. And once more, in almost dreamlike repetition, two figures above them slowly rose to their feet. "They seemed so shaky," said Dave, "that I shouted to them to stay where they were until I could get to them. Which they did. And when I arrived they were lying prostrate on a little shelf of snow. As they spoke to me it was very slowly and with much effort, and their faces were a deep ashen blue."

Dave and Girmi quickly unlimbered their extra oxygen bottles and hooked them up to the two men's masks. After a few minutes their talk became more coherent and their color changed from blue to a more normal pink. Presently they were standing. The four were starting down. Lute and Barry were lurching and stumbling, with Dave and Girmi assisting them. And it was as if an old moving picture film were being re-run, with ironic changes; for three weeks before it had been Lute and Barry who had played the role of escort, accompanying Norman and Big Jim and Gombu and Ang Dawa down from the heights, while Everest's summit receded behind them. . . . That had been their day of disappointment and sacrifice. But they had had a second chance. They had risen to it. They had reached their goal. And now it was others who were sacrificing for them.

Indeed, the sacrifice was more total, for Dave Dingman and Girmi Dorje would *not* have another chance. Every step they were descending on the peak was a step they would never regain. It had been at about 27,700 feet that they met Lute and Barry and turned around, with the mountaintop a mere 1300 feet higher. It seemed highly probable that, on that bright and windless day, they could have reached it—just as Barry Corbet, if he had had the chance, could have gone all the way with Willi Unsoeld and Tom Hornbein. But it was not to be for Barry, and it was not to be for Dave and Girmi. It was no one's fault. It was the luck of the game. And Dave and Girmi, as they now descended, were not complaining. They were helping their companions. They were belaying the rope. They were saying, "Come on—to the right here—now the left. Steady now—that's it—you're doing fine."

That is the mountain way.

When they reached Camp VI, Willi and Tom were resting in sleeping bags in one of the tents. And now Lute and Barry rested too, while Nima Dorje, the Sherpa who had remained at the camp, melted ice into water. None of the summit four had any stomach for solid foods, but in an enormous craving for liquids they downed cup after cup of lemonade, coffee, tea and hot chocolate. Then, about ten o'clock, they were off—now in a procession of seven—and in about two hours, moving slowly but steadily, they reached Camp V on the South Col. Here the Sherpa Pemba Tenzing was waiting. There was more rest. More to drink.

Then they continued on down.

Over the Geneva Spur. Over the Yellow Band. Across the Lhotse Couloir, the Lhotse Face. (And it was an old familiar route to Barry, Lute and Dave, but to Willi and Tom, the pair from "the other side," it was all brand new.) As they moved on, so did the day—from early, to mid- to late afternoon. And at about five, on the Lhotse Face, they paused, and Willi brought out his walkie-talkie to see if he could again make contact with Advance Base. He could and did. Indeed, not only did he reach A.B. but Base Camp as well, and he was able to tell Norman himself where they were and what had happened, and that both the summit teams were now descending the mountain—if not exactly in the pink, at least alive and victorious.

Then came something even better. It was the hour at which Base had its regular daily contact with Kathmandu, and Dan Doody, operating the radio, was able to effect alternating conversations with the men on the mountain and the waiting crowd in Bill Gresham's shack. This was the day—May 23—on which Jolene Unsoeld and Lila Bishop were back at the shack for the third time, still hoping for word of their husbands. And this time, at last, they had it in full measure; for though Lhotse Face and Kathmandu could not speak directly, Dan was able to relay messages back and forth within a matter of seconds. Said Willi and Barry, both: "We're all right—greetings—love." Then, mindful of his "promises to keep," Willi added: "Truly, I promise this will be my last big climb." To which Jolene replied by way of Dan: "This time I have a lot of witnesses."

There was airborne jubilation in Kathmandu, at Base, at Advance Base—even among the worn and beaten men still on the mountainside.

"And what, please," Sally Dyhrenfurth inquired, happily asking the unanswerable of her husband, "are you going to do for an encore?"

Then, while those below continued their palaver, the summit teams signed off and continued their descent. Shortly they came to Camp IV on the Lhotse Face, and here again they rested and drank. But not for long; for they were determined to reach Advance Base that same day, no matter how many hours it took them, and soon they were again moving down the vast walls of ice and snow. For a while, the euphoria generated by the radio messages moved with them. "It was one long schuss," said Willi Unsoeld—half picnic, half triumphal procession. But this, alas, was not to last for long, for presently the grimmer realities of life, and Everest, began to reassert themselves, and the four summiteers again knew themselves for what they were: a straggle of battered, exhausted, debilitated men barely escaping with their lives down the mountain.

Indeed, for all except Tom Hornbein, there now began to be an extra dimension to their misery. And the dimension was pain. Throughout the day, Barry, Lute, and Willi had stumped down the endless slopes on frozen feet that had lost all vestige of sensation. But now at lower levels their feet were thawing, and each step, multiplied into thousands of steps, brought a new and increasing agony. Their pace grew slower and slower. It was dark before they reached Camp III near the foot of the Lhotse Face.

But still they kept on, down the Western Cwm, threading the maze of the crevasses with the aid of Dave Dingman's feeble flashlight, and at last, at 10:30 at night, they stumbled into what seemed to them then the veritable metropolis of Advance Base. Jimmy Roberts and Maynard Miller, who had held the fort there for the past ten days, had gone down that afternoon to Camp I, to be in position to receive them on their further descent the next day. But the West Ridge support team—Barry Corbet, Dick Emerson, Al Auten and their Sherpas—were now down to take their place. It had been only a few hours before, as they were ending their descent from Camps 4W and 3W, that they had seen a procession of dots on the Lhotse Face, and, by counting the dots, had reached the conclusion that all the top climbers were present and accounted for. And now their welcome to Willi and Tom was one of the great and moving events of the expedition. A lot of water had flowed under the bridge—or over the mountain—since they had last seen them, high on the North Face, some fifty-four hours earlier.

In the tents of Advance Base, crampons and overboots and boots and layers of stockings came off at last, and Dave Dingman examined the feet of the four summiteers. Though feeling—excruciating feeling—was returning to them, Willi's and Barry's were dead white, hard as iron, and icy to the touch. Lute's, too, were frozen, though not so badly, leaving Tom as the only one who had suffered no serious damage. All had frostbitten fingertips, in varying degrees, but in no case had they been affected as badly as the frozen feet. Dave did what he could for them—which was mainly to relieve their ever-growing pain, and then the four exhausted men turned in for the night.

The next morning, with gritted teeth, they managed to get their footgear back on. They managed to rise, to move. And, after almost eight weeks of service as expedition nerve center, Advance Base was finally evacuated. The goraks croaked a beady-eyed farewell; then turned their attention to what foodstuffs had been left behind to keep them victualled for the coming summer, while, through the morning, the last echelon of AMEE plodded down through the lower Cwm. At Camp I Jimmy Roberts and Maynard Miller were waiting, and the summit climbers, who except for Tom were now hobbling miserably, were given another chance to rest. And here it was Maynard's turn to make one of the expedition's notable "sacrifices"—though this was of a rather different sort from those of most of the others. The top foursome were still badly dehydrated, desperately thirsty. But there were no liquids available—or at least none designed for drinking. All that was on hand was a precious (for Maynard) collection of bottles containing melted ice which, during the past ten days, he had laboriously drawn from successive annual layers of the Cwm's glacier, and which were to be analysed for tritium and other chemical content on his return home. As of then and there, one suspects, there must have been a few difficult moments for AMEE's glaciologist. But the humanitarian in him overrode the scientist. For presently out came the bottles, and in a twinkling a fair percentage of his rare specimens was vanishing forever down parched gullets.

Then it was off again. Down through the Icefall. While the second wave of climbers had been up high, the spring thaw had continued its work on these lower levels, and in spite of the work of the Sherpa maintenance crew, the steep icy labyrinth was in worse chaos than ever. Only a day or two before, at a key point in the route just below the Cwm's entrance, a huge complex of ice had collapsed, leaving a gaping chasm; and the best the Sherpas had been able to do was to bridge it with a 150-foot length of rope, which slanted down through thin air over a bottomless pit. Down this flimsy strand, everyone now had to slide, using the technique known as a Tyrolean traverse, in which one leg is hooked over the rope, and the body, hanging beneath it, is propelled by hands and arms. For the crippled summiteers it was a cruel ordeal, but in the end they made the passage. Through the afternoon the now long procession wound its way on down through the maze of the Icefall. And at last, as dusk was falling, they trudged into Base Camp on the Khumbu Glacier.

Two months and two days after the first climbing had begun, the last of the expedition was down off the mountain.

During many phases of the siege of Everest movement had been so slow, so little appeared to be happening, that it seemed almost as if the whole enterprise had ground to a halt. Now, in contrast, so many things were happening, and so quickly, that the impression was that of a moving picture film racing wildly through its sprockets. With the exception of the small group who had gone off to the

Mingbo Glacier, all personnel was now at Base. To it had been added the 275 low-level porters who had just come up from the Solu Khumbu villages to help in the march out. And to men who a mere two days before had moved through the solitudes of earth's summit, it was as if they had come suddenly into Times Square or an Indian bazaar. The first order of the day—or night—was celebration: a welter of handshakes and embraces, of food and drink, of joking and shouting, of laughter and tears. Then came the complex, frenetic preparations for departure. For this was the evening of May 24; the next day, the twenty-fifth, was the date long since set for evacuation; and everyone was determined that in this the expedition would hew to its schedule.

Moreover, and of the greatest importance, it was now obvious that the more badly frostbitten of the summit climbers must be got out to civilization and hospitalization as fast as was humanly possible. Even before their arrival, Norman, after a morning walkie-talkie report from Dave Dingman at Advance Base, had radioed Kathmandu with the emergency request that the U.S. AID helicopter be dispatched to Namche Bazar on the morning of the twenty-seventh. And now a renewed examination of the men's feet by Dave and Gil Roberts made it clearer than ever that time was of the essence. The elfin Tom Hornbein was, incredibly, almost as good as new. He appeared perfectly capable of packing his 125 pounds right back up the mountain again and taking off from the top in his flying saucer. Lute Jerstad's feet, though bad, were not *too* bad. Though half crippled, half blinded and totally battered, he would not, in the doctors' judgment, need hospital treatment. But for Willi Unsoeld and Barry Bishop it was another matter, for their frostbite was deep and deeply serious. The best medical treatment was essential. It must be administered quickly. Though the expedition had taken a leisurely eight days (not counting the stopover for five at Thangboche) to move up from Namche Bazar to Base Camp, Norman was resolved that it would get down in two.

The next morning the tents were struck. The radio aerial, the meteorological instruments and the American flag were down. Loads were packed and hoisted, and the caravan was on its way: no longer a millipede but only a multicentipede, less than a third of its original length, winding down among the *névés penitentes* of Phantom Alley. As on the approach march, progress was in a single column, with the team members and high Sherpas spread among the rank-and-file Sherpas—men, women and children—who carried the bulk of the loads. Among these were twelve men whose loads were human: four each for Willi, Barry and Lute, whom they carried in relays for periods of twenty minutes each. At first the crippled climbers rode backwards, sitting in baskets slung over the porters' shoulders; but in this position the jolting was unendurable, and soon they had changed to a simple piggyback, which was more comfortable, if less dignified.

Indeed, there was little dignity—at least of the outward variety— anywhere in the plodding procession; little indication that this was a group of men returning from a bright and glittering triumph. It was a tatterdemalion lot: the porters stooped and ragged, the climbers scruffy, bearded, emaciated—three of them unable even to walk —as they moved down the glacial valley, looking back now and then at the mountain on which they had struggled and aspired.

And *conquered*, one might add.

But it would not be these men who would add it. Not then— nor ever. For these men were mountaineers. They would say, with George Leigh-Mallory, "Have we vanquished an enemy? None but ourselves." They would say, with Barry Bishop, "When the battle ends, the mountain remains unvanquished. There are no true victors, only survivors."

Plus one who was not a survivor. And presently they were to bid good-bye to him; for they had come to the place called Gorak Shep, beside the Khumbu Glacier, which on their upward trip had been a wilderness of ice and snow, but was now, in late spring, a rocky vale beside a mountain lake, in which grew tiny alpine flowers, as high as any in all the world. The trail passed close by the lake—and also by a large rock near its shore on which a stone cutter from one of the Sherpa villages, hired by the expedition, had been at work for a few weeks past. His work was now finished, and on the rock was carved:

IN MEMORY OF

JOHN E. BREITENBACH

AMERICAN MOUNT EVEREST EXPEDITION 1963

Slowly, in single file, the other men of Everest passed by and moved on toward the world below.

16. WORLD BELOW

"WELL DONE! Congratulations!"

And this was praise from Caesar; for, appropriately, it was Sir Edmund Hillary, whose expedition was still doing its educational and medical work in the Solu Khumbu villages, who was the first to greet the expedition as it emerged from the mountain fastnesses.

It had, as planned, reached Namche Bazar in two days, having been joined en route by the Mingbo Glacier party of Barry Prather, Dick Pownall, Gombu, and their accompanying Sherpas. It had camped on a hillside terrace above the town. And at 6:30 on the morning of May 27, while everyone was just coming awake in the tents, there was a humming and whirring in the sky and the helicopter from Kathmandu set itself down on a flat hilltop nearby. It was a visitation from another world—an almost forgotten world—and the expedition moved quickly up to it, followed by most of the population of Namche and environs. Aboard it were its pilot, a young Norwegian named Knut Solbakken, and, as passenger, Tom Abercrombie, a staff photographer of the National Geographic Society, who had been assigned to fill in for Barry Bishop on the march back to Kathmandu. In a welter of excitement and confusion

Barry and Willi Unsoeld were carried up from camp and took their places in it. But there, happily, confusion ended, for there was no such mishap as had marked the Clinch-Huestis saga, and in short order the chopper was up, off and away.

For more than three months Barry and Willi, as members of AMEE, had fought their way, day by day, mile by mile, step by step, to the summit of the world. Now in a matter of seconds, expedition, mountain, all of it, had vanished into the past.

At nine o'clock on that morning the helicopter set them down at the gates of Shanta Bhavan, the site of the American-run United Mission Hospital in the outskirts of Kathmandu. By lucky happenstance, which was a great mitigation of their miseries, they were two of the three expedition members whose wives were in Nepal, and a moment later they were in the arms of Lila and Jolene. Then they walked—for they could still walk—to the hospital steps and, sitting there flanked by their wives (and Willi by his four children as well), they talked to the host of friends and press and radio and television crews and many others who had come to see them. They were worn and bearded; they were still wearing their mountain clothes and boots and layers of socks; the crowd stared at them as if they were men from another planet—which in a way, indeed, they were. And they in turn looked back with the eyes of men who were seeing something other than what was before them.

At Shanta Bhavan they came under the devoted care of the senior surgeon, Dr. Robert E. Berry of Philadelphia. And two days later Melvin M. Payne, the executive vice-president of the National Geographic Society arrived from Washington, D.C., bringing with him Dr. Eldred D. Mundth, of the U.S. Naval Reserve, a specialist in frostbite who thereafter assisted Dr. Berry with counsel and the most modern drugs. The major areas of both Willi's and Barry's feet responded quickly and well to treatment, and it was soon apparent that they would eventually heal. But all their toes, gangrenous from loss of circulation, were now an angry purplish black, and much time would have to pass before it would be known whether or not they could be saved.

Meanwhile there would be the ordeal of treatment, of pain, of confinement, of waiting. And, helping them face it, the love and companionship of their wives.

Back in Namche Bazar on May 27, the rest of the day was devoted to heroic chang and arak drinking by the Sherpas and a general drawing of deep breaths by their sahibs. Then the next morning came a fond and sad farewell to those of the high Sherpas who were staying behind in their home villages, and the main body of AMEE began the long trek to Kathmandu. It had taken Willi Unsoeld and Barry Bishop ninety minutes to get there. It would take the walkers thirteen days. But at least that was three days faster than the time taken for the approach march.

There was no lingering good-bye to Everest. From the time they had come down off the glacier, it had been lost behind them, swathed in cloud and mist; and in Namche it was learned over the radio that the advance storms of the summer monsoon had begun moving into the Everest region on the very day on which the expedition had left Base Camp. Again AMEE had been blessed with good fortune. For if the last summit climbers, who had had such fine weather during their final push, had been even a day or two later in their descent of the mountain, they would probably have been caught in a cauldron of wind and storm and drifting, crumbling snow.

As the caravan now marched off from Namche Bazar down the gorges of the Dudh Kosi, it was not snow that threatened, but rain. And soon it cut off to the west over a higher route than the one it had taken in, for the river was high and raging and one of the principal bridges was out. Up the procession went to lofty passes, then down to lower valleys; up again, down again, through the hours and the days. And for most of the hours the monsoon rains now beat down, drumming at night on the nylon of the tents, drumming by day on the mud of the trail. At last those improbable umbrellas purchased months before in Kathmandu were brought into use as the ultimate item of expedition equipment. Other triumphant campaigners returning from their wars carry flags, banners and trophies as tokens of conquest. But for AMEE the standards of victory were a line of black dripping bumbershoots.

Up, down. Down, up. Only now there was more down than up.

Off to the north, the great sweep of the Himalaya, so clear and beckoning during the approach march, was now, like Everest itself, largely hidden in cloud. There were only the hills and the valleys, the rain and the muck. But for men down from the frozen heights there was beauty even in these, for all around them, too, there was now the wondrous, all-but-forgotten miracle of green and growing life.

The trail unrolled. The villages came up out of distance, in reverse order—Ringmo, Junbesi, Sete, Changma; Those, Yersa, Kirantichap, Manga Deorali. At Junbesi the travelers were greeted by Mrs. Pashi Sherpa, the once terribly burned woman who had been sent by helicopter to the hospital in Kathmandu and who a few weeks before had at last been able to return home. She brought with her, as a gift, a basket of fresh eggs garnished with iris blossoms. Her face had healed; she was well and happy. And it was no little satisfaction to AMEE to know that, if it had lost a life in its pilgrimage to its mountain, it had also done its share in helping to save one.

Down, up. Up, down. It was a procession of gaunt and soggy scarecrows. But after where the scarecrows had been, the roller coaster of central Nepal was like a paved highway, and bony legs devoured the miles. For several days Lute Jerstad, with his semifrozen feet, had been carried by Sherpas, then had ridden a pony, but now the feet were better and he walked with the others. Tom Hornbein practically trotted. Dan Doody and Balu Prather, who a few weeks before had rubbed elbows with death, kept pace without tiring. Jim Lester, the expedition tyro, who had hobbled through the approach march on tender and blistered underpinning, was now a case-hardened mountaineer swinging along in full stride. Down, up. Up, down.

Will Siri and Maynard Miller kept an eye cocked on the porters who were carrying their precious specimens. Jimmy Roberts kept his cocked in all directions. And doctors Gil Roberts and Dave Dingman were again conducting their itinerant clinic, treating the aches and ailments of the countryside. Stretched out along the line of march were the others: Jim Whittaker, Dick Pownall, Barry Corbet, Al Auten, Dick Emerson. And, interspersed with them, the Sherpas: Gombu, Ang Dawa, Girmi Dorje and their brethren.

Sometimes at the head of the column, sometimes in its middle, sometimes at its end, was the general of the tattered army, Norman Dyhrenfurth. As on the approach march, he was in a state of suspension between the world behind and the world ahead: marching, stopping, eating, sleeping, rising, marching on again in almost mechanical sequence. So much had happened between approach and exodus—in labor and adventure, in tragedy and achievement— that mind and emotion were not yet able to encompass it.

They came to Risingo, to Chaubas, to Dolalghat. It grew warmer. Day by day mountain clothing was discarded, until the expedition uniform was boots and socks, a pair of shorts, and an umbrella. But now, in the last days of the march, the rains mercifully ceased and umbrellas were furled. On June 9, the date set weeks before for arrival in Kathmandu, the sun, in the spirit of the day, beamed from a stainless sky. And at midmorning, with another Cecil B. DeMille crowd waiting to greet it, AMEE arrived at the field in Banepa from which it had departed for Everest 109 days before.

The facts of Kathmandu were still there. But in different perspective.

To put first things first, there was beer. Then there were jeeps, trucks, buildings, rooms, baths, tables, chairs. There were women. There was clean underwear. There were letters, cables, greetings, reunions, and talk talk talk into the middle of the nights. There were visits to Shanta Bhavan to see Willi and Barry. There was another fond and sad leave-taking from more Sherpas. There was a spate of rushing about in the causes of finance, plane tickets, freight shipments, customs clearances. For Norman, there was Sally. For Dave Dingman, there was his wife Jan, who arrived from the States on the same day the expedition came in.

There was more beer. There was food food food. There were stomach-aches. There was confusion. And there were parties. King Mahendra of Nepal greeted the team at a reception. Ambassador and Mrs. Stebbins gave a dinner. The American community in general gave another. Boris and Inger Lissanevitch of the Hotel Royal gave a combined party-reception-dinner-celebration that seemed to go on for a week. Not the least of the good cheer was that Willi and Barry were able to attend most of the festivities, making their entrances and exits perched jauntily on stretchers.

There were a few more stomach-aches. There were preparations for departure. There were the painted eyes on the temples of Kathmandu, and the eyes asked, "Little men, what now?"

Two team members were to stay in Nepal: Jimmy Roberts, because it was his permanent home, and Willi Unsoeld, who would resume his work as deputy director of the Peace Corps as soon as he was out of the hospital. (Indeed, Willi was already deep in his paperwork on his bed in Shanta Bhavan.) For Barry Bishop, arrangements were made by our Embassy whereby a United States military plane with a built-in bunk would evacuate him to New Delhi, whence, with Lila, he would be flown home to Washington. And for the rest, too, the first stop would be New Delhi, before the flight homeward through Europe.

Not only the team would be going; there would be guests as well. Through a grant from the State Department's Bureau of Educational and Cultural Affairs funds had been provided to bring six non-American members of the expedition on a visit to the United States, and the selection of the men had been made by Norman with the concurrence of the team. One who of course would come was Nawang Gombu. Another was Norman's Ang Dawa. A third was liaison officer Noddy—who for such an occasion merits his full name of Captain Prabakher Shumshere Jung Bahadur Rana. The remaining three were the Solu Khumbu Sherpas, Girmi Dorje, Ila Tsering and Nima Tenzing (of Thami), who had so distinguished themselves on the heights of Everest.

The departure from Kathmandu was in stages, determined by who could be fitted into what plane. But on June 17 and 18 most of the expedition was reunited in New Delhi, where we were received by Prime Minister Nehru and the then American Ambassador to India, J. Kenneth Galbraith. Also—and very memorably—we were feted by the Indian Mountaineering Foundation, which had planned and executed the two almost successful Indian attempts on Everest in 1960 and 1962. And there was not a member of AMEE who was not well aware, as we received the openhearted welcome of its members, that, had it not been for a mischance here, a trick of fate there, they too would have won the victory for which they were now paying us tribute.

From New Delhi, the journey home was piecemeal. The nucleus of the expedition, headed by Norman with the Sherpas in tow, went by way of Italy, Switzerland and France. Others took other routes. There was a pause, a hiatus.

And then the epilogue.

On July 8, as guests of the National Geographic Society, the seventeen returned members of the expedition, plus most of their wives and their Asian guests, assembled in Washington and in the Rose Garden of the White House were presented with the Society's Hubbard Medal by President Kennedy. The rarely awarded prize had previously been given only to individuals—Peary, Byrd, Lindbergh and the like—and never to a group. But Norman had insisted that in the case of AMEE it must be to everyone or no one. And to everyone it was. The original gold medal went to the expedition as such, with Norman as custodian. Replicas went to the other surviving team members, to Jake Breitenbach's widow, to Noddy Rana, to Nawang Gombu, to the other high Sherpas as a group, and to Sally Dyhrenfurth and Chuck Huestis, who in their multiple capacities had done as much for our venture as any who actually climbed on Everest. From most of us, as we received our award, the reply was a simple "thank you." But Gombu did better than that. Out from his pocket, just as had happened on earth's summit, came a *kata*, the symbolic friendship scarf of the Buddhist faith, which, in traditional fashion, he draped about the President's neck, while the audience applauded, cameras clicked and whirred —and it was hard to tell if President or Sherpa had the warmer smile.

There were more parties. (And if the Sherpas missed their chang and arak, they politely made do with American substitutes.)

Then there was dispersal. To the Pacific Coast, to the Rocky Mountain West, to the Midwest, along the Atlantic Seaboard. To homes and families. To offices, laboratories, hospitals, classrooms —and depleted bank accounts. All that was now left of AMEE as a unit were the five Sherpas and Noddy Rana, who, with Jim Lester as mentor, set out on an eight-week transcontinental tour of the United States. Traveling by station wagon, they visited New York, southern New England, Cincinnati, St. Louis, Denver, the Teton Mountains of Wyoming, Seattle, San Francisco, Los Angeles; and at each stop their hosts were expedition members who lived in that area. They rubbernecked, window-shopped, dined out, attended all manner of receptions, and each day answered a thousand questions—half reasonable, half foolish. They made acquaintance with revolving doors, automats, television, traffic cops, baseball, hamburgers, planetariums, and Disneyland. Gombu learned to swim, and all of them—more or less—to bowl. With Barry Corbet as guide, they climbed Wyoming's Grand Teton. With expedition wives as guides, they went to the top of the Empire State Building; and though they were unimpressed by the molehill view, they conceded that it was the fastest thousand feet they had ever ascended. "Are there no poor people in America?" they asked. And they were shown. But the slums of Harlem and elsewhere baffled rather than convinced them. Even there they saw curbs lined with cars, big buildings, with roofs on them, and store windows filled with merchandise. They saw fat people, fully clothed people, no one barefoot, no one starving in the street. And as men from the heart of Asia, they asked incredulously, "You call *this* poor?"

As on Everest—as anywhere—they kept their inner thoughts and feelings to themselves. But they smiled, they laughed, they charmed. They made friends everywhere they went. And when at last they flew homeward, after a week with Norman in Los Angeles, every member of AMEE was the better for having known them and the sadder for their departure.

Home—

For some, their functions as team members ended with their return. For others, work would continue almost as actively as when they were on the mountain. The scientists would be busy collating and evaluating their research for months, even years, to come. There was the expedition book to be written, plus articles for magazines and journals, and many of the men were soon involved in the lecture circuit. Barry Bishop, frozen feet and all, was waist deep in the 25,000-odd photographs that had been taken, and Norman worked at the giant task of turning miles of moving picture film into a presentation for television and theatre showings. Also—and mostly on Norman's shoulders (with help from Chuck Huestis)—there were such matters as getting freight shipments home, making reports to expedition backers, clearing up finances. And ahead was the important business of converting the American Mount Everest Expedition into the American Mount Everest Foundation, dedicated to the support of scientific research in mountaineering ventures of the future. It was not long before the Bara Sahib was breathing as hard as when he was struggling up the Southeast Ridge above Camp VI on that fearsome May Day of 1963.

For most of the men there were to be no lasting ill effects from their ordeal on the mountain. But Barry Bishop and Willi Unsoeld were not so lucky. After long treatment at the Bethesda Naval Hospital—during which he resolutely kept working on photographs —Barry suffered the loss of all his toes, plus the tips of both of his little fingers; and Willi, back at the United Mission Hospital in Kathmandu, lost all his toes except one. Further, while convalescing from this, he developed a severe case of hepatitis, and in the early fall of 1963 he was flown home, also to become for a while a patient at Bethesda. Now both men are up and about again. They are living their normal lives. After months in bandages and sandals, they are again wearing shoes and are mastering a new skill—the balance that must be learned by the toeless. Both will undoubtedly climb again, if Lila and Jolene allow them. And perhaps even if they don't.

Yet—the toes are gone. They have paid a stiff price for standing, each for his few minutes, on the summit of Everest. And the inevitable question remains (at least for the non-mountaineer): Was it worth it? The final answer must be their own, not anyone else's. But, as a tentative one, perhaps the best is that they were *not* non-mountaineers. They were not only mountaineers; they were Everesters. No man is happy to lose a part of his body, a part of his normal functioning. But many men have risked as much and lost more in lesser causes. As against how many who have realized the dream of a lifetime?

The weeks and months pass. Soon the years will pass. And what is left of it all?

For the mountaineering historian there is a spate of records and "firsts"; and among these, pre-eminently, there are the climbing of the West Ridge, the crossing of the summit, the descent by the South Col. At expedition's end Norman said: "For decades it has been the dream of mountaineers to do a major Himalayan traverse. We are particularly happy and proud that this was not only the first Himalayan traverse, but that the traverse was on Everest." For all, that happiness and pride will endure.

There were other achievements as well. Among them: most men on top of Everest in one expedition; most men on top in one day; most team members and Sherpas to heights of 26,000, 27,000, and 28,000 feet; the first moving pictures at the summit; the first radio communication from the summit; the highest "night out" in history; and the first time that any of the world's great mountains had ever been tried—let alone climbed—simultaneously from two directions.

So far, so good. It will look well in the record book. But so will the feats of those who preceded us and those who will follow us. AMEE on its mountain was, in the long view, not an exploit whole and complete in itself, but part of a continuing story, a continuing adventure. In the struggle for earth's summit, we were not alone but in companionship with the British, the Swiss, the Indians— yes, even the Chinese—and any and all who will come after.

What will be ours uniquely will be more than records, more than a chapter in history. It will be what a group of men, collectively and individually, gave and received on a great adventure; and this will be so no less for those who got halfway or three-fourths or nine-tenths of the way up the mountain than for those who were chosen to stand on its top. "We want no damn heroes," said Norman. And in the end there were no heroes. There were mountaineers—and men.

Now they are back in what Norman calls the "other life": in the world below. They are at their desks and test tubes and operating tables and typewriters and cash registers. They are in their family dining rooms, their family cars. They look out at the landscapes of New England, Maryland, Ohio, Michigan, Colorado, Wyoming, Washington, Oregon, California. To the east of Norman's house in Santa Monica, California, are low brown hills; to the west is the Pacific Ocean, sweeping thousands of miles toward Asia, India, Nepal, the Himalaya. It was the glint in Norman's eye, the thrust of Norman's jaw, the dedication in Norman's heart, that moved AMEE across those miles, to its distant goal—and back again. For that is now the fact of life: back again. Mission completed. The glint in the eye is supplanted by a slight glaze as he looks about him at a room filled with letters, bills, forms, invoices, stacks of photographs, cans of film—the accumulated residue of a dream fulfilled.

But there is something else in his eyes as well. No longer a glint, perhaps, yet not a glaze. And it is in the eyes, too, of all the other men of AMEE, wherever they are, whatever they are doing: the light in the eyes of men who have seen and felt things they will never forget.

They see them still—

The tow head, the grin, the easy stride of Jake Breitenbach, as he moves up toward the Icefall on that second day at Base Camp. (Well, at least he is where he would have wanted to be.) The white chaos of the Icefall and the white stillness of the Cwm. The fluted walls of Nuptse, the savage ridge, the fangs of Lhotse. The tall face of Lhotse, gleaming in sunlight, raging in storm. The desolation of the Col; the thrust of the ridge beyond; the thrust of the West Ridge, rising, rising, rising; the kick-kick-kick of feet, the whack-whack-whack of axes; at last the ridges converging, the mountainsides converging, the whole of earth converging, until finally there is only the ultimate crest of earth in its radiant pinnacle, with its snow plume streaming in the winds of space.

The light in the eyes is not quite the same as that which touched them on that now long-gone morning in a DC-3 flying from Calcutta's Dum Dum Airport to Kathmandu, when a vision rose up out of the sky to the north. Then the light was prospective. Now it is retrospective. But, still, the two lights are not so different, for both are very strong and very pure.

The adventure is past. The vision remains.

PART II

THE COMPONENTS

1. WHO'S WHO

AMEE Members
(All facts and figures are as of the time of the expedition.)

ALLEN C. AUTEN

Home:	Denver, Colo.
Personal statistics:	Age 36, 5 ft. 11 in., 154 lb., married.
Occupation:	Assistant Editor, *Design News*.
Education:	Electrical Engineering, University of Denver. Radio and Television, University of Denver. B.S. Physical Science, Colorado State University.
General:	Electronic Technician; holder of First-Class Commercial Radio-Telephone License, Amateur Radio License, Amateur Extra-Class License; motion picture cameraman and sound engineer; National Ski Patrolman; Radio and Communications Committee Chairman, Southern Rocky Mt. Division, National Ski Patrol System.
Mountaineering:	Since 1952. Humboldt Peak, Crestone Needle,

No. Maroon Peak, Steam Boat Rock, Pyramid Peak, Snowmass Mountain, Mt. Elbert, Quandare Peak, Mt. Harvard, Columbia Peak, etc., Colo.; Shiprock, N.M.; Devil's Tower, Wyo.; Mt. Rainier, Wash.; Popocatepetl, Iztaccihuatl, Orizaba, Mexico; Mt. Victoria, Assiniboine, Mt. Temple, Bugaboo Spire, Canada; etc.

Expeditions: Kilimanjaro and Ruwenzori, Africa.

BARRY C. BISHOP

Home: Washington, D.C.

Personal statistics: Age 31, 5 ft. 7 in., 165 lb., married.

Occupation: Photographer and Geographer, National Geographic Society, Washington, D.C.

Education: B.S. Geology, University of Cincinnati, Ohio.
                     M.S. Geography, Northwestern University, Evanston, Ill.

General: Scientific Advisor on staff of Rear Admiral Richard D. Byrd, Antarctic Projects Office; United States Observer, 1956–57 Argentine Antarctic Expedition; Academic Honors: Omicron Delta Kappa, Sigma Gamma Epsilon, Sigma Xi, McKibben Medal.

Mountaineering: Western United States; Mexico; Canada; Swiss, Austrian, French and Italian Alps; Alaska; Nepal Himalaya.

Expeditions: 1951: Mt. McKinley Expedition (first ascent via Western Buttress).
                     1956–57: Argentine Antarctic Expedition.
                     1960–61: Himalayan Scientific and Mountaineering Expedition, led by Sir Edmund Hillary. First ascent of Ama Dablam, 22,494 feet.

JOHN E. BREITENBACH

Killed on Everest, March 23, 1963.

Home: Jackson, Wyo.

ENTRE-ACTE

CELEBRATION

—both of victory and of Norman Dyhrenfurth's birthday.

PHYSIOLOGIST WILL SIRI

GLACIOLOGIST MAYNARD MILLER

Photograph by William F. Unsoeld, AMEE

CAMP 4W ON THE WEST RIDGE

4W IN STORM

Photograph by William F. Unsoeld, © 1963 NATIONAL GEOGRAPHIC SOCIETY

DEEP FREEZE

Unsoeld after the storm.

TERRA INCOGNITA

The Diagonal Ditch slanting up the North Face.

FIRST OF ALL MEN

The Hornbein Couloir—
Tibet Below

Photograph by Allen C. Auten, AMEE

Photograph by William F. Unsoeld, AMEE

—Yellow Band Above

Camp 5W

(all of it)

Approaching the Yellow Band

The Miles of Tibet

Looking down the North Face
to the Rongbuk Glacier.

Hornbein on a West Ridge Crag
at More Than 28,500 Feet

Photograph by William F. Unsoeld, AMEE

From Right to Left: Chamlang, Lhotse, Everest's South
Summit, the Summit Ridge—and Hornbein's Oxygen Bottle

Photograph by William F. Unsoeld, AMEE

WIND ON THE SOUTH COL

WIND ON THE PEAK

LAST OUTPOST

Photograph by Richard Pownall, AMEE

JERSTAD AT VI

Photograph by Barry C. Bishop, © 1963 NATIONAL GEOGRAPHIC SOCIETY

FOUR ON TOP

Barry Bishop

Lute Jerstad
—with movie camera.

Tom Hornbein

Willi Unsoeld
—more or less.

FROM THE SUMMIT OF THE WORLD

EAST PAST MAKALU AND CHOMOLÖNZO TOWARD DISTANT KANGCHENJUNGA

SOUTHWEST PAST NUPTSE OVER AN OCEAN OF CLOUD

SOUTHEAST PAST LHOTSE TOWARD THE PLAINS OF INDIA

(The cornice in the foreground is similar to the one that gave way during the Whittaker-Gombu descent.)

NORTH OVER THE RONGBUK GLACIER INTO TIBET

Photograph by David L. Dingman, AMEE

CHAOS REVISITED

Roping down on the last descent through
the wilderness of the Icefall.

"ON EVEREST THERE ARE NO VICTORS"

Photograph by Gilbert Roberts, AMEE

GOOD-BYE TO A FRIEND

JERSTAD BEING CARRIED OUT

Photograph by James W. Whittaker, AMEE

A PRICE TO BE PAID

Bishop and Unsoeld, with frozen feet, waiting to be flown out to Kathmandu.

"TIGERS" ALL

The Sherpa brigade at Namche Bazar.

THE TEAM AT NAMCHE

In front (kneeling, squatting and sitting on ground): Dingman, Siri, Dyhrenfurth, Prather, Gombu, Pownall. *Seated:* Bishop, Unsoeld, Hornbein, Jerstad. *Standing:* J. Roberts, G. Roberts, Miller, Whittaker, Lester, Auten, two Sherpas, Knut Solbakken (helicopter pilot), Emerson, Corbet, Doody.

The Way Out

Return to Banepa

Sally Dyhrenfurth greets her husband.

Welcome Home

President Kennedy presents the team with the
National Geographic Society's Hubbard Medal.

Personal statistics: Age 27, 5 ft. 11 in., 155 lb., married.

Occupation: Mountain Guide; Part-Owner, Skiing and Moun-
                      taineering Equipment store.

Education: Pre-Med studies, Dartmouth College, N.H.
                      Physics major, University of Washington.
                      B.S. Mathematics, Oregon State University.

General: Graduate Assistant in Mathematics, Oregon State
                      University; Radio-Electronics, Automobile Me-
                      chanics, Photography; Mountain Guide, Tetons,
                      Wyo.

Mountaineering: Since 1949. Olympics, Wash.; Oregon Cascades;
                      Washington Cascades; Colorado Rockies: Arapa-
                      hoe Peak, E. Face of Longs Peak, the Maiden,
                      Flatirons, etc.; Wind Rivers, Wyo.; Tetons, Wyo.
                      (incl. No. Face of Grand, No. Ridge of Teewinot,
                      first ascent, Jensen Ridge of Symmetry, So. But-
                      tress of Mt. Moran, Fourteen Hour Pinnacle,
                      first ascent, etc.).

Expeditions: 1958: Mt. McKinley, Alaska (West Buttress).
                      1959: Mt. McKinley, Alaska (first ascent, West-
                            ern Rib of South Face).
                      1961: St. Elias Range: Attempt on Mt. Steele.

JAMES BARRY CORBET

Home: Jackson, Wyo.

Personal statistics: Age 26, 6 ft., 180 lb., married, one child.

Occupation: Mountain Guide and Ski Instructor; Owner, The
                      Alp Horn Lodge; Part-Owner, Skiing & Moun-
                      taineering Equipment store.

Education: Geology Major, Dartmouth College, N.H.

General: Lecturer on mountaineering; Instructor of Uni-
                      versity Extension courses in mountaineering.

Mountaineering: Numerous ascents in Tetons, Wyo., including:
                      No. Face of Grand, So. Buttress of Moran, No.
                      Face of Teewinot (first), E. Buttress of Middle
                      Teton (first), No. Face Red Sentinel (first), etc.;
                      Devil's Tower, Wyo.; Yosemite, Castle Crags,

Calif.; Canadian Rockies, incl. Mt. Rundle, Head
Peak (first); So. Coast Range, B.C.; Alaska.

Expeditions: 1959: Mt. McKinley, Alaska (first ascent, Western Rib of South Face).

DAVID L. DINGMAN, M.D.

Home: Baltimore, Md.
Personal statistics: Age 26, 6 ft., 175 lb., married, two children.
Occupation: Physician.
Education: B.S., Dartmouth College, N.H.
                     M.D., Medicine, University of Michigan.
General: Internship, University Hospital, Baltimore, Md.;
                     Residency, surgery, University Hospital, Balti-
                     more, Md.; Mountain Guide, Tetons, Wyo.
Mountaineering: Since 1951. Rocky Mountain National Park; Ore-
                     gon Cascades; Washington Cascades; Tetons,
                     Wyo. (incl. six first ascents); Wind Rivers, Wyo.
                     (incl. first ascent, No. Face Mt. Squaretop);
                     Alaska; Peru; Bolivia.
Expeditions: 1958: North American Mt. McKinley Expedition
                     (first ascent of *both* summits in one day).
                     1959: Cordillera Blanca Expedition, Peru, with
                     Leigh Ortenburger (5 peaks of 20,000 feet);
                     Huayna Potosi, Bolivia (solo).

DANIEL E. DOODY

Home: North Granford, Conn.
Personal statistics: Age 29, 6 ft. 2½ in., 185 lb., single.
Occupation: Film Maker.
Education: B.S. Agricultural Mechanics, University of Wy-
                     oming.
                     M.A. Cinema, University of Southern California.
General: Television Film Editor; Cameraman; Associate
                     Producer of "True Adventure."
Mountaineering: Since 1956. Devil's Tower, Wyo.; Needles, S.D.;
                     Tetons, Wyo. (incl. No. Face of Grand); Ship-
                     rock, N.M.; Agathlan, Ariz.; Tahquitz Rock, So.

Calif.; Wind Rivers, Wyo.; Shawangunks, N.Y.;
E. Face of Mt. Whitney, Calif.; Mt. Temple, Mt.
Victoria, Mt. Eisenhower, Mt. Edith Cavell (No.
Face, first ascent), etc., Canada.

NORMAN G. DYHRENFURTH (Leader of Expedition)

Home: Santa Monica, Calif.
Personal statistics: Age 44, 6 ft., 190 lb., married, one child.
Occupation: Motion Picture Producer-Director; Explorer.
Education: Matura, Kant. Gymnasium Zurich, Switzerland.
                       Diploma, Kant. Handelsschule Zurich, Switzerland.
General: Supervisor and Assistant Chief of Motion Pictures, General Dynamics-Astronautics, San Diego, Calif. (until 1960); Host of "Expedition," weekly TV show on Channel 13, KCOP, Los Angeles (until 1960); Lecture Tours: United States, Canada, Switzerland, Italy (until 1957); Fulbright Research Grant in Motion Pictures, Italy (1953–54); Associate Professor, UCLA (Head of Motion Picture Division), (1948–53); Cameraman-Director; Mountain Guide and Ski Instructor.
Mountaineering: Since 1928. Swiss, Austrian, Italian and French Alps; Chugach Range, Alaska; Tetons, Wyo. (incl. CMC route on Moran, E. Ridge of Grand, Nez Percé traverse, So. Teton—Cloudveil Dome traverse, etc.); White Mountains, N.H.; Sierra, Calif.; Storm King, N.Y.; Patagonia, Argentina; Nepal Himalaya.
Expeditions: 1938: Mt. Marcus Baker, Alaska (Bradford Washburn, Leader).
                       1938: Harvard Alaskan Expedition (Co-Leader).
                       1952: Swiss Mt. Everest Expedition.
                       1955: International Himalaya Expedition (Leader).
                       1958: Slick-Johnson Snowman Expedition (Dep. Leader).

1960: Swiss Dhaulagiri Expedition (first ascent of Dhaulagiri, 26,975 feet, highest peak ever scaled without oxygen, by eight team members).

RICHARD M. EMERSON, Ph.D.

Home: Cincinnati, Ohio.
Personal statistics: Age 38, 6 ft. 1 in., 184 lb., married, two children.
Occupation: Assist. Professor of Sociology, University of Cincinnati, Ohio; Senior Research Associate, Dept. of Psychiatry, University of Cincinnati.
Education: B.A. University of Utah.
                         M.S. Sociology and Psychology, University of Minnesota.
                         Ph.D. Sociology and Psychology, University of Minnesota.
General: Instructor, University of Minnesota (Ford Foundation College Teaching Internship); Teaching and Research Assistantships, University of Minnesota; Park Ranger, Grand Teton National Park (Mountain Rescue Operations).
Mountaineering: Since before WW II. Wasatch Range, Utah; Camp Hale, Colo. (Instructor, United States Mountain Infantry); Seneca Rocks, W.Va. (Instructor, United States troops); Italian and Austrian Alps (Supervisor, Advanced Mountaineering Training); Dolomites, Italy; Swiss Alps; Chamonix Aiguilles, France; Tetons, Wyo. (incl. No. Face of Grand).
Expeditions: 1960: American Pakistan Karakoram Expedition to Masherbrum, 25,660 feet.

THOMAS F. HORNBEIN, M.D.

Home: San Diego, Calif.
Personal statistics: Age 32, 5 ft. 7 in., 140 lb., married, five children.
Occupation: Physician (Anesthesiologist).

Education:	B.A. Geology, University of Colorado.
	M.D. Medicine, Washington University, St. Louis, Mo.
General:	Internship, King County Hospital, Seattle, Wash.; Residency in anesthesiology, Washington University, St. Louis, Mo.; U.S. Public Health Service Post-Doctoral Research Fellow; Instructor, Division of Anesthesiology, Washington University; Phi Beta Kappa, Earth Science and premedical honoraries; lieutenant in United States Navy, released in time for Expedition.
Mountaineering:	Since 1944. Front Range, Colo.; San Juans, Shiprock, N.M.; Tetons, Wyo.; Cascades, Wash. (incl. new route up Mowich Face, Mt. Rainier); Alaska; Pakistan.
Expeditions:	1957: Alaskan Expedition (S.E. of Mt. McKinley).
	1960: American Pakistan Karakoram Expedition to Masherbrum, 25,660 feet.

LUTHER G. JERSTAD

Home:	Eugene, Ore.
Personal statistics:	Age 26, 5 ft. 8 in., 155 lb., married, one child.
Occupation:	Speech Instructor, University of Oregon.
	Mountain Guide, Mt. Rainier National Park.
Education:	B.A. Speech, Theatre, Pacific Lutheran University.
	M.A. Speech, Theatre, Washington State University.
	Ph.D. in Theatre in preparation, University of Oregon.
General:	High School Teacher; Coach, basketball and golf; Basketball: Varsity Team, Pacific Lutheran University; Inspirational Award Winner in 1958; Played two years A.A.U. basketball in Northwest League; State Title 1959–60; Organizations: National Collegiate Players, several Lettermen's Clubs.

Mountaineering:	Since 1953. Washington Cascades, incl. 35 ascents of Mt. Rainier over various routes; Colorado Rockies; Oregon Cascades; Mt. Rainier Summit Guide.
Expeditions:	1961: McArthur-Logan Expedition, Yukon. Co-leader.
	1962: Mt. McKinley Expedition, Alaska.

JAMES T. LESTER, JR., Ph.D.

Home:	Berkeley, Calif.
Personal statistics:	Age 35, 6 ft. 1 in., 186 lb., divorced, no children.
Occupation:	Clinical Psychologist.
Education:	B.S. Psychology, Northwestern University.
	M.A. Psychology, UCLA.
	Ph.D. Psychology, UCLA.
General:	Clinical Internships: Langley Porter Neuropsychiatric Institute, San Francisco, and Brentwood V.A. Neuropsychiatric Hospital, West Los Angeles, Calif.; Instructor, University of Maryland Overseas Program, Munich, Germany; Director of psychological Services, Orthopaedic Hospital, Los Angeles; Project Director, Federal Office of Vocational Rehabilitation Research Grant; Private practice of diagnostic testing and psychotherapy; Musical arranger, trombonist, pianist, vocalist.
Mountaineering:	San Gorgonio, San Jacinto, Mt. Whitney, Calif.; Mt. Rainier pre-Expedition Training Camp, Wash.

MAYNARD M. MILLER, Ph.D.

Home:	East Lansing, Mich.
Personal statistics:	Age 41, 6 ft., 168 lb., married, two children.
Occupation:	Associate Professor (Glaciology, Geomorphology, Glacial Geology and Photogrammetry), Dept. of Geology, Michigan State University.
Education:	B.S. Geology, Harvard University (*Magna cum laude*).

M.A. Geology, Columbia University.

Ph.D., Cambridge University.

General: Director, Summer Institute of Field Sciences, Alaska; Exec. Director, Foundation for Glacier Research, Inc.; 1954 United States Junior Chamber of Commerce selection as "One of America's ten outstanding young men"; former staff member, Dept. of Geography, Cambridge University; visiting staff member, Swiss Federal Institute for Snow and Avalanche Research; lectured extensively throughout United States, Canada, and Europe.

Mountaineering: Since 1933. Olympics and Cascades, Wash.; Coast Range, B.C.; Selkirks, Canada; Fairweather Range (incl. first ascent of Mt. Bertha), St. Elias Range (incl. second ascent of Mt. St. Elias), Alaska; Tetons, Wyo.; Mt. Rainier summit guide; White Mountains, N.H.; California Sierras; Shawangunks, N.Y.; Argentina, Chile, Peru, Canadian Arctic, Greenland, England, Norway, Switzerland, Wales, Scotland, India, etc.

Expeditions: 1940: Alaskan Expedition (Bradford Washburn).

1942: Selkirks, Harvard Mountaineering Club— Army QMC Test Expedition (Leader).

1946: St. Elias Range, Harvard Mountaineering Club—USAF Expedition to Alaska.

1947: Juneau Icefield Research Program.

1948: Arctic Institute's "Snow Cornice" Expedition, Yukon.

1948: Juneau Icefield Research Program.

1949: Joint American Geographical Society— Museo Argentino de Ciencias Naturales Expedition to Patagonia.

1949–51: Alaska-Canada Boundary Range Expeditions.

1952: Greenland and Ellesmere Island Expedition.

1953: Juneau Icefield Research Program.

1958–62: Juneau Icefield Research Program

RICHARD POWNALL

Home:	Denver, Colo.
Personal statistics:	Age 35, 6 ft., 180 lb., married, two children.
Occupation:	Mathematics and P.E. Instructor.
Education:	B.S., Iowa State.
	M.A., University of Colorado.
	M.S. in Mathematics under preparation, University of Colorado.
	Ph.D. in Physical Education under preparation.
General:	Mountain Guide, Grand Teton National Park; Football and Track Coach; Athletic Director; Certified Ski Instructor.
Mountaineering:	Since 1944. Tetons, Wyo. (incl. first ascent of direct No. Face of Grand); Wind Rivers, Wyo.; Oregon Cascades; Colorado Rockies; Canadian Rockies; Austrian, Swiss, Italian Alps.

BARRY W. PRATHER

Home:	Ellensburg, Wash.
Personal statistics:	Age 23, 6 ft., 210 lb., single.
Occupation:	Aeronautics Engineer.
Education:	Physics major, Dartmouth College.
	B.S., Physics, Central Washington State College.
General:	Staff Geophysicist, Foundation for Glacier Research; Assistant to Director, Summer Institute of Field Sciences, Alaska; Engineering representative for Northwest, Potter Aeronautical; Amateur radio operator; Holder of Commercial Operator's License.
Mountaineering:	Since 1956. Numerous ascents in Washington Cascades, including Sunset Ridge of Mt. Rainier, N.E. Ridge of Mt. Stuart (second and third ascents), N.E. Ridge of Ingalls East Peak (first ascent), two winter ascents of Mt. Adams, Chimney Rock E. Face (first ascent); spent two months on summit of Mt. Rainier.
Expeditions:	1958, 1960, 1961, 1962: Juneau Icefield Research Program.

GILBERT ROBERTS, M.D.

Home:	Berkeley, Calif.
Personal statistics:	Age 28, 6 ft. 2 in., 185 lb., married.
Occupation:	Physician.
Education:	B.A. Psychology, Stanford University. M.D., Stanford University.
General:	Internship, Minneapolis General Hospital; Aviation Medicine, United States Air Force; Flight Surgeon, Stead AFB, Reno, Nevada; Air Force Survival School; Captain, USAF (separated from Service Oct. 6, 1962).
Mountaineering:	Since 1946. Sierra Nevada; Yosemite, Tahquitz Rock, Mt. Whitney, Mt. Shasta, etc., Calif.; Mt. Rainier, Wash.; Canadian Rockies: Mt. Edith Cavell, Mt. Smythe (first ascent), Mt. Athabaska, Mt. Victoria, Bugaboos Spine, Snowpatch Spine, Mt. Robson (Cain route), Mt. Columbia; E. Buttress of Mt. Whitney, Calif. (winter ascent); Tetons, Wyo.; Matterhorn, Switzerland.
Expeditions:	1954: Stanford Expedition, B.C. Coast Range (Mt. Tiedman, Serra I, Serra III, Mt. Munday).
	1957: Mt. Logan Expedition. Leader (E. Ridge Mt. Logan, first ascent).
	1958: Hidden Peak Expedition, Pakistan.

JAMES OWEN M. ROBERTS, Lt. Col.

Home:	Kathmandu, Nepal.
Personal statistics:	Age 45, 5 ft. 10½ in., 164 lb., single.
Occupation:	Lt. Colonel, British Army (ret.). Military Attaché.
Education:	Graduate, Royal Military College, Sandhurst, England.
General:	Commissioned as 2nd Lt., 1st Gurkha Rifles, Indian Army (1936); Gurkha Parachute Battalion, Burma and Assam (World War II); since 1947

	India Partition with Gurkha Rifles, British Army in Far East.
Mountaineering:	Since 1930. Great Britain; European Alps; Karakorams, Pakistan; Punjab Himalaya, India; Sikkim Himalaya; Nepal Himalaya.
Expeditions:	1938: British Masherbrum Expedition, Karakorams.

1940–45: Punjab and Sikkim Himalaya Expeditions.

1946: Eastern Karakorams Expedition.

1950–60: Six Nepal Himalaya Expeditions, incl.

1953 British Mt. Everest Expedition (oxygen).

1954 Dhaulagiri Himal Expedition.

1957 British Machapuchare Expedition (Leader).

1960 Joint British-Nepalese-Indian Army Expedition to Annapurna II (Leader).

1962 Dhaulagiri II Expedition (Leader).

WILLIAM E. SIRI, Ph.D. (Deputy Leader)

Home:	Richmond, Calif.
Personal statistics:	Age 44, 5 ft. 8 in., 150 lb., married, two children.
Occupation:	Physicist.
Education:	B.S. Physics, University of Chicago. Ph.D. Physics, University of California.
General:	Physicist, Donner Laboratory, University of California; Research, biological and medical physics; Application of Radio-Isotopes and physical principles to basic problems in normal and pathological physiology; Major areas of research: (1) formation of red blood cells, (2) respiration, (3) metabolism of fat and water, (4) instrumentation. Professional Societies include: Amer. Phys. Soc., Amer. Assoc. for Advancement of Science, Biophys. Soc., Amer. Assoc. of Physicists in Medicine, Sigma Xi, Cal. Board of Reg. for Prof. Engin., Arctic Inst. of No. America.

Mountaineering:	Since 1945. Sierra Nevada; Wind Rivers, Wyo.; Pacific Northwest; Canadian Rockies (incl. Mt. Robson); Coastal Ranges, B.C.; European Alps; Peruvian and Bolivian Andes; Nepal Himalaya; Antarctic.
Expeditions:	1950: University of Calif. Peruvian Expedition.
	1952: University of Calif. Peruvian Expedition (Leader).
	1954: Calif. Himalayan Expedition to Makalu (Leader).
	1957: University of Calif. Bolivian Expedition (Leader).
	1957–58: International Physiological Antarctic Expedition (Field Leader).

JAMES RAMSEY ULLMAN

Home:	Boston, Mass.
Personal statistics:	Age 55, 5 ft. 10 in., 150 lb., married, two children.
Occupation:	Writer.
Education:	B.A., Princeton University.
General:	Author of many books, including: *The White Tower, Tiger of the Snows, High Conquest, The Age of Mountaineering, Banner in the Sky, River of the Sun, Windom's Way, The Sands of Karakorum, Island of the Blue Macaws, The Day on Fire, Fia Fia, Where the Bong Tree Grows, Kingdom of Adventure: Everest, The Other Side of the Mountain;* contributor of short stories and articles to magazines; former newspaper reporter; New York theatrical producer (*Men in White, Blind Alley*); executive of Federal Theatre Project; Officer in American Field Service in World War II.
Mountaineering:	Since 1927. European Alps (incl. Matterhorn twice, twenty-five years apart); American and Canadian Rockies; Tetons, Wyo. (incl. E. Ridge of Grand, traverses of Nez Percé and South Teton–

Cloudveil Dome); Andes, So. Amer.; Popocatepetl and Iztaccihuatl, Mexico; Kilimanjaro, E.
Africa; Himalayan foothills, Nepal.

WILLIAM F. UNSOELD, Ph.D.

Home:	Corvallis, Ore. Kathmandu, Nepal.
Personal statistics:	Age 36, 5 ft. 10 in., 160 lb., married, four children.
Occupation:	University professor (philosophy and religion). Deputy Director, Peace Corps, Nepal.
Education:	B.S. Physics, Oregon State College. B.D. Theology, Pacific School of Religion, California. Ph.D. Philosophy, University of Washington.
General:	Assist. Prof., Dept. of Philosophy and Religion, Oregon State University; Teaching Assistant in Philosophy, University of Washington; Assist. Minister, Methodist Church; Director of Boys' Club, First Presbyterian Church, Oakland, Calif.; Academic Honors: Sigma Pi Sigma, Phi Kappa Phi; Member of American Philosophical Association.
Mountaineering:	Since 1939. Began climbing with the Boy Scouts. Oregon and Washington Cascades; Rock climbs in New York State, Kentucky, Missouri, Tetons, Wyo.; Swiss Alps; Instructor, University of Washington, Mountaineering Course; Garhwal Himalaya; Mountain Guide, Tetons, Wyo. (7 seasons); Nepal Himalaya; Karakorum, Pakistan.
Expeditions:	1949: Nilkantha Expedition, Garhwal Himalaya. 1954: Californian Himalaya Expedition, Makalu. 1960: American Pakistan Karakoram Expedition, Masherbrum, 25,660 feet.

JAMES W. WHITTAKER

Home:	Redmond, Wash.
Personal statistics:	Age 34, 6 ft. 5 in., 200 lb., married, two children.
Occupation:	Manager, Recreational Equipment Inc., Seattle.

Education:	B.S. Biology, Seattle University.
General:	Mountain Guide, Mt. Rainier Guide Service; Certified Ski Instructor; Member, Northwest Underwater Research Group.
Mountaineering:	Began climbing in 1943 as a Boy Scout; Graduate, Seattle Mountaineers; Climbing and Ski Instructor, United States Army Mountain and Cold Weather Training Command; All major peaks of Washington and Oregon; many ascents in California and Colorado; Mt. Rainier, Wash. (55 ascents by various routes, incl. ski descent); Alaska.
Expeditions:	1960: Mt. McKinley Expedition, Alaska (West Buttress).

AMEE Board of Directors

Norman Barker	Vice-President, United California Bank
Norman G. Dyhrenfurth	Documentary film producer
Charles B. Huestis	Vice-President and Treasurer, Hughes Aircraft Company
Joseph Kaplan	Professor of Physics, UCLA Chairman United States National Committee, International Geophysical Year
John W. Miner	Deputy District Attorney, County of Los Angeles
Bestor Robinson	Attorney-at-law
William E. Siri	Research physicist, University of California
Lowell Thomas	Author and commentator
James Ramsey Ullman	Author

Advisory Council

George I. Bell

Nuclear physicist
Leader, 1960 American
Pakistan Karakoram Expedition

Günter Oskar Dyhrenfurth

Professor emeritus,
geology and palaeontology
Leader, 1930 and 1934,
International Himalayan Expeditions

Albert Eggler

Attorney-at-law
Leader, 1956 Swiss Everest-Lhotse
Expedition

Melville Bell Grosvenor

President and Editor
National Geographic Society

Sir John Hunt

Leader, 1953 British
Mount Everest Expedition

Warren G. Magnuson

United States Senator

2. AN EVEREST CHRONOLOGY

(All expeditions prior to World War II were on the northern, or Tibetan, side of the mountain. Since then, all have been from the southern, Nepalese side, except for one Chinese expedition and three small, unauthorized ventures by Westerners.)

1852   Everest discovered by the Survey of India to be the highest mountain in the world. Height first computed at 29,002 feet; figure later changed to 29,141, then to 29,028, which is currently accepted.

1921   British reconnaissance, carrying to the North Col, at about 23,000 feet.

1922   First full-scale British expedition, reaching 27,300 feet. Marked by first use of oxygen in mountaineering.

1924   British expedition, reaching more than 28,000 feet. Disappearance of Mallory and Irvine.

1933   British expedition, again reaching more than 28,000 feet.

1934   Solo attempt by Englishman Maurice Wilson, resulting in Wilson's death below North Col.

311

1935   British reconnaissance-in-force, again carrying to the North Col.

1936   British expedition; hampered by bad weather and getting only slightly above the Col.

1938   British expedition; reaches about 27,000 feet.

1947   Solo attempt by Canadian Earl Denman; falls short of North Col.

1950   First approach to Everest from the south. H. W. Tilman and Charles Houston reach the foot of the Khumbu Icefall.

1951   (1) British reconnaissance expedition to south side; reaches entrance of Western Cwm at top of Icefall. (2) Solo by a Dane, R. B. Larsen, starting from southern side but carrying over to northern, on which he reached North Col.

1952   (1) First major non-British expedition—by the Swiss. Pioneer route to South Col and summit ridge, reaching height of about 28,200 feet. (2) Swiss return in autumn for second attempt, but are stopped at about 26,300 feet, above South Col.

1953   *First ascent of Everest.* Summit reached on May 29 by New Zealander Edmund Hillary and Sherpa Tenzing Norgay on expedition led by John Hunt.

1956   *Second ascent of Everest.* Swiss place four men on top, in two teams on successive days, and also make first ascent of neighboring Lhotse.

1960   (1) Indian expedition; climbs to within 700 feet of summit. (2) Chinese expedition on north side of mountain. Announce that three climbers reach summit, but claim doubted by most Western mountaineers.

1962   (1) Second Indian expedition; again falls a few hundred feet short of summit. (2) Group of three Americans and one Swiss make unauthorized attempt from north, reaching about 25,000 feet.

1963   *Third authenticated ascent of Everest* by AMEE.

3. AMEE TIMETABLE

June, 1960	Application for permission made by Norman Dyhrenfurth to Government of Nepal.
July, 1960 to Jan., 1963	Organization and financing of expedition.
Sept., 1962	Training and testing of equipment on Mount Rainier, Washington.

1963

Jan. 2–4	Psychological and physiological examination of team members at Institute of Personality Assessment Research, University of California.
Jan. 14	Advance guard of expedition leaves Los Angeles by air for Nepal.
Feb. 3	Main body of expedition leaves San Francisco by air for Nepal.
Feb. 13	Advance guard and main body join forces in Kathmandu, Nepal.

Feb. 20   Expedition truly begins with departure afoot from Kathmandu.

Mar. 7   Arrival at Namche Bazar.

Mar. 9–20   From Namche Bazar toward Base Camp. Acclimatization and training climbs.

Mar. 21   Base Camp established at 17,800 feet.

Mar. 22   Climbing of Everest begins with entrance into Icefall.

Mar. 23   John E. Breitenbach killed in Icefall.

Mar. 29   Advance party surmounts Icefall.

Mar. 30   Camp I established at 20,200 feet at entrance of Western Cwm.

Apr. 2   Advance Base (Camp II) occupied, at 21,350 feet in Western Cwm.

Apr. 3–12   Reconnaissance of West Ridge route. Climbers establish Camp 3W (23,800 feet) on Apr. 7 and reach site of prospective 4W (25,100 feet) on Apr. 12.

Apr. 3–16   Forging of route up Lhotse Face. Establishment of Camps III (22,900 feet) and IV (24,900 feet). South Col, at 26,200 feet, first reached on Apr. 16.

Apr. 17–26   Stocking of camps on Col route.

Apr. 27–30   Col route assault teams, starting from Advance Base, move up camp by camp for first summit attempt.

Apr. 29   First assault team at Camp V on South Col.

Apr. 30   First assault team establishes Camp VI at 27,450 feet on Southeast Ridge.

May 1   *James W. Whittaker and Nawang Gombu reach summit of Everest at 1 P.M. Descend to Camp VI.*

May 2–3   Assault teams descend to Advance Base and Base Camp.

May 4–11   Most of expedition at Base Camp. Work continues on preparation of West Ridge route.

May 6   Unsoeld and Hornbein, of West Ridge team, up from Base Camp for summit push.

May 12   Jerstad and Bishop leave Base Camp for second summit attempt via South Col route.

May 15   West Ridgers occupy Camp 4W, at 25,100 feet.

May 16   Unsoeld and Hornbein reconnoiter above 4W.

May 16–17   Major storm. West Ridgers forced to descend to Camp 3W.

May 18–19   West Ridgers recuperate at 3W.

May 18–20   South Col team moves up from Advance Base to South Col.

May 20   West Ridgers reoccupy 4W.

May 21   Col team to Camp VI. West Ridgers pitch Camp 5W at 27,250 feet.

May 22   *Luther G. Jerstad and Barry Bishop, of Col team, reach summit of Everest at 3:30 P.M. William F. Unsoeld and Thomas F. Hornbein, of West Ridge team, reach summit at 6:30 P.M.* Unsoeld and Hornbein traverse summit, descend via Col route, and meet Jerstad and Bishop on Southeast Ridge at about 10 P.M. Four continue down together.

May 23   Summit climbers halt descent and from 12:30 to 6 A.M. spend night out at about 28,000 feet. Then continue descent via South Col route with support climbers, reaching Advance Base at 10:30 P.M. Unsoeld, Bishop and Jerstad suffer frostbitten feet.

May 24   Descent continues to Base Camp. Entire expedition down from mountain.

May 25   Base Camp evacuated.

May 26   Arrival at Namche Bazar.

May 27   Unsoeld and Bishop flown by helicopter from Namche Bazar to Kathmandu.

May 28   Rest of expedition begins march out from Namche Bazar.

June 9   Expedition arrives in Kathmandu.

June 14–16 Expedition leaves Kathmandu. During next few weeks proceeds home individually and in various groups.

July 8   Expedition received by President Kennedy at White House. Award of National Geographic Society's Hubbard Medal.

4. FINANCE

by Charles B. Huestis

THE INVENTION OF THE TELEPHONE is an event which I generally regard with some disfavor, and this feeling is not diminished by early Saturday morning calls. So I was, perhaps, not very cordial to the Western Union girl at the outset, on that February 16, 1963—and much less so when she had read me the message:

"Nepalese government demanding payment of all expenses while in Nepal in dollars. Please rush via American Express Travelers' Checks maximum funds available. Signed, 'Dyhrenfurth.'"

Though no amount was specified, it was obvious that Nepal was refusing to accept some $32,000 in Indian rupee funds as payment for porter and Sherpa wages, bonds, transportation, hotel costs, miscellaneous supplies, and the numerous other items to be paid by the expedition while in that country. There was less than $20,000 in the expedition bank account, and sizable sums were scheduled for payment within the next few months.

"Any way we slice it," I told Norman Barker of the United California Bank on Monday morning, "this means we've got to raise at least $25,000 more before June to get the team home."

I wasn't particularly concerned about our ability to do so, and over

317

the week end had developed some thoughts as to how we might go about it. In the meantime, though, almost a thousand people were due to start the trek from Banepa within less than forty-eight hours, and the whole timetable, it seemed to us—perhaps the whole expedition—was in serious jeopardy.

By noon that Monday we had combined $17,000 from the expedition bank account with a $15,000 loan from the United California Bank and had cabled the total check authorization to Kathmandu. A second cable from Dyhrenfurth was received the next day, too late to stop the transfer which his negotiations with the Nepalese government had made unnecessary. But, although it had taken only a few hours to get the funds on the way, it was three weeks before the entire process was reversed, the money safely back in our Santa Monica account, and the bank loan repaid.

The fact that we were able to send $32,000 "on demand" to a team in trouble pointed up the unparalleled financial support this expedition had received. And this had been translated into a financial posture that permitted a highly satisfactory banking relationship with the United California Bank in Los Angeles. This relationship was further cemented by the fact that Barker, a vice-president of the bank, had long since been a member of the expedition's board of directors.

In the weeks immediately preceding the last-minute emergency, we had handed the bank, along with our board members, two financial reports. The first, a special budget and funding estimate, prepared for our board meeting just before Christmas, disclosed that we were, if budgetary estimates were valid, finally fully funded with a slight reserve. This we considered our final budget, against which we ultimately would make cost comparisons—and it exceeded the original estimates which Dyhrenfurth had made in 1961 by $216,783.

When first published, the original budget had included no costs for scientific programs whose performance depended on receipt of funding. It had also been made up for a fifteen-man team instead of for one of twenty. Further, it did not contemplate the scope of the documentary film contracted and paid for by the National Geographic, nor could it foresee the Sherpa tour of the United States under the terms of our grant from the U.S. State Department.

One other significant change took place in the organizational expense category: the board voted Dyhrenfurth a salary as corporate president and expedition leader. He had already, at the time of this board action in the fall of 1962, not only invested all of his own personal resources in the enterprise but completely divorced himself from all income opportunities for a period of almost two years. This salary, together with administrative and fund-raising expenses that mounted with the expanding size of the effort, more than doubled the operating costs of the corporate entity. I was pleased, nevertheless, to see this figure stay at about 12½ per cent of the total, which I knew to be an acceptable "overhead" rate in the eyes of several of our sponsors.

The funding portion of the report pointed up another significant change from the original plan. As our support grew, not only in dollars but in terms of individuals, companies, and private and government agencies, it became apparent that, if we followed the practice of previous major expeditions in our financial record-keeping, we would be ignoring some of our largest supporters—the equipment and food suppliers who were generously providing the majority of our needs in these respects free or at only a token charge. We therefore added to our budget, and credited in our funding reports, more than $70,000 in noncash donations; that is, equipment, clothing, food and services. While this caused some misleading comparisons of costs with other expeditions, we felt the result contributed to both accuracy and equity.

The corporate balance sheet as of December, 1962, which was presented in January to our board and to the bank, was also required by several of our governmental funding sources. In the preparation of the year-end report, we analyzed the terms of each contractual relationship whereby funds were to be furnished us and then recorded performance reserves as liabilities. These reserves were amortized only as the expedition's progress and the scientific investigators' achievements assured our meeting the commitments we assumed when executing contracts or accepting grants.

Although a great deal of our equipment and supplies were carried as inventory in our asset accounts prior to the team's departure, all but the scientific equipment was expensed off during the course of the expedition. Final physical inventorying of the mountaineering, scientific, and photographic equipment brought back resulted in a small residual value being restored on our postexpedition books.

Despite apparent complete funding and a reasonable balance sheet, we still shared some of the financial problems of other expeditions in terms of actual cash availability. Several of our grants and contracts called for progressive payments, some for payment only on completion of performance, and the result was a cash pinch early in June, 1963, which required, in classic expedition manner, a transmittal of funds "to get the team home."

Again we called on the United California Bank, which advanced a loan of $20,000 to be repaid out of receipts expected later in 1963 and 1964. The first repayment of $5,000 was made as scheduled, early in September.

It is still too early to render the last financial report. Although the actual cost totals almost precisely the final budget figure in the report shown herein, additional costs are still to be incurred and recorded. Expenditures are expected to exceed $430,000. The firm pledges shown in the funding report of December 31, 1962, have been realized in terms of cash or contractual documentation. In addition, an $11,327 grant was received from the National Aeronautics and Space Administration in support of the physiology program, and cash contributions continued coming in early in 1963 to the extent of about $3,000. Both cost and funding figures will increase further by some $60,000 as a result of additional effort for and funding by the National Geographic. Most of the increase relates to a still further expansion of the documentary film program.

With scientific programs that will not be completed until 1965, literary and photographic projects, and numerous lecture opportunities, the business of the corporation continues with little abatement, and no fine line can be drawn to show that prior to this point costs were expeditionary and beyond it, postexpedition affairs.

Under the terms of individual contracts with each team member, the income from writings and lectures is being divided between the corporation and the author or speaker. Our contract with the Geographic for the film will yield further income after all costs have been paid. These intangible assets eventually will result in a "profit" for the expedition in its corporate entity. Since our articles of incorporation stipulate that no profits may accrue to any individual but must be disbursed only for purposes consistent with the stated objectives of the corporation, we ultimately will face the problem of disposition of this income. Whether its disbursement will be connected with the dissolution of the present corporation or through the vehicle of a continuing and permanent foundation remains to be seen.

In either event, both science and mountaineering, already so spectacularly advanced by the "Americans on Everest," will be further served.

SCHEDULE I—BUDGET

Item	Original budget July 31, 1961	Budget Dec. 31, 1962	Actual costs Recorded through Nov. 30, 1963
Organization and administration	$16,500	$50,788	$52,283
Medical	*	7,074	3,595
Mt. Rainier camp	3,500	3,219	3,259†
Equipment and clothing	41,100	83,824	92,850
Oxygen equipment	14,950	22,673	22,203
Travel and accommodations	44,798	38,610	45,872†
Freight and handling	3,379	22,607	37,745
Wages	22,195	27,728	36,189†
Food	12,600	18,559	20,532†
Still photography	4,345	6,615	4,047
Documentary film	6,200	30,660	37,237
Direct costs—scientific programs	...	54,950	32,920
Sherpa Tour of United States	...	25,000	13,104
Contingency and miscellaneous	16,957	11,000	3,427
	$186,524	$403,307	$405,263

* Included in "Equipment and clothing."
† Final costs.

SCHEDULE II—FUNDING

Total Budget December 31, 1962		$403,307

Received to date
  Contributions ... $ 13,961
  Equipment donations ... 54,950
  Food donations ... 12,378
  Services donations ... 5,723
  Executed contracts and grants
    Life magazine ... $ 9,750
    National Geographic Society ... 114,719
    Air Force Office of Scientific Research ... 10,000
    National Science Foundation ... 24,700
    Office of Naval Research ... 35,190
    J. B. Lippincott Company ... 6,750
    UCLA ... 3,520
    Explorer's Club ... 1,000
    Total contracts and grants ... 205,629

Firm Pledges
  Life and N.G.S. (film processing) ... 1,500
  National Science Foundation (physiology) ... 11,600
  Quartermaster Corps (general support) ... 10,000
  U.S. State Department (exchange program) ... 82,000
  Sawyer's Inc. (3-D photography) ... 2,500
  Ski Magazine (article) ... 1,000
  Other ... 4,300
  Total firm pledges ... 112,900

Total Funding December 31, 1962 ... $405,541

SURPLUS—Funding over budget ... $ 2,234

SCHEDULE III—BALANCE SHEET

ASSETS

	Dec. 31, 1962	Nov. 30, 1963
Cash	$ 17,521	$ 5,361
Marketable securities	1,493	2,321
Accounts receivable	...	1,640
Contracts receivable	71,457	25,349
In process contract costs	18,624	...
Expedition inventories	90,999	12,143
Scientific equipment	4,944	6,025
Deposits and deferred charges	1,139	1,946
Total assets	$206,177	$54,785

LIABILITIES AND SURPLUS

	Dec. 31, 1962	Nov. 30, 1963
Notes payable	$ 5,981	$15,000
Accounts payable	13,353	12,524
Accrued taxes payable	4,252	767
Total current liabilities	$ 23,586	$28,291
Reserves for contract performance	185,209	45,476
Total liabilities	$208,795	$73,767
Capital		
Operating deficit Inception to date	(2,618)	(18,982)
Total liabilities and capital	$206,177	$54,785

5. *FOOD*

by Richard Pownall

IN APPROACHING the problem of high-altitude diet and expedition menus, one finds that there is little agreement among the authorities in the field. Each expedition has its own unique problems of food requirements, and within each expedition further uniqueness is dictated by the individual members of the team. There are, however, certain guide lines that can be established in the early planning stages of any expedition prior to the formulation of the actual diet. These are:

1. Number of man-days involved
2. Maximum weight allowance
3. Budget allotment for food
4. Number of calories-per-day intake (partially governed by elevation and number of days in the field)

Beyond these specifics one must procure, assemble and package a menu that hopefully will be compatible with the desires and whims of the expedition personnel.

Owing to the size of AMEE and its date schedule, it was necessary to preship literally all the foodstuffs from this country well in advance. Smaller expeditions to the Himalaya have been able to procure a good portion of their diet from native sources. This idea was considered, but abandoned, both because of the volume of food required and the possibility that food would not be available since we would be approaching Everest in early March, which is in advance of the harvest season for most of the local produce.

Certainly one area of agreement in diet requirements of climbers is the need for liquid. Because of increased dehydration of the body at high altitudes, a large liquid consumption is essential. Although a variety of liquids were available in our ration stores, it was tea and lemonade that were the big favorites among climbers and Sherpas.

Food preferences were determined by sending out to each team member, for comments and rating, a list of all foods that had been taken on previous expeditions and other foods that could be taken. All foods received a rating from each expedition member on a graded response of 1 to 3, indicating a range from "a real favorite of mine" to "I do not like this food." Food lists of the following major expeditions were examined in detail prior to drawing up our own: 1953 American K2 Expedition, Fairweather Range Expedition of 1962, 1960 American-Pakistan Karakoram Expedition to Masherbrum, 1953 British Everest Expedition, and the British Cho Oyu Expedition of 1952.

From the responses received on this original grading scheme, a Menu Proposal #1 was evolved. This in turn was sent to all team members for further comments and suggestions, and from these the final menu was eventually resolved. In using this system, one could foresee the possible gloomy consequence, on a twenty-man expedition, that once out of twenty meals each man would get one he liked. But fortunately there was general agreement on those foods which were disliked and general agreement on a vast variety of preferred foods. Indeed, there was such a wide range of foods that received ratings of 1 and 2 that it was possible to discard all foods that received a 3 rating.

In view of the length of time we were to be in the field, it was generally felt that the approach menu should be as close to a normal diet as possible. Weight limitations did not affect the selection of foods for this portion of the journey, since these foods would be consumed quite early, and the expense of the extra carrying power required would be small in the overall picture. Hence, there was a gradual transition to the so-called mountain menu, in which weight of food and calorie intake held precedence over pure foods of choice.

The Base Camp rations were packed in bulk-stores, but all the rest were packaged into man-day units or multiples thereof. The advantages of this system on an expedition are that the sorting and making up of loads and the distribution of rations are greatly simplified; shortages of essential items due to overconsumption or pilfering are avoided; there is less chance of contamination of food by flies and in handling; and *complete* meals are readily available by opening only one container. The task of organizing and packaging this vast quantity of rations (10 tons) was contracted out to Universal Services Inc. of Seattle.

Our mountain diet was probably more varied than previous high-altitude menus, due to the new freeze-dried process of food preservation; and a variety of freeze-dried meats and vegetables were used generously to supplement the high-altitude diet. Preparation of these foods generally required ten minutes of soaking in water and then warming. Since these foods are extremely light and reconstitute with a minimum of cooking (usually just a warm-up), there was double-saving in the weight department, thanks to the minimal fuel required for preparation.

For purposes of planning, packaging and rationing, our foods and menus were divided into the following major categories:

1. Approach march rations
2. Base Camp rations
3. Mountain assault rations
4. Summit assault rations
5. Return march rations
6. Sherpa rations

In spite of all research and individual consultation in planning menus for an expedition, one must assume from the beginning that all climbers will not be pleased at all times with the food provided. True, this situation could occur at sea level as well as on a mountain; but the basic variation in likes and dislikes is further complicated by changes in individuals as they live for a long period at high altitude. Past experience has shown that above certain heights—varying with the states of acclimatization—climbers' appetites undergo marked deterioration. On Cho Oyu in 1952, the daily energy value of the food eaten between 19,000 and 22,000 feet averaged 3200 calories, as compared with 4200 calories on the approach march. Above 23,000 feet on Everest in 1953, the calorie intake was calculated to be about 1500 calories. Some men become intolerant of fatty foods; some crave special foods which may not be available. High on Everest in 1933, Shipton had a craving for a dozen eggs; Smythe wanted frankfurters and sauerkraut; in 1924 Somervell's favorite diet was strawberry jam and condensed milk; on Cho Oyu, Hillary wanted pineapple cubes and Secord wanted tinned salmon.

On our expedition, Jim Whittaker had cravings for tossed green salad, and almost unanimous cries for charcoal grilled steak could be heard on various occasions. Strangely, the most appetizing meal I myself can remember was at Advance Base Camp, when Jerstad and I returned from a siege on the Lhotse Face and Danu the cook served us rice covered with two or three greasy fried eggs. A surprise food that proved extremely popular with sahibs and Sherpas alike, were pancakes, which we consumed in quantity. A popular and true statement which was reiterated many times was: "To go high, eat." But it wasn't always easy.

There was general agreement that more dehydrated foods could have been used by cooking with pressure cookers. Quite often the freeze-dried foods were poorly prepared by the Sherpa cook, who mistook them for dehydrated foods (they were similar in appearance), boiling them for many minutes, until the end product was tough, dry, and almost inedible. Certainly more gravies and cream sauces should have been available to supplement the various menus; and crackers, too, should have been on hand in larger quantity.

On the lower levels, local produce was a pleasant change from our own rations. Chickens, which were small and tough, were quite delicious after a session in Danu's pressure cooker. On occasion, we feasted on yak, goat and mutton, which were good morale boosters. Potatoes and rice were abundant on the return march.

A vitamin supplement was used daily. These vitamins were not prepackaged with our rations but were available in a large bottle with each meal. Two vitamins were used to supplement the diet, vitamin C and the R-A Formula. The special R-A Formula is a high-level water-soluble therapeutic vitamin which is high in ascorbic acid and other water-soluble ingredients, helping to prevent depletion of vitamin reserves during strenuous activity.

I. *Approach March*

An attempt was made here to have an ample, almost luxurious menu. A well-rounded diet was deemed important in getting the climbers to the mountain in the best possible health. Weight was not a limiting factor since the extra porters could be discharged in the early stages as the provisions were consumed. The weight of each meal, for the twenty team members, averaged slightly more than 30 pounds. Menus were repeated every eight days, and consisted largely of the sorts of foods that would be used on a normal camping trip back home.

A TYPICAL DAY'S MENU:

Breakfast

V–8 Juice
Raisin bread
Spiced wafers and strawberry apple jelly
Coffee
Hot chocolate

Lunch

Grapefruit juice
Protein Plus cereal and milk
Bread and butter
Sliced Tillamook cheddar cheese
Coffee
Hot chocolate
Food supplement powder
Dried prunes

Dinner

Vegetable soup
Chicken and noodle dinner
Peas and carrots
Jellied cranberry sauce
Bread, butter and honey
Bartlett pear halves
Coffee, tea, milk

II. *Base Camp*

No specific menus were prepared for Base Camp rations, since Base Camp occupancy would vary considerably. A large kitchen commissary was established there with a vast variety of foods unpacked and shelved so that meals could be selected and varied to meet individual desires. In addition to the basic necessities, there was included a generous sprinkling of special luxury items, such as artichoke hearts, cookies, mixed nuts, canned fruit, boned chicken, kipper snacks, smoked salmon, etc.

III. *Mountain Assault*

The Mountain Assault rations were packaged to provide a full one-day's ration for six men in one package. It is referred to as the six-man-day ration. Since this was the largest single food group (over 2800 man-days), a special attempt was made to provide as much variety as possible and still maintain nutritional value and caloric content within weight limitations. Each six-man-day ration weighed approximately 25 pounds. There were four basic menus within this group, and they were of course simpler than those for the approach march and Base Camp, consisting largely of lightweight and easily preparable dehydrated and freeze-dried items.

A SAMPLE MENU:

1¼ lb. hot cereal
8 oz. whole powdered milk
6 oz. sugar
1 15-oz. can sweetened condensed milk
1 No. 2½ can sliced peaches
6 indiv. pkg. 1 oz. Ovaltine
6 6 oz. pkg. Jell-O
4 6½-oz. cans tuna fish
6 pkg. Metrecal cookies
3 5-oz. cans fruit cake
1 box matches
1 can pepper
Pkg. of salt
4 pkg. malt crunch
12 oz. vacuum-pack peanut brittle
12 pkg. tea
24 6-oz. pkg. sugar
12 indiv. pkg. jam
6 pkg. chicken noodle soup
1 1-lb. can white bread
2 cans potato soup mix
1 can onion soup mix
1 No. 2½ can chicken meat
1 pkg. frying potatoes
3 pkg. chocolate Sustagen
2 pkg. lemonade mix (1 qt. each)
2 pkg. instant pudding, vanilla flavor

IV. *Summit Assault*

The Summit Assault ration was packaged to provide sustenance for two men for one full day. It was referred to as the two-man-day ration.

Much care was taken in selecting food not only for its appropriateness for the environment, but also for its nutritional value and high calorie content. Weight was also an obvious factor.

The two-man-day summit assault ration weighed only 4 pounds 1 ounce, and contained 10,542 calories, or 5270 calories for each of the two men. Each ration contained:

2 pkg. Metrecal cookies (9 per pkg.)

Breakfast cereal consisting of: 4 oz. dry cereal, 2 oz. coconut, 2 oz. whole powdered milk, 1 oz. freeze-dried banana or peach slices

2 8-oz. pkg. Sustagen, 1 chocolate and 1 vanilla flavor

2 6-oz. pkg. Jell-O

1 meat bar

1 can pemmican

2 1-oz. pkg. Ovaltine

2 pkg. soup mix

1 pkg. lemon juice mix

2 pkg. indiv. consomme

1 12-oz. can mixed nuts

assorted hard candies

16 indiv. pkg. tea

Packaging

All food items and rations were specially packed in 416 boxes, each measuring 28 by 16 by 12 inches and weighing an average of 63 pounds apiece. The boxes were numbered, inventoried, and color-coded. The foods were protected within the boxes by being enclosed in heavy-gauge polyethylene bags.

6. CLOTHING AND EQUIPMENT

by James W. Whittaker

MY SELECTION as equipment coordinator for the expedition was based on my position as Sales Manager for Recreational Equipment, Inc., a mountaineering supply firm in Seattle, Wash. On the basis of this experience and Norman Dyhrenfurth's Himalayan background, we compiled the lists of needs and requested samples from various manufacturers. In September of 1962 we had a clothing and equipment shakedown on Mt. Rainier. The entire team made suggestions, went over the complete lists, and made the final selections.

One of the principal features of the clothing and many other expedition items was the great use made of nylon. This synthetic material proved to be very strong and made up not only our ⅜-inch climbing ropes and slings, but our tents, wind pants and parkas, pack sacks, ponchos and overboots. The heavier 4.4-ounce nylon fabric worked well for overboots and packs, as it was more abrasion resistant and had greater water repellency. For this reason it was also used in the Base Camp tents and middle-altitude tents. The 2.3-ounce nylon cloth was ideal for the high-altitude tents, and since it was wind- and snowproof, it was used for our down pants, down parkas and sleeping bags as well. We had special dye lots run on the cloth to provide colors of high visibility

330

and good photographic value. The Sherpa clothing was in different color combinations from the sahibs', for identification at distances.

J. P. Stevens & Co. provided all our nylon fabric, working against a very tight schedule to get the goods to the various manufacturers. These in turn were pressed into rush schedules in order to make the items in time to be crated and put aboard an American Mail Lines ship leaving Seattle in November for Calcutta.

The clothing was carefully selected by the entire team, as was the other equipment. An effort was made to please everyone—a not-too-easy task with an expedition of twenty men, each of whom has his own preferences in such matters.

For underclothing we had two-layer cotton-wool underwear, fishnet cotton underwear, and finally down underwear. Wool pants came in both knicker and ski pants styles, with large cargo pockets. Our heavy wool jacket shirts were worn over cotton turtle-neck T-shirts. The down overpants made of rip-stop nylon also had cargo pockets which sealed with velcro tape, and the overlapping down parka had a wolverine fur-trimmed hood with both nylon zipper and velcro fastening. All items containing down were supplied by Eddie Bauer of Seattle.

Along with the usual heavy wool mitts and shells, we had a light-weight nylon glove, so that cameras and hardware could be handled without the metal sticking to the skin. Over these were worn down mittens with leather-faced palm; and the hand could be slipped either between two layers of down for maximum warmth, or next to the leather face for dexterity. Several of the team tied the gloves together with a long string passed through the sleeves of the parka to eliminate any chance of losing them or "misplacing" them because of hypoxia.

Frostbite is one of the greatest dangers of high-altitude climbing, and special attention must be paid to the selection of footgear. For the approach march most of the team wore old boots, already broken in, or carried a pair of light *kletterschuhe* to alternate with new boots. This worked well over terrain where most of the porters went barefoot, but above Base Camp we resorted to a sturdy full-time boot that had insulation as well. Our middle-altitude footgear was the Lowa Eiger double boot. It has a removable felt inner boot and a very stiff, heavy leather outer boot, with a thick, narrow-welted, vibram sole. An extra felt inner boot was provided, so one pair could be worn while the other dried.

The high-altitude footgear was the Dolomite Reindeer boot. It consisted of a reindeer-fur knee-length upper, lined with felt at the foot area, and a shallow cleated rubber sole. Both boots were sized large enough to accept two to three pairs of heavy wool socks.

Both Norman and I preferred the fit of the Eiger Boot, because our Reindeer boots pinched a bit in the toe, and while wearing them, I myself suffered a touch of frostbite when putting in Camp IV. So rather than risk worse damage, I wore the Eiger to the summit. Additional protection for the feet was provided by nylon knee-length over-boots worn over the regular boots—over which went, in turn, twelve-point Grivel crampons.

The frostbite, and subsequent loss of toes, suffered by Barry Bishop and Willi Unsoeld was felt to be primarily due to exposure, rather than inadequate footgear.

Among the most important items on any expedition are the tents. For the Mount Everest climb we paid particular attention to our "homes away from home," because we would be using them from the start of the approach march to our highest camp, 27,450 feet on the Southeast Ridge—and back.

Fifty-two tents were taken on the expedition. Of these, forty-two were of the Draw-Tite design in which the tent itself is supported from an external trapezoidal aluminum wand suspension. Four special designs were developed by Draw-Tite inventor Robert L. Blanchard and team member Barry Bishop.

On our rush order Eureka Tent and Awning Company concentrated their entire staff and factory to produce two 12' by 12' tents, six 10' by 10' tents, ten 2-man assault tents, and twenty-four 4-man assault tents. The 12' by 12' tents and the 10' by 10' tens were of the umbrella type and were used in Base Camp and Advance Base for medical, mess, and communications purposes.

The two- and four-man assault tents were double-walled to provide added warmth and reduce condensation. The external shell, made of 2.3 ounce rip-stop nylon, was dyed burnt orange. The pastel green 2-ounce inner cotton liner was held taut by shock cord attachments.

The external aluminum frame on all the Draw-Tites provided sturdy support and easy erection even in high winds. The tents could be moved about without being collapsed when ice under the floor became irregular or crevassed. Elastic shock cord ties from the aluminum frame to the tent fabric eliminated sharp pulls or jerks against the cloth in high winds. The floors were of waterproof nylon.

In addition to the Draw-Tite tents we had ten 2-man assault tents with tunnel entrances supplied by Gerry Mountain Sports, of Boulder, Colorado. These were of the conventional modified A-frame, or Meade, design and were bright orange in color.

Of all the tents used on the expedition, the four-man Draw-Tite tent proved to be one of the most durable. Three of these tents withstood very high winds in the South Col at 26,200 feet for four weeks.

All tents were made of nylon and were dyed burnt orange for easy visibility on the snow. Nylon's lightness of weight and its ability to resist tearing more than made up for its reduced water repellency. In the lowlands during the heavy rains of the monsoon, we used rubberized nylon rain flies.

The sleeping bags used on both approach march and on the mountain were mummy-shaped down bags with rip-stop cover and lining. The lighter bag consisted of 2 pounds of down and had no zipper. It was almost too warm on the approach and return march, and a few nights we slept on top of the bag. The outer bag was extra long and had a total of 3½ pounds of down. It was adequate by itself in the coldest temperatures, although some used it with an inner bag in extreme cold or when they had no air mattresses.

The air mattresses were the usual style made of nylon with tubular construction. In conjunction with them we used single-celled foam Ensolite pads. Quite often these ³⁄₁₆-inch pads were used without air mattresses and seemed to offer enough insulation from cold, though with not quite the softness of the combination.

Cooking stoves, lanterns and space heaters all operated on butane, which came pressurized in various sized containers capable of burning from 10 to 72 hours. The space heaters were used in the medical and laboratory tents and kept them at a comfortable, working temperature. In addition to the butane stoves, we had the usual kerosene primus to back them up in case of failure or shortage; but our experience with the butane stoves was wonderful. Not only did they ignite without priming; they also required no pumping and had enough pressure for operation even at Camp VI at 27,450 feet.

Many items which would not be taken on small climbing trips helped to make our expedition comfortable during its long journey and climb.

Norman Dyhrenfurth's experience on previous expeditions into the Himalaya proved invaluable toward outfitting the team. Whereas many people would have taken a short air mattress to save weight, he wisely recommended that we take a full-length mattress and pad, because this would be our bed for almost four months and would more than make up for the weight in comfort. We also took folding aluminum chairs and tables, umbrellas for protection from sun as well as monsoon rain, tent brooms, and even hot water bottles. All these items helped provide the difference between the bare minimum and actual comfort.

We also knew the problems we would face in the Icefall, and in Seattle constructed six 6-foot sections of aluminum ladder which could be bolted together into one long ladder. It was used at the top of the Icefall to negotiate the final wall leading into the Cwm. With ice screws and Jumar ascenders, we prepared the walls, installed fixed ropes and established the routes.

To package all our food and equipment into 65-pound porter loads, we relied on stout cardboard rather than the wood cartons of previous expeditions. Manufactured by the Georgia-Pacific Co. the cardboard was processed to withstand the monsoon rains and rough handling and carries, and it held up better than wood under the shocks of dropping and jarring. In addition to steel banding, the boxes were secured by nylon tape, then stenciled and marked according to the elevation at which they were to be opened. The weight saved using cardboard rather than wood was well over a ton.

7. TRANSPORT AND SHERPAS

by Lt. Col. James O. M. Roberts

WHEN PEOPLE in Kathmandu asked how we were going to transport over 900 porter-loads of food and equipment to the foot of Mount Everest, I used to reply that I did not know. Past experience and careful preparation breed confidence; but there were times during those mid-February days of 1963, when the expedition seemed to consist of no more than a jumbled mountain of boxes on the apron of Kathmandu's airport, that I suffered from nightmares of the missing-the-train variety. All this and nineteen Americans too.

The task, then, was to deliver our 900-odd loads to Base Camp, and the problem was the recruitment of a large number of porters and the availability of food, track space and night accommodation for them on the trail to Everest. The first two of these problems were largely solved by the importation of 500 Sherpa and Khampa porters from Solu Khumbu. This left only 400 Tamangs to collect locally, and I gave orders that the Khumbu men should each carry a load of food from their homes to be dumped at set places along the route to Kathmandu, for later consumption. Despite much advice to the contrary I was determined we should march as one army and not in two or more parties on successive days. In the event, everyone seemed to be able to tuck

335

themselves away for the night even in drizzling rain in the most un-promising staging sites, and the congestion along the trail, although considerable, caused no serious delay.

For control, we divided the porter corps into nine legions of 100, each under a *naiki* (headman), Sherpa or Tamang, assisted by one of our own "climbing" Sherpas. The *naikis* brought up the rear, while a Sherpa went ahead and checked the loads as they arrived in camp. In camp each porter party had its own separate dump, and thus the stack-ing of loads in the evenings and distribution in the mornings was simpli-fied. Each porter had a tag, numbered from 1 to 909, and the tag num-ber was noted against the load number in a much-thumbed book.

All this seems quite simple, and the friends who came to see us off at Banepa on February 20 were kind enough to describe the departure as "organized chaos." Along the way complications inevitably arose. Sahibs and Sherpas consumed at least four loads of food a day, and every few days we discharged about fifteen Tamangs. Others dropped out, sick or tired, and there was a constant changeover of loads. The book was soon a bit of a mess, and I just hoped that nothing important was missing. Fear of theft and pilfering was of course a constant anxiety in such a large party, but ironically it was not until we entered "Sherpa-land" that bits and pieces began to disappear. Only one load was actually lost on the way to the base, the youth carrying it having suc-cumbed to a surfeit of chang below Namche. Inevitably it had to con-tain a valuable scientific instrument, the only one of its kind with the expedition. However, Maynard Miller and Barry Bishop never agreed as to the ownership of this instrument, and we seemed to get along all right without it.

Anxiety among the porters about shortages of food and accommodation at the end of the day caused a general speeding up on the march. Never have I known such early starts. At about 3 A.M. the sounds of the army bedding down would merge into the morning medley of flickering fires, coughing and spitting, talk, the weeping of children, wood smoke, and the clash of cooking pots. After an hour or so of this racket the sahibs could be heard grumbling in their tents, awaiting the first dread flash-ing of the butane lanterns and the note of Danu's shrill whistle, the summons to Weet-a-bix and fruit juice consumed standing up and shivering in the cold dawnlight. On most mornings camp would be clear at 7 A.M., the first loads having left at least an hour earlier. Those of us that could do so would get ahead of the mob. If caught in the crush, it was usually best to sit and quietly wait for an hour or so and bring up the tail.

The Tamangs returned from Namche, and it was fortunate, for their threadbare clothing and worn or nonexistent footgear were ill-suited to the rigorous winter conditions which lay ahead. After some days of snow at Thangboche even the Khumbu army began to dwindle, and we had to resort to relaying loads the remaining stages to Base Camp. The actual stocking of Base was thus spread over several days, but from the beginning there was sufficient food and equipment at hand to prevent delay in starting work on the mountain.

Now at Base Camp, with the expedition delivered more or less intact, I turn with some diffidence to the subject of our Sherpa high-altitude porters. I say "with diffidence," as the deeds of the Sherpas have already formed an integral and important part of this narrative; but perhaps I can dot some *i*'s and cross some *t*'s in this Sherpa story, which I myself believe is probably unique in Himalayan climbing history.

Norman Dyhrenfurth and I had corresponded on the subject of the composition of the Sherpa team for nearly two years before the expedition, and the result was a highly competent bunch of toughs. There were inevitably some weak links. Our sirdar hailed from Namche Bazar and was really a political choice, as that metropolis can give large expeditions a rough passage if it wishes. He was a good shouter until he lost his voice, and he soon became sick on the mountain. We had no trouble from Namche, but I grudged him his large pay packet. The virtual sirdar on the approach march was Angcherring, of Khumjung, although it was difficult to convince some of the Americans that Gombu, with his knowledge of basic English, was not the power behind the transport scenes.

Despite various pressures, I closed the roll when it numbered thirty-two Sherpa names and kept five vacancies for younger men to be recruited in Khumbu. Young Sherpas often put up outstanding performances on their first expeditions; and although the two-day selection program I planned had to be compressed into a wet half-hour at Thangboche, this young entry produced two out of the five Sherpas who did the great carry to 5W, at over 27,000 feet, on May 21.

Under the regulations of the Government of Nepal, mountaineering expeditions are obliged to make their arrangements for the employment of Sherpas through an agency known as the Himalayan Society. Often criticized, the Society in fact these days usually performs its duties not inefficiently. One of the guiding principles of its policy is that Sherpas resident in Nepal should be given preference in employment over those who have emigrated to India. This is not the place to discuss the rights and wrongs of this policy, and in practice there is no difficulty in including a few chosen Darjeeling men in a Sherpa team. It has, however, tended at times to draw attention to the rift and rivalry existing between Khumbu- and Darjeeling-based porters.

It is easy to exaggerate these differences, which are certainly no more serious than those existing between the two main rival Sherpa factions in Darjeeling itself, or than the intervillage feeling between Namche and Khumjung.* Such friction as existed during the expedition was caused more by the clash of personalities than by differences of habitat, and by the favored treatment accorded, rightly or wrongly, to two of the Darjeeling men. Tempers openly flared, and for a very short time, only above 26,000 feet, when even the best of friends may come to blows if they still possess the necessary energy.

There was some delay in the buildup of the South Col route before the first Sherpa carry of six loads on April 24; and since about thirty loads in all were required on the Col, this necessitated the concentration for a time of our best men on that route. I had hoped to pull a few of our proven Tigers after only one trip to the Col to help the West Ridge team maintain momentum on their advance. But on April 26 a vital carry of seven loads got no further than the Yellow Band (in fact a great effort under very bad weather conditions), and consequently nearly all our remaining porter strength had to be thrown into the assault on the Col route. During the subsequent days nineteen Sherpas reached the Col, many for the second time, and ten went on to Camp VI at 27,450 feet.

Between summit assaults, work continued on the lower part of the West Ridge route; and in the Icefall and on up to Camp II we employed twelve extra porters, most of whom were fairly experienced men, who provided their own somewhat old and threadbare clothing and equipment for an additional fee. These men did great work carry-

* There was considerable disagreement on this point among expedition members, with several feeling that some of the Solu Khumbu Sherpas had a built-in animosity toward those from Darjeeling. There is no doubt, however, that at least some of this was resentment of Gombu's and Ang Dawa's status as "semi-sahibs."—J.R.U.

ing up the Icefall, day after day, in all weathers and unescorted. Indeed I do not think that our Sherpas were ever specifically escorted at any time during the expedition, although they often, of course, climbed in the company of sahibs when a route was being opened for the first time, or later, as partners during the summit and support operations.

At first, as I watched the little dots strung out on the Lhotse Face, I was myself a bit doubtful about this break with normal Himalayan tradition. However, the Sherpas have come a long way during the past few years, and they themselves said they did not require escorts. Most important, it worked, and over a long period. Nevertheless, I think that if the sahibs had undertaken more routine carries with the porters instead of sitting about in the Cwm and at Base, it would have improved both their physical fitness and knowledge of the Sherpas. I speak of general principles. In fact, of course, no shortcomings in these respects interfered with final success on the mountain.

For the second two-pronged summit assault, it was to be my function to move up with Dave Dingman as support for the Col team of Bishop and Jerstad. During this period I also had the task of deploying the Sherpa strength, and in particular of persuading the men who had carried once to Camp VI from the Col that it would now be a good thing to start climbing the mountain a second time after a week's rest, this time by a new route. They responded nobly, but had already given of their best, and it was left to younger men to carry the top camp on the West Ridge. Following the great West Ridge storm of May 16–17, ten Sherpas dribbled down into Camp 2 from out of the clouds. Most had had enough, but two, Ila Tsering and Tenzing Gyalsto were persuaded to return up the ridge after a day's rest; Ang Dorje, Passang Tendi and Tenzing Nindra had remained at 3W and it was these five, three of them on their first expedition, who carried to 27,250 feet on May 21 and set Willi Unsoeld and Tom Hornbein on the way to their great traverse.

At this stage, our supporting resources were of the shoestring variety. Lute and Barry had three Sherpas with them, of whom two went up to Camp VI, and Dave only one, Girmi Dorje. I was now going badly, and Dave very strongly, so I gave Nima Dorje over to him so that he'd have a chance at a summit attempt with Girmi Dorje. They would probably have succeeded on May 23, had they not had to help the summit pairs of May 22 down to Camp VI and below, after the latter's overnight bivouac.

Having read this tale of outstandingly successful cooperation between sahibs and Sherpas, some might presume that perfect harmony prevailed throughout the expedition. In fact, of course, we had our occasional arguments and differences of opinion with the porters; and it would have been unnatural had we not. At least such rows as we did have left no ill feeling. They followed a familiar pattern, and sometimes I suspect that no self-respecting Sherpa considers an expedition complete unless it is enlivened by one or more time-honored disputes.

First, there was the matter of the weights of loads to be carried above Base. Up to Base the high-altitude porter is a privileged person carrying only a light rucksack; above, his work begins. I have usually reckoned in the past that about 40 pounds is a reasonable load to expect a Sherpa to carry on fairly difficult ground above Base on a big mountain and over a long period. Some spare clothing, food, a water bottle and rope will probably bring his total burden to about 50 pounds. Logistical planning this year, however, required a useful load of nearer 50 pounds to be carried into the Cwm; and an argument blew up between the two strongish characters, Tom Hornbein and Chotari, about the number of oxygen cylinders a Sherpa might fairly be expected to carry. Four cylinders, which Tom considered the proper load, weighed 52 pounds, with a carrying frame and other extras bringing the total burden to about 60 pounds; and Chotari maintained that this was too much. However, by the time I reached the scene to help mediate, the Sherpas were carrying their four cylinders with fairly good grace.

On the whole, a good balance was kept between the requirements of the sahibs and the interests of the porters. It was unreasonable to argue, as some did, that the team members were carrying heavier loads and that the Sherpas should therefore follow suit. Some sahibs did indeed occasionally carry 60 pounds or more when moving up to an established Camp, but this is a different matter from the tedium of daily and exhausting routine portages. It is a careful balance which must be struck between the conflicting necessities of maintaining pressure during the buildup stage on a high mountain and husbanding the Sherpas' strength for the supreme effort which is to come later. From the Col to Camp VI the loads were still of four cylinders, though now one was being breathed, and at Camp 4W on the morning of May 21 there were no arguments, no weighing of loads.

Now the sleeping bag row. Whereas in the matter of the loads I felt that the Sherpas' grievances merited at least a sympathetic hearing, in the case of the sleeping bags I felt no sympathy at all and was disappointed by their behavior. Perhaps I should have known better. Equipment is the Achilles' heel of the Sherpas, and any imagined short-dealing or removal of cherished items which have, of course, an excellent resale value are, at any rate in a large expedition, a sure source of trouble. But on our present expedition, the issue of clothing and equipment to the Sherpas had been on a scale so lavish and of such good quality that I was not prepared for the minor revolt which took place when it became known that second sleeping bags were not available to supplement the very excellent, large, warm bags issued to the Sherpas in Kathmandu. (The sahibs were given second inner bags soon after arrival at Base, and this sparked off the complaint, which was quite irrelevant, as the extra bags were never carried above Base.)

The sirdar presented the men's grievance most inconsiderately at suppertime, and I tried to judge in the half-light who were the ringleaders. I accused the Sherpas of demanding inner sleeping bags (which anyway we had not got) for barter and told them that they had already received small fortunes in the form of equipment. They replied with dignity that the single bags they had received were not warm enough and that they would feel cold on the mountain. After a time I grew fed up and called a meeting for the following morning. There were some rather ashamed-looking men on parade, obviously only too willing to withdraw their demands, providing this could be achieved without undue loss of face. Among mutual declarations of admiration and good faith we agreed that we would pay for local porters to go down to the men's villages to bring up their own sleeping bags to supplement the inadequate equipment provided by the expedition. Later some greasy and motheaten old cotton quilts appeared in Base Camp. I don't think they were ever taken higher.

We had ordered porters to take us back to Namche to arrive at Base on May 24, and the last ten loads came down the Icefall the following morning. What with this rush and celebrations among the Sherpas, the next few days were rather chaotic. Apart from my temper, we were lucky to lose only two items of equipment: a star camera base belonging to Maynard Miller valued at several thousand dollars, unique of its kind, and a kit bag belonging to Dick Pownall. The camera base which looked exactly like a dirty old Sherpa cooking stand, we later recovered from a hut in Pheriche. Dick's kit bag containing all his high-altitude clothing was, alas, never found.

SOME SHERPA PERFORMANCES

Individual	Achievement on mountain
Nawang Gombu	to the summit
Ang Dawa IV	to about 28,200 feet
Girmi Dorje	above Camp VI; South Col three times
Chotari	Camp VI; South Col three times
Nima Tenzing (of Pangboche)	Camp VI; South Col three times
Phu Dorje	Camp VI; South Col twice
Kancha	Camp VI; South Col twice
Nima Dorje	Camp VI; South Col twice
Pemba Tenzing	Camp VI; South Col twice
Dawa Tenzing	Camp VI; South Col twice
Lhakpa Sonam (in middle fifties)	Camp VI; South Col twice
Tenzing Nindra*	Camp 5W; South Col twice
Ang Nyima	Camp 4W; South Col twice
Angcherring II	Camp 4W; South Col twice
Nawang Dorje	Camp 4W; South Col twice
Ila Tsering	Camp 5W; South Col
Passang Tendi*	Camp 5W; South Col
Tenzing Gyalsto*	Camp 5W; South Col
Ang Dorje	Camp 5W
Kalden	South Col three times
Nima Tenzing (of Thami)	South Col twice
Tashi (in middle fifties)	Camp 4W (three times); South Col

Passang Temba and Urkien also carried to the South Col. Annulu performed remarkable work keeping the Icefall route open for eight weeks.

Collective achievement

19 Sherpas carried to over 27,000 feet
 4 reached the South Col three times
11 reached the South Col twice
 8 reached the South Col once
23 reached the South Col in all

* Men on their first expedition.

8. HEALTH AND MEDICINE

by Gilbert Roberts, M.D.

I. *Preparations*

All expedition members submitted medical histories and received complete physical examinations. In addition they were immunized against cholera, tetanus, yellow fever, smallpox, typhoid, paratyphoid, polio (oral vaccine), typhus and diphtheria. Just before leaving the United States gamma globulin was given to each man for protection against hepatitis during the early portion of our travels.

II. *Supplies*

A decision about what particular types and quantities of medical supplies should be taken along is invariably a compromise. On the one hand, a major Himalayan expedition may encounter almost any conceivable medical problem there is; on the other, the limiting factors of weight and bulk must be taken into account. We ended up with about 200 pounds of medical equipment, exclusive of the oxygen paraphernalia and the water filter. All our medical supplies were donated by various pharmaceutical houses, which, without exception, responded generously and promptly to our requests.

The medical items began arriving at my home months before they

343

were due to leave for India. They were all subsequently repackaged in plastic vials and bottles to prevent breakage and unnecessary weight. Dressings and instruments were sterilized and sealed in plastic to avoid contamination. The final loads were so organized that the loss of any one of them would not mean the loss of all of any essential item. In addition twenty first-aid kits were packed—these to be issued to each climber on the mountain. Three "doctors' boxes," which the MDs were to carry with their personal gear, made up the rest.

The following is a partial list of the types of supplies taken:

Antibiotics (several types). Used in greatest quantity was a combination short- and long-acting penicillin which was very useful for "one-shot" treatments of patients who gathered for sick call. A sulfa preparation which required only one or two tablets a day was also utilized under similar circumstances. Tetracycline was used extensively for bronchitis, sinusitis and diarrheas. Chloromycetin was of real value on a few occasions in the treatment of very severe and potentially fatal infections.

Analgesics. Aspirin and APC tablets are used for virtually everything, and one never has enough if one dispenses them as we did for placebos in symptomatic relief among the local population. Aspirin compound with codeine was not only extremely useful as an analgesic and for treatment of severe headaches at altitude, but also to suppress coughs and diarrheas. We took 500 tablets and could have used double that amount. Stronger narcotics such as demerol and morphine were taken for emergency use but were only required as premedication for minor surgical and dental procedures on a few occasions.

Upper Respiratory Symptomatic Medication. A good long-acting decongestant is essential, and large quantities were used. Virtually every member of our entourage of a thousand had a cold during the trip to the mountain. Many of these colds persisted on the mountain, with sinusitis, chronic sore throats, laryngitis and coughs being the rule rather than the exception among the climbers. A cough lozenge with expectorant and codeine was very useful.

Sedatives. Several different barbiturates were taken, and response to them varied. Most members of the expedition occasionally required fairly large doses of barbiturates for sleep at high altitude.

Gastro-intestinal Medication. An antispasmodic preparation was frequently utilized, and antacids were occasionally valuable for the dyspepsia encountered at altitude. Diarrheas were common and mostly responded to codeine, antispasmodics and, if severe, sulfa or tetracycline.

Emergency Drugs. These included vasopressors, rapidly acting injectable digitalis preparations, aminophylline, a mercurial diuretic, injectable hydrocortisone, adrenalin, an injectable antihistamine and heparin. These items were available in quantities large enough so as to be distributed in the various medical boxes and in the smaller doctors' boxes higher on the mountain.

Skin Preparations. Several antibiotic and steroid ointments were taken as well as a number of hotel-sized bars of germicidal soap, which were probably more frequently used than anything else in the treatment of skin disease among the Nepalese villagers. A number of different sunburn preventives were taken, and individuals differed in the protection they required. Everyone was agreed, however, that high on the mountain the only agents which were completely effective were those which mechanically blocked all the sun's rays.

Eye Medicine. Fairly large quantities of antibiotic eye ointments were taken for the treatment of ophthalmic infections which are common among the natives. Steroid and anaesthetic medications were also brought for snow blindness, but very few cases occurred.

Antiparasitic Agents. All expedition members took prophylactic chloroquine during the trip for malaria prevention. We had large amounts of chloroquine and atabrine, but encountered only one case of clinical malaria. Large quantities of piperazine were used in the treatment of round worm infections such as ascariasis among the native population. Amibiasis was treated with chloroquine and carbarsone, but we saw very little acute amoebic dysentery during the expedition itself.

Dressings. We had more than adequate supplies of gauze, orthopedic plaster and band-aids which are a favorite among the porters. Although we took large amounts of adhesive tape, it soon was in short supply, due to the fact that it invariably ends up being used for any number of purposes other than medical. Skin toughener and mole skin were in demand during the approach march in the treatment of the inevitable blisters.

Surgical Equipment. We had three small instrument packs which would enable each doctor to suture small lacerations or perform a tracheotomy. We also had a major instrument set with adequate instruments for an appendectomy or the repair of a ruptured viscus or decompression of an intracranial injury with a trephine. Besides these we had a nasal gastric tube, Foley catheters (which could also be used as chest tubes), some endotracheal tubes, a laryngoscope, sterile gloves, sutures, etc.

Dental Supplies. These included two pairs of universal forceps, a dental curette for root extraction, and zinc oxide and euginol for temporary fillings.

Anesthetic Supplies. We took ether with a mask to use with our oxygen equipment, a spinal anesthesia setup, pentathol and suxxinyl-choline as a relaxant.

Fluids. We had dextran and serum-albumin for temporary expansion of blood volume. In addition we had blood collection bags, and blood types had been determined on all expedition members previously so that emergency transfusion could be given. We had a total of 10 liters of intravenous fluids (normal saline and dextrose and water), and we could have used more. Some of the fluids were taken in 500-cc plastic blood-bags, each of which was sealed in an additional plastic bag. These could be thawed in warm water, were not breakable, and proved extremely useful. I think future expeditions should package all intravenous fluids in this fashion.

Lab Equipment. Thanks to the large scientific program, we had available for medical use a microscope and other equipment which enabled us to do blood counts, urinalysis and bacterial smears.

Immunization Materials. We took tetanus toxoid, but had to have smallpox vaccine flown in when we came across an epidemic in the Solu Khumbu area.

First-aid Kits. Each member was given a small first-aid kit which included dressings, tape, a wire splint, anesthetic eye ointment, a rapid-acting digitalis preparation with detailed instructions for treatment of pulmonary edema, morphine syrettes, sleeping tablets, APC, codeine tablets, an antispasmodic, a decongestant, salt tablets, injectable penicillin, cough lozenges and achromycin capsules. The items were carefully labeled and members were instructed in use of the contents. Drugs were thus available for emergency use in the absence of a physician. On several occasions doctors were able to advise via radio, and medicines were then taken accordingly, speeding up initiation of treatment.

III. *Problems*

On the march we saw up to fifty local people and porters each day. Their problems ranged from enthusiastic partiality for tablets, band-aids and a look at the sahibs to a large variety of incurable diseases for which we could do little. These included chronic heart failure, cancer of the breast, a large abdominal tumor, a chronic osteomyelitis of the leg, and many others. Respiratory diseases from colds to pneumonia were common. We saw many cases of suspected tuberculosis, both pulmonary and other, including a tuberculous abdomen. Diarrheas and various abdominal complaints, many of them probably parasitic, were seen. Occasional eye infections were encountered, but not much trachoma, which is more prevalent in the Karakoram region of Pakistan (presumably because of the veil which the Moslem women use to wipe their children's eyes). Dental problems were common, and we became quite proficient at extractions. Particularly memorable was a house call made in the apartment of the High Lama of Thangboche. After two cups of salted buttered tea, His Holiness made it known that he had a toothache. Fortunately we were able to pull the offending tooth without difficulty. When we returned to our camp afterwards, several of the Sherpas approached us regarding the pulled tooth and were disappointed to find that we had not kept such a valuable relic.

Among the climbers, the most frequent approach-march problems were respiratory infections and diarrheas. Many also suffered from blisters during the first few days, and several had an acute viral gastroenteritis with extreme nausea, vomiting etc., lasting twenty-four hours. One climber developed a recurrence of an old bursitis of the shoulder, which improved following local injection with cortisone. Several porters sustained minor bruises, sprains and lacerations in the collapse of a chain bridge. Amazingly no more serious injuries were suffered despite the 15- to 20-foot fall onto rocks.

At Junbesi a local woman came to us with five-day-old 20 per cent third-degree burns of arms and face. We treated her with antibiotics and analgesics, and arrangements were made for her evacuation to Kathmandu by helicopter, where skin grafts were done. On our return she met us with eggs and arak—the local firewater.

A few days later a young boy appeared with smallpox. He was isolated in a local home but unfortunately died. We were able to have vaccine flown in after several very anxious days of waiting, during which no more cases of smallpox appeared. We vaccinated about 500 people above Namche, and Sir Edmund Hillary's group, to whom we sent some of our vaccine, immunized even more. Even so, in our return from the mountain we saw many people recovering from the disease and were told that there had been about forty deaths in the area, including possibly some of our porters who had left us before the arrival of the vaccine.

At Namche, Chotari, our assistant sirdar, developed the classic symptoms of appendicitis. We were preparing to do an appendectomy, but before it became necessary he responded to large doses of intravenous chloromycetin. He recovered completely without surgery. At the same time an eighteen-year-old Sherpani developed a severe bilateral pneumonia. She too was treated with large doses of penicillin and chloromycetin and was given oxygen. After an anxious night for the doctors, she began to improve, and three months later she came up to Base Camp to help carry on the return march. To complete our stay in Namche, one of our porters broke an arm. We reduced the fracture and immobilized it in a plaster cast.

On the mountain, the usual high-altitude problems of insomnia, headache, nausea, weight loss, chronic colds, coughs and sinusitis occurred. One man had to return to Base Camp twice because of vomiting but eventually acclimatized and did very well. Antibiotics and decongestants served to combat the purulent postnasal drip that plagued many of us. It tended to return however, when medication was stopped. Norman Dyhrenfurth and one Sherpa had severe laryngitis for several weeks and could speak only in whispers. One Sherpa came down with acute hepatitis. Many had vague abdominal complaints, some with bloody stools which were treated as of helmenthic or amoebic origin, with good recoveries in most cases.

On March 23 Jake Breitenbach was killed when an ice wall collapsed. In the same accident Dick Pownall suffered some painful rib contusions and Ang Pema several severe facial lacerations and a probable basal skull fracture. He had cerebrospinal fluid leaking from his nose for three days. He recovered completely without developing any infection, thanks to his rugged constitution, antibiotics, and the relatively sterile atmosphere of Base Camp.

Maynard Miller fractured a metatarsal bone in his foot when a rock overturned on it on the moraine. He was treated with a tight boot, and after a few weeks of hobbling around on ski poles healed very well (as shown by an X-ray on our return to Kathmandu).

Dan Doody developed a deep thrombophlebitis of the leg at Advance Base Camp. Since there have been several episodes of thrombophlebitis and other thrombotic phenomena at high altitude on other expeditions (presumably due to the combination of polycythemia, dehydration and minor trauma to the legs), we were prepared for the problem. He was kept at Advance Base because of the hazards of evacuation by litter and because oxygen was available. He was anticoagulated with heparin (which required frequent determination of clotting times). He was also given intravenous fibrinolysin and dextran, which has recently been advocated for treatment of peripheral thrombosis. He did well, developed no signs of embolism, and was able to return to Base Camp in ten days.

Barry Prather, our youngest man, aged twenty-three, developed acute pulmonary edema at Camp IV after hard work breaking trail the previous day. He had no history of previous cardiac problems. He felt tired and remained at IV while his companion, fortunately an MD, pushed on toward the Col with two Sherpas. Bad weather turned them back, and on their return to Camp IV a few hours later they found Prather dyspnoic and somewhat confused, with a rapid pulse and pulmonary rales. He was given digoxin and amynophylin by injection and began improving almost immediately, even before oxygen, which had been buried in the snow, could be located and administered. Although this was the only case requiring therapy, pulmonary edema is probably more common at high altitude than realized. Many of us developed a cough, more rapid pulse and slight dyspnea at the end of a particularly difficult day's work. These symptoms cleared within a few hours but may well have represented minimal pulmonary edema.

There were a few cases of minor frostbite with slight loss of sensation or peeling of skin of faces, fingers or toes. During the second summit assault and its ensuing bivouac, two members were severely frostbitten. They were treated conservatively. Parts that had not already thawed were rewarmed in warm water at Advance Base, and they were carried from Base to Namche, where they were evacuated by helicopter to Kathmandu. Micromolecular dextran was given, but no definite conclusions can be drawn as to its effectiveness at this time. Anticoagulants and vasodilators were not used, since recent evidence suggests that they are of little value. Subsequently Barry Bishop lost all his toes and the first joint on both fifth fingers. Willi Unsoeld lost the first two joints of all toes except one little one. Amputation was not carried out until many weeks after injury, so that the extent of tissue damage could be clearly ascertained. In general, skin changes early in frostbite appear worse than total tissue injury, and early amputation, unless forced by the development of infection, is apt to result in removal of tissue which may be viable.

The march out was relatively uneventful medically, and everyone enjoyed good health except for minor reactions to the extreme heat, which were treated with salt and fluids. The large number of upper respiratory infections encountered on the approach march fell to almost zero, presumably due to the warmer weather and smaller number of porters. Diarrheas were not much of a problem until our return to Kathmandu. On the march all drinking water was filtered with a Millipore filter which removed all particles of bacterial size and above, and the water was also treated with globaline (iodine water purification tablets). However, on return to civilization and its rounds of parties and the inevitable relaxation of personal food and water discipline, enteric pathogens began to take their toll and over 50 per cent of the expedition developed diarrheas. On return to the United States one member was found to have typhoid organisms, and several had amibiasis. One developed hepatitis, but at this writing all have recovered.

9. OXYGEN

by Thomas F. Hornbein, M.D.

ALTHOUGH OXYGEN was used as early as 1922 by a British Everest Expedition, it was another thirty-one years before development of sufficiently light and reliable oxygen breathing apparatus led to the successful attainment of the highest point on earth. Without oxygen man has climbed to a little above 28,000 feet on the North Face of Everest. No one knows how much higher he can go, nor what would be the consequences of prolonged exposure to such extreme oxygen deficiency.

The sheer necessity of oxygen for uphill movement at 29,000 feet is only too apparent to most Himalayan mountaineers. Beyond this, the use of oxygen increases the distance a climber can travel in a day and thereby ultimately shortens the time of his stay at very great heights. It adds immeasurably to his safety and clearness of judgment. It even permits him to derive a certain modicum of pleasure and aesthetic appreciation from his endeavor and the beauty of his surroundings. Without oxygen, each step at great heights is virtually a maximal effort; there is no reserve with which to face the unexpected. With oxygen there is a striking sensation of release, a spring in the step, a capacity to make a rapid movement, a desire to gaze elsewhere than at the slow alternate plod of each foot.

The greater the concentration of oxygen breathed, the greater the benefit derived. A closed-circuit system in which the climber breathes 100 per cent oxygen, the expired air being recirculated past a chemical absorbent for removal of carbon dioxide, would provide at 29,000 feet a pressure of oxygen more than equivalent to that attained breathing air at sea level. The single use of such a system was by Bourdillon and Evans, of the British Expedition of 1953. The advantage in terms of rate of climb was impressive. But complexity and poor reliability resulted in failure of one set near the South Summit of Everest. This single experience, coupled with the proven reliability of open-circuit units, has left the closed-circuit system pretty well abandoned to the present time.

Thus the open-circuit set has been used exclusively in reaching the summits of all the earth's highest peaks. This set operates on the principle that the climber breathes predominantly outside air enriched by a small percentage of oxygen. It possesses the great advantage of simplicity and reliability, though necessarily supplying a lower concentration of oxygen to the climber than does the closed-circuit system. In the past, flow rates of oxygen were used which supplied the climber with an oxygen-air mixture roughly simulating an altitude of 17,000 to 19,000 feet, the maximum height at which a person is thought to be able to function effectively for fairly prolonged periods of time. For example, an exercising climber at 28,000 feet (one-third atmosphere pressure) may breathe 100 liters of gas each minute. At an oxygen flow of 4 LPM (liters per minute, expressed in terms of sea level pressure) only 12 per cent of his total ventilation would be pure oxygen. The concentration he receives deep in his lungs will depend therefore on a number of factors including altitude, oxygen flow rate, and minute volume of ventilation.

I. *Apparatus*

The typical open-circuit set consists of a high-pressure oxygen source, a pressure-reducing and flow-regulating device, a rubber delivery tube, a bladder or other economizer for storage of oxygen, and a mask in which air and oxygen are mixed during inspiration.

Bottles. The oxygen bottles used on this expedition were aluminum alloy cylinders wound with steel piano wire. Of French manufacture, they weighed 9.9 pounds empty and carried nearly 3 pounds of oxygen.

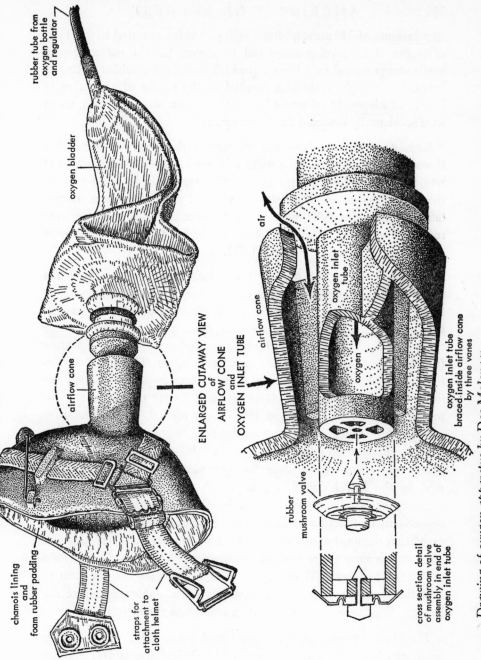

rubber tube from oxygen bottle and regulator

oxygen bladder

airflow cone

chamois lining and foam rubber padding

straps for attachment to cloth helmet

ENLARGED CUTAWAY VIEW
of
AIRFLOW CONE
and
OXYGEN INLET TUBE

air

airflow cone

oxygen inlet tube

oxygen

oxygen inlet tube braced inside airflow cone by three vanes

rubber mushroom valve

cross section detail of mushroom valve assembly in end of oxygen inlet tube

Drawing of oxygen apparatus by Dee Molenaar

At a pressure of 230 atmospheres (3300 psi) this amounted to 920 liters of oxygen at sea level pressure and 15 degrees C. The outlet of each bottle was protected by a brass cap which contained a rubber O ring to provide an airtight seal. This resulted in the saving of a number of bottles which would otherwise have lost pressure when the valve knobs were accidentally loosened during transport.

Regulators. The regulator was attached to the oxygen bottle with a threaded metal adapter. An airtight seal was achieved by the rubber O ring, permitting the regulator to be easily screwed in by hand without the need of wrenches. The regulator weighed about 12 ounces. It contained a Bourdon tube pressure manometer, a single-stage pressure reduction section, and a flow control calibrated to deliver continuous oxygen flows of ½, 1, 2, 3, and 4 LPM.

Oxygen Bladder. The oxygen flowed from the regulator through a length of rubber tube to a 1.5-liter latex rubber bladder attached directly to the mask. The bladder served as a collection chamber for the oxygen, storing it for use during each inspiration. A valve in the mask prevented entry into the bladder of the climber's expired air, where the moisture from the breath would have condensed and frozen. The demand function of the bladder resulted solely from changes in pressure within the mask during breathing, the positive pressure during expiration tending to seal the valve firmly shut as the bladder refilled, and the negative pressure during inspiration sucking the oxygen from the bladder into the lungs along with outside air. In theory this system, though simpler, lighter and more reliable than the spring-loaded bellows economizer used by the British in 1953, possesses the disadvantages of a lower efficiency of oxygen conservation at low breathing rates and possible impairment of function in high winds. Studies performed prior to the expedition demonstrated that the bladder would function at near 100 per cent efficiency at the ventilatory volumes associated with even mild work at high altitude. Winds up to 70 miles per hour did not seem to alter this function even though there was considerable flapping of the bladder. Experience on the mountain confirmed these tests.

The Mask. The classical open-circuit mask contained directional valves for inspiration and expiration, usually of sufficient size and/or number as to minimize breathing resistance for the very high ventilatory flow rates occurring during climbing at high altitude. An additional valve prevented entry of expired air into the oxygen bladder. Altered from existing aviation masks, the resistance in many cases still remained uncomfortably high. Of even greater consequence was the problem of ice formation under all but the most ideal weather conditions. Freezing of moisture from the breath would gradually impair function of the expiratory valves, making exhalation more and more of an effort. More serious was the condensation of water from the breath over the oxygen valve. This water would either descend into the bladder when the valve lifted during inspiration, or it would freeze on the valve, obstructing the flow of oxygen and causing the bladder to distend to basketball-size proportions. Little imagination is required to envision the difficulty of unscrewing the valve mount, removing the delicate valve and scraping the ice from it while the wind whistles coolly by and while deprived, for this interval of repair, of the use of oxygen. Problems of just this type played a major role in the failure of the 1960 Indian Mount Everest Expedition a scant few hundred feet below the summit.

For the present expedition a mask was created specifically to fulfill the requirements for high-altitude mountaineering; namely, simplicity, comfort and reliability. Devising a means of molding the mask as a single unit, as well as its final manufacture, were a contribution of the Maytag Company of Newton, Iowa. Their two-year effort emanated largely from the personal interest, intellectual curiosity, and deep spirit of adventure of the late Fred Maytag.

The Maytag mask (see p. 353) contains only a single valve to prevent rebreathing into the bladder. Inspiration and expiration take place through a valveless "airflow cone" placed concentrically about the oxygen inlet tube. The dimensions of the airflow cone were determined by the requirements for a low breathing resistance coupled with adequate conservation of oxygen for use during inspiration. The latter function was abetted by use of an exceedingly low resistance valve over the oxygen inlet. The result was a mask which possessed lower resistance to breathing than any mask previously used, while still being about 10 per cent more efficient in oxygen usage during climbing than prior masks utilizing a bladder for oxygen conservation. Since the oxygen valve lay directly in the stream of expired air, it was kept warm by the breath. During the climb we noticed that the thin film of moisture over the valve would freeze within seconds when the mask was removed. This was easily thawed by merely replacing the mask on the face and breathing through it for a few breaths. Any condensation would roll off the valve and down the airflow cone, rather than entering the bladder. Since the entire mask was molded as a single unit of rubber, the ice which gradually accumulated at the lower rim of the airflow cone could be easily dislodged by an occasional squeeze of the cone with the mittened hand. The extreme simplicity and nonrigid construction of the Maytag mask made it essentially indestructible, even by those most adept with ice ax or crampons.

In actual use the mask performed to the best of expectations. Because of the low breathing resistance very little training was required to become accustomed to its presence while climbing. As a matter of fact, a few windy days soon demonstrated its virtue as excellent face protection even when oxygen was not being used. The mask was made in a single large size. By use of chamois-lined foam pads it could be adapted to the great variety of facial contours existing within our climber and Sherpa population. Fogging of goggles due to mask leak was minimized by good fit and by the low resistance to expiration through the airflow cone. The fogging which occasionally did occur seemed to be unrelated to the presence of a mask and was most likely a result of poor ventilation of the goggles. Among other fringe benefits of the Maytag mask was the discovery that the icicles which accumulated at the rim of the airflow cone provided an excellent means of quenching one's thirst during the day's climb. The final virtue of the mask lay in skillfully concealing the countenances of those who over a period of weeks failed to maintain a presentable social appearance.

The mask used for sleeping was a lightweight, polyethylene "K-S" mask (Ohio Chemical & Surgical Equipment Co.). Operating on the rebreathing principle, it afforded more efficient utilization of oxygen, and so long as it was kept inside the sleeping bag no problems with freezing resulted. The pliable construction of the mask permitted sleeping in any position without difficulty. It took a while to become accustomed to the warmth and moisture in the mask, but this was soon offset by the improvement in sleep and feeling of significant rest provided by a night's oxygen at the high camps.*

* Here, again, is a point on which not all team members were in agreement. Some of them, as well as some Sherpas, were never happy with the "flexible aquariums" and preferred to use their regular masks for sleeping as well as climbing.—J.R.U.

Oxygen played a role in the successful treatment of cases of pneumonia, thrombophlebitis, and high-altitude pulmonary edema during the course of the expedition. The sleeping mask was used for medical administration of oxygen, using a considerably higher flow than for other purposes.

II. *Logistics*

There was a total of 200 French bottles containing 920 liters of oxygen each and 16 Draeger (German) bottles of 1000-liter capacity. Since the latter were considerably heavier, they were reserved primarily for medical use. In anticipation of emergency medical needs, each camp was stocked with at least six bottles prior to its occupation.

Oxygen requirements were based on the previous experience of the British in 1953 and the Swiss in 1956. Oxygen was used for climbing above Camp III at 22,900 feet and Camp 3W at 23,800 feet. A flow of 2 LPM was used up to 26,000 feet and 3 or occasionally 4 LPM above that altitude. For sleeping a ½-LPM flow was adequate at Camps III, 3W, IV, and 4W, with a 1-LPM flow being used for sleep at the higher camps. Normal sleeping requirements were calculated on the basis of an eight-hour usage, one bottle being shared by each pair of climbers. For the summit attempts each climber carried two bottles, sufficient for eight hours at the maximum flow of 4 LPM.

The South Col teams followed the habit of their predecessors by caching the first bottle below the South Summit for use on the way down. Unfortunately the summit team of May 1 dropped their bottles too early and were forced to return from the summit to them without the use of oxygen. The team approaching from the West Ridge, contemplating a traverse, used their first bottles to exhaustion before jettisoning them. It required constant care to ration the supply so it would not be exhausted before the uphill climb was completed. Oxygen was limited to a flow of 2 LPM while climbing and was generally turned off during intervals of belaying when moving one at a time. It is obvious that a balance must be maintained between supply and demand lest the climber suddenly find himself perched breathlessly at some breezy height without the ability to continue on. This was achieved by constant monitoring of the pressure within the bottles as a measure of oxygen usage; flows were adjusted accordingly. Even at flows of 2 LPM it was found that climbing could be performed with a certain amount of dexterity and pleasure.

Oxygen was used only by those Sherpas destined to make the final carries to the high camps on each route. In order to conserve strength for the following day, the eight high Sherpas on the Col route used oxygen for the carry from Camp IV to the South Col and slept at the Col on a flow of 1 LPM. They carried to Camp VI at 27,450 feet on a flow of 3 LPM. Similarly the five Sherpas who made the long carry to Camp 5W slept on oxygen at Camp 4W and carried to 27,250 feet on 2 to 3 LPM of oxygen.

Of the 200 French bottles, 12 were used for the reconnaissance of the West Ridge with 63 more being allotted for the actual climb on the assumption that there would be six camps and two 2-man summit teams. The South Col route required 16 bottles for the preparation of the Lhotse Face plus 95 bottles planned for the summit attempts by two 4-man teams and one 2-man attempt on Lhotse. Following the initial effort, 7 more bottles were added for the second ascent via the Col three weeks later.

This account has dealt primarily with problems related to oxygen usage unique to the present expedition. For a more complete background on the subject the reader is referred to the appropriate sections in *The Conquest of Everest* by Sir John Hunt and *The Everest-Lhotse Adventure* by Albert Eggler.

10. *STILL PHOTOGRAPHY*

by Barry C. Bishop

DURING THE PAST SIXTY YEARS photography has become an increasingly important consideration on mountaineering expeditions. Even before the turn of the century that outstanding pioneer in mountain photography, Vittorio Sella, had created a standard that is today hard to equal. He did this with equipment that was heavy, bulky, and difficult to operate. But since Sella roamed four continents with his 30- by 40-cm Dallmeyer plate camera, photographic equipment has been vastly improved. Cameras are now smaller and lighter. A vast choice of high quality interchangeable lenses permits the photographer great flexibility in treating a subject. Moreover, an infinite variety of both black-and-white and color films are available. But even more important, the average mountaineer is an exceptionally fine photographer. Mountains and mountaineering offer breath-taking photographic possibilities, and it is the rare climb or expedition today that is not well photographed.

Ever since the reconnaissance of 1921, past expeditions to Mount Everest have done a masterful job of photography. The standard set by our predecessors would be difficult to duplicate on the American Mount Everest Expedition, but this we hoped to do. Not only did we wish to make a thorough photographic record of AMEE for our own personal pleasure and satisfaction (often an expedition is more enjoyable in retrospect than in fact, and good pictures always make waxing nostalgic the more enjoyable) but, like all modern expeditions, we had many obligations which had to be satisfied by photography. Press photographs, illustrations for magazine articles, books and scientific reports had to be supplied, as well as photographs of hundreds of pieces of equipment for manufacturers who cooperated with the expedition. Moreover, we felt an obligation to our friends, fellow climbers and the general public, who would not have the opportunity of visiting the high Himalaya, for many of us had already been on expeditions to that part of the world. Now we were going to "the granddaddy of them all," 778 feet higher than the second highest mountain, K2.

We knew how drained of energy we would be, struggling under heavy loads as we balanced on some steep icy traverse, our lungs screaming for oxygen while the wind made us unsure of our balance. Photography under such conditions requires a great deal of motivation. While the mind might be strong, the body all too often is weak. The climber recognizes a wonderful scene or situation that should be recorded, but he cannot muster those extra few calories of energy necessary for removing the camera from the kangaroo pocket of the parka, lifting it to his eye while making the necessary exposure calculations, setting the shutter speed and lens opening, and depressing the shutter. Usually he rationalizes the situation by saying to himself, "I'll get it next time I feel a bit stronger. Perhaps the light will be more interesting then." But we also knew that one never feels better and that the light usually will never be more interesting.

We hoped, however, to overcome this common roadblock to photography in the Himalaya—the climber's own lethargy—by increasing his motivation for taking pictures.

On the Mount Rainier shakedown in September, 1962, we decided to select one 35-mm camera with which we could standardize on the expedition. This would allow members of the team to interchange lenses among themselves, it would assure, hopefully, a higher standard of photographs. And for many of us it would mean that we would come away from the expedition with photographic equipment of a much higher quality than what we previously possessed.

Selecting the "official camera" of the expedition could have created a major problem. Mountaineers are outspoken individualists, particularly when it comes to the question of equipment—any equipment. This was the case with our team. Some favored the single-lens reflex camera while others favored the view-finder, range-finder camera. Some preferred the 35-mm format while others preferred 2¼ by 2¼ inch, or larger, format. Some preferred to work only in color while others preferred black and white. But all knew that the choice of photographic equipment is always a compromise, and our expedition was no exception.

We finally selected the Nikon F single-lens reflex camera. It was fairly lightweight for such a camera, was easy to operate, and offered an infinite variety of high quality lenses.

Nippon Kogaku K.K., of Tokyo, Japan, makers of the Nikon, outfitted each member of the expedition with a model F camera, 50-mm f/20 Nikkor lens, and 28-mm f/3.5 Nikkor wide-angle lens. This equipment was winterized at the factory and thoroughly tested in a cold chamber prior to our picking up the equipment in Japan en route to Nepal and the Himalaya. We were assured that the shutter speeds and mirror reflex mechanism as well as the automatic lens diaphragms would function normally down to −22 degrees F. In addition several other Nikkor lenses were supplied, ranging from 21 mm to 200 mm.

This standardized camera system with group lenses allowed the climbers to exchange items throughout the expedition. In addition, each member of AMEE was encouraged to bring his old camera with which he had worked in the past and whose operations and idiosyncrasies he knew well.

Several additional cameras both large and small were also taken. Six Olympus Pen-S cameras, taking 72 frames on a standard 36-exposure cartridge of 35-mm film were taken for use high on the mountain and on the actual summit assault. This split-frame camera could be operated with one hand and required film changing only half as often as a standard 35-mm camera. This feature had definite advantages when we operated in cold temperatures amidst windblown snows that saturate the open back of a camera in a matter of seconds.

A 4- by 5-inch Linhof camera system was taken for large negative photography. Because of its weight it saw limited action and was never taken past Advance Base. Such also was the case with camera systems taken along for testing purposes like the Zeiss Ikon Conarex whose weight precluded it from being carried high on the mountain.

A great deal of film was taken on the expedition, in order to encourage the members to use their cameras as much as possible. Each climber was furnished with 30 rolls of Kodachrome II color film. More than 20,000 exposures on 35-mm film were made during the course of the expedition as well as several thousand exposures with larger negative size.

We designed a simplified logging system. With it each member of the expedition could keep a running record of the rolls of film he shot. On 3½- by 5½-inch pads were spots to enter the photographer's name, roll number, film type, date and description of subjects photographed. The team member kept a carbon copy and folded the original into the film can. In this manner each of us had a permanent record of all the pictures we took, and a log stayed with the film for identification purposes.

Film was sent out with the mail runners every two weeks and usually was processed in the United States four weeks after leaving Base Camp. The National Geographic Society acted as custodian for the film while we were in the field.

During the expedition, lens hoods and ultra-violet filters were used at all times. The latter was as helpful in protecting the front lens element as in filtering ultra-violet rays.

Another valuable piece of photographic equipment each member of the expedition carried was a lightweight aluminum ice-ax clamp. Machined in the workshop of the National Geographic Society and fitted with a small Leitz ball and socket head, this clamp slid over the pick of the ice ax all the way up to the shaft where it could be held in place by a set screw. The set screw had wings on it, so that it could be operated with mittened hands. This piece of equipment converted our ice axes into unipods. With it we could steady our cameras when using long focal-length lenses or when operating in very high winds. The ice-ax clamp unipod was also used in conjunction with the small magazine-type motion picture cameras high on the mountain.

When working primarily with 35-mm film size (24 by 36 mm), it was absolutely essential to get sharp pictures if they were to be enlarged twenty to forty times. We were able to almost eliminate unsharp pictures due to camera movement by using a shutter speed 1/250 second. On Mount Everest we found that with Kodachrome II film, normally there was more than enough light to use this shutter speed.

Standard exposures between Base Camp and the summit were f/8.0 to f/11.0 at 1/250 second for scenes with foreground subject material and f/11.0 to f/22.0 at 1/250 second for general scenics.

In fact there was so much light high on the mountain that there was a tendency to overexpose. We attempted to overcome this problem by taking three exposures of any subject: the exposure we thought to be correct, then one exposure either side of the supposed optimum. After a few weeks on the mountain we became familiar with the light values and used a light meter when confronted with unusual lighting situations.

During the expedition we were able to carry out more photography above 25,000 feet on Mount Everest than any previous climbing party. All our photographic equipment functioned well—both the winterized Nikons and the other nonwinterized equipment. We wore the Nikons around our necks without a case and exposed to the elements and had no freeze-up problem; nor did we have any trouble with film becoming brittle at low temperature and tearing. This, we feel, was partially due to the fact that we were normally working within an ambient air temperature range of 20 degrees to −20 degrees F.

High on the mountain we found that we did not have to keep our cameras inside our sleeping bags at night. The temperature inside the tents was warm enough to permit our leaving them on a piece of down clothing or an insulate pad, but not on the nylon tent floor immediately above the snow.

Condensation on the lenses took place when the cameras were taken back and forth between the cold outdoors with low humidity and the warmer, more humid interior of a tent where snow would forever be melting. If photography was not planned inside the tent, the fogging problem could be eliminated, at least with the winterized Nikons, by leaving them outside in a pack for the night.

Prior to going high on the mountain, such as onto the South Col, I found it extremely helpful to "preflight" the photography I intended to do. Rather than trust my fuzzy thought processes at high altitude, I made lists of those scenes which I wished to photograph, even to the point of noting the elevation at which a certain picture would be taken. The most rudimentary calculations of exposure become oversized mental gymnastics high on the mountain and therefore were determined beforehand in the comfort and comparatively thick air of Base Camp. This system seemed to work quite well.

When I climbed to the summit, I carried two still cameras. Around my neck was an Olympus Pen-S split frame camera which I used en route and which gave surprisingly high-quality results. In my pack was a Nikon reflex with a 35-mm P.C. lens. This was used for all still photography taken on the summit.

Judging from the results, we feel that the approach we took with still photography was a good one and that we were successful also in this aspect of the expedition.

11. CINEMATOGRAPHY

by Norman G. Dyhrenfurth

FOR MANY YEARS the scientist, the educator, the explorer, and the mountaineer have been separated from the theory, practice, and practitioners of professional film making. And yet the men and women in the first group have often wished they could make effective and useful film records, as well as documentary films of professional quality.

One of the most important aims of a good film maker is to tell a story largely in visual terms, rather than in a lecture with a few pictures thrown in haphazardly to accompany his words. If much scientific or other factual information must be transmitted verbally, a good series of slides or film strips will generally serve the purpose much better than a film. We know from experience that audiences cannot absorb spoken words and visual images simultaneously unless they are closely interrelated. Unless the events to be filmed are entirely unforeseen and cannot be restaged, it is always a good idea to plan scenes, sequences, and, if at all possible, the entire picture on paper before beginning photography. In the case of a Himalayan expedition this is obviously not always possible, but the film maker—particularly if he has been on similar expeditions before—should start out with a reasonably accurate concept of what the final film should look like.

With very few exceptions, important scenes should be covered in long shots, medium shots and close-ups. A long shot may include anything from a whole landscape to a group of full-length figures; a medium shot includes figures from the knees or waist up; a close-up, head and shoulders, and even less in the case of an extreme close-up. The camera angle should be changed as the photographer moves in closer. If the camera is kept in one place and its optics changed from wide-angle to long-focus lens, the slightest difference in spatial relationships of objects within the frame, brought about by the time lapse between long shot and close-up, will result in very awkward and annoying mismatchings of action, or "jump-cuts." By changing the angle from one camera position to another, perspectives are changed, and slight discrepancies in spatial relationships will be less noticeable. In addition, all action should—wherever possible—overlap from one angle to another. This will avoid "jump-cuts" and protect the film editor who has to put the scenes together.

If some action takes a long time and cannot be condensed, every possible advantage should be taken of the motion picture's control over the time-space continuum. One might start a sequence with a long shot, followed by a number of different angles which present varying perspectives—including close-ups and extreme close-ups of people and tools or equipment used by them—and finally cut back to a medium or long shot of the last stages of the operation. The result will be an interesting, well-conceived sequence which gives the audience an illusory feeling of having witnessed the entire operation in a very short time. The secret of this type of coverage is the cameraman's or director's understanding of the *principle of significant selection*. The amateur will usually attempt to photograph the whole event from one fixed camera position in order to "get it all on film." Every time the camera's spring motor runs down, he feverishly rewinds it and again pushes the button. The end result is a very dull and incomplete record, with a great many disturbing "jump-cuts" wherever the camera unwound or ran out of film. Reaction shots frequently have greater impact than the action itself and enable the film maker to control the pace and intensity of a given sequence. Another much-used method of shortening action is by means of cut-away shots which may or may not have any direct relationship to the scene at hand. Most expedition films lean rather heavily on this cinematic "crutch," and ours is no exception. Example: Dick Emerson is busily shoveling snow to uncover the power winch. Since this particular activity, if fully recorded on film, would sorely try the viewer's patience, the editor intercuts a shot of our special friend, the gorak. This bird was nowhere near Emerson and his winch at the time, but the illusion created is that of intense interest in Dick's exercise in self-control.

One important characteristic of good film making is the planning and use of effective transitions between sequences (scenes related by time or place). In addition to purely optical devices such as fades and dissolves (gradual darkening or superimposition of scenes, which can be made through optical effects photography or A & B roll printing), there is a great wealth of other bridges of space and time such as ideological, audio, texture to texture, color to color, shape to shape, motion to motion, and simple camera movement transitions. Any of these may be used in straight cuts, or in conjunction with dissolves. A few examples will illustrate this: To get a person from one location to another, he may simply walk toward the camera until the screen is blacked out. The next sequence starts with his back close to the lens, then moving away from the camera, thereby revealing a new location. Or, if a car approaches the camera (as unlikely as this may be in the Western Cwm), one may cut as it fills the screen, pick up the same car at some other place as it again fills the screen, and turn, or "pan," with it to reveal a new background. Another transition frequently used shows a man walking into the frame, looking up at a tall building, tree, or mountain. The camera tilts up into the sky, following his gaze. This cuts to a sky of similar "texture" somewhere else, the camera tilts down and reveals the same man, but in a new location. There are hundreds of similar transitional devices which may help the film maker in getting his characters from one place to another without disturbing the smoothly flowing continuity of his film. A man's feet, train wheels, car wheels, flowing water, telephone wires and power lines, traveling shots through town and countryside, aerial photography—all of these lend themselves to bridging gaps in space and time. Care must be taken, however, not to go overboard on the use of such transitions. They must have a definite purpose; they must be more than mere playthings for the budding film maker. If they are too farfetched and excessively "arty," they will be nothing but pyrotechnics which interfere with the story.

The scientist, however, while granting that considerations of spatial relationships and transitions may be of value to the creative producer of dramatic documentaries and feature pictures, may wonder how it could possibly apply to the factual film record of an anthropological, ethnological, or glaciological expedition. The answer is that the application of such basic principles of good film making will result in an interesting, well-coordinated story-telling film which otherwise might be nothing but an amateurish and boring illustrated lecture. The taking of excessive "cinematic license" which might falsify important scientific information, or, as in the case of a summit climb where no motion picture camera was carried, is in no wise indicated.

Excessive camera movement should be avoided. Nothing is more annoying and tiresome to an audience than to sit through a long succession of jerky, unmotivated pan and tilt shots, scenes in which the camera moves horizontally or vertically on a stationary pivot. There must be some logical motivation for camera movement, such as traveling in a vehicle, following a car, an animal or a human being.

It is difficult to itemize ideal equipment for an expedition, since this depends so largely on budget, desired results, and available manpower. Rather than present a comprehensive listing of every existing piece of motion picture equipment, I shall concentrate on those items used by our Expedition:

1. *Cameras.* One 16-mm Arriflex camera with 6 lenses ranging from 10- to 300-mm, "wild" and synchronous motors, rechargeable nickel-cadmium and heavier dry-cell batteries; two 70 DR Bell & Howell Filmos; one 70 KM Bell & Howell Filmo; three 50-foot magazine-load Bell & Howell Model 200, as "summit" cameras.

During the approach march most of the filming was done with the Arriflex (with 400-foot magazines) and one of the 70 DR's. Although the Arriflex was taken as far as Advance Base (21,350 feet), the 400-foot magazines were left at Base Camp. Due to Dan Doody's illness very little photography was done with the Arriflex. I used a 70 DR camera as high as Camp VI (27,450 feet) on the Southeast Ridge of Everest. In fact, we carried this camera and the small Miller Fluid Head to 28,200 feet but were unable to use it this high due to the severity of the storm and our own physical deterioration. The 50-foot magazine-load cameras, though basically nothing more than amateur cameras for family use, were chosen as "summit" cameras for reasons of size, weight, compactness, and simplicity to load and operate. At extreme altitudes and in strong wind, oxygen-starved men would be unable to thread film through a camera's gate without suffering frost-bite, and the camera would be full of snow in a matter of seconds. These magazine-load cameras performed extremely well in the hands of Barry Corbet, up to an altitude of 27,200 feet on the West Ridge, and of Lute Jerstad all the way up to the summit. All cameras were specially prepared and lubricated with a silicone fluid which guaranteed their operation at temperatures ranging from minus 65 to plus 125. During the 1952 Swiss Mount Everest Expedition, we encountered difficulties with the 50-foot magazines which had a tendency to freeze up after a run of only a few seconds. This time the magazines were specially pre-pared for cold-weather operation by Eastman Kodak in Rochester, and the film itself was "waxed" to prevent static electricity and assure its smooth passage through the gate.

Static electricity markings can ruin the best scenes and are generally caused by friction of the film coming in contact with the cold metal of the camera, particularly when film and camera are of different tempera-tures. It is therefore important to keep both camera and film at the same temperature and to prevent condensation when loading or un-loading. When cameras are brought from the outside cold into a warm tent—something one need not be overly concerned with when camped on the South Col or above—condensation is formed which takes a long time to dry. Lenses and filters may become fogged, while the film be-comes moist and, on drying, will stick together or develop static marks. Condensation on the back element of a lens is particularly hard to detect when using a camera without through-the-lens viewing. Frequent examination of front and rear elements of all lenses is highly recom-mended. There is also the problem of filters cracking or "bleeding" at high altitudes, and several of our #85 Conversion Filters had to be re-placed.

2. *Tripods.* 1 Miller Fluid Head, heavy duty; 1 Arriflex Gyro Head; 1 CECO Fluid Head; 1 Miller Fluid Head, light duty, on Schianski light-weight metal legs; 1 Arriflex baby tripod with friction head; 1 Linhof lightweight panoramic head.

For all-around production work as far as Advance Base (21,350 feet), the heavy-duty Miller Fluid Head proved to be outstanding. The Arriflex Gyro Head, though a fine piece of equipment, did not offer sufficient resistance when panning or tilting. Many scenes requiring slow and even camera movement were ruined by excessive speed. The far greater resistance offered by standard fluid in the Miller Head resulted in uniformly smooth camera movement. The CECO Fluid Head, though previously used by me on Dhaulagiri, cannot compare with the somewhat heavier Miller, and required "breath-holding" to such an extent as to render it impractical at high altitudes. While moving up as part of the first assault team, I used the lightweight Miller Head with a thinner fluid which had been successfully tested in cold chambers at temperatures of 60 degrees below zero. Although not quite as smooth as the heavy-duty Miller, this special high-altitude tripod performed exceedingly well, and panoramic shots taken from Camp VI in a strong wind are remarkably steady and evenly paced. These scenes are undoubtedly the highest ever taken from a professional tripod.

Lute Jerstad was equipped with a lightweight Linhof panoramic head which could be attached to his ice ax by means of a special bracket. The quality of his panorama from the summit of Everest is amazingly good, the more so when one considers the impact of sudden gusts of wind on a severely stressed and exhausted man behind the camera. The mere physical and psychological effort to set up a camera, and to operate it under such extreme conditions on earth's highest pinnacle, is more than most humans could carry out, and Lute's accomplishment is truly remarkable.

3. *Exposure Meters.* 1 Combi-500 incident-light meter, with high and extreme low-range reading capability; 4 Norwood "Director" incident-light meters (in addition to a large number of reflected light meters used by team members for still photography).

For average exposure readings, an incident-light meter is preferable to a reflected-light meter, which presents the amateur with a greater margin for error. If, on the other hand, reflecting surfaces exhibiting an excessive brightness range are to be photographed, reflected-light measurements will be valuable. It must always be remembered that any kind of light meter is nothing but a mechanical device with no brains of its own. It takes a certain amount of interpolation on the photographer's part to analyze and augment the readings given by the exposure meter, depending on the reflecting surfaces of the scene to be photographed, and the desired effect.

To determine correct exposure for scenes to be taken with a telephoto lens such as a 152-mm or 300-mm lens, the abundance of ultraviolet light causes overexposure. UV filters and intentional underexposure (from ⅔ to 1 lens stop in the case of brilliant snow scenes) will bring the desired results. When shooting scenes in a heavy snow storm, reduce exposures as suggested by an incident-light meter by as much as 1½ to 2 stops. To trust your incident meter under such conditions would result in serious overexposure.

4. *Sound Recording Equipment.* 1 Perfectone EP6A synchronous magnetic tape recorder; 1 Stellavox synchronous magnetic tape recorder; 1 collapsible microphone "fishpole" with extension cables; 1 RCA BK5A microphone with windshield and bracket; 2 RCA BK6B microphones; 1 Ryder single-dial Modular Mixer.

While the Perfectone recorder was not carried beyond Base Camp where some "lip-sync" dialogue sequences were shot, the extremely lightweight Stellavox was taken as far as Advance Base. Perfectone operates on regular flashlight batteries, and Stellavox on rechargeable nickel-cadmium batteries; but both recorders were affected by low temperatures to such an extent that sound recording in synchronization with the Arriflex camera was not always practical. A proper warm-up period —in a sleeping bag or by means of butane heat lamp—provides a solution to the problem.

Although I had high hopes of making extensive use of synchronous tape recorders during the Expedition, I regret to say that with very few exceptions they served no other purpose than the recording of my diary. For this, a less expensive and lighter piece of equipment, such as UHER recorders used by other team members which run at speeds slower than 7½ inches per second, would have been preferable. If, on the other hand, it is important to record sound effects, native voices, dialogue, radio conversations, etc., in synchronization with the visual image, the Perfectone and Stellavox will do an excellent job.

5. *Film.*   Close to 28,000 feet of 16-mm Ektachrome Commercial film (in 100-foot and 400-foot rolls, as well as some 50-foot magazines for the "summit" cameras) were exposed. This emulsion is balanced for a color temperature of 3200 degrees Kelvin and, when used with a #85 conversion filter, has a speed rating of ASA 16. No special precautions were taken in shipping the film to and from Nepal. Although *Americans on Everest* will be distributed in 35 mm, we decided against the use of 35-mm Eastman color negative. Negative color films are less stable than Reversal emulsions such as Kodachrome or Ektachrome. Whereas it is possible on a big-budget feature film production to ship exposed negative in refrigerated containers to the laboratory every day, this would obviously be impossible on an expedition to Mount Everest. The latent image would deteriorate rapidly due to subtropical heat and humidity while being carried to Kathmandu by runners. There is also the matter of additional weight and greater cost. The 16-mm Ektachrome Commercial with its greatly improved latitude and gradation can be blown up to 35 mm with very satisfactory results, as evidenced by the quality of Walt Disney's "True Life Adventures."

There are many more problems which a film maker may encounter on Himalayan expeditions, but to mention them all would go far beyond the limits of this discussion. The important thing is to remember the basic tools of the creative film maker and to make use of them to their fullest extent. One must not rely on the sound track alone to tell the story, but make every possible attempt to tell it visually in a smoothly flowing continuity.

12. COMMUNICATIONS

by Allen C. Auten

IN PLANNING COMMUNICATIONS for the expedition, the first step was to decide who had to talk to whom. It soon developed that we actually needed two communications systems: one to talk to the outside world, the other to allow expedition members to talk to each other between camps. We also needed a radio to give us a source of news, plus the Everest area weather forecast from All India Radio. First considerations were size and weight. These were followed closely by performance.

For the Base Camp set used to talk to the outside, several choices were possible. We could keep the equipment very simple and use code transmission, which would have had the advantage of covering long distances with relatively low power. The disadvantage was that only those members of the expedition familiar with code would be able to use the radio. Such an arrangement would have kept the radio officer in Base Camp, so continuous wave (CW) was ruled out as a primary means of communication. CW did remain a desirable feature for possible use in an emergency. Other choices were amplitude modulation (AM) or single-sideband (SSB) radio-telephone communications. This raised a question: the AM transmitters generally are simpler and easier to fix, but, on the other hand, transmission efficiency using SSB is greater

373

and, for a given result, takes less power. The decision finally went to the single-sideband equipment.

The next step was to determine how much primary power was necessary to operate the radio. Most equipment available today can be operated either from a storage battery or commercial power lines. Usually, the power in watts used by the equipment will be nearly the same. Because we would be making all our own power, good equipment efficiency was necessary. The last item considered, but by no means least important, was unit cost. In the end, weighing all the factors, the expedition purchased a KWM-2 transceiver, manufactured by Collins Radio.

The next problem concerned what equipment to use for the inter-camp communications. These were the units that would enable Base to talk to men at camps farther up the mountain. Most of the people using these would have no technical knowledge, so the unit must be nearly foolproof. Most important was performance. Size or weight would not matter if the equipment would not perform after it had been hauled up the mountain. If performance were marginal, it would not be long before the walkie-talkies were left behind.

With the advent of Citizens Band radio, a large number of walkie-talkies became available. In fact, the large number was one of the major problems in selecting equipment. Several points became apparent. Many of the units were being built to a price, were poorly designed, and were housed in flimsy cases which would not stand the rough handling they would receive. Most of these units also operated on dry batteries. This would have required a large number of spares brought in by porters, plus adding the problem of poor battery performance at cold temperatures.

Instead of trying to check all the catalogs, we set down what features were necessary and then attempted to find units to match. We felt our ideal set should use a full superheterodyne receiver circuit, including an RF amplifier and more than one stage of IF amplification. The set should have good automatic volume control characteristics and a squelch circuit which would ungate with very low input signals. The audio output should have enough power to let the set be heard easily above loud surrounding noise. The transmitter should be capable of full modulation with low distortion and should have as much carrier power as possible. At the time equipment was being selected for the expedition, several units were found having transmitters with a 1-watt input—one even had a 5-watt input. The final choice went to the 1-watt Osborne which has low audio distortion in the transmitter and receiver circuits and uses a crystal controlled, dual conversion superheterodyne receiver. One additional piece of equipment arrived late in April, a 27-pound experimental transmitter-receiver built by Hughes Aircraft, the model HC-162, Manpack. This was the set used to call for evacuation of Bishop and Unsoeld. Although we were unable to establish two-way communication, Kathmandu picked up our Manpack transmission and dispatched the helicopter to Namche Bazar.

Our next concern was to provide primary power. At about this time, needs of the scientific programs also entered the picture. The expedition carried a centrifuge for spinning blood samples, a scintillation counter and an EKG machine. These units all needed 110-volt 60-cycle a-c. This power could have been provided directly from an alternator, or converted from 12-volt d-c. System efficiency would be increased if the power were generated as a-c. This approach would have required that the generator be operable any time the equipment was in use. Therefore, we sacrificed some efficiency for a greater margin of safety. The generator selected provided 12-volt d-c with a sea level rating of 300 watts (about 150 watts in Base Camp). The output charged a nickel-cadmium storage battery rated at 20 ampere-hours. The scientific equipment, in turn, was operated from a 12-volt d-c to 110-volt 60-cycle a-c inverter. The KWM-2 transceiver was supplied with a 12-volt d-c mobile-type power supply working directly from the battery. The same type of power supply was used for the walkie-talkie Base set. By using the storage battery, the expedition would be able to maintain communications for a time in case the generator did break down. This happened, in fact, on the return march to Kathmandu. A radio schedule had been set up, but when the time came, the gasoline for the generator was missing. The schedule was held, using only storage-battery power. And by talking fast, we did get our messages through.

The expedition also had two "Tiny Tiger" generators. These were rated at 120-volt a-c, 300 watts, and could be carried in one hand. At our high elevation, the air-stream-operated governor allowed an output closer to 160 volts. Despite this, a "Tiny Tiger" was used to operate the centrifuge. Because of the high elevation, the "Tiny Tiger" had been supplied with a special fuel containing a large quantity of castor oil for lubrication. Unfortunately, the oil congealed at night. This made it necessary to flush the carburetor at the end of each run to make restarting possible.

A major concern of the communications officer is to obtain the necessary licenses or permits for the use of transmitting equipment in a foreign country. Perhaps the most direct approach is to get help through United States Embassies or Consulates located in the countries concerned. Obtaining the necessary permits is perhaps the most important single piece of business and should be regarded as a number one priority problem.

After arrival in Kathmandu, introductions were arranged with the two American amateur operators living in Nepal: Lt. Col. William Gresham, military attaché to the United States Embassy, and Father Marshall D. Moran, S.J., a longtime Kathmandu resident.* Tentative schedules were set up with them and frequencies agreed upon. Our license request had asked for use of the 20-meter amateur band and the frequency used by the Nepal Net (7010 kc).†

Use of the 27 mcs intercamp walkie-talkie circuit began informally. After reaching the Khumbu Valley, expedition members made some short side trips, climbing several of the nearby pinnacles. Walkie-talkies were taken along and schedules agreed upon at the last moment. After Base Camp was set up, schedules for the walkie-talkie circuit simply evolved. The usual times were eight in the morning and six in the evening, though this was flexible, depending on the needs of any given day. The receiver in Base Camp was left turned on throughout the day so that a call from one of the higher camps could be taken at any time. This Base Camp set also had a voice-operated recorder connected to it so that all conversations on the walkie-talkie circuit were preserved. This was part of the sociological program, but was also a useful reference when long lists of the equipment needed at upper camps began to come through.

Operation of the equipment was good. The single-sideband transceiver performed well throughout the entire expedition. The walkie-talkies provided Base Camp with probably 80 per cent communication. The chief shortcoming seemed to be battery life. Eleven walkie-talkies

---

* The expedition is greatly indebted to the unfailing help given us by these two men.

† The frequencies used in the United States for the 40-meter amateur band are reserved for shortwave broadcast in the Far East.

were in use, but during a moment of false economy, only twenty rechargeable batteries were purchased. This meant that all batteries were either in use or being recharged. This gave us no charged spares in the higher camps which could be put into use when a set's batteries began to run low. For future expeditions, a minimum of three batteries per set would seem reasonable.

Spare parts and tools were also taken. A complete set of tubes was included for the KWM-2 and a set of parts for the walkie-talkies, plus their Base set. In addition, we took a small carbon resistor kit, a 5-watt wire-wound resistor kit and a selection of electrolytic capacitors. Also included were some disc ceramic capacitors and a box of assorted hardware. None of the spare parts actually were needed, though it was a great comfort to have them with us. Among the hand tools was a small electric soldering iron, a 1-pound roll of solder, and a large pair of parallel-jaw, slip-joint pliers, which proved useful for getting the lids off the 5-gallon gasoline cans.

Fuel has been mentioned briefly in connection with the "Tiny Tiger." Fuel for the main generator turned out to be a major problem. The generator's engine was designed for operation on 90-octane regular gasoline. In East India, "regular" gasoline is closer to 70-octane. The expedition purchased 70-octane regular and 120-octane aviation gas in a ratio of three to one. The gasoline was supplied in 2-gallon (Imperial) cans. Unfortunately, most of these gas cans leaked. This made it necessary to transfer the fuel to surplus 5-gallon jerry cans. These cans were purchased locally and had evidently been stored outside since the end of World War II. Future parties should plan on taking the new lightweight plastic 5-gallon cans from the United States. The cost will be no more and the fuel will not be contaminated. A tube of "Permatex" gasoline-proof gasket sealer would also have helped seal the fuel cans.

The communications equipment was carried to the mountain in the boxes used for shipping it overseas. In retrospect, we would have done better to have set up an operating station in one of the expedition foot lockers. This would have given us one box to unpack for the station, another for the power supply, and a third for the antenna and its associated parts. As it was, all the communication boxes (seven in all) had to be opened every time to assemble the various bits and pieces. A spray can of day-glow paint was taken along and used to mark the boxes. On the few occasions during the approach when equipment was needed hurriedly, this was a great help in locating the necessary cartons from the tremendous piles of expedition gear. Unfortunately, several others had the same idea. For this reason, several colors should be taken so that after enough people have borrowed your paint, you can switch colors and continue to identify your own boxes.

After the expedition, it is easy to look back and see how things might have been done differently. As it worked out, the communications plan was effective and greatly simplified the logistics problem present in any undertaking of this size.

13. *PHYSIOLOGY*

by William E. Siri, Ph.D.

THE BODY is a remarkably well-regulated assembly of biological machinery. Under ordinary conditions it looks after the proper balance of its internal affairs with a precision and reliability that any automation engineer could envy. Within limits, it also actively accommodates itself to circumstances somewhat removed from the ordinary, among them cold, heat, altitude, exercise, and disease. Man probably has been aware of these elementary facts from the time he first evolved human insight, but physiological regulation under normal and abnormal conditions still remains a compelling subject for scientific research. For the most part only the effects have been described, while much of the underlying mechanism remains obscure.

Men engaged in climbing the highest mountains are in some respects unique subjects for research on the body's regulatory mechanisms. Driven by intense motivation, climbers subject themselves for extended intervals to submarginal environmental conditions that would not be tolerated in a contrived laboratory setting. Prolonged exposure to severe hypoxia (oxygen deficiency) combined with fatigue, cold, insomnia, diminished appetite, and psychogenic factors must ultimately lead to progressive deterioration when physiological reserves for adjustment are exhausted and

379

the crucial balances in the body's functions and chemistry can no longer be maintained. These conditions may evoke responses in our regulatory machinery that are ordinarily inaccessible to study.

The studies on Mt. Everest were designed to examine the responses of two of the body's vital components that participate in adjustment to stressful conditions. The first involved the production of red blood cells, which is greatly stimulated by the hypoxia of altitude. The second part of the study dealt with response of the adrenal gland and its many control hormones that help regulate the body's functions, metabolic processes, and chemical balances.

Before the expedition took to the field, two laboratory studies were needed to give meaning to observations made on the climbers during the ascent of Mt. Everest. In one test, normal values of physiological parameters were determined for each member of the team at sea level. Without these "base line" values, data gathered at high altitudes would have no points of reference and therefore little meaning. These measurements were made at the Donner Laboratory, University of California, a month before departure.

The second test was more elaborate and somewhat different in nature. It was designed to examine the responses evoked by sudden exposure to an altitude comparable to that of Base Camp on Mt. Everest. Later, these responses could be compared with those occurring in the slow ascent during the three-week journey from Kathmandu to Base Camp. For this comparative test, a member of the expedition was rapidly taken to 17,000 feet in the Donner Laboratory high-altitude chamber and kept at this altitude for four days. Before, during and after his incarceration in the chamber, his reactions were continually assessed by physiological and biochemical tests and by clinical observations. The responses to sudden exposure to altitude are far more dramatic during the first few days than those encountered in climbing high peaks, even when the peak is Mt. Everest.

Among physiological responses to high altitude, the "thickening" of blood is probably one of the most familiar. This thickening is due solely to an increase in the number of red blood cells (erythrocytes); the plasma volume does not change appreciably. In the healthy person at sea level about 0.8 per cent of the red cells are replaced per day. New cells formed in the bone marrow are balanced by removal of old red cells from the circulation. Thus, nearly a constant and "normal" total volume of about 35 milliliters of red cells per kilogram of lean body weight is maintained. Ordinarily, red cells make up 40 to 50 per cent of the blood volume, and hemoglobin, the red pigment that carries oxygen, amounts to 14 to 16 grams per 100 milliliters of blood.

Under the stimulus of hypoxia, red cell production increases. Precisely how this happens is still obscure except that it is known to be mediated by an elusive hormone called erythropoietin. The amount of erythropoietin normally circulating in the blood and excreted in the urine, even at moderately high altitudes, is too small to be detected by the relatively insensitive assay methods available. However, the hormone is sometimes found in high concentrations in persons with very severe anemia, and it is readily detected in laboratory animals during the first two or three days they are exposed to high altitude. A similar response was demonstrated in the expedition member who was acutely exposed to 17,000 feet in the high-altitude chamber. It is perhaps significant that erythropoietin level and the severe symptoms of altitude sickness subsided together after three days at altitude.

On Mt. Everest there was no expectation of finding erythropoietin in men acclimatized to the elevation of Base Camp (17,800 feet). Climbers who ascended from Base Camp to 23,000 feet within a few days seemed the most promising candidates for demonstrating an acute response, such as that seen in the chamber test. Moreover, to see if erythropoietin ever remains consistently elevated, climbers who spent extended intervals at 21,400 feet and 23,000 feet were also tested. For the climbers the procedure was simple; they merely collected urine in a bottle for a day. When the bottles were returned to Base Camp, the urine was passed through special filters to concentrate the hormone for later assay in the laboratory.

Research conducted in a tent is never so impersonal as it frequently is in the laboratory. In some respects this was regrettable. The special filters for processing the urine would tolerate neither drying nor freezing. Storing them in quart bottles of water solved the former problem, but more heroic measures were needed for the latter. Sharing a sleeping bag every night with three or four hard, cold, and sometimes damp bottles seemed at times an inordinate sacrifice in the name of science.

Negative results are always anticlimactic even when they are meaningful. This was the case for erythropoietin. None of the climbers who were tested had produced measurable quantities of the hormone. In contrast, the subject in the pre-expedition chamber test produced a high concentration of erythropoietin at only 17,000 feet, but he did this only when symptoms of hypoxia were extremely severe. Such symptoms were never as severe on Mt. Everest as those experienced in the chamber. For reasons that are still not entirely clear, climbers never experienced the same degree of distress—even without oxygen near the summit of Mt. Everest—that they would have suffered had they been brought suddenly to Base Camp from sea level.

Although erythropoietin evaded detection, it was unquestionably there in greater than normal concentration prodding the bone marrow into ever greater production of red cells with increasing altitude. Fortunately the production rate could be measured with somewhat greater confidence than the stimulating hormone. Iron is the key element in hemoglobin, the red oxygen-carrying pigment that forms 60 per cent of the red cell. When more red cells are manufactured, correspondingly more hemoglobin is synthesized and more iron utilized. It is a long but reasonably direct chain of events from iron to circulating red cell; hence, if the rate of use of iron is measured, as it can be with radioactive iron, the production of red cells can be estimated. In principle the method is simple; the subject's own plasma is mixed with radioactive iron, injected back into his veins, and then blood samples are taken at intervals for several hours to determine how rapidly the radioactivity is removed from the plasma to form new hemoglobin. With a portable counter generously provided by Nuclear-Chicago Corporation, measuring radioactivity on the slopes of Mt. Everest was no more difficult than making a pot of tea.

This was never a popular test, and the ready willingness of team members to cooperate was gratifying. The victim spent the better part of a day confined to camp with a 4-inch long needle with a stopcock set in a vein in his arm, much the same as a spigot in a cask. With all its complications and discomforts—when done in a small tent on snow—the experiment was highly informative. It showed that at 17,800 feet man produces red cells nearly twice as fast as at sea level, and at 21,400 feet his production rate is 2.5 to 3 times as fast. It also showed that the total volume of red cells had nearly doubled and that the plasma volume had not changed.

Conventional blood tests, unlike that with radioactive iron, could be made repeatedly to follow the changes in red cell concentration as the team progressed to higher altitudes. Hemoglobin, for example, followed roughly the gross pattern of increasing altitude but with a two-week delay. However it never exceeded 24 grams per cent (normal: 14 to 16). The moment the Expedition left Base Camp on the return march, the response was immediate. Hemoglobin concentration dropped precipitously. The body simply stopped producing red cells when informed by the drop in altitude that we were returning to Kathmandu—where iron in the blood is needed less than cast iron in the stomach.

The adrenal glands are two small flattened bodies perched, one each, atop the kidneys. The inner portion (medulla) of these bits of tissue secrete adrenalin, the "panic" hormone that gives us a momentary boost when suddenly confronted with danger. However, it was the outer layer, the cortex of the adrenal gland, and more particularly its multitude of hormones that commanded the attention of the physiological studies. Among the many hormones secreted by the adrenal cortex, one of the most important is the familiar substance hydrocortisone.

The importance of the adrenal cortex as a regulatory organ is firmly established. The cortical secretions, some of which are controlled by ACTH from the pituitary gland, exercise a controlling influence over the body's chemistry, the heart, and the circulatory and respiratory systems. In response to such challenges as disease, injury, environment, or psychogenic factors that tend to disturb the body's normal physiological balances, it is the adrenal cortex that acts to restore equilibrium. Until the balance is restored, according to one widely held view, a state of stress exists that manifests itself in physiological, chemical, and psychological changes that may be profound. Physiological reserves that can be called upon to meet a challenge may seem large but they are not unlimited. If the demand continues beyond the capacity to adjust, deterioration and ultimately death ensue. The extreme conditions encountered in Himalayan climbing made it reasonable to assume that Mt. Everest would induce in her assailants an advanced state of stress and thus provide the rare opportunity to observe how and to what extent the adrenal cortex copes with such problems.

The cortical hormones are excreted, some in slightly modified form, in the urine, making their collection easy for the investigator and painless for the subject. Once more, as in the search for erythropoietin, the quest for urine was pursued over the faces and ridges of Mt. Everest. The Sherpas could well understand our using bottles in camp at night, but carrying the bottle while climbing perplexed them, and carrying the full bottles back to Base Camp was beyond all comprehension. Twenty-four hour collections were obtained under a variety of circumstances, all of them, we felt, involving stressful conditions. At the end of the first day's collection the climber received an injection of ACTH to stimulate his adrenal glands to maximum output of certain members of the hormone group, among them hydrocortisone. The second day's urine collection would then reveal his adrenocortical reserve. Such collections were obtained from nearly all the summit climbers, their support teams, and from men living at 21,400 feet and 23,000 feet for prolonged intervals. Before we disclose what was found in this accumulation of fluids, a few observations on some of the collateral tests are needed.

Basal pulse rate and resting blood pressure increased as expected almost immediately as the Expedition moved to higher elevations on the approach march, and they remained higher than normal for several weeks after arriving at Base Camp. But as acclimatization progressed, pulse and pressure slowly returned to the values they had had at sea level. The pulse or the systolic pressure, or both, for some climbers ultimately dropped below their normal values although diastolic pressures always remained higher than normal.

The response of the heart and circulation to moderate exercise was tested by observing the rise and recovery in both pulse and blood pressure following a three-minute step test. The general character of the recovery pattern did not seem to change much during the course of the expedition, although there were exceptions. However, the rise in pulse and pressure produced by the exercise changed progressively with acclimatization. In the first week at altitude, when symptoms of hypoxia were most evident, the responses were greater than at sea level. During the two months that followed, the pulse and pressure responses to the exercise decreased steadily until they were decidedly smaller than they had been in the pre-expedition test. The cardiovascular system had obviously made important adjustments to meet the challenge of hypoxia.

Most members of the team felt their capacity for heavy work was significantly reduced by the time Base Camp was abandoned. Subjective observations of this kind often contain a large measure of truth, but they are always difficult to assess; they are compounded of many unweighable factors and subject to no small measure of unintentional self-deception. We can only report the existence of this effect as a conviction, although there is indirect support for it.

Climbers around the world are acutely conscious of the need to maintain fluid balance because of the debilitation and hazards that accompany dehydration. The American Expedition subscribed to the rule followed by the British Mt. Everest Expedition in 1953 at the urging of Dr. L. G. C. Pugh—that each man must have 5 to 7 pints of fluid per day. The rule was practiced as well as preached because there were few signs of chronic dehydration. The inevitable exceptions were acute in nature, involving primarily the summit climbers who had no practicable means of securing fluids during the twelve to twenty hours they were above the highest camps when fluid loss, unfortunately, was greatest and most critical.

Nutrition has received, if anything, more emphasis than proper hydration, but it is far more difficult to manage in practice. The principles are clear enough, but they cannot resolve the practical problems of logistics, limited acceptability of highly processed foods, appetites that both diminish and become more selective with increasing altitude, and perhaps certain insidious effects of hypoxia about which little is known. With more than sufficient experience in semi-starvation on previous expeditions, and no desire to repeat it, we were determined to have ample quantities of food, particularly foods high in protein, and in such limitless variety that even the most jaded appetite could not help but find something appealing. The result was without doubt the most elaborate menu ever offered on Mt. Everest.

In spite of a varied and well-stocked larder, weight loss during the expedition followed a familiar pattern. The 10 to 15 pounds everyone lost on the approach march could well be spared. Exact measurements of fat, water and protein made on members of the team in the pre-expedition laboratory tests showed that fat constituted one-eighth to more than one-quarter of their weights. Weights stabilized before Base Camp was reached and for a week after arrival, but when men moved to higher camps weight loss once again resumed its persistent course. Much of the weight loss during the ascent was unquestionably fat, the loss of which would do relatively little harm, but convincing signs of muscle wasting became evident even before fat reserves were exhausted. The debilitating effects of lean tissue wasting on health and physical performance are well known. It would not seem the best condition in which to enjoy a climb of Mt. Everest.

It is now evident that in the operations above Base Camp everyone suffered for want of protein as well as total calories. Depressed appetites, the ever present difficulties of preparing foods, and occasional food shortages could perhaps explain the weight losses without further inquiry. However, two additional factors may be far more important than we have heretofore realized. Monotony of diet for one can have devastating results, particularly under stressful conditions. Highly processed, concentrated foods seem to have this quality built into them. With continued use processed protein foods, especially meat products and concentrates, seem to lose much of whatever acceptability they may have had at the outset. This is less true of some fats and carbohydrates, butter and sugar, for example. In contrast, unprocessed foods of almost any description, old tough goat, eggs of doubtful vintage, and local potatoes were always consumed with keen appetites. Perhaps it was only the contrast and change that stimulated appetites, but it is also possible that under hypoxic conditions low acceptability of highly processed foods could contribute significantly to the weight loss and debilitation suffered by most high-altitude expeditions.

There remains a second facet of nutrition at high altitude about which little is known. This concerns the absorption and utilization of food we do manage to consume. If hydrolysis of fats and proteins in the gastrointestinal tract is impaired, or if absorption of digested food in the intestine is impeded, then one could starve in the midst of plenty. Malabsorption or faulty metabolism could be a more insidious factor with greater and more persistent influence on health and performance than depressed appetite and fussy preferences in food. Even forced feeding, as conscientiously practiced by Hornbein and Unsoeld, would then be of little avail.

Evidence to support this contention, admittedly, is both meager and contestable. It consists for the most part of nonspecific signs and symptoms such as the steadily declining weights even when food consumption seemed adequate; the distressingly large quantities of gas in the gastrointestinal tract soon after eating, suggesting faulty digestion; and bulky, perhaps abnormal stools daily, even during protracted periods of inactivity. There can be little doubt but that everyone on the expedition suffered from undernutrition, and it is likely that those who spent much time above Base Camp were also subjected to malnutrition. Nothing in the data collected on Mt. Everest, however, makes it clear which of the factors discussed above is mainly responsible; probably all are involved to some extent.

If for no other reason than the appalling environment at high altitudes, one would expect in men climbing Mt. Everest an advanced state of stress that all but exhausted their physiological resources. The feeling of chronic exhaustion, the slow and painful effort to perform even the smallest task at high altitude would seem to attest to this. Certainly the appearance of the summit climbers on their return would suggest it. Moreover, there is a widespread conviction among authorities on the subject that the limiting altitude to which man can acclimatize lies somewhere between 20,000 and 22,000 feet. Beyond this he deteriorates progressively faster with altitude. No one would argue that without oxygen life expectancy at 29,000 feet could be anything but short.

Yet the pages of physiological data from the Expedition seem to form a picture somewhat different from the one we had anticipated. We have looked through the test data in vain for unequivocal evidence of physiological stress that could be called severe, or for most of the climbers, even moderate. Certain of the white blood cells that often signal the existence of stress are unchanged; the cardiovascular responses to exercises are much the same as for team members who remained at the lowest camps, and all show good acclimatization; and the key electrolytes, sodium, potassium, and chloride, in blood and urine are all within the normal range. Finally, and most damaging to preconceived ideas, the adrenal cortex seems little disturbed by the experiences on Mt. Everest. The assays of the adrenocortical hormones are incomplete at the time this is written but the data at hand show little that is abnormal in the excretion rates of the hormones. The adrenal cortex also responds in a normal healthy manner to ACTH. Exceptions and differences exist, but no one is near the brink of physiological disaster.

Conclusions drawn before the results of a study are fully assessed are extremely hazardous and rarely offered. If compelled however to voice at least an impression that at this point seems to sum up the observations, it would have to be this: the climbers were physically debilitated by the time they left Mt. Everest, but they exhibited few signs of extreme physiological stress. The expedition, probably like those before it, seems to have been the victim mainly of semi-starvation, and we do not know why.

A final note is added here on a subject that was not part of the physiological studies but is nevertheless relevant to this expedition and perhaps all others with 8000-meter-peak aspirations. The possibility that the central nervous system, particularly the higher brain centers may be damaged by exposure to extreme altitudes is frequently discussed, occasionally debated, but rarely if ever brought under scientific scrutiny. Throughout the history of Himalayan climbing there is from time to time suggestive evidence of brain damage, in some instances perhaps permanent, in climbers exposed to altitudes greater than 8000 (26,250 feet) meters without oxygen. The effects are said to be expressed as impaired memory and personality changes, particularly chronic depression.

The six climbers of the American Expedition who reached the summit of Mt. Everest spent intervals ranging from four to twelve hours without oxygen above 28,000 feet, and four exhausted their oxygen on the summit. All told, eleven men, excluding Sherpas, climbed higher than 27,000 feet. Everyone appeared to experience acute psychic effects of hypoxia at the time, but once the expedition left the mountain no apparent evidence of brain damage could be seen from casual observation. During the months that followed, however, many members of the expedition have reported subjective signs of memory impairment, and some have experienced periods of depression. A variety of other, less well-defined symptoms have also been described. In one respect their reports are identical: they have frequent difficulty in recalling once familiar names, and a need now to search out words that formerly were often and easily used.

On the basis of these subjective impressions it is not possible to assess the nature, extent and duration of cerebral injury, or even to assert unequivocably that it exists. If the evidence in climbers is less than overwhelming, there is still reason to believe brain damage is possible, even probable, at extreme altitude if for no other reason than the well-known intolerance the brain has for anoxia. One conclusion is incontestable: the subject needs more study and less conjecture. It is one that future expeditions might well pursue in the interest of the welfare of high-altitude climbers.

As every scientist knows, it takes funds as well as effort to do research. Or to paraphrase a quotation from "Rum Doodle" often used on the expedition, "Gathering data is one thing, supporting it is quite another." For the task of gathering physiological data, support was gratefully received from the U.S. Atomic Energy Commission through the Donner Laboratory, University of California, and as research grants from the National Science Foundation, the U.S. Air Force Office of Scientific Research, and the National Aeronautics and Space Administration.

14. *PSYCHOLOGY*

by James T. Lester, Jr., Ph.D.

I MET Norman Dyhrenfurth in April of 1961, at the home of a mutual friend. When he began to talk about his plans and hopes for getting an American team to Everest, I was taken by his enthusiasm and conviction and realized that he was in some ways a different sort of person from most that I had known. The more I considered the kinds of things which might be investigated on the climb, the more convinced I became that there really was a chance of contributing something worthwhile to the results of the expedition as well as a chance of sharing in the experience. Not long after our first meeting Norman and I had agreed that I should join the expedition, provided we could raise the necessary funds—which were then estimated at $10,000 per team member. The only way such a sum could be raised for my participation would be from a research grant.

The first thing I had to do if I were to obtain a grant was to write to a number of psychologists in other parts of the country to find out whether any of them was engaged in similar work, whether I'd be duplicating anyone else's research. Progress was slow at first, principally because I was busy as head of the Psychology Department at Orthopaedic Hospital in Los Angeles and was also developing a private prac-

390

tice in the evenings. But gradually the correspondence piled up, I learned of many books and articles bearing on my proposed research, and, most importantly, I received considerable encouragement. In early 1962 I felt I had a workable notion of what could be done, and how to go about doing it, and submitted a proposal through AMEE to the Office of Naval Research. Their acceptance of the proposal made it possible for me to become a member of the expedition.

The idea of the United States Navy's invading the Himalaya sounds incongruous. The basis for the Navy's interest was not, of course, the mountain environment as such, but simply the hardship conditions under which the team members would be living for a fairly lengthy period of time, conditions similar to those endured by a group of men isolated at an Arctic post, and not dissimilar to those experienced by a crew of a long-submerged atomic submarine or astronauts on a space voyage. From the point of view of psychological science, the great appeal of the American Mount Everest Expedition was that it would be a real-life rather than a laboratory situation in which men would be under considerable stress for a prolonged period, during which something might be learned about the effects of stress on the behavior of these men.

Some of the first questions that came to mind were: Do some men, or types of men, hold up better under stress than others? Do some men experience less of a feeling of stress than do others? How much might a man's behavior be expected to change when the environment is changed so drastically? Can men who are going to experience, or create, difficulty be spotted *before* the trip by means of interviews and psychological tests?

As I write this, the expedition is only recently over, and the final stage of the study—the organizing and analyzing of the results into conclusions—has yet to be carried out. However, I can describe the methods used to obtain my fundamental observations, on which all conclusions will later be based.

First, in order to judge how predictable behavior might be during the climb, it was necessary to assess the personalities of the climbers before they left the United States. This was accomplished in an intensive three-day period at the University of California's Institute of Personality Assessment and Research, in Berkeley. During these three days (which some of the team approached with eagerness and others with considerable misgiving) the climbers were subjected to an almost un-interrupted series of techniques: paper and pencil tests; personality questionnaires; ink-blot tests designed to reveal aspects of a person's subconscious; interviews concerning their life histories and their interest in climbing; a group technique designed to indicate the tendency to be influenced by group opinion when it is in conflict with one's own; experimental tests of perception, of interest, of values; and group dis-cussions which were observed and rated by teams of psychologists. The point of these tests was to gather as much information as possible about the ways in which the men differed from one another psychologically, so that later differences in behavior on the mountain might be more meaningful. A by-product of this body of information will be its use in comparative studies with other groups who have been studied similarly at the Institute, such as Air Force officers, scientists, artists, and writers.

While the team was actually in the field, I was busy collecting four kinds of information. (1) Each man was regularly asked to rate all his fellow team members, with regard to how much he liked them at the time of the rating. He was also asked to make guesses about how each of the *other* men was rating *him*. Perhaps the most complex rating I requested was one in which the climber made guesses as to how certain other team members were rating the members of the group. As a final item in this category, each man several times checked a group of adjec-tives, out of a long list, which seemed to him to best describe each of the other men. With all these data, I hope to have obtained a basis for understanding the kind of feelings and attitudes present among the group and how these changed as the climb progressed.

(2) At irregular intervals I made a point of spending time alone with each man, interviewing him about his mood, his feelings about the progress of the climb, his attitudes toward himself and other team members, and the topics uppermost in his mind at the time. With this information I was in a better position to understand the ratings made by the man and to assess personally the degree of stress he might be experiencing and his particular way of coping with it.

Some men were eager to discuss their personal reactions with me and in many instances came to *me* for talks; while others, perhaps less interested, or more cautious, found the appearance of my face at their tent opening the occasion for a sour grimace. Everyone, however, was most cooperative in accepting my activities as an integral part of the expedition.

(3) I made informal observations of events taking place, of situations arising among team members, of remarks made around camps or during a day's hike, which seemed to me to add to my information about differences among the men.

(4) I collected as many of the dreams that occurred, during the approach march and through the summit attempts, as the men could recall. Dreams are the way in which we think when we are in the altered state of mind known as sleep, and the thoughts that come at that time are often more revealing of our mood, our preoccupations, or the general drift of our feelings than are our conscious waking thoughts. Hence my interest in them. It was more difficult to sustain my interest when I discovered that the only way I could get the dreams was to approach the men first thing in the morning, while they were eating what we often laughingly called breakfast. I suspect a good part of the 40 pounds I lost was due to missing the morning meal.

The first of three things that remain to be done is to turn the four kinds of basic data listed above, which are rich and varied but somewhat disorganized, into a coherent set of descriptions of the events during the climb that were of special interest to psychology. Guesses as to the meaning and implications of various things that took place will have to be made; individuals will have to be rated on certain dimensions, summaries prepared of personality characteristics reflected in behavior during the climb, judgments made concerning the nature of, and changes in, relationships within the group. The talents and cooperation of other psychologists will be called upon in an effort to achieve greater objectivity. Raw data from the field observations will be presented to them, on the basis of which they will be asked to make inferences, judgments, ratings, comparisons, and the like. Out of these will come the descriptions on which final conclusions will actually be based.

The second remaining task is to score, tabulate, compare with norms for different groups, and otherwise analyze the information about personality differences gathered at IPAR. This set of scores will then be related to the descriptions of events on the climb.

The final task will be to assess the overall effect of the experience on the team members. I know that being part of the team has had a significant influence on the course of my own affairs, and I suspect that I am not alone in this. I will be following the lives of this exceptional group for some time, hoping to study some of the long-range effects of their experience.

The inevitable question arises: Why *do* men climb mountains? In response to the question asked seriously, I can only reply that the question was not really a central one in my study and that in any case until the data analysis is carried out I will be unable to say anything about it with conviction.

But the question is not too often asked seriously; it is more often asked as a way of asserting something; namely, that mountain climbing is foolish, or perhaps mad. This assertion can be a starting point for intriguing reflections, and I would like to mention a few of my own. (1) the range of motives for climbing mountains probably varies between healthy and unhealthy in about the same way as do motives for any other action; the activity itself is not the criterion for judging the possible "madness" involved. Another way to put this is: there are as many reasons for *not* climbing mountains as there are for *doing* so, some of which are healthier than others. (2) We all recognize that in order to climb a significant mountain one has to be dedicated to and absorbed in the job; otherwise the energy simply will not be there. Often in thinking about the W*hy* question, I wonder if the assertion behind the question isn't really this, at least in part: It's wrong to devote so much energy to any one thing—play it safe, don't put all your eggs in one basket, etc. Following this line of sheer speculation (not about *why* men climb but about the *question* why they do), I sometimes feel that the amazement many of us feel in contemplating mountains and their climbers has its roots in an enfeebled ability to devote oneself to, to become absorbed in, an activity—in a word, to enjoy living with responsive vitality.

What I am trying to say is not that climbing insures a greater enjoyment of life, for climbers seem to have as much difficulty with that as any of us, but rather that many of the psychological qualities characterizing the man climbing a difficult mountain are qualities that could greatly enrich anyone's daily life. The strong interest so many people seem to have in such energetic and adventurous enterprises strikes me as a rather poignant longing for these qualities; and the rejection of climbing so often found in the *Why* question seems very likely to come from a sense of futility about achieving them. How sad!

Henceforth, by the way, I intend to try to achieve them in my own life without going any higher than is required to get in some decent skiing—say, ten thousand feet!

15. *SOCIOLOGY*

by Richard M. Emerson, Ph.D.

IN BOTH MOUNTAINEERING AND SCIENTIFIC CIRCLES there is mixed opinion about the advisability of combining research and climbing on major expeditions. Some climbers feel very strongly that "research" encumbers their mountaineering enterprise. Many scientists doubt that valid and meaningful studies can be carried out in the midst of high-altitude climbing. Through both of these objections may run a note of cynicism. Since "science" can help to justify the trip, provide some of the financing, etc., there lurks the suspicion that it might not be pursued for its own sake.

Yet, despite such objections, research of some type has become almost a conventional part of large expeditions. Why? The cynic may have part of the answer in some of the cases, but two facts remain. First, climbers include a remarkably large number of scientists of one kind or another. And second, large expeditions of this type do, in fact, offer numerous opportunities for important research.

Research on expeditions can be divided into two classes. Most common are studies of the unusual environment encountered, including geology, geography and cartography, botany, climatology, radiation, etc. These studies frequently have no inherent connection with the climbing process. They may add equipment to, and draw manpower from, the climbing enterprise. The second (and less common) class of study is that of *human performance* under extreme environmental conditions. With the exception of studies in physiology, this area has been almost entirely neglected by mountaineering expeditions. It is in this area that research must of necessity be intimately wed to actual climbing.

We made a number of resolutions very early in our planning: (1) mountaineering success would be the uncompromised objective; (2) we would explore research opportunities previously overlooked; and (3) we would design our studies and weave our methods into the fabric of climbing routine, thus minimizing dislocations in the mountaineering process. Most important, our research programs were so conceived that their success depended upon a vigorous and unencumbered assault on the mountain. The mountaineering program *was* carried forward to notable success. Thus, point (3) was accomplished as well. While our research activities were often a nuisance or inconvenience to team members, they did not seriously interfere with the climb.

My study, along with Jim Lester's program, represents the first major excursion into psychological and social-psychological research on a mountaineering expedition. It is well to remind ourselves, however, that meaningful research is an attempt to unravel principles which have broad application. Thus, we do not ask, "Why do men devote so much energy to climbing Mount Everest?" The general, and more important, question is, "What governs the amount of energy men will mobilize to accomplish an objective?" Therefore the researcher is interested in Mount Everest only as an extreme case in point: the Everest research was worthy of support* because it had a bearing upon human endurance.

No climber will be surprised when a psychologist states that if the achievement of a goal is uncertain, enthusiasm for that goal is increased. Climbers generally do not select peaks that are either very easy or clearly out of reach. Such is the nature of aspiration. We are concerned here with that aspect of man which seeks and responds to challenge. The essence of challenge is also the tendency to explore. For in attempting to scale Everest's West Ridge, the object was not so much to "conquer" the mountain by reaching the top (the Col route was

* The expedition would like to acknowledge the full support of The National Science Foundation in making this study possible.

better suited to this purpose), rather, it was to explore, to find out, to resolve uncertainty.

We were interested in studying the motivating power of "uncertainty" and the social and psychological processes which produce and prolong it.

Uncertainty about the outcome of an endeavor is a mental state midway between certainty of success and certainty of failure. Such mental states are a result of (1) the information which a person has available to him pertaining to eventual success or failure, and (2) the way his mind receives and organizes that information. When these two factors leave the person in doubt about the outcome of an effort, he will funnel maximum energy into the effort. If he becomes either very pessimistic *or* very optimistic, his devotion to the task will diminish. Thus, information, and its organization in the human mind, becomes an important topic to study if we are to understand the sources of prolonged human effort.

In any group endeavor, a member receives information about eventual success or failure from two sources: from the environment in which the group is working and from his fellow group members. One part of this study is focused upon communication and its effect upon optimism-uncertainty-pessimism and, hence, team effort. The central question was: What information will a communicator select and transmit to fellow group members? Will it be optimistic or pessimistic in import, and under what conditions? Our theory suggested that when group members are not suffering undue stress: (1) they will communicate largely optimistic information when the environment provides largely pessimistic conditions, and pessimistic information when the conditions seem predominantly favorable; (2) if a member shows signs of optimism (or pessimism), he will receive pessimistic (or optimistic) information from fellow team members.

If these theoretical hunches are correct, their result should be maximum and prolonged uncertainty throughout the group. Communication offsets environmental information which might otherwise have led to premature pessimism or optimism (individual and collective). At the same time, communication promotes maximum team effort. For example, on the West Ridge of Everest the uncertainty of outcome was prolonged until 6:30 P.M. on May 22! The intense motivation accompanying it was prolonged and maintained for months. It is my task to assess the importance of communication processes in this prolonged effort.

These hypotheses about communication are stated with one qualification: they hold only if psychological stress is not too intense. Under stress, the challenge of uncertainty in achieving a goal is offset by the desire to escape from threat, and uncertainty may become intolerable anxiety rather than tantalizing challenge. Some forms of stress may make the mind, in effect, blind to optimistic signs, while other types of stress may lead a person to overlook or rule out the pessimistic information available.

Thus, my research bears upon some important aspects of mental health. When Maurice Wilson attempted to scale Everest alone, he was certainly responding to some challenge. But was he sane? We cannot say. But certainly, in 1934, with what was commonly known about Everest, he was not fully "in touch with reality." His optimism could not have been founded on an adequate and objective appraisal of the information available to him. In Freud's terms, there must have been a breakdown in "reality testing."

If we turn from Freud to basic psychology, we find that principles of perception can explain very nicely how the mind distorts the information it has available. Apply these principles to climbers assessing the feasibility of the mountain, and we come to some strange conclusions. Once the climber starts to entertain the hypothesis "it can be climbed," these principles indicate that he will be more likely to notice the optimistic signs. This will strengthen his growing belief in its climbability, which further increases his "blindness" to the pessimistic side, and so on. The same holds for the climber who might start with the hunch "it can't be climbed." In either case, these processes of perception lead to distorted appraisals, to a "loss of contact with reality."

These principles of perception have been well tested.* They apply in all areas of conduct, showing themselves in prejudices (prejudgments) of all sorts which are stubbornly impervious to "facts."

All our hypotheses about communication mentioned above are predicated on this notion of "reality testing." Consequently, validation of this theory is being sought in data concerning group communication and in the communicative behavior of those members of the team ex-

* See, for example, Leo Postman, "Toward a General Theory of Cognition" in Rohrer and Sherif, *Social Psychology at the Crossroads.*

posed to intense stress of one form or another. Since stress produces a breakdown in reality testing, predictable consequences may show up in these data.

The foregoing notions were formulated before going into the field, and a number of research procedures were designed to obtain the pertinent data. For instance, a running record had to be obtained for each climber, showing his level of optimism-uncertainty-pessimism concerning our mountaineering objectives. Levels of enthusiasm for these objectives likewise had to be assessed. Especially prepared diaries were provided for this purpose, calling for daily entries including estimates by each climber of the likelihood of success, his own and others' enthusiasm, weather conditions at the time, etc.

In addition, recorders were used to preserve the communication during planning sessions, conferences, all radio communications, etc. Of particular importance to the research design was the following procedure (revealed now to most climbers for the first time): In the course of normal conversation I turned the topic to eventual success or failure, if necessary, then made a pessimistic or optimistic comment in natural context, and recorded the response on tape or in notes. This was done at least once with every climber, using both optimistic and pessimistic "stimulus statements." With most climbers it was done many times.

The use of convenient and reliable apparatus for recording was, of course, an important factor. Agfa PE 65 "Super-thin" magnetic tape, the "Walkie Recordall" made by Miles Reproduction Company, and the Minifon recorder manufactured in West Germany, all contributed substantially in obtaining these data.

At the time of this writing, analysis of the data has only just begun, and it will be a long process. Meanwhile, it can be stated with assurance that a high-altitude Himalayan climb provided an exceptionally fine setting for a study of this nature. Certainly, the events of this expedition in particular give the study every chance to succeed by providing the kind of data needed. Most important to research success was the fine cooperation of all expedition members. The completion of the diaries, for instance, with their often complex questions, required great will power as well as dedication to the scientific aims of the expedition. In the long run, the success of scientific inquiry on mountaineering expeditions hinges on the dedication of the team to its research commitments.

16. GEOLOGY AND GLACIOLOGY

by Maynard M. Miller, Ph.D.

A QUARTER OF A BILLION YEARS AGO, well before "uplift" of the present Himalayan range, the ancient Tethys or Himalayan epicontinental sea bordered the then main land mass of Southern Asia, separating it from the Indian subcontinent. The situation was comparable to the separation of Europe from Africa today by the Mediterranean. It was in and on the margins of this ancient sea that lithologies found on the upper reaches of Everest today were laid down as fine-grained clastic sediments, intermixed with living calcareous ooze.

Our summit climbers, on both routes, encountered a difficult section of rock climbing above the 25,000-foot level. These steep cliffs of iron-stained limestone (or paramarble) have been referred to by earlier assault teams as the "yellow bands." The presence of these strata is indisputable proof of a marine origin of much of the Everest series, deposited in the Tethys Geosyncline long ages ago. This vast central sea retained its character for the whole of Mesozoic time and gave rise to a continuous sequence of sediments from upper Paleozoic (roughly 300 million years ago) to early Cenozoic time (upwards of 60 million years ago).

About 70 million years ago, the sea began to narrow and became shallower. At the beginning of the latest Geologic period, the Tertiary, it completely disappeared as immense forces in the earth began to take effect. The first phase of this disturbance resulted in a shifting and crumbling of the marine sediments and development of deep-rooted and tightly compressed major folding. At the earth's surface there was upwarp—the birth of the Tibetan Marginal Mountains. In the earth's crust at depth, the axes of the largest fold structures became tilted. Some even overturned at low angles. On the surface flanks of this upwarp, pioneer stream channels began to develop with major drainage lines to the south.

Since there have been numerous reports of low-angled fractures in rock units of the Indian Himalaya (Garhwal) as well as in Nepal, it is clear that later immense masses of these recumbent beds were sheared over each other and thrust southward. Accompanying, or following, this horizontal thrust, the sedimentary horizons bordering the Tibetan Marginal Mountains to the north were elevated to become the highest of the mountain chains at that time (i.e., probably 15,000 to 18,000 feet). Thereafter, the older stream channels were rejuvenated, with these rivers being powerful enough to maintain their southerly courses across the continually rising Himalayan block, the locus of far greater uplift at a later date.

There followed an even more powerful uplift, with the root zone of the great overfolds, or nappes, being pressed upward nearly two miles. Thus some of the former sea-bottom rocks now exposed on the higher massifs are ones once subjected to intense heat and pressures at great depth in the earth's crust. This is corroborated by the metamorphism observed in samples collected high on Mt. Everest. In fact, most of the summits of 25,000 feet or more which we first saw in magnificent array through the aircraft windows on our descent through the mid-February haze to Kathmandu are located in the uplifted root zone of these ancient folds. And yet, the uprising of this crestal zone, including Mt. Everest, is still going on today.

Associated with this uplift is a hinge effect, expressed by relief features farther south in the region of the Nepal Midlands and the lesser Himalayan range of the Mahabharat. Here linear sections of the crust have even become depressed, probably by normal faulting, which may explain the development of the Duns, or great undrained interior valleys of Nepal. In recent time some of the rivers which formerly found egress south to the Gangetic Plain became dammed by the Mahabharat barrier. In the Kathmandu and Panch-khal areas, lacustrine deposits over which we passed were the product of such impounding. Related to this were deposits of coarser detritus in tributary valleys, indicative of intensified pluvial (wet) conditions at the end of the Ice Age. These and the lake deposits are geologically the most recent of all.

The Geology of the Chomolongma Massif. On the precipitous walls of Mt. Everest itself the root zone of the once deep-seated fold structure and their associated low-angled thrust fractures were dramatically revealed as we trekked up the Khumbu Valley in mid-March.

The rocks exposed on the lower flanks of the great peaks from Lobuje to Everest are light-colored massive gneiss, apparently of sedimentary origin but highly altered to a granitic rock by permeating and replacive metasomatism most probably accompanying the early phases of orogeny in the linear center of uplift. The evidence for granitization lies in the existence of numerous relict transverse structures of dark sedimentary and metamorphic rock with gradational transitions into the crystalline facies. Also, the granogneisses are characterized by strong lineation parallel to unreplaced segments of the layered sedimentaries. The upper Khumbu Glacier has cut so deeply into this basement material that its present bed grinds across almost continuous granite. Although in this lower section much of the detailed structure of the old sediments has been destroyed, several thousand feet up the cliffs of Lingtren (21,972 feet) and Khumbutse (21,785 feet) segments of the ancient recumbent folds can be seen. Small portions of these isoclinal folds are also exposed along the base of the south wall of Everest, bearing out the concept that the Everest massif lies in a huge overturned fold system or nappe-root zone.

The summit cliffs of Lhotse, including most of the massive south precipice of Everest visible from the camps in the Western Cwm, consist of a series of former sedimentary lithologies. As shown by the work of A. M. Heron, N. E. Odell and L. R. Wager* they are primarily of late-Paleozoic and Mesozoic Age. Although it is desirable to stress the sedimentary structure involved, these rock units reveal some undulations of secondary order and, in places, normal fault structures (seen in the photographs of the Nuptse-Lhotse ridge). Except for the calcareous "yellow bands," they mostly comprise a schistose pelitic sequence (clay

---

* Geologists, respectively, on the British 1921, 1924 and 1933 expeditions to the Tibetan side of Mt. Everest.

sediments), somewhat locally granitized with a few strata of intercalated quartzite (altered sandstone).

The degree of metamorphism attenuates at higher stratigraphic levels, with the actual summit rocks of Everest being units which have quite well retained their bedding structure. Actually, one may refer to them either as a highly indurated, partially altered, sedimentary cover, or as a series of low-grade metamorphic strata (meta-sediments). A. Lombard, geologist on the 1952 Swiss Everest Expedition, refers to this whole structural unit (i.e., stratigraphically at least 8000 feet thick) as the "Tibetan slab," the base of which is a gneissic granitized zone supporting an exceptionally thick series of sedimentary formations farther north in Tibet. This slab, a segment of which comprises Lhotse as well as Everest, is a massive block which has been thrust from the north up and over two other major tectonic units of the Chomolongma massif, as described below.

The first of the overlapped units we saw as a huge anticlinal structure again largely granitized and lying beneath the metamorphic-sedimentary unit of Everest. Along the crest of Nuptse, however, are relict sections of metamorphic rock which also show sedimentary continuity. The field relationships indicate that a massive discontinuity lies above these ridge-top segments, separating them from the lower Everest gneiss. Probably this is a thrust plane, as Lombard has suggested, although a more apt description is a thrust surface since it is by no means planar, having been deformed as well by the regional stressing involved. The same situation pertains beneath the meta-sedimentary cover of Lhotse. The trace of this huge, steeply inclined locus of overthrust appears to pass across the Cwm and to parallel the prodigious north wall of Nuptse. On this basis, the impressive face is a thrust-line scarp. As a result, the sculptured form of the gorge of the Cwm has been controlled by this important tectonic surface, bearing out that structure as well as lithology has affected the morphology of the great Everest massif. To the southwest, the thrust zone has been destroyed by erosional development of the Khumbu Valley. A separate but roughly parallel thrust surface can be traced along Nuptse's southern wall where it plunges beneath an imbricated wedge of metamorphics in this sector.

Farther down valley, the granitized fold structure of the Nuptse massif in turn rests on a sequence of sedimentary remnants and associated schist and gneiss, again revealing the thrust slice nature of the tectonic units.

These rocks are similar to schists, orthogneisses, quartzites and marbles crossed during the latter days of our journey up the Imja Khola Valley from Namche Bazar. They are apparently also the rock types which underlie the layered summits of Cho Oyu (26,750 feet), Gyachung Kang (25,990 feet) and other great peaks to the west, rising beyond the misty ramparts of Gauri Sankar (23,440 feet) which provided such impressive views during the early days of our approach.

Here then, sketched in outline, is the geological foundation of the high glaciated surfaces of the roof of the world into which the Khumbu and other high glaciers of the Mahalangur Himal have deeply eroded their courses.

Ancient Glaciation in the Everest Region. The problem of ancient glaciations in the Himalaya is an especially intriguing one because of the lack of field evidence of any large-scale former ice limits very far from the areas of presently existing glaciers. In fact, in the region north of Everest, none of the early observers in Tibet has given any evidence of a former Tibetan ice sheet. The lowest definite ancient moraine reported in the Rongbuk Valley is at 16,000 feet, only 5 miles beyond the present terminus of the Rongbuk Glacier. South of Everest the first evidence we observed was as we entered the district of Solu Khumbu while crossing the 12,000-foot pass west of Junbesi.

Here, sporadic felsenmeer ("rock sea") surfaces were crossed in shallow depressions, nivation hollows of former perennial snow. This terrain had once been subjected to intense frost shattering and Arctic-type mass wastage, but today the boulders are lichen-covered, and scattered talus is stabilized by a thick mantle of sedge and moss. From here northeastward, the soil was of wind-borne loessial clay, with a leached surface and a further stabilizing cover of grass, again indicative of colder and formerly drier conditions. The implication is that of former desert conditions similar to those on the Tibetan plateau today. Later we found that this proof of a drier climate in Glacial time fitted into our other observations on the character of the late-Pleistocene in the inner Himalaya.

Two days later we climbed a steep trail approaching the village of Kharikhola, but 35 miles south of Everest. At 6400 feet, on the threshold of a hanging valley high above the Dudh Kosi, we saw patches of cultivated winter wheat growing in soils of unquestionable glacial origin. The most convincing proof was the presence of unweathered, glacially grooved slabs of gneiss. Nearby, an irregular line of boulders crossed the steep fields, apparently part of an ancient lateral moraine. The glacier which had produced it once filled a sloping basin on the ridge to the east. One distinct glacial boulder lay as low as 6200 feet, probably close to the snout of the old moraine. This source basin represents the lowest identifiable Pleistocene cirque we were to find during the course of the expedition.

The amphitheatre floor, a measure of the prime nourishment level of this former glacier, we estimated at an elevation of 8500 feet, about 12,000 feet lower than the present level of accumulation we were to record on the Khumbu. The snow-line depression indicated by this feature is staggering when compared with Pleistocene limits of other mountain regions of our earth. Furthermore, the terminus, so close to an elevation of 6000 feet, is the lowest ancient glacial limit reported in the Everest region. It is, of course, in great contrast to the elevation (16,000 feet) of the oldest moraines known on the Tibetan flank of this range. These facts suggest that maximum early glaciation in the Mahalangur Himal was asymmetrical, with the greatest thickening of ice taking place well south on the more maritime Nepalese flank.

On the other hand, the least elevation of existing glaciers in the Everest region is 14,000 to 15,000 feet, and 13,000 for termini of present glaciers in the Kangchenjunga region. This means that the present glacier limits are at least 7000 feet higher than those of the lowest former glaciation in Eastern Nepal and Sikkim.

North of Kharikhola numerous main and side-valley moraines occur at progressively higher levels. From observations of these moraines and associated outwash deposits, the reconstructed picture of former maximum glaciation in the region immediately south of Everest is seen as one of many ice centers, each with its own regime and fluctuation pattern, dependent on altitude and position. The situation was similar to that pertaining today in the main region of present glaciation at higher levels, i.e., a series of partially connected mountain-valley glaciers with substantial areas of exposed bedrock on spurs and broad ridges, rather than an ice-flooded landscape involving contiguous ice sheets. On many of these rock surfaces loess deposits, of the type we had seen while traversing the high ridges west of the Dudh Kosi, had formed. Again this aeolian material bears out the influence of strong continental winds so characteristic of the dry cold climate of that time.

Near timber line in the high valley of the Imja Khola we reached a remarkable series of moraine embankments, all extensively mantled with lichen. These multiple moraines occur at 13,000 to 15,000 feet in the Pangboche-Pheriche area and line the valley flanks to heights of several hundred feet. They are recessionals from an extinct composite glacier system once partly fed by ice out of the Khumbu Valley. The youngest and highest moraine passes beneath marginal detritus of the modern moraines of the Khumbu Glacier near its present terminus. The oldest segments in this sequence occur 10 miles down valley from the present ice, at a point where they interfinger with outwash from the Mingbo Valley, east of Pangboche. The magnitude of these features dwarfs any previously noted.

Were they but part of a long sequence of normal retreat from the older down-valley moraines, or did it mean that a zone of former glacial concentration had shifted upward and northward in more recent time? Of one thing we are sure. At the upper end, the highest moraines merged with present bodies of ice, and at the lower end they were no more than 14 miles from the absolute southern limit of valley ice which we had seen in the Dudh Kosi canyon. Again, the reconstructed picture is one of isolated centers of glaciation, all contributing to the complexity of the glacial history in the Everest region.

The modern Khumbu Glacier lies behind a steep mountain of fresh moraine less than a century old, hence far younger than the aforementioned system. The glacier's snout rests at the head of the broad gravel-filled valley of Pheriche, a summer yak pasturing ground of the Sherpas lying at an elevation of 14,000 feet. Its impressive terminal moraine is multiple, with a dozen or more fluctuational ridges boldly displayed. The ice-contact side of the moraine is at an elevation of 16,000 feet. The base of the oldest section and related outwash fan below is at 14,500 feet. In the intervening mile, every conceivable rock type of the Chomolongma group is found, from the calc-pelites of the Everest-Lhotse summits to the granitized lithologies of the Nuptse thrust zone in the Western Cwm. Admixed, of course, are all the facies of the Khumbu nappe structure exposed along the lower section of this glacier system.

The debris-charged ice surface for 6 miles above the terminus is a no-man's land of hidden crevasses, treacherous ice ponds, 30- to 60-foot high radiation pinnacles and a thin mantle of constantly sliding ablation moraine. From our 16,000-foot camp below Lobuje Peak (20,076 feet), we commenced the glaciological investigation of the Khumbu Glacier which was to be carried to the upper nourishment zone in the Western Cwm.

The Glaciological Program. Glaciological studies were made from the middle of March until the last week of May, primarily on the Khumbu Glacier from its terminus at 15,000 feet to the Lhotse Face at 23,000 feet, a distance of 12 miles longitudinally along the glacier surface. The main studies were conducted from the expedition Base Camp (17,800 feet), at Camp I (22,000 feet) and at Advance Base (Camp II, 21,350 feet). Because of injuries and illness in the geological team, resulting in a loss of several valuable weeks of field time, the studies were carried out as a reconnaissance of the glacio-physical character of this glacier and the gross atmospheric factors affecting its state of health. Limited observations and measurements were made on the glacier's surface morphology, its regime characteristics, englacial structure, temperature and surface movement. Basic meteorological records were obtained at the Base and Advance Base Camps, with supplementary data at Gorak Shep and Camp I providing a climatological profile from 17,000 to nearly 22,000 feet.

Geophysical measurements were made via gravity surveys of the glacier's depth on six across-glacier transects: at Profile I (16,000 feet), II (17,000 feet), III (17,800 feet), IV (20,200 feet), V (21,500 feet) and VI (22,800 feet). A set of longitudinal traverse points were also occupied between the upper four profiles. Gravity data were also obtained at selected sites on a northeasterly traverse across the Nepal Midlands to the Khumbu Valley during the approach march, but because of lack of precise position surveys the results are of provisional value. The seismic records, obtained on several key transects, are of interest in shallow ice. They are of limited value otherwise because insufficient energy could be generated with the sledge-hammer technique made necessary by political exigencies forbidding the use of dynamite.

The pre-Monsoon névé line (glacier snow line) in the high Khumbu Valley in 1963 was found to lie at 18,500 feet. Measurements of net accumulation were made above this level with a positive accumulation budget recorded at and above 20,000 feet. Contrary to previous belief, we found that most of the accumulation in the Cwm is by direct snowfall rather than by avalanche snows. Katabatic winds off the Lhotse face deplete, and in some years largely remove, the snow cover from the Cwm surface above the 22,500-foot level, i.e., on the ice apron below the Lhotse face. This deflated accumulation, however, is redeposited by winds in the middle and lower sections of the Cwm. The zone of maximum total accumulation over the past decade has rested in the lower one-third of the Cwm at about 21,000 feet. The greatest thickening of ice along the Pumori-Khumbutse rampart also lies at this level. Over the past decade the annual net accumulation in this zone has averaged approximately 3.5 feet water equivalent, most of which is monsoon snow deposited between June and September.

Retained firn and ice covering the last seventeen years of accumulation in the Western Cwm give a stratigraphic thickness of 60 feet. Melt samples from each of these strata were obtained for laboratory analysis of the nature and origin of wind-deposited material. One phase of this investigation is an attempt to measure relative quantities of H_3 or natural tritium, in an effort to detect any significant variations of this light isotope of hydrogen known to be produced in periodic outbursts of flare activity on the surface of the sun. We hope that such may provide useful information on the variations of solar energy over the past two decades. This phase of the analyses is being carried out by Dr. W. E. Libby of the Department of Chemistry, University of California, for whom we also collected corollary glacier samples on the Taku Glacier, Alaska, immediately upon our return from Everest.

Preliminary evaluation of the geophysical results indicates a thermophysical character of the upper Khumbu Glacier verging on Polar conditions (i.e., in the Western Cwm where both ambient and englacial temperatures are continually well below freezing, with little if any propagated melt water). Subpolar to almost Temperate glacio-thermal conditions (that is progressively warmer, with the glacier throughout being at the freezing point for Temperate ice) apparently exist in the glacier at lower elevations. The general state of health points to an equilibrium regime verging on slight down-wasting and retreat, but the changes are affected in an oscillating manner. Regionally, this condition prevails on other glaciers in the surrounding Himalaya. Although A. Desio on the 1954 Italian K-2 expedition cited a few cases of advancing glaciers in the Karakoram, our observations indicate that the only advances to be expected under current regime conditions in the Eastern Himalaya will be on very small glaciers and only on the northern flanks of the higher massifs. Our distant views of the West Rongbuk and adjoining glaciers in Tibet, however, indicate that all the main ice tongues from Everest, regardless of orientation, are continuing a trend of equilibrium at higher level and slow retreat at their termini.

Our movement records on the Khumbu suggest a somewhat slower rate than expected in view of the active crevasse patterns and gradients (a slope average on the lower glacier of 9 degrees), i.e., no more than 600 feet per year, or a maximum of 1 to 2 feet per day at the base of the Khumbu Icefall. This is in line with F. Müller's report from the 1956 Swiss expedition of 450 feet per year on the lower middle section of this glacier. These rates are well below those found in comparable Alaskan glaciers and are probably an effect of the low englacial temperatures encountered in the accumulation zone, as well as partly the result of a negative regime condition below the Cwm.

The glaciological-climatological relationship is interesting because of the high solar radiation recorded, the low humidity, and the extremely arid, Arctic-desert conditions experienced during the spring observation period. Above 19,000 feet, the propagation of melt water was found to be negligible with ablation at the glacier surface largely in the form of evaporation. This, too, is a direct result of the intense radiation. Up to 24,000 feet, however, slight melting was observed on ice adjacent to bedrock exposures, but this only for one to two hours in the afternoon. The total effects, regimewise, are considered to be nil.

An evaluation of the meteorological records has not yet been made, except to note that the lowest temperatures encountered at Base Camp in March and April were from −10 to −15 degrees F, rising to maxima in the range of +10 to +20 during the afternoons. Increases in daytime temperatures after the first week in May brought some melt water to the surface streams as runoff at and below 18,000 feet. During May at the Cwm camps ambient temperatures persisted below 15 degrees F and at night invariably dropped below zero. During April temperatures at Advance Base ran 10 to 15 degrees colder than at Base. On the day of the May 1 summit assault, temperatures at the South Col (26,200 feet) registered 18 below zero. Although because of strong differences in orographical control, lapse rates cannot be considered pertinent in extrapolating temperatures at these higher levels, it is presumed to have been at least 10 degrees colder, i.e., about 30 below zero, at the time Whittaker and Gombu attained the summit.

Generally, temperatures were not as low as anticipated. Provisional evaluation of the spring weather record compared with previous expeditions on Mt. Everest suggests conditions warmer and drier than in the 1920's. Presumably, the world-wide climatic amelioration of the past half century has affected this part of the Himalaya and has been expressed by a regional shift of storm tracks somewhat to the south. Such is corroborated by the record for March and April. At Base Camp light snow showers fell daily, but through them, over the Lho La, we continually noted blue skies on the Rongbuk side of the Lingtren ridge. This was towards the North Col where the early British expeditions of the 1920's and 1930's had reported violent snow squalls every afternoon during these months. Perhaps allied to this changed condition is the seemingly later arrival of the monsoon season in the period since the early 1950's, as opposed to the reports of expeditions 30 to 40 years ago.

In spite of the severe down-wastage observed on the lower Khumbu, the Cwm sector appears to be in a healthy state. Because of its great elevation, in spite of its restricted area (4 square miles), this portion of the ice mass should continue to thrive even under present warmer climatic conditions. A vigorous resurgence of the terminus, however, can not be expected until a cooler trend ensues, i.e., one which brings the freezing level and mean snow line of the monsoon to a level well below its present limit of 17,000 to 18,000 feet. Such cooler conditions a half century ago, and again in the early part of the nineteenth century, probably affected the latest main resurgences of this glacier system which produced the double set of fresh-appearing moraines found in the terminal sector.

Two interesting facts are noted: (1) that these two very latest expanded positions of ice in the main Khumbu Valley are indeed not far from the present glacial surface; and (2) that the corresponding scour zones and associated lateral moraines along the valley walls suggest that these were as vigorous advances as have occurred probably at any time in the last 5000 years. It follows that the development of a strong upward and northward shift in maximum glacial position could explain the lack of ice-cut shoulders, older cirque basins and moraine deposits of earlier vintage at or above these latest ice limits. However, in the long fugue of strictly climatic events, a northward shift of centers of accumulation is not compatible with climatic theory nor with the storm-track trends which have been indicated. This leaves the tantalizing possibility that recent tectonic uplift and resultant climatic changes on these high slopes explain the paradox that the most extensive glaciation has developed here late in the Ice Age, as opposed to the early Pleistocene Maxima known to have occurred in formerly glaciated regions elsewhere on earth.

This connotes, of course, uplift sufficiently rapid to balance out deglaciation effects of the world-wide climatic amelioration which has been so well documented elsewhere in so-called "post-Glacial" time. It furthermore requires a Himalayan upwarp of sufficient magnitude to maintain this elevated land in a glacial condition quite out of phase with the natural climatic trend.

Certainly, the exceptionally depressed position of ancient snowlines and terminal ice limits, when compared with those of the far northwestern provinces of the Himalaya, suggests that other than normal climatic changes have occurred in the border region of Nepal and Tibet. A maximum glaciation in recent time also frames the present glacial position and its Polar characteristics in a category only slightly less severe than the most expanded conditions of the Glacial Age. One is, therefore, tempted to conclude that today a most significant event in diastrophic history is affecting the high border of southern Asia and that for this reason abnormal glacial conditions characterize the Mahalangur Himal and Mt. Everest in a manner not revealed anywhere else on earth.

Acknowledgment is made to the Committee for Research and Exploration of the National Geographic Society for its support of the geological and glaciological program. For information important to the interpretations of regional geology discussed in this chapter, the writer is indebted to the published works of T. Hagen, A. M. Heron, A. Lombard, N. E. Odell and L. R. Wager. Acknowledgment is also extended to P. Aufschnaiter, B. Bishop, A. Gansser, T. Hagen and F. Müller for helpful discussions relating to their previous studies in the Himalaya.

Appendix I

Acknowledgments

THE AMERICAN MOUNT EVEREST EXPEDITION 1963 wishes to express its indebtedness and thanks to the following agencies, companies, organizations and individuals, whose contributions of products, services or money made the whole venture possible. In a listing of this size there are bound to be a few inadvertent omissions, and AMEE offers its sincere apologies to any contributors who have been overlooked.

Agencies Supporting Major Expedition Programs

National Aeronautics and Space Administration	Physiology Research
National Geographic Society	Documentary Film Glaciology Research Solar Radiation Research
National Science Foundation	Physiology Research Sociology Research
Office of Naval Research	Psychology Research
United States Air Force, Office of Scientific Research	Physiology Research Psychology Research
United States Atomic Energy Commission	Physiology Research
University of California at Berkeley	Physiology Research
University of California at Los Angeles	Ice Dating
United States Department of State, Bureau of Educational and Cultural Affairs	General support of scientific and cultural exchange objectives including U.S. tour by Expedition Sherpas

Companies Contributing Products or Services

Abbott Laboratories Chicago, Ill.	medical supplies

413

Acme Iron Works Seattle, Wash.	aluminum ladder aluminum rappel pickets
Acme Steel Company Seattle, Wash.	miscellaneous equipment
Chas. Clise Agent, Inc. Seattle, Wash.	warehouse
AGFA Inc. Rockleigh, N.J.	magnetic recording tape
Alfa Candy Corporation New York, N.Y.	Acerola Rosehips Jel Bars
Allgäu Imports Montrose, Calif.	Eiger special boot (Iowa)
Aloe Division Brunswick Corp. Chicago, Ill.	medical supplies
Alpine Crafts Co. San Francisco, Calif.	socks lip salve
American Bread Company Nashville, Tenn.	canned bread and fruit cake
American Crystal Sugar Company Denver, Colo.	sugar
The American Tobacco Company New York, N.Y.	cigarettes
Anderson & Thompson Seattle, Wash.	bindings, goggles, sweaters, boot wax
L'Appareil Médical de Précision Paris, France	oxygen and oxygen apparatus
Application Des Gaz Paris, France	stoves, lanterns, space heaters, fuel (Butane)
Armour & Co. Chicago, Ill.	medical supplies
ASTRA Pharmaceutical Products Worcester, Mass.	medical supplies
B & J Equipment Co. Seattle, Wash.	winch
B & K Manufacturing Company Chicago, Ill.	multimeter
Balzers A. G. Liechtenstein	goggles, lenses
Eddie Bauer Seattle, Wash.	all down clothing all sleeping bags
Baxter Laboratories Morton Grove, Ill.	medical supplies
Beard Instrument Co. Houston, Texas	gravity meter (loan)

Bedayan Co. Orinda, Calif.	carabiners
Bell-Art Products Pequannock, N.J.	plastic "tees" for sleeping sets
Bell Aerosystems Co. Buffalo, N.Y.	packs, experimental
Bell & Howell Chicago, Ill.	four cameras (loan)
Best Foods New York, N.Y.	Knorr soups
Thomas Black & Sons Port Glasgow, Scotland	anoraks
Black Manufacturing Co. Seattle, Wash.	pants: wool, cotton shirts: wool, cotton
The Borden Company New York, N.Y.	milk
Boyle-Midway, Div. of American Home Products New York, N.Y.	Woolite cold water soap
R. D. Bradshaw & Sons Wendell, Idaho	honey
Brown Best & Co., Ltd. London, England	packs, rucksack, cairn
Brown & Haley Candy Company Tacoma, Wash.	candy
Burroughs Wellcome & Co. Tuckahoe, N.Y.	medical supplies
California Packing Corporation San Francisco, Calif.	Del Monte canned foods—fruits and fish
Campbell Soup Company Chicago, Ill.	canned Red Kettle soups; Franco-American dinners
The Carnation Company Seattle, Wash.	mashed potatoes, packages of hot chocolate
Cello Bag Company Seattle, Wash.	Cello bags
CIBA Pharmaceutical Co. Summit, N.J.	medical supplies
Collins Radio Co. Cedar Rapids, Iowa	KWM-2 Transceiver
Community Industries Sullivan, Ill.	jelly bars
Cramore Products, Inc. Point Pleasant Beach, N.J.	fruit beverages, Dri-syrup
Crescent Manufacturing Company Seattle, Wash.	1-pound tins and vacuum packing

Patrick Cudahy, Inc. Cudahy, Wisc.	canned dried beef
Cutter Laboratories Berkeley, Calif.	medical supplies
J. L. Darling Co. Tacoma, Wash.	waterproof field notebooks and meteorological and glaciological data forms
The Dickinson Company Portland, Ore.	fruit, preserves
Dietiene Company Minneapolis, Minn.	milk shakes
La Dolomite Montebelluna, Italy	boots: high altitude, approach march, camp
Dri Lite Foods South Gate, Calif.	Spanish rice, Malt Crunch, Tropical Bar
Duofold, Inc. Mohawk, N.Y.	underwear
Dynalab Corp. Rochester, N.Y.	medical supplies
El Molino Mills Alhambra, Calif.	Cara-Coa fruit brownies Cara-Coa instant drink whole grain flour
Elam Mills, Div. of National Bakers Services, Inc. Broadview, Ill.	Elam's Mix, whole wheat flour
Electrodynamic Instrument Co. Houston, Tex.	lightweight Interval Timer (loan)
Eureka Tent & Awning Binghamton, N.Y.	tents
Fearn Soya Foods Melrose Park, Ill.	pancake mix, high protein food
Robert Fisher Bakersfield, Calif.	"R-A Formula" vitamins vitamin supplement
Food Farmacy Riverside, Calif.	canned bread
Foods for Life Bakery Glendale, Calif.	canned bread
Foundation for Glacier Research Seattle, Wash.	meteorological, radiation and ice coring equipment, field microscope (loan)
The R. T. French Company Rochester, N.Y.	instant potatoes
Geigy Pharmaceutical Co. Ardsley, N.Y.	medical supplies
General Foods Corporation White Plains, N.Y.	Jell-O, tapioca, rice Tang, Grape-Nuts

General Magnetics Corporation Hollywood, Calif.	magnets for avalanche detector
General Mills, Inc. Minneapolis, Minn.	Betty Crocker products, multi-purpose foods
General Motors Corporation Oldsmobile Division Lansing, Mich.	automobiles made available to expedition members
Georgia-Pacific Corporation Portland, Ore.	containers: corrugated pulp board cartons
Gerry Mountain Sports Boulder, Colo.	tents, wind parkas, cable ladders, headlamps
Glaciological Institute Michigan State University	Brunton compasses (loan)
The Grist Mill Los Angeles, Calif.	breakfast cereal
Grivel Frères Courmayeur, Italy	crampons
S. Gumpert Company, Inc. Jersey City, N.J.	packaged foods: eggs, puddings, punch, fruit drinks
Hall-Sears, Inc. Houston, Tex.	geophones and cables (loan)
Hamilton Watch Company Lancaster, Pa.	precision chronometer equipment (loan)
H & H Engineering Co. Denver, Colo.	design and construction of the tent radio antenna mounts
H & M Packing Corporation Glendale, Calif.	pemmican
Head Ski Co., Inc. Timonium, Md.	skis, poles, sleds
Heublein, Inc. Hartford, Conn.	Maypo oat cereal
Hills of Westchester Brentwood, Md.	canned fruit cakes
Horlicks Ltd. Slugh, Buckinghamshire, England	candy
Irvington Machine Works Portland, Ore.	winch
Johnson & Johnson Menlo Park, Calif.	medical supplies
Jumar-Steigbugel Reichenbach, Switzerland	ascenders
Keeps, Inc. Greenwich, Conn.	canned breads
The Kelling Nut Company Chicago, Ill.	canned nuts

Kellogg Company Battle Creek, Mich.	Kellogg's Concentrate
R. C. King Co. Seattle, Wash.	socks, headbands
Waldes Kohinoor, Inc. Long Island City, N.Y.	zippers
Lab Geodetics Corp. Falls Church, Va.	Zenith star camera
Lederle Labs Pearl River, N.Y.	medical supplies
Liana Incorporated Edinburg, Tex.	freeze-dry corn, chicken, spinach
Eli Lilly & Co. Indianapolis, Ind.	medical supplies
Linhof Nikolaus Karpf K. G. Munich, West Germany	Linhof camera, 4″ x 5″
Lion Packing Company Fresno, Calif.	raisins
McCormick & Co., Inc. Baltimore, Md.	coffee, tea, spices, potatoes, milk
Majesty Ham Imports Los Angeles, Calif.	canned ham, bacon, lunch meats
Mark Products Division, Dynascan Corp. Chicago, Ill.	communications antennas
The Maytag Company Newton, Iowa	oxygen masks, development and manufacture
Mead Johnson Laboratories Evansville, Ind.	Sustagen, Metrecal cookies
Mechanical Products Co. Phoenix, Ariz.	packs: frame, cruiser
Merck, Sharpe & Dohme West Point, Pa.	medical supplies
Miles Laboratories Elkhart, Ind.	medical supplies
Millet Annecy, France	rucksacks
Millipore Filter Corp. Bedford, Mass.	medical supplies
Minnesota Mining & Manufacturing Co. St. Paul, Minn.	magnetic recording tape, pressure banding
Mustang Manufacturing Co. Seattle, Wash.	cooking equipment

National Biscuit Company, Special Products Division Portland, Ore.	Cream of Wheat
Nippon Kogaku K. K. Tokyo, Japan	twenty Nikon cameras with appurtenances
Nuclear Chicago Corp. Des Plaines, Ill.	portable radioactivity counter
O-U Sports Seattle, Wash.	headgear, laces
Ocean Spray Cranberries, Inc. Hanson, Mass.	cranberries
Olivetti-Underwood Corp. New York, N.Y.	typewriter
Omega, Louis Brandt et Frère S. A. Bienne, Switzerland	watches
Ohio Chemical & Surgical Equip- ment Co. Madison, Wisc.	K-S disposable sleeping masks
Ora-Dent Corporation Lodi, Calif.	Foamettes brushless dentifrice
Ortho Pharmaceutical Co. Raritan, N.J.	medical supplies
Osborne Electronics Corporation Hawthorne, Calif.	handie-talkie transceivers, communications equipment
Ovaltine Food Products Villa Park, Ill.	Ovaltine
Pacific Laboratories, Ltd. Vancouver, B.C., Canada	sun lotion

Pacific Marine Supply
Seattle, Wash.
	rope: $\frac{1}{4}$ in. Goldline
	        $\frac{3}{8}$ in. Goldline
	        $\frac{1}{4}$ in. Manila
	        $\frac{5}{16}$ in. Manila

Pacific Match Company Tacoma, Wash.	matches
Parke Davis & Co. Detroit, Mich.	medical supplies
S. S. Pierce Company Boston, Mass.	canned butter, fruits, vegetables, and assorted groceries
V. Pincetich Hollywood, Calif.	motion picture tripods
Plus Products, Inc. Los Angeles, Calif.	milk food products
Procter & Gamble Company Cincinnati, Ohio	vegetable oil shortening

The Ralston Purina Company St. Louis, Mo.	breakfast foods
Recreational Equipment, Inc. Seattle, Wash.	climbing equipment, clothing, cooking gear, pack bags
Rexall Drug Co. Los Angeles, Calif.	medical supplies
Reynolds Metals Company Richmond, Va.	aluminum for cruiser frames
Richter Bros., Inc. New York, N.Y.	dried vegetables and Grunkern soups
Riker Laboratories, Inc. Northridge, Calif.	medical supplies
Robins Co., Inc. Richmond, Va.	medical supplies
S & W Fine Foods, Inc. San Francisco, Calif.	artichoke hearts
Sanborn Company Waltham, Mass.	medical supplies
Sandoz Pharmaceutical Co. Hanover, N.J.	medical supplies
Schering Corp. Bloomfield, N.J.	medical supplies
Scott Paper Company Everett, Wash.	all paper products
Sea and Ski Co. Reno, Nev.	medical supplies, sunglasses
Ad. Seidel & Son, Inc. Elk Grove Village, Ill.	Kwik-Shake
Seymour Foods, Inc. Topeka, Kan.	Quik-Egg
Sicks Ranier Brewing Company Seattle, Wash.	beer
Siebe Gorman & Co., Ltd. Chessington, England	fittings for oxygen masks
Claudius Simond Chamonix, France	ice axes
The Ski Hut Berkeley, Calif.	repair materials, rum fudge bars
Smith, Kline & French Philadelphia, Pa.	medical supplies
Squibb & Sons New York, N.Y.	medical supplies
Standard Brands, Inc. New York, N.Y.	peanuts, coffee

Stebco Industries, Inc. Chicago, Ill.	air mattresses
J. P. Stevens & Co., Inc. New York, N.Y.	fabric
Stokely-Van Camp, Inc. Seattle, Wash.	canned juice, fruit, beans, peas, corn, carrots, beets, tomatoes
Swiss Foundation for Alpine Research Zurich, Switzerland	helmets for oxygen masks
Texas Pharmical Co. San Antonio, Tex.	medical supplies
Thermex Co. of California San Francisco, Calif.	stoves
Tillamook County Creamery Assoc. Tillamook, Ore.	cheese
Tissot Le Locle, Switzerland	watches
Chocolat Tobler, Inc. Berne, Switzerland	chocolate bars
Town Food Company Riverside, Calif.	canned bread
Traeger Manufacturing Co. Seattle, Wash.	gaiters, overboots, pack bags
Uncle Ben's Rice Houston, Tex.	rice
William Underwood Company Watertown, Mass.	liver, deviled ham
Union Carbide Corp. San Francisco, Calif.	batteries
United Fruit Co. Boston, Mass.	complete line of Wagerized freeze-dried fruits, vegetables, seafoods, meats, and poultry
Universal New York, N.Y.	Stanley containers, vacuum, electric toothbrush
Universal Services, Inc. Seattle, Wash.	food packaging
Vacu-Dry Company Emeryville, Calif.	canned fruits
The Van Brode Milling Co., Inc. Clinton, Mass.	breakfast cereal
Varian Associates Palo Alto, Calif.	M-49 Magnetometer (loan)
Vemp Food Company Denver, Colo.	pancake mix

Visking Company   Vistend bags
Seattle, Wash.

W I S Pharmaceuticals   medical supplies
Rochester, N.Y.

Wallace and Tiernam Co.   precision aeneroid barometers
Belleville, N.J.   (loan)

W. L. Weiss   nylon wind pants
Redmond, Wash.

Westclox Division   travel alarm clocks
General Time Corporation
La Salle, Ill.

Wild Heerbrugg Instruments Inc.   precision theodolite equipment
Port Washington, N.Y.   (loan)

Wilson & Co., Inc.   freeze-dried pork chops,
Chicago, Ill.   hamburgers and meat bars

Winpower Manufacturing Company   gasoline electric plant
Newton, Iowa

R. S. Winters Co.   duffles, containers, G.I.
Seattle, Wash.   gloves

Winthrop Laboratories   medical supplies
New York, N.Y.

Wyeth Laboratories   medical supplies
Philadelphia, Pa.

Zion Countryside Bakers   fig bars
Zion, Ill.

Companies, Clubs and Foundations Contributing Cash

American Alpine Club   The Cascadians
New York, N.Y.   Yakima, Wash.

Appalachian Mountain Club   Christies, Inc.
Boston, Mass.   Albany, Ore.

Alpha Stationers   The Colorado Mountain Club
Santa Monica, Calif.   Denver, Colo.

Bacon's Market   C. S. U. Mountaineers
Albany, Ore.   Fort Collins, Colo.

Bruin Mountaineers, University of   Duofold Inc.
    California   Mohawk, N.Y.
Los Angeles, Calif.   Loveland Basin Volunteer Ski
Burbank Rotary Club   Patrol
Burbank, Calif.   Golden, Colo.

Cahners Publishing Company   Marsh-McClennan-Cosgrove & Co.
Boston, Mass.   Los Angeles, Calif.

Carnegie Tech. Explorers Club   The Mazamas
Pittsburgh, Pa.   Portland, Ore.

The Mountaineers
Seattle, Wash.

Ski Magazine
New York, N.Y.

The Mount Everest Foundation
London, England

The Stans Foundation
Los Angeles, Calif.

New Mexico Mountain Club
Albuquerque, N.M.

Sub Sig Outing Club
Lexington, Mass.

The Pittsburgh Climbers
Pittsburgh, Pa.

Table Mountain Gun Club
Denver, Colo.

Plus Products
Los Angeles, Calif.

University of Wyoming Outing Club
Laramie, Wyo.

Potomac Appalachian Trail Club
Washington, D.C.

Wittenberg Outing Club
Springfield, Ohio

Rocky Mountain Rescue Group
Boulder, Colo.

Yakima Rotary Club
Yakima, Wash.

Sierra Club, San Diego Chapter
San Diego, Calif.

Yale Mountaineering Club
New Haven, Conn.

Individuals Contributing Cash

Thomas R. Aasum, Jr.
Mr. and Mrs. Charles Alexander
Paul Alexander
Briggs M. Austin
Dr. George Austin
J. E. Baker
Richard Baldinger
Neil Baldwin
Mrs. Richard H. Baldwin
Ralph W. Ball
Richard J. Bates
Mrs. Roy E. Bates
Mrs. H. F. Bauer
Ralph and Janice Baxter
Jack O. Benson
John W. Berggren
Melvin J. Bernstein
David D. Bidwell
Mr. and Mrs. John L. Biehn
Douglas Bingham
Barry and Lila Bishop
James G. Bjorgen
Thomas R. Bjorgen
Ronald Blair

Carl Blaurock
Warren T. Bleser
E. H. Braunsworth
A. James Bravar
Alexander H. Bright
Harvey Broome
Janet L. Brown
Roger Brown
Helen I. Buck
Mr. and Mrs. Carl H. Builder
Richard E. Burdett
Norman S. Calvo
Fred A. Camp
Dr. Frank C. Campbell
Adams Carter
Don Christiansen
Nicholas B. Clinch
David C. Collins
Myrtle Connelly
Hallam Burr Cooley
Lt. Paul A. Cornett, USN
Ursula Corning
Julian Crafts
Neal E. Creamer

Carole Crisetti
Georgia and Eaton Cromwell
George L. Crosson
Richard DeKay
Christian Drake
Jack Edwards
Maury Englander
T. L. Englund
Francis and Marjory Farquhar
William Field
J. C. Firey
Joel E. Fisher
E. A. Fortier
Placido S. Fortino
David Foster
James F. Fox
Dr. Alfred L. Frank
H. W. Franklin
Mrs. Anne S. Frantz
Betty Sue Frary
James Fredsall
Karen Fryklund
Carlton P. Fuller
Dr. Frank E. Gaebelein
Rev. Donald J. Gardner
Dr. and Mrs. William Georgiades
Lillian Gest
Mr. and Mrs. E. A. Goodell
Dr. S. Jackson Gossett
John D. Graham
Walter L. Gregory
Keith Gunnar
Alfred S. Gutman
N. I. Hall
John R. Hanson
Robert C. Harper
John L. J. Hart
Howard Head
John Helmer
Kenneth A. Henderson
Horst von Hennig

Hal Higdon
Robert W. Hillerby
E. H. Hilliard, Jr.
John H. Hitchcock
Dave Hotaling
Donald Hubbard
Eliot Hubbard
Mr. and Mrs. John M. Huebner
Mr. and Mrs. Charles B. Huestis
John S. Humphreys
R. L. Hunt
Howard A. Ingall
Mr. and Mrs. Jack R. Irwin
Keith H. Jacobson
Martin Jezer
Douglas Johnson
Horton Johnson
Janet M. Johnson
Douglas E. Johnston
Earle M. Jorgensen
Walden R. Joura
Pierre Juillerat
John Kaczorowsky
Mr. and Mrs. Clifford C. Knight
Elizabeth Knowlton
Dr. Hans Kraus
Mr. and Mrs. Kermit Kuebler
Jack Kuusela
George P. LaBorde
Henry F. Lacy, Jr.
Jeannette Lasher
Omar L. Latum
W. Robert Leach
Francis and Margaret LeBaron
Mrs. Philip A. Leighton
Arthur Leins
King Leopold III of the Belgians
Lois F. Lindley
M. Albert Linton
Harold McBride
Henry L. McClintock

W. J. McGarvey, Jr.
David Byrd McGlone
Paul C. Manchester
Henry Mandolf
Vincent N. Manuel
Mr. and Mrs. Jack Marler
Joel and Bertha H. Massie
J. Alex Maxwell
Elizabeth F. Maynard
John D. Mendenhall
Mary H. Merrick
Bruce Meyer, M.D.
Mr. and Mrs. Marsh Meyers
Mrs. George S. Moe
Cornelius M. Molenaar
Dee Molenaar
A. F. Moody
Mary A. Moore
Terris Moore
Laura M. Mosley
Mr. and Mrs. K. J. Nelson
Art C. Newman
Mike O'Haver
Mary Caroline Orr
Edwin R. Page
Arthur K. Peters
Mr. and Mrs. B. B. Peterson
O. X. Pitney
Robert Polesie
Edward C. Porter
Rose Pullara
Al and Frances Randall
Dr. Charles F. Rapp
Peter Rathburn
Ronald Reagan
Mr. and Mrs. Richard Ream
Christine L. Reid
Adam Rhodes
Dr. W. K. Rieben
Mrs. Florence Roser
John D. Sancher

Edmund Savoie
Edith W. Sayre
Miriam R. Schantz
Charles W. Schmidt
E. W. Schnitzer
Hugo Schramm
Leslie P. Seyb
Richard Sideman
John L. Siemens
Francis B. Silsbees
Dudley T. Smith
Judge Macauley Smith
Nancy B. Smithson
William L. Souvey
Robert Spenger
Mr. and Mrs. Arthur Sperber
Mrs. Lyman Spitzer, Jr.
Dr. David H. Stern
Paul Stettner
Mrs. Robert L. Stevenson
Walter G. Sutton, Jr.
Mrs. Mary Sylvander
Samuel F. Thomas
William H. Thomas
Dr. J. Monroe Thorington
Samuel Tierney, Jr.
Paul W. Trousdale
Fred C. Tuttle
Richardson J. Twohy
Dr. Ralph L. Uber
Martha A. Valliant
A. Van Norman
Bruce B. Vester
Donald H. Vetterlein
Ernestine E. Voss
Elizabeth Wallace
Miss E. A. Ward
Thomas J. Watson
Charles J. Webb, II
Mr. and Mrs. Ernest Wegener
Thomas C. Wendell

Charles Wettling
Dr. and Mrs. J. A. Weyandt
Mr. and Mrs. Theodore White
Hassler Whitney
Harold Widsteen

Paul W. Wiseman
Gertrude B. Woodward
John A. Woodworth, M.D.
John Swindell Wright, Jr.
Kenneth Wright

AMEE also wishes to express its appreciation to the following individuals and companies for special services rendered:

The Honorable Stewart Udall
Secretary of the Interior

The Honorable Clair Engle
U.S. Senator from California

The Honorable Warren G. Magnuson
U.S. Senator from Washington

The Honorable Phillips Talbot
Assistant Secretary of State

Mr. W. Clyde Dunn
Deputy Director, Near Eastern and South Asian Programs
Department of State, Bureau of Educational and Cultural Affairs

Mr. S. A. Carapiet
James Warren & Co., Ltd.
Calcutta, India

Mr. Paul Chapas
(formerly Universal Services, Inc., Contract Manager
Seattle, Wash.)

Mr. Fred Dunham
Ephrata, Wash.

Miss Betty Frary
Seattle, Wash.

Miss Jean Ann Hirschi, Attorney
Palm Desert, Calif.

Mrs. Kathryn P. Huestis
Palos Verdes Estates, Calif.

Mr. Walter Scott, CPA
Los Angeles, Calif.

Miss Sally Smith
Design News
Denver, Colo.

Mr. Roy Dickerson, Mr. Thomas G. Harding and Mr. Hugh Mitchell of the First National City Bank of New York

Mrs. Dorothy Devine, Mr. Coye L. Hampton, Mr. Jack R. Irwin, Miss Pat Parsons, Miss Mary Poprac and Mr. and Mrs. Edwin P. Ramsey of the Hughes Aircraft Company

The Hughes Aircraft Company, for miscellaneous transportation and services and for the loan of their experimental HC-162 Manpack transceiver, with which the expedition called for the helicopter evacuation of Bishop and Unsoeld

The several individuals and companies who contributed to the development and testing of the Maytag oxygen mask including: Mr. Keki Bunshat, Dr. Robert Elsner, Dr. John Coates, Mr. Charles E. Fess, Dr. Jurg Marmet, McDonnell Aircraft Company, General Dynamics Astronautics, U.S. Naval Air Station at North Island, and Indian Oxygen, Ltd., Calcutta

Appendix II
Glossary of Mountaineering Terms

(F indicates French derivation, G German, W Welsh)

belay—securing of a rope by hitching it over a projection or passing it around the body.

bivouac—a temporary impromptu camp.

chimney—a steep, narrow cleft in a wall of rock or ice.

col, F—a pass, or the low point of a ridge.

cornice—a projecting mass of snow or ice, as on the leeward side of a ridge.

couloir, F—a gully, usually in an up-and-down direction.

crampons, F—steel frames with projecting spikes that are attached to the soles of boots to prevent slipping on steep snow or ice.

crevasse, F—a deep crevice or fissure in a glacier, caused by its downward movement.

cwm, W—a hollow in a mountainside; a deep ravine.

firn—granular snow at the top of a glacier; névé.

fixed rope—rope attached to a mountainside, as against that which is used to tie climbers together.

icefall—the steepest section of a glacier, usually taking the form of a wildly jumbled mass of ice.

ice screw—a form of ice piton (see below) which is screwed, instead of hammered, into place.

Jumar ascender—a mechanical device for gripping a rope, with the same function as a Prusik knot (see below).

karabiner (or *carabiner*), G—a metal snap ring, usually used in conjunction with a piton, through which a rope may be passed for greater security during difficult climbing.

428

kletterschuhe, G—lightweight climbing shoes, usually with rubber or rope soles.

la—the Tibetan word for *pass* or *col.*

moraine—rock and debris carried down by a glacier. Depending on their position, moraines are known as medial, lateral or terminal.

névé, F—a snow field lying above the snow line, usually the source of a glacier.

névé penitente, F—an ice tower, or serac, of a form thought by the Alpinists who coined the name to resemble a praying or "penitent" human figure.

pitch—a short, steep section of a mountainside.

piton, F—a metal spike designed to give support in steep climbing to hand, foot or rope. Pitons are made in varying sizes and shapes: some designed for use on ice, some for driving into cracks in rock.

Prusik knot—a special hitch used in a small-diameter rope to assist in the ascent of a fixed climbing rope.

rappel, F—roping down. The maneuver of letting oneself down a steep place by means of a supplementary rope.

rappel picket—a stake used for affixing a rappel rope; usually used in snow.

saddle—the low point of a ridge. A col.

sérac, F—a tower of ice, usually found on a glacier.

traverse—the horizontal or diagonal crossing of a mountainside. Also the crossing of a peak or pass from one side to the other.

MOUNT EVEREST
29028

South Summit
28750

Northeast Ridge

Camp VI
27450

Yellow Band

South
2620

Camp 3 West
21250

West Ridge

Camp V
26200

CHANGTSE
24780

Camp 4 West
25100

Camp 3 West
23800

KHUMBUTSE
21785

West

(Advance
Base Camp)

Camp
21350

*Rongbuk
Glacier*

Lho La (Pass)
19705

Camp I
20200

PUMORI
23442

Khumbu

Icefall

Base Camp
17800

Camp

Khumbu Glacier